Curriculum Connections

Picture Books in Grades 3 and Up

Carol Otis Hurst
Lynn Otis Palmer
Vaughn Churchill
Margaret Sullivan Ahearn
Bernard G. McMahon

A Publication of THE BOOK REPORT & LIBRARY TALK
Professional Growth Series

Linworth Publishing, Inc.
Worthington, Ohio

Published by Linworth Publishing, Inc.
480 East Wilson Bridge Road, Suite L
Worthington, Ohio 43085

Copyright©1999 by Linworth Publishing, Inc.

Series Information:
 From The Professional Growth Series

All right reserved. Reproduction of this book in whole or in part, without permission of the publisher, is prohibited except for not-for-profit educational use in the classroom, in the school library, in professional workshops sponsored by elementary and secondary schools, or other similar not-for-profit activites.

ISBN 0-938865-70-6

5 4 3 2

Table of Contents

INTRODUCTION VII

THEMES AND CURRICULUM CHART IX

PICTURE BOOKS 1

    Ackerman/Gammell - **Song and Dance Man** 1
    Agee - **The Incredible Painting of Felix Clousseau** 4
    Alexander/Hyman - **The Fortune-Tellers** 7
    Altman/Sanchez- **Amelia's Road** 10
    Avi/Henry - **The Bird, the Frog and the Light** 13
    Baillie/Wu - **Rebel** 16
    Baylor/Parnall - **If You Are a Hunter of Fossils** 19
    Baylor/Parnall- **The Table Where Rich People Sit** 22
    Birchman/San Souci - **Jigsaw Jackson** 25
    Birdseye/Chen - **A Song of Stars** 28
    Bodkin/Rose - **The Banshee Train** 31
    Breathed - **Goodnight Opus** 34
    Brett - **Armadillo Rodeo** 37
    Buehner - **Fanny's Dream** 41
    Bunting/Shed - **Dandelions** 44
    Bunting/Minor - **Red Fox Running** 47
    Bunting/Himler - **Train to Somewhere** 50
    Cannon - **Stellaluna** 53
    Climo/Heller - **The Egyptian Cinderella** 56
    Coerr/Young - **Sadako** 59
    Cooney - **Eleanor** 62
    Cooney - **Island Boy** 65
    Emberley - **Three Cool Kids** 68
    Goble - **Death of the Iron Horse** 71
    Goble - **The Girl Who Loved Wild Horses** 74
    Grifalconi - **The Village of Round and Square Houses** 77
    Griffith/Stevenson - **Georgia Music** 81
    Hall/Moser- **The Farm Summer 1942** 84
    Hall/Moser - **I Am the Dog; I Am the Cat** 87
    Hall/Moser- **Old Home Day** 90
    Heide/Lewin - **Sami and the Time of Troubles** 93
    Hopkinson/Ransome - **Sweet Clara and the Freedom Quilt** 96
    Houston/Lamb - **My Great-Aunt Arizona** 99

Table of Contents Continued

Howard/Himler - **The Log Cabin Quilt** 102
Isaacson/Zelinsky - **Swamp Angel** 105
James/Vojtech - **Blow Away Soon** 108
Johnston/Ludwig - **The Cowboy and the Black-Eyed Pea** 111
Khalsa - **How Pizza Came to Queens** 114
Kidd - **Almost Famous Daisy** 117
Kindersley - **Children Just Like Me** 120
Kotzwinkle/Catrow - **The Million-Dollar Bear** 123
Lobel - **Fables** 126
Lobel - **Ming Lo Moves the Mountain** 129
London/McLoughlin - **Voices of the Wild** 132
Lyon/Catalanotto - **Cecil's Story** 135
Macaulay - **Black and White** 138
Macaulay - **Rome Antics** 141
Martin/Carpenter - **Washing the Willow Tree Loon** 145
McLerran/Carle - **The Mountain that Loved a Bird** 148
Mollel/Morin - **The Orphan Boy** 151
Moser - **Tucker Pfeffercorn** 154
Pilkey - **Dog Breath** 157
Polacco - **Aunt Chip and the Great Triple Creek Dam Affair** 160
Polacco - **The Keeping Quilt** 163
Polacco - **Pink and Say** 167
Romanova - **Once There Was a Tree** 169
Rosen - **Purr: Children's Book Illustrators Brag About Their Cats** 172
Rylant/Moser - **Appalachia: The Voices of Sleeping Birds** 175
Rylant/Brown - **The Old Woman Who Named Things** 178
Say - **Tree of Cranes** 181
Say - **Grandfather's Journey** 184
Scieszka/Smith - **The Stinky Cheese Man** 187
Segal/Zelinsky - **The Story of Mrs. Lovewright and Purrless Her Cat** .. 190
Sewall - **Pilgrims of Plimoth** 193
Shelby/Halperin - **Homeplace** 196
Siebert/Minor - **Sierra** 199
Steptoe - **Mufaro's Beautiful Daughters** 202
Steptoe - **The Story of Jumping Mouse** 205
Stevenson - **I Had a Lot of Wishes** 208
Swope/Root - **The Araboolies of Liberty Street** 211
Thompson - **How to Live Forever** 214
Turner/Himler - **Dakota Dugout** 217

Table of Contents Continued

Turner/Desimini - **Heron Street** 220
Turner/Himler - **Nettie's Trip South** 223
Van Allsburg - **Bad Day at Riverbend** 226
Van Allsburg - **The Stranger** 229
Van Allsburg - **Wreck of the Zephyr** 232
Watson - **The Butterfly Seeds** 235
Wells/Jeffers - **Waiting for the Evening Star** 238
Yolen/Shannon - **Encounter** 241
Yolen/Cooney - **Letting Swift River Go** 245
Yolen/Baker - **Honkers** 248
Yolen/Young - **The Seeing Stick** 251
Yolen/Nolan - **Wings** 254
Young - **Lon Po Po: A Red-Riding Hood Story from China** 257

TITLE, AUTHOR & ILLUSTRATOR INDEX 261

SUBJECT & SKILLS INDEX 275

Introduction

It wasn't so long ago that picture books were the province of very young children. Too young to listen to complicated plots without ample illustrations to fascinate and hold their attention, these children and their parents and teachers treasured the volumes dedicated to them. There are still many delightful picture books that fall into this category, of course, but increasingly authors and illustrators have been turning their attention toward the picture book with more mature audiences in mind. It is toward these books that we have turned our attention here.

There are multitudes of reasons for using picture books with older students. Students from third grade up can gain artistic and literary insights through picture books which, in turn, can delight, amuse and enlighten. Teachers using such picture books with their students will find that, in a very few minutes, an entire group of children can focus on a subject or area, a result that usually involves much more extensive reading. Cross-curriculum activities become readily apparent. Literary devices such as plot, character, setting, climax and resolution can be pointed out in a picture book more easily than in more complicated text, but understanding these devices can later be applied to complex text. Various skills and strategies that need to be addressed by some students can be followed up after a picture book has provided the means or the motivation in that direction. Areas necessitating further reading and research become obvious when an important picture book has been discussed, and connections between various parts of the curriculum are easily bridged with the right picture book reading as entries to the subjects.

In this book we have chosen many picture books with an eye to the older readers. For each book we give a brief summary of the book, some information about the art, and point out connections that can be made from this book to various areas of the curriculum. We also highlight connections to longer narratives and novels and themes that this picture book brings to mind. The chart that follows will allow you to quickly see strong points in the curricula for the picture books. A word of caution belongs here, however; intended age groups for those novels vary widely, and careful choices must be made to offer appropriate novels for the age group with which you are working.

Obviously no teacher or group of children will want to pursue every possible avenue from a given picture book. To do so would belabor and drag down the book. But by picking carefully from the choices outlined and by using our suggested activities as spurs for your own creativity, you will find this book can provide positive experiences with picture books in the classroom.

Books, Themes and Curriculum Strengths

AUTHOR/TITLE	PAGE	POSSIBLE THEMES & CURRICULUM TIES	Language Arts	Mathematics	Science	Social Studies	Art	Music
Ackerman - Song and Dance Man	1	Grandparents / History of the 1920s	■		■	■		
Agee - Incredible Painting of Felix Clousseau	4	Famous artists	■				■	
Alexander - The Fortune-Tellers	7	Dreams & ambitions	■		■	■	■	
Altman - Amelia's Road	10	Migrant Workers	■			■	■	
Avi - Bird, the Frog and the Light	13	Fables / Mythology	■		■			
Baillie - Rebel	16	Rebellion / Dictators	■			■		
Baylor - If You Are a Hunter of Fossils	19	Geology / Fossils & Rocks	■		■			
Baylor - The Table Where Rich People Sit	22	Values	■	■		■		
Birchman - Jigsaw Jackson	25	Tall Tales	■			■		
Birdseye - Song of Stars	28	Astronomy / Myths and Legends	■		■	■		
Bodkin - The Banshee Train	31	Legends / Storytelling	■	■	■	■		
Breathed - Goodnight Opus	34	Parodies & Extended Fairy Tales	■	■	■			
Brett - Armadillo Rodeo	37	Texas & the West	■		■	■	■	■
Buehner - Fanny's Dream	41	Women's Roles / Homesteading	■			■		
Bunting - Dandelions	44	Home / Westward Expansion	■	■	■	■		

Books, Themes and Curriculum Strengths (continued)

AUTHOR/TITLE	PAGE	POSSIBLE THEMES & CURRICULUM TIES	Language Arts	Mathematics	Science	Social Studies	Art	Music
Bunting - **Red Fox Running**	47	Foxes Food Chains	■		■			
Bunting - **Train to Somewhere**	50	Moving Westward Expansion	■			■	■	
Cannon - **Stellaluna**	53	Mistaken Identities Bats	■	■	■	■		
Climo - **The Egyptian Cinderella**	56	Cinderella Stories Ancient Egypt	■		■	■		
Coerr - **Sadako**	59	World War II	■		■	■	■	
Cooney - **Eleanor**	62	Biographies	■			■		
Cooney - **Island Boy**	65	Family History	■			■	■	
Emberley - **Three Cool Kids**	68	Proverbs Urban Areas	■		■			
Goble - **Death of the Iron Horse**	71	Culture Conflict Westward Expansion	■			■	■	
Goble - **The Girl Who Loved Wild Horses**	74	Transformation Plains Indians	■			■	■	
Grifalconi - **The Village of Round and Square Houses**	77	Pourquoi Stories - Customs of Various Cultures	■		■	■		
Griffith - **Georgia Music**	81	Rural vs. Urban Environment	■	■	■	■		■
Hall - **The Farm Summer 1942**	84	Farms World War II	■	■	■	■		■
Hall - **I Am the Dog; I Am the Cat**	87	Perspective	■		■			
Hall - **Old Home Day**	90	Changes	■		■	■		

Books, Themes and Curriculum Strengths (continued)

AUTHOR/TITLE	PAGE	POSSIBLE THEMES & CURRICULUM TIES	STRONGEST CURRICULUM AREAS					
			Language Arts	Mathematics	Science	Social Studies	Art	Music
Heide - Sami and the Time of Troubles	93	Effects of War Lebanon	■			■		
Hopkinson - Sweet Clara and the Freedom Quilt	96	Slavery	■			■	■	
Houston - My Great-Aunt Arizona	99	Teaching/Education Appalachia	■	■	■			
Howard - The Log Cabin Quilt	102	Quilts Westward Expansion	■			■	■	
Isaacs - Swamp Angel	105	Strong Women - Regions of U. S. - Occupations	■	■		■		
James - Blow Away Soon	108	Life Cycles	■	■	■	■	■	
Johnston - The Cowboy and the Black-Eyed Pea	111	Impossible Tasks Regional Customs	■		■	■		
Khalsa - How Pizza Came to Queens	114	Food	■	■		■		
Kidd - Almost Famous Daisy	117	Art Travel	■	■		■	■	
Kindersley - Children Just Like Me	120	Children Around the World	■	■		■		
Kotzwinkle - The Million-Dollar Bear	123	Wealth & Value	■	■		■		
Lobel - Fables	126	Fables	■		■			
Lobel - Ming Lo Moves the Mountain	129	Trickster Tales Meeting Challenges	■		■	■		
London - Voices of the Wild	132	Perspective Wilderness	■		■	■		
Lyon - Cecil's Story	135	Civil War Time	■		■	■	■	

Books, Themes and Curriculum Strengths (continued)

AUTHOR/TITLE	PAGE	POSSIBLE THEMES & CURRICULUM TIES	STRONGEST CURRICULUM AREAS					
			Language Arts	Mathematics	Science	Social Studies	Art	Music
Macaulay - **Black and White**	138	Perspective Ecosystems	■		■		■	
Macaulay - **Rome Antics**	141	Ancient Rome Architecture	■			■	■	
Martin - **Washing the Willow Tree Loon**	145	Pollution	■		■			
McLerran - **The Mountain That Loved a Bird**	148	Love & Nurturing Ecosystems	■		■		■	
Mollel - **The Orphan Boy**	151	Trust & Betrayal - Masai Culture - Astronomy	■		■	■	■	
Moser - **Tucker Pfeffercorn**	154	Fairy Tale Extensions Coal Mining	■			■		
Pilkey - **Dog Breath**	157	Eccentric Characters Wordplay	■		■			
Polacco - **Aunt Chip and the Triple Creek Dam Affair**	160	Value of Reading	■			■		
Polacco - **The Keeping Quilt**	163	Heritage & Tradition Immigration	■	■		■	■	
Polacco - **Pink and Say**	167	Civil War Friendship & Sacrifice	■			■		
Romanova - **Once There Was a Tree**	169	Trees History	■		■	■	■	
Rosen - **Purr: Children's Book Illustrators Brag About Their Cats**	172	Pets Writers	■	■		■		
Rylant - **Appalachia: The Voices of Sleeping Birds**	175	Appalachia Regional Study	■		■	■		■
Rylant - **The Old Woman Who Named Things**	178	Loneliness Problems of the Elderly	■	■		■		
Say - **Tree of Cranes**	181	Cultures Japan	■			■	■	

Books, Themes and Curriculum Strengths (continued)

AUTHOR/TITLE	PAGE	POSSIBLE THEMES & CURRICULUM TIES	Language Arts	Mathematics	Science	Social Studies	Art	Music
Say – Grandfather's Journey	184	Culture Clash / Immigration	■		■	■		
Scieszka – The Stinky Cheese Man and Other Fairly Stupid Tales	187	Satires / Fairy Tale Extensions	■			■		
Segal – The Story of Mrs. Lovewright and Purrless Her Cat	190	Reality vs Dreams / Loneliness	■			■		
Sewall – Pilgrims of Plimoth	193	Community / Pilgrims	■			■		
Shelby – Homeplace	196	Home / Discoveries & Invention	■			■	■	
Siebert – Sierra	199	Perspective / Ecosystems, Geology	■		■	■		
Steptoe – Mufaro's Beautiful Daughters	202	Beauty / Cinderella Stories	■		■	■		
Steptoe – The Story of Jumping Mouse	205	Quests / Native American Folklore	■			■	■	
Stevenson – I Had a Lot of Wishes	208	Memories / History of the 1930s and 1940s	■			■		
Swope – The Araboolies of Liberty Street	211	Conformity / Community	■			■		
Thompson – How to Live Forever	214	Time / Libraries	■	■		■		
Turner – Dakota Dugout	217	Prairie Homes / Westward Expansion	■			■		
Turner – Heron Street	220	Ecology / Change	■		■	■	■	
Turner – Nettie's Trip South	223	Slavery / Letters	■			■		
Van Allsburg – Bad Day at Riverbend	226	Puzzles / Illustration	■				■	

Books, Themes and Curriculum Strengths (continued)

AUTHOR/TITLE	PAGE	POSSIBLE THEMES & CURRICULUM TIES	STRONGEST CURRICULUM AREAS					
			Language Arts	Mathematics	Science	Social Studies	Art	Music
Van Allsburg - **The Stranger**	229	Seasons Strangers			■	■	■	
Van Allsburg - **Wreck of the Zephyr**	232	Ambition - Vanity Mythology	■		■	■		
Watson - **The Butterfly Seeds**	235	Immigration	■		■	■		
Wells - **Waiting for the Evening Star**	238	Life Cycles	■		■	■		
Yolen - **Encounter**	241	Columbus World Explorers	■			■		
Yolen - **Letting Swift River Go**	245	Cost of Progress Local History - Water	■		■	■		
Yolen - **Honkers**	248	Farm Changes	■		■			
Yolen - **The Seeing Stick**	251	Disabilities	■		■	■	■	
Yolen - **Wings**	254	Mythology Ancient Greece	■		■	■		
Young - **Lon Po Po**	257	Fairy Tales	■		■		■	

Song and Dance Man

by Karen Ackerman
Illustrated by Stephen Gammell
Knopf, 1981
ISBN 0-394-99330-6

SUMMARY

This Caldecott Award winner tells a simple story of a grandfather who takes his grandchildren to the attic where he opens a trunk full of costumes and props from his days as a song and dance man. There, under the spotlight provided by an old bridge lamp, he performs part of his vaudeville act. We join the grandchildren in the glimpse of his younger days. The story is told from the point of view of the grandchildren.

ILLUSTRATION

The colored pencil illustrations show Gammell's usual unkempt and slightly grotesque people who are somehow familiar. The shadows cast by the various lamps in the house highlight and cover some of the action. Crafted line drawings have been executed with color pencils and are fundamental to Gammell's illustrations. He achieves a full sense of the third dimension with his mastery of the value scale. Line is built upon line and color is mixed with color to create this range of values that read as solid forms. The mood of joy and celebration is established by the use of bright colors. Together the brightly costumed and likable characters are Gammell hallmarks.

CONNECTIONS

NOVEL

Mavis Jukes' short novel **Blackberries in the Dark**, illustrated by Thomas B. Allen (Knopf, 1985. ISBN 0-394-87599-0 Grades 3-6), would go well with this loving look at a grandfather. In **Blackberries in the Dark**, a young boy spends his summer vacation with his grandmother shortly after the death of his grand-father. When they share the sorrow and the joy of the man's life, they can begin to enjoy each other.

THEMES

▶ Careers
▶ Grandparents

CURRICULUM CONNECTION

▶ SOCIAL STUDIES – History of the 1920s and 1930s

Language Arts

SIMILES

▶ Karen Ackerman uses several similes in this book. Substitute other similes for hers.

"his tap shoes make soft, slippery sounds like " _____

"does a new step that sounds like " _____

"his voice is as round and strong as" _____

▶ Make up your own similes. What's the softest thing you know? Can you make a simile out of two soft things: this cotton is as soft as ____. Look at Eve Merriam's poem "Clichés." It may inspire you to search for other, less common, similes.

GRAMMAR

▶ Change part of the story to past tense. Do you like it better? Why do you think the author used the present tense?

EVALUATING LITERATURE

▶ This book got the Caldecott Award. Find out what that is and decide which of the books in your classroom deserve such an award. Have your own award ceremony.

WRITING

▶ Many elderly people live in nursing homes. Establish contact with a nursing home and exchange postcards and letters with residents there.

Math

▶ Figure out how old grandpa might be based on the pictures.

▶ Figure out how old grandpa might be by finding out when vaudeville was popular and then how old a veteran of those times might be now.

Science

▶ This grandfather obviously loves entertaining his grandchildren and enjoys his life. Why do some elderly people appear to be able to do this while others seem so depressed and unhappy? What things do you think make for better lives for elderly people?

▶ Think about the experiences that an older person might have had. Develop a list of five questions you would like answered by such a person. Interview a person about the same age as this grandfather. Ask the questions. Go back and think about the answers you got and develop three more questions to ask based on what you now know. Re-interview the person with those questions. Think about those answers and think of one question you could now ask that would reveal even more information. Ask it. Find a way to share what you now know with others.

Social Studies

▶ Find out more about vaudeville and other song and dance performers.

▶ Interview some retired people about the work they used to do and the work they are doing now. What changes in society are they most concerned about? Why?

▶ Get permission to investigate an attic, garage or basement of an older home. What's the oldest thing you can find there? What evidence can you find in such a place that shows what people once did?

▶ Some eras in U. S. history have been named: the Gay Nineties, the Roaring Twenties, the Fabulous Fifties, for instance. How did those eras get those names and what name would you give to the 1990s?

Fine Arts

▶ Find and listen to some recordings of music that might have been used for song and dance routines.

▶ Work up some song and dance routines.

▶ Look at some old movie musicals such as Singing in the Rain, Meet Me in St. Louis and Easter Parade. Which of the people in them would you call song and dance people?

RELATED BOOKS

NOVELS

Jukes, Mavis. **Blackberries in the Dark**.
Illustrated by Thomas B. Allen Knopf, 1985.
ISBN 0-394-87599-0 Grades 3-6
A young boy spends his summer vacation with his grandmother shortly after the death of his grandfather. When they share the sorrow and the joy of the man's life, they can begin to enjoy each other.

Klaveness, Jan. **Beyond the Cellar Door**.
Scholastic, 1991. ISBN 0-590-43021-1 Grades 4-8
When Grandfather comes to stay, he and Jeff battle almost from the beginning. Then Jeff finds a Victorian house with mysterious and constant changing decor and discovers his grandfather in a different way.

Lasky, Kathryn. **The Night Journey**.
Illustrated by Trina Schart Hyman. Warne, 1981.
ISBN 0-670-809357 Grades 3-8
A great-grandmother tells the story of her family's escape from a pogrom. Her audience is a very modern little girl, but the connection between the generations is a strong one.

Murrow, Liza Ketchum. **Dancing on the Table**.
Holiday, 1990. ISBN 0-8234-0808-6 Grades 4-8
This short novel revolves around the impending remarriage of a beloved grandmother and her granddaughter's attempts to stop the wedding.

Slepian, Jan. **Pinocchio's Sister**.
Philomel, 1995. ISBN 0-399-22811 X Grades 5-7
Mr. Rosedale, a ventriloquist on the vaudeville circuit in 1928, devotes his time and attention to his dummy rather than to his daughter, Martha, who vows to eliminate the puppet once and for all. The connection here is with vaudeville.

PICTURE BOOKS

Bunting, Eve. **The Wednesday Surprise**.
Houghton, 1989. ISBN 0-9-89919-721-3
The little girl and her grandmother are planning a surprise for her father. Eventually we learn the secret that she has taught her grandmother to read.

Greenfield, Eloise. **William & the Good Old Days**.
HarperCollins, 1993. ISBN 0-06-021093-1
Illness changes a woman, a little boy, a family and a neighborhood.

Griffiths, Helen. **Grandaddy's Place**.
Greenwillow, 1987. ISBN 0-688-06254-7
A little girl visits her grandfather and learns about her mother as a child, her grandfather and herself.

Kesselman, Wendy. **Emma**.
HarperCollins, 1985. ISBN 0-06-443077-4
An elderly woman is shown as a person of talent and abilities as well as a person with wonderful independence.

Stroud, Virginia. **Doesn't Fall Off His Horse**.
Dial, 1994. ISBN 0-8037-1634-6
A Kiowa man tells his granddaughter how he got his name.

OTHER BOOKS BY KAREN ACKERMAN

Araminta's Paint Box.
Simon & Schuster, 1990. ISBN 0-689-31462-0
A little girl's paint box travels west, but not with her.

By the Dawn's Early Light.
Simon & Schuster, 1994. ISBN 0-689-31788-3
Rachel tells us about her family and about her mother, who works all night.

OTHER BOOKS ILLUSTRATED BY STEPHEN GAMMELL

Haseley, Dennis. **The Old Banjo**.
Simon & Schuster, 1990. ISBN 0-689-71380-0
An old farm comes alive with music as all the abandoned instruments on it begin to play.

Blos, Joan. **Old Henry**.
Morrow, 1990. ISBN 0-688-09935-1
When Henry moves into the old house, the neighbors hope he'll fix it up, but he doesn't.

Rylant, Cynthia. **The Relatives Came**.
Simon & Schuster, 1985. ISBN 0-02-777220-9
Relatives arrive in a mountain home for an old-fashioned family reunion.

The Incredible Painting of Felix Clousseau

by Jon Agee
Farrar Straus & Giroux, 1988
ISBN 0-374-33633-4

SUMMARY

A rather scruffy looking painter named Felix Clousseau paints pictures which, compared to those painted by his contemporaries, seem a tad plain and dull. However, Felix Clousseau's works of art come to life, often at the strangest times. When the powers-that-be find out about Clousseau's talent, they make increasingly uncomfortable demands on him until he deserts the real world and literally goes back to his work.

ILLUSTRATION

These illustrations offer a wonderful study of the visual element of value. Agee uses deep, dark and somber color tones in contrast with selected areas of bright and colorful spaces to focus attention on the story's key characters and events. He also uses contrasting sizes of objects and characters to create a sense of space and place. The contrasting sizes of frames and pictures imply the importance of the words. The pictures of the museum rooms capture the feeling of enormous scale and how the place might be experienced by a visitor. This is a textbook of successful illustration lessons.

CONNECTIONS

NOVEL

William J. Brooke's **A Brush With Magic** (HarperCollins, 1993. ISBN 0-06-022973-X) also concerns a magical relationship between the artist and his work. In it, a boy uses a magic brush to paint things that come to life. He is brought to the Emperor's palace where he is asked to use his talent to satisfy the Emperor's greed.

THEMES

▶ Inanimate objects coming to life
▶ Transformations

CURRICULUM CONNECTION

▶ ART – Art and artists

LANGUAGE ARTS

GETTING MEANING FROM ILLUSTRATION

▶ Note that the impact of Felix Clousseau's paintings is all done visually; the text does not inform the reader of what the paintings do. Retell the story using only the illustrations. Now compare your story with the story presented in the text. Do the two stories correspond? Can either story stand alone or is each one enhanced by the other? Look for other picture books that truly require both text and illustrations to tell the complete plot. Are those books more enjoyable to read?

▶ Compare the first and last pages. Do the illustrations found there provide you with any information about where Felix came from?

USING IDIOMS

▶ The last page of the book informs us that Felix "...returned to his painting." The illustration shows him quite literally returning into the work of art itself. Explore other expressions (idioms) that we don't (usually!) take literally. For example, we might say that Felix is "gets into his work."

▶ Fred Gwynne's books (see Related Books) may give you some other ideas. Try your hand at illustrating an idiom literally. Discuss what would happen if you really did take those expressions word for word. Peggy Parish's Amelia Bedelia books (see Related Books) might be fun to share.

WRITING

▶ What happened to all the other painted objects which came to life? Write or tell their stories.

▶ Invent titles for paintings you would want to come to life and tell the resulting story.

▶ Retell the story from Felix's point of view. Where did he come from? Why does he have the ability to paint things that come alive? Is Felix a part of a painting that someone else has created?

▶ Illustrate a Felix Clousseau painting and write a story about what happened to the person who bought it.

▶ Find a large poster of a landscape scene. Now "walk into it." That is, describe the setting in terms of their senses. Given that setting, what would one feel, see, touch and taste?

▶ It was fortunate that the king had a Clousseau painting on guard. Write letters to the king providing advice on protecting his property.

VOCABULARY DEVELOPMENT

▶ The inside flap of the book jacket states that "art imitates life." What does that mean?

COMPARING RELATED LITERATURE

▶ Compare this book to other books where things come to life such as Jumanji and the Indian in the Cupboard (see Related Books).

ART

▶ Find a famous work of art into which you would want to climb. Research the work and the artist. Explain why you have chosen that particular work of art.

▶ Is it possible to determine about when this story takes place by looking at the type of paintings that were presented at the art show?

▶ Experiment with several art media: oil paint, poster paint, watercolors, chalk, pastels, crayons. Make a sample book for each medium showing your work as well as copies of works by famous artists who employ the featured medium.

▶ Experiment with printing materials: cardboard, potatoes, sponges, linoleum, wood.

▶ Look carefully at favorite picture books. How were the illustrations done? Would the use of a different medium have changed the impact of the illustrations?

RELATED BOOKS

NOVELS

Brooke, William J. **A Brush With Magic**.
HarperCollins, 1993. ISBN 0-0- 022973-X
A boy uses a magic brush to paint things that come to life and is brought to the emperor's palace where he is asked to satisfy the emperor's greed.

Fenner, Carol. **Randall's Wall**.
Bantam, 1991. ISBN 0-553-48021-9 Grades 5-9
Randall's home situation is appalling, and he is shunned by most of his teachers and classmates. But one teacher and one friend discover his amazing artistic abilities and succeed in tearing down a bit of the wall behind which he hides.

Say, Allen. **The Ink-Keeper's Apprentice**.
Houghton, 1979. ISBN 0-395-70562-2 Grades 5-8
Allen Say has slightly fictionalized his life story from the time when he became apprentice to a master cartoonist in Japan until he emigrated to America.

PICTURE BOOKS

Cazet, Denys. **Frosted Glass**.
Simon & Schuster, 1987. ISBN 0-02-717960-5
Gregory has art in his head all the time. He draws on frosted glass; he sees dinosaurs in heavy construction work; he sees rocket ships in a vase of flowers.

DePaola, Tomie **Bonjour, Mr. Satie**.
Putnam, 1991. ISBN 0-399-217827
Mr. Satie is called upon to judge an art contest between Pablo and another artist with equal fame but vastly different technique. Careful looks will also disclose Gertrude Stein and Alice B. Toklas, Josephine Baker, Isadora Duncan (complete with scarf), Ernest Hemingway, Edith Sitwell and lots of others.

Gwynne, Fred. **The King Who Rained**.
Aladdin, 1988. ISBN 0-671-66744-0 and
A Chocolate Moose for Dinner.
Aladdin, 1988. ISBN 0-671-667416
These are two of a series of books by Gwynne that illustrate literally and amusingly idioms and homonyms.

Johnston, Tony. **The Last Snow of Winter**.
Morrow, 1993. ISBN 0-688-10749-4
Gaston Pompicard, the great artist, lives in a small town and, inspired by the first snow, he makes a snow sculpture for the village. Later, when he falls ill, they repay the favor.

Kesselman, Wendy. **Emma**.
Harper, 1985. ISBN 0-440-40847-4
Emma is a 72-year-old grandmother who loves to have her family visit. Unfortunately, they don't stay very long and she is often lonely. Secretly, Emma begins to paint pictures of the things she loves most and becomes famous. Surrounded by her paintings, she is never lonely again.

Parish, Peggy. **Amelia Bedelia**.
HarperCollins, 1992. ISBN 0-06-020187-8
Amelia Bedelia begins working for the Rogers family. They leave her alone on her first day. Unfortunately, she follows instructions exactly to the letter, causing some very funny things to happen. This is one in a series of rather silly stories about Amelia Bedelia, who always takes things literally.

Rylant, Cynthia. **All I See**.
Orchard, 1988. ISBN 0-531-08377-2
A boy watches an artist painting beside a peaceful pond as the man paints whales because, he explains, it's all that he sees.

Small, David. **Paper John**.
Farrar, 1987. ISBN 0-374-35738-2
Whatever John makes with his skills at origami becomes real.

Van Allsburg, Chris. **Jumanji**.
Houghton, 1981. ISBN 0-395-30448-2
A board game comes to life and gets a little too real for its two players.

The Fortune-Tellers

by Lloyd Alexander
Illustrated by Trina Schart Hyman
Dutton, 1992
ISBN 0-525-44849-7

SUMMARY

This book is set in Cameroon, West Africa. The works of a brilliant artist and a master storyteller combine to create a fascinating and humorous tale. A young carpenter seeks a fortune teller to learn about his future. Will he be rich, famous and happy? Will he find his true love? He is conditionally assured of a very bright future. Soon after their meeting, the fortune teller mysteriously disappears. The carpenter abandons his hammer and saw, and through a humorous twist of fate, all his dreams come true. The amusing story and enchanting illustrations combine to provide a glimpse of the wit and wisdom of a beautiful country.

ILLUSTRATION

These illustrations are the result of pen line drawings that have been packed with a variety of watercolor washes. The result is a series of brightly colored compositions that capture the flavor of West African culture. Color is a dominant element in the crafts and dress of the region. The illustrator employs subtle changes in color to link the carpenter's current status with his imagined fortunes. Brighter colors establish the carpenter's present circumstances, while soft and muted color washes reference the imagined results of good fortune. Native crafts, such as fabric design and batik, saturate these compositions.

CONNECTIONS

NOVEL

There are many books about a character's ability or inability to predict the future. Betsy Byars' **Tarot Says Beware** (Viking, 1995. ISBN 0-670-85575-8 Grades 3-6) is a light mystery with scary moments. Herculeah finds the body of her friend Madame Rosa, the fortune teller and, although both her mother and father forbid any further action on her part, Herculeah is soon the intended second victim of the murderer.

THEMES

▶ Achieving one's dreams
▶ Biographies

CURRICULUM CONNECTION

▶ GEOGRAPHY – Cameroons, Africa

LANGUAGE ARTS

CAUSE AND EFFECT

▶ This book lends itself to speculation:

What if the fortune teller's predictions were frightening and alarming?

What if the carpenter hadn't returned to the fortune teller's room?

What if the cloth merchant's wife hadn't believed in miracles?

What if the old fortune teller had returned to the village?

Record different reactions from the class to these "what ifs."

VOCABULARY DEVELOPMENT

▶ Prepare a vocabulary list of interesting words from the story. Can you find antonyms or synonyms for any of them? Possible words to use are: profit, trifle, demise, seer, scrubby, codger, fraud, savanna, benefactor.

▶ Which parts are funny in the book? Are some of the words funny in and of themselves?

WRITING

▶ Compose some chants to be used before foretelling the future.

▶ Write humorous fortunes for various classmates stated in a manner similar to those in the book.

▶ Make a list of materials (bat wings, spider webs, etc.) to be used in a potion for telling the future.

▶ Write a completely different ending for the story and for each fortune teller.

FINDING DETAILS

▶ It's sometimes fun to spot minor characters in picture books. Examine each illustration and count the chameleons (lizards) found on the various pages.

▶ Collect other books in which animals/people appear on selected pages. Some examples are **Company's Coming**, **Goodnight Moon**, and the books by Chris Van Allsburg.

▶ Add another category in which the characters are cleverly hidden, as in **Where's Wallace?** and the **Where's Waldo?** series.

▶ Find some objects in the fortune teller's room that might have been used to foretell the future. Begin with the crystal ball.

▶ Find the two pages depicting the dream of the carpenter coming true. Do they resemble the events that really happened?

SEQUENCE

▶ Make three columns, listing the important events in each character's life. Fill in some events that could have happened that are omitted.

Carpenter	Fortune Teller	Cloth Merchant's Wife
Visits a fortune teller	Tells a great fortune	Meets the carpenter

SOCIAL STUDIES

▶ Locate Cameroon on a world map. Which countries are its neighbors? How far away is it from where you live? What language is spoken there?

▶ Find out about the weather and identify other countries of the world with the same climate and time zones.

▶ Decide on the various occupations of the people in the story.

▶ Identify the river that swept away the real fortune teller.

SCIENCE

▶ Examine the illustrations. Find and name each animal.

▶ Research and identify flowers, fruit, plants and trees that appear in the book.

▶ Try foretelling the future of our country, favorite sports team, super heroes. The story uses a crystal ball as a way of foretelling the future. Some other popular methods are astrology, palmistry, cards and consulting spirits of the dead. Do they work? Research these methods. Choose one type to dramatize.

▶ Find the lizards on the first page and identify the species.

▶ Except for the first page, all the other lizards in the book are green. Identify the type. Are they chameleons? Why or why not?

▶ Categorize all animals found in the book.

ART

▶ Examine the intricate and many-hued costumes of the natives. Choose some patterns to duplicate for things other than clothes (cards, wrapping paper, wallpaper).

▶ Scrutinize the jewelry worn by the men, women and children. Determine the materials used. Design pieces of jewelry. Identify the materials and for whom they were created.

RELATED BOOKS

NOVELS

Byars, Betsy. **Tarot Says Beware**.
Viking, 1995. ISBN 0-670-85575-8 Grades 3-6
This is a light mystery with scary moments. Herculeah finds the body of her friend Madame Rosa, the fortune teller and, although both her mother and father forbid any further action on her part, Herculeah is soon the intended second victim of the murderer.

Peck, Richard. **Blossom Culp & the Sleep of Death**.
Dell, 1994. ISBN 0-440-40676-5
The Dreadful Future of Blossom Culp.
Dell, 1987. ISBN 0-440-42154-3
The Ghost Belonged to Me.
Viking, 1987. ISBN 0-670-33767-6
Ghosts I Have Been.
Dell, 1979. ISBN 0-440-92839-7 Grades 3-6
This series of novels centers around the clairvoyance of Blossom Culp.

PICTURE BOOKS

Berson, Harold. **The Thief Who Hugged a Moonbeam**. Seabury, 1972. ISBN 0-395-28767-7
A man tricks a thief on his roof. He makes the robber believe in a magic wand and a moonbeam and disaster results.

Brown, Marcia. **Stone Soup**.
Simon & Schuster, 1979. ISBN 0-874-88953-X
Three soldiers trick the peasants into cooperating with them. The villagers believe that the soup was made from stones.

Fletcher, Jane Cowen. **It Takes a Village**.
Scholastic, 1993. ISBN 0-590-46573-2
Yemi is in charge, but at the market she loses her brother Kakow. Her search involves the entire village.

Shub, Elizabeth. **Clever Kate**.
Illustrated by Anita Lobel.
Simon & Schuster, 1973. ISBN 0-02-782490-X
A new bride gives her husband's gold away. This is but one of her many mistakes. Ultimately Kate redeems herself and truly becomes "clever."

Zemach, Margot. **It Could Always Be Worse**.
Farrar, Strauss, 1977. ISBN 0-374-43636-3
A poor man goes to his rabbi to ask for advice about his crowded household. Amazingly his life gets worse and he learns to count his blessings.

Amelia's Road

by Linda Jacobs Altman
Illustrated by Enrique O. Sanchez
Lee & Low, 1993
ISBN 1-880000-04-0

▶ SUMMARY

Amelia hates roads and maps because roads always lead to someplace else and, whenever her father takes out the maps, she knows the family will soon be loaded into the truck to move on to the next place to pick vegetables. This time she particularly hates to leave because she has a teacher who has learned her name and who has liked a drawing Amelia did, even putting a star on it. When Amelia finds an abandoned road, she buries her treasures in a metal box beside it, knowing this is a place to which she can return. This time she doesn't cry when her father gets out the map.

▶ ILLUSTRATION

These traditional compositions mirror the straightforward nature of the text. Outlined objects and figures are filled with a complete range of muted colors. The colors are used with usual references to red tomatoes, blueberries and green lettuce. Paint application is so subtle that the woven texture of the canvas can be seen beneath the thin application of the mixed medium. Delightful images of fruits and vegetables are selectively placed on pages of text as though separated from a larger still-life arrangement for emphasis. For example, notice how the pears, peaches and strawberries are carefully modeled in such a manner.

▶ CONNECTIONS

NOVEL

There are many good novels about migrant workers. One of the strongest has been around a long time but is still in print. Doris Gates' **Blue Willow** (Puffin, 1982. ISBN 0-14-030924-1 Grades 3-7) revolves around a blue willow plate which belonged to her mother and represents home for Janey, the child of migrant workers.

THEMES
▶ Belonging/ Home
▶ Migrant Workers

CURRICULUM CONNECTION
▶ SOCIAL STUDIES – Migrant Labor

LANGUAGE ARTS

COMPARING LITERATURE

▶ Look at **Working Cotton** (see Related Books), another picture book about migrant life. Compare the two books in as many ways as possible: illustrations, character and story. What do you think each author and illustrator is trying to say?

▶ Compare the lives of Amelia and Shelan to that of Anna in **Apple Picking Time** (see Related Books) who picks but does not travel. What things can Anna do that Amelia and Shelan cannot? What things can Amelia and Shelan do that Anna cannot?

EXTENDING THE BOOK

▶ Amelia buries some treasures to make one spot feel like home. What could you bury in a similar container that would show what you are? Take a small basket or box similar to the one Amelia used and go around your home for a few days deciding which things you could put in. Bring your boxes to school and take five minutes apiece to explain the meaning behind each of your choices.

WRITING

▶ Amelia's dream house is rather simple. What would yours be like? Write about it first and then draw it. Make both the writing and drawing as detailed as possible. Is yours different from Amelia's? Why?

MATH

▶ Go to the local market and price apples. Find out how much the market pays the farmer for those apples. What amount goes to the market? What are the market's expenses?

SCIENCE

▶ Is there an area of this country where pickers would not have to travel in order to find work all year long? What crops are available there?

▶ One of the dangers in the lives of migrant farm workers is the use of pesticides in agriculture. Which pesticides are used in the farms nearest you? How safe are those pesticides? What alternatives are possible to the use of pesticides? Are they economically feasible?

▶ Most of us have heard about the dangers of overexposure to sunlight and take precautions. Do migrant workers and other field workers take similar precautions? How could you go about finding that information? What would you tell Amelia about this?

SOCIAL STUDIES

▶ What crops in your area are picked by migrant workers? Which crops are not picked by migrant workers? Who picks those crops?

▶ Talk to some people who live as migrant workers. What do they like and dislike about their jobs and life?

▶ Find out why farm owners use migrant labor. What would they do if no families were willing to live this way?

▶ What rights do migrant workers have? Why do many of them allow children to work in the fields? What do you think about this? What further rights would you give them? Which rights would you take away?

▶ Find out about the life of Cesar Chavez (see Related Books). What changes did he try to make? Is the life of migrant workers any better now than it was before Chavez began his work?

▶ Would you say that Amelia and her family are homeless? Why? What do they have in common with some homeless people?

RELATED BOOKS

NOVELS

Gates, Doris. **Blue Willow**.
Puffin, 1982. ISBN 0-14-030924-1 Grades 4-7
The blue willow plate belonged to her mother and represents home for Janey, the child of migrant workers.

Peck, Robert Newton. **Arly**.
Walker, 1989. ISBN 0-8027-6856-3 Grades 4-8
Set in 1927 in a migrant labor camp in Florida, this story tells of a young boy's future being changed through the actions of a teacher.

Peck, Robert Newton. **Arly's Run**.
Walker, 1991. ISBN 0-8027-8120-9 Grades 4-8
This sequel to **Arly** is set in the early 1900s and centers around life migrant workers had at that time in Florida.

PICTURE BOOKS

Slawson, Michele. **Apple Picking Time**.
Illustrated by Deborah K. Ray. Crown, 1994.
ISBN 0-517-58971-0
Anna's family picks apples, but they are not migrant workers. She tells of the hard work and the satisfaction of a day in the apple orchard.

Thomas, Jane Resh. **Lights on the River**.
Hyperion, 1994. ISBN 0-7868-0004-6
Maria's family carry their house on their backs from farm to farm and their life gets a harsh portrayal in this picture book.

Williams, Sherley Anne. **Working Cotton**.
Illustrated by Carole Byard. Harcourt, 1992.
ISBN 0-15-299624-9
Shelan works with her family in the cotton fields of central California and tells us of one long day in the fields with her family. The illustrations are breath-taking.

NONFICTION

Altman, Linda. **Migrant Farm Workers: The Temporary People**.
Watts, 1994. ISBN 0-531-13033-9
This is a carefully documented, unemotional look at the statistics and facts about migrant farm workers in America today, with most of the focus on Mexican labor.

Ashabranner, Brent. **Dark Harvest: Migrant Farmworkers in America.**
Shoe String Press, 1993. ISBN 0-200-02391-7
Among the many pieces of information in this book are maps indicating the travels of some of the migrant workers.

Atkin, S. Beth. **Voices from the Fields: America's Migrant Children**.
Nine children tell about their lives as migrant families and often as workers themselves. Black and white photographs and poems and writings of the children are interspersed with the narratives.

Brimmer, Larry D. **A Migrant Family**.
Lerner, 1992. ISBN 0-8225-2554-2
The central character in this nonfiction book is Juan Medina, whose Mexican-American family lives in a migrant labor community in southern California.

Holmes, Burnham. **Cesar Chavez**.
Raintree, 1992. ISBN 0-8114-2326-3
This brief biography talks about Chavez's organizing of farm workers and of the many trials and triumphs of his life.

The Bird, the Frog and the Light

by Avi
Illustrated by Matthew Henry
Orchard, 1994
ISBN 0-531-06808-0

SUMMARY

This is a fable in which the frog, a self-proclaimed king, is alone with his underground treasures. The bird, who has been singing to wake up the sun, catches the attention of the pompous frog and is invited underground so that the bird might feel the frog's treasures: his crown, army, palace and great library, among other things, and become aware of the frog's importance. He then sends the bird back to the sun to bring a ray of light into the cave, the better to view his treasures. In the cold light of truth, however, the crown is revealed as a bottle cap, the marble palace a smooth stone, and the great library a torn page from the telephone book that the frog cannot even read. The light, however, will continue since the frog asks the bird to teach him to read.

ILLUSTRATION

A fantastic lesson on texture appears in this book. Most of the compositional elements can be seen in the illustrations, but texture is dominant. Mastery of technical means to create the myriad textures is evident at the turn of each page. The delight is in the details, and Matthew Henry has packed the pages with them.

CONNECTIONS

NOVEL

There is also a connection here between Lois Lowry's **The Giver** (Houghton, 1993. ISBN 0-395-64566-2 Grades 5-9) and this picture book. **The Giver** is, in a sense, the giver of light and that light points out the flaws and the reality of that "ideal" society.

THEME
▶ Search for Truth

CURRICULUM CONNECTION
▶ LANGUAGE ARTS – Myths and fables

Language Arts

INVESTIGATING LITERARY GENRES

▶ The book jacket tells us that this is a fable. Discuss the nature of fables. Is there a moral to this story? Find and read other fables with the same or similar message.

EXTENDING THE STORY

▶ List character traits of the frog and of the bird. Which would you prefer to have as a friend? Why?

▶ The bird is using the telephone book to teach the frog to read. Use the guide words in old telephone books to determine which pages students' own names would appear on. Create appropriate yellow pages for a frog.

WRITING

▶ In teaching the frog to read, the bird informs the frog that "R is for reading." Design an alphabet book for the bird to use as a teaching tool based on reading. For example, *A* could be for advertisement, *B* for book and *C* for comic.

VOCABULARY DEVELOPMENT

▶ Return to the word *light* in the title. What do you think it refers to? Discuss the idiom, "seeing the light."

▶ The word *light* is a multiple-meaning word. Can you think of other multiple-meaning words? Have students provide at least two meanings for words such as *branch*, *fall*, *spring*, *trip*, *bank*, *pitcher*, *match* and others.

▶ Avi writes wonderful descriptions in this book. Find examples of descriptive phrases throughout the story. Re-read the text without showing the illustrations. Is Avi's text complete enough to allow one to "picture the story" or are the illustrations required? Review the description of the items the frog had in his kingdom. Are there other objects that would have felt the same?

▶ Make a list of things that couldn't be done in total darkness. Take a class vote on what would be missed the most if you lived in darkness. Graph the results.

▶ Is it possible that Frog made up his whole kingdom just to force Bird to teach him to read? If so, why didn't Frog simply ask for Bird's help?

COMPARING LITERATURE

▶ Investigate frogs in literature. Find other examples of frogs wishing to be more than mere frogs.

Science

▶ Investigate frogs. Do frogs ever really go underground?

▶ What animals are associated with darkness? Could a mole have been in the frog's role in this story? Why or why not?

▶ Determine the type of bird in the book using bird field guides.

▶ Bird's song brought the sun every day. Listen to bird songs and hold Grammy Awards for "the best of..." in categories generated by the class.

Social Studies

▶ Frog named objects he claimed to have in his dark kingdom. What other items are needed for daily life?

▶ The story ends with Frog starting to learn to read. Why is reading important? What activities, hobbies and jobs require reading?

RELATED BOOKS

NOVELS

Avi. **Nothing But the Truth: A Documentary Novel.**
Thorndike, 1994. ISBN 0-7862-0131-2 Grades 6-9
A boy's attempt to unnerve a teacher sets off a series of events that quickly put the original prank out of the picture and eventually involve everybody but the boy and the teacher. The outcome is what neither of them wanted.

Henkes, Kevin. **Words of Stone.**
Greenwillow, 1992. ISBN 0-688-11356-7 Grades 4-8
Two children deal with the truth and friendship. The stones referred to in the title are set in a circle under that Blaze has buried several imaginary friends that failed to help him deal with his mother's death. Joselle is trying to deal with a mother who has no time for her.

Lowry, Lois. **The Giver.**
Houghton, 1993. ISBN 0-395-64566-2 Grades 5-9
The society seems ideal: no disease, full employment, loving families, until the flaws come slowly to light. They do so through Jason, a young boy who has been selected to receive the memories of that society from The Giver, the keeper of the past.

PICTURE BOOKS

Bunting, Eve. **Terrible Things: An Allegory of the Holocaust**. Illustrated by Stephen Gammell. Jewish Publication Society, 1989.
ISBN 0-8276-0325-8
The forest creatures refuse to protect each other when the Terrible Things come to take them away, species by species. Where they go and what happens to them is unknown and the survivors wait for their turn.

Grimm, Jacob and Grimm, Wilhelm. **The Frog Prince**
Many versions are available of this fairy tale of a frog who demands royal treatment from a very selfish princess.

Gwynne, Fred. **Pondlarker**.
Simon and Schuster, 1992. ISBN 0-671-70846-5
Pondlarker the frog has grown up listening to the story of the Frog Prince and is convinced that he himself is on the brink of metamorphosis.

McFarland, John. **The Exploding Frog and Other Fables from Aesop**. Little, 1981
This book contains several of Aesop's fables delightfully illustrated by James Marshall.

Scieszka, Jon. The **Frog Prince, Continued**.
Penguin USA, 1991. ISBN 0-670-83421-1
Here's what happened after the princess and the frog prince married and supposedly lived happily ever after.

Vesey, A. **The Princess and the Frog**.
Atlantic Monthly, 1985
In this story, the frog is not an enchanted prince but a freeloader.

Rebel

by Allan Baillie
Illustrated by Di Wu
Ticknor & Fields, 1994
ISBN: 0-395-69250-4

SUMMARY

A general marches his troops and tanks into a small village in Burma. He declares that he will now control the lives of all the villagers. As he is giving his speech, a child's thong is thrown at him. The general orders all the school children to be brought before him and his troops to search for the child who is wearing only one thong. Instead of finding the "rebel," the general sees a large pile of thongs and every one of the children and their teachers bare footed. Having lost face and now being the laughing stock of the village, the general and his troops depart. The book jacket states that this story is based on an incident that occurred in Rangoon.

ILLUSTRATION

Drawing skill is the basis for these successful illustrations. The many portraits are accurate accountings of individual likenesses. They are similar to courthouse drawings where the interest is in a visual record of people and events. Watercolor washes of soft muted hues make up the forms that are drawn with soft-textured pencil lines. The narrative is similar to a newspaper account of events. The illustrations are similar to editorial cartoons.

CONNECTIONS

NOVELS

Two novels for older students by Robert Cormier fit in well with the plot of **The Rebel** in that they deal with a gang of bullies and one child who dares to rebel against them. They are **The Chocolate War** and **Beyond the Chocolate War** (see Related Books).

THEMES

▶ Bullies
▶ Community
▶ Courage

CURRICULUM CONNECTION

▶ HISTORY – Dictators, resistance

Language Arts

Vocabulary Development

▶ What is a rebel? What are some synonyms for rebel? Name some famous ones. Are rebels always right?

▶ Re-read the first page and then the page where the general and his army are retreating. What words have changed? How have these changes affected the meaning of the text?

▶ The footwear in this book (thongs) is one type of shoe. What other footwear is worn and for what reasons? Do we wear any shoes similar to thongs?

Interpreting the Text

▶ Discuss the mood of the story. How does it change? What events create turning points in the mood of the story?

▶ Take a character in the story (the general, a villager, a teacher, a student) and tell that person's feelings and how they changed throughout the story.

▶ How would the story have been different if the child who threw the thong had been discovered? How might the story have been different if the child had not thrown the thong?

▶ Are there any other ways that the villagers could have protested the general's presence and actions?

▶ Given the illustrations and the general's speech, what does the reader know about the people in this book?

Extending the Book

▶ Every school has at least one bully. Brainstorm ways to deal with bullies. Consider using role playing to illustrate appropriate ways to cope with someone who is unkind or unfair. Make up situations (such as a bully trying to take lunch money, a bully starting a fight, a bully who is cruelly teasing another student) and act out the roles. Expand the situations to include other If... then... statements.

Social Studies

▶ Locate Burma (renamed Union of Myanmar in 1989) on a map. Investigate the country. Does a general rule the country?

▶ The Armed Services depicted in the book wear uniforms. What other jobs require uniforms? What purposes are there for wearing uniforms? Sometimes current fashions become almost a type of uniform. Discuss whether your students dress in common. Can your students design a uniform to wear to school?

▶ In the book, government was by force. How is our government formed? Perhaps an elected official from your area could speak to your class about his or her role in government and how he or she got that job.

▶ Consider holding a class election to determine the class color or mascot. Have students prepare and give speeches in favor of their choice and design campaign posters. Vote by secret ballot.

▶ In the book, the general states his "rules." Were these rules fair to the villagers? Why or why not? Review school or classroom rules. What reasons are there for making rules? What could you do if you felt that a rule was unfair? Are there some rules common to most people in our society?

▶ During World War II, in countries under Nazi rule, Jews had to wear the Star of David on their clothing. Find out what one king did to show support for the Jews and to confuse their captors.

▶ Look for similar acts of defiance and group actions in accounts of the women's suffrage movement, antiwar demonstrations, labor strikes and environmental protests.

RELATED BOOKS

PICTURE BOOKS

Briggs, Raymond. **The Tin-Pot Foreign General and the Old Iron Woman**.
Little, 1985. ISBN 0-316 10801-4
This is a scathing satire about the Falklands war in picture book format.

NOVELS

Banks. Lynne Reid. **The Fairy Rebel**.
Avon, 1989. ISBN 0-380-70650-4 Grades 3-6
This novel is about the naughty rebellion of Tiki, a fairy who defies her queen in order to help a childless couple.

Cormier, Robert. **Beyond the Chocolate War**.
Dell, 1986. ISBN 0-440-90580-X Grades 6-9
This is the sequel to **The Chocolate War** (see Related Books). In this volume, the dictatorship and power structure of the school are challenged by the group, and when Brother Leon is hit in the face with a tomato, the class elects the thrower of that tomato class president.

Cormier, Robert **The Chocolate War**.
G K. Hall, 1988. ISBN 0-8161-4528-8 Grades 6-9
This powerful book for older students explores the abuses of power by the head of a boys' school, Brother Leon, and the gang he controls, The Vigils.

NONFICTION

Bonvillain, Nancy. **Black Hawk, Sac Rebel**.
Chelsea, 1993. ISBN 0-7910-1711-7
When U. S. army general Edmund P. Gaines was sent to force the Indians removal from their home in Illinois, Black Hawk rebelled.

Shirer, William L. **The Rise and Fall of Adolf Hitler**.
Random, 1967. ISBN 0-394-90547-4
Hitler's dictatorship caused worldwide repercussions and remarkably little rebellion amongst his people.

Stern, Philip Van Doren. **Henry David Thoreau**.
Harper, 1972. ISBN 0-690-37715-0
Thoreau rebelled in deeds when he refused to pay his taxes and in his writing when he protested against society's injustices.

Wright, David K. **Burma**.
Childrens, 1991. ISBN 0-516-02725-5
This is a clear nonfictional source for material on Burmese history, geography, religion and culture. The reading level will be challenging for some readers.

Zane, Alex. **Osceola: Seminole Rebel**.
Chelsea, 1994. ISBN 0-7910-1716-8
Osceola fought against the removal of the Seminoles from Florida.

OTHER BOOKS BY ALLAN BAILLIE

Adrift. Puffin, 1994. ISBN 0-14-037010-2
In this short novel, a boy and his sister are carried out to sea in their makeshift boat.

Bawshou Rescues the Sun. Illustrated by Michelle Powell. Scholastic, 1992. ISBN 0-590-45453-6
Retelling a tale by Chun Chan Yeh, Baillie tells a story of primeval China and a youth that grows under the protection of the phoenix.

Drac and the Gremlin. Illustrated by Jane Tanner. Puffin, 1992. ISBN 0-14-054542-5
A child's playtime becomes an imaginary adventure.

If You Are a Hunter of Fossils

by Byrd Baylor
Illustrated by Peter Parnall
Simon & Schuster, 1984
ISBN 0-689-70773-8

SUMMARY

In first-person narrative the book tells of a child exploring a mountain in the desert, which once was part of a vast sea. She finds the fossils of sea creatures and imagines the time long past when the sea was there. The book is a treasure of terms from geology and paleontology embedded in a poetic text.

ILLUSTRATION

It takes time and care to see and appreciate all of the subtle images that are woven into Peter Parnell's compositions. The color-filled linear shapes are inviting compositions apart from their function as illustration for this story. Various elements of nature meld or blend with one another to create mixed forms. Land, sea and sky blend together with human figures to form unique relationships in composition. Hidden forms can be discovered or seen in new relationships imagined by the reader or intended by Parnall. While pen and ink drawing and watercolors are traditional tools for illustrators, they are used by Parnall with extraordinary imagination and skill.

CONNECTIONS

NOVEL

Pam Conrad's **My Daniel** (HarperCollins, 1989. ISBN 0-06-021818-2 Grades 5-9)
 deals with the intense competition for dinosaur fossils that took place at the turn of the century.

THEMES
▶ Deserts
▶ Prints and printing

CURRICULUM CONNECTION
▶ SCIENCE – Rocks and fossils

LANGUAGE ARTS

VOCABULARY

▶ The study of fossils is called paleontology. Use a dictionary to find out what the prefix paleo and the suffix ology mean.

WRITING

▶ At the end of the book, when the child is walking home, holding a rock, Baylor says, "You always hold onto that long chain of life as you go." Find an interesting rock. It's nice if it's a fossil but it doesn't have to be. Can you imagine the chain of life it represents? Write its possible life story.

MATH

▶ Find out when a sea existed in what is now the desert of southwestern United States. Make a time line showing what creatures existed elsewhere in the world during that time.

SCIENCE

▶ Make fossil-like shapes by flattening a piece of plasticene about two inches thick and turning up the edges to form a solid ridge. Coat a shell with Vaseline and push it into the plasticene to form an imprint. Remove the shell and pour plaster of Paris into the plasticene. After it hardens, remove the clay. Both the clay and the plaster shapes are fossil-like. Are they fossils? Why or why not? What substance would be the plasticene in real fossils?

▶ Byrd Baylor mentions many prehistoric creatures in the text. Choose one of them and find out all you can about it.

▶ Baylor also mentions limestone, the kind of rock that is apt to contain this kind of fossil. Dinosaur footprints are often found in shale. Shale and limestone are just two of the many kinds of rock, which you can learn to identify. One way of identifying rocks is by using a streak test. You do this by rubbing a mineral sample across a piece of unglazed porcelain. Use the backside of a piece of porcelain tile. Rub a spoon across it first. What color is the streak? It should be the same color as the mineral that scratched it if that mineral were ground into powder. The spoon scratch is probably gray. Try it with other rocks and minerals for one clue for identifying it.

▶ Find some rocks that you think might be limestone. Pour soda water onto the rock. What happens? If it is limestone, the liquid will bubble and fizz.

▶ Another way to identify a rock is by its hardness using Moh's hardness scale. Classify some rocks using these guidelines:

Hardness 1. You can scratch it easily with a fingernail.

Hardness 2. You can scratch it with a fingernail but it's hard to do so.

Hardness 3. You can scratch it with a penny.

Hardness 4. You can scratch it with a knife. Limestone is this hardness.

Hardness 5. You can scratch it with a knife but you have to bear down hard.

Hardness 6. It will scratch a knife.

Hardness 7. It will scratch glass.

Hardness 8. It will scratch quartz.

Hardness 9. It will scratch topaz.

Hardness 10. Diamond will scratch any other rock

SOCIAL STUDIES

▶ Find out about people who hunt fossils for their life's work. What do they call themselves? How do you train to become one? Who pays them?

ART

▶ Create sandscapes to mimic the layers of rock. Collect sand from several sources and compare the differences in the color. You can add food coloring to tint some of the sand for greater contrast. Pour the different colors into a glass jar. Use a knitting needle along the side of the jar to lift a small amount of sand up or push it down. Fill the jar completely before you put on the lid so that the sand layers will stay.

RELATED BOOKS

NOVELS

Boston, Lucy. **The Fossil Snake**.
Atheneum, 1975. ISBN 0-689-50037-8
A fossilized snake comes to life and changes a young boy's life.

Butterworth, Oliver. **The Enormous Egg**.
Dell, 1987. ISBN 0-440-42337-6
This book touches on political and scientific satire as it tells the funny story of a dinosaur egg that hatches and becomes both a treasure and a threat.

Conrad, Pam. **My Daniel**.
HarperCollins, 1989. ISBN 0-06-021818-2 Grades 5-9
Julia Creath Summerwaite, age 80, has come from Nebraska to take her grandchildren to the natural history museum. During their frequent rest stops the old lady tells them of her brother Daniel, who became obsessed with finding the fossil bones that, ultimately, caused his death.

Lasky, Kathryn. **The Bone Wars**.
Morrow, 1988. ISBN 0-688-07433-2 Grades 6-9
This challenging novel is set in the 1870s when the competition for fossil remains almost equaled that for gold. Two teenagers, fed up with the actions of the paleontologists they work for, resolve to make public their latest discoveries.

PICTURE BOOKS

Baylor, Byrd. **Everybody Needs a Rock**.
Simon, 1974. ISBN 0-684-13899-9
The various properties of rocks are explored in a beautiful and poetic manner.

NONFICTION

Arnold, Caroline. **Trapped in Tar: Fossils from the Ice Age**. Houghton, 1987. ISBN 0-8991- 415-X
The La Brea tar pits are described and explored with photographs and text.

Horner, Jack. **Digging Up Tyrannosaurus Rex**.
Crown, 1992. ISBN 0-517-58783-1
In 1990, a family made the first discovery of a complete skeleton of the huge dinosaur. Here the laborious excavation is described and woven into information about the dinosaur itself.

Lindsay, William. **Prehistoric Life**.
Knopf, 1994. ISBN 0-679-86001-0
This Eyewitness book concentrates more on the creatures as they lived, but there is some good fossil information as well.

Rhodes, Frank. **Fossils: A Guide to Prehistoric Life**.
Western, 1962. ISBN 0-307-24411-3
Although this book has been around for a while, it's a good guide to the most common plant and animal fossils.

Roberts, Allan. **Fossils**.
Childrens, 1983. ISBN 0-516-41678-2
This is far simpler and easier to read although, of course, less complete than the Eyewitness book listed below.

Taylor, Paul. **Fossil**.
Random, 1990. ISBN 0-679-90440-9
Part of the Eyewitness series, this book covers concisely but in significant depth information about the creation and recovery of fossil forms and the information humans have obtained from them.

Other Books by Byrd Baylor and Peter Parnall
See page 24.

The Table Where Rich People Sit

by Byrd Baylor
Illustrated by Peter Parnall
Simon & Schuster, 1994
ISBN 0-684-19653-0

▶ SUMMARY

A young girl has called a family meeting to discuss their lack of money. The family gathers around their homemade table for the discussion, which quickly turns from cash-oriented to what they reckon as real wealth—the ability to see sunsets, hear coyotes and walk canyons. One by one they give each of these perks a dollar value and their wealth quickly accumulates as our narrator, their list-maker, totals it all on paper.

▶ ILLUSTRATION

Parnall uses unique pen line and watercolors that capture the American Southwest. While the colors are bright and raw, they never appear garish, and while many of Parnall's shapes are abstract, we never have difficulty identifying them.

▶ CONNECTIONS

NOVEL

Eleanor Estes' **Hundred Dresses** (Harcourt, 1974. ISBN 0-15-642350-2 Grades 3-6) is a very short novel (or long short story) about a much maligned girl at school who claims to have 100 dresses at home but prefers the worn one she always wears.

THEMES

▶ Family
▶ Needs
▶ Values

CURRICULUM CONNECTION

▶ MATH – Adding large numbers

LANGUAGE ARTS

WRITING

▶ The girl in the book considers herself the family's list maker. Make a list of lists—possible lists you could make. Start with logical ones but don't be afraid to go out on a limb a bit. For instance, you could make a shopping list, a list of things to pack for various occasions, but you could also make a list of favorite smells, sights, and sounds, or a list of people with whom you'd like to change places. Compare your list of lists with those of others in the class. Feel free to copy any of their good ideas.

▶ The narrator of this book finds herself with a list of things that make her family wealthy. Do the same for your own family.

EXTENDING THE TEXT

▶ This family thinks that the first thing a baby sees should be important and beautiful and so they show their first child a desert mountain and their next child an ocean with a jungle coming right up to it. If you become a parent some day, what are the first sights you'd like your child to see?

FINDING THEMES

▶ Look through some of the books listed below by Byrd Baylor, especially *Guess Who My Favorite Person Is* and *I'm in Charge of Celebrations* (see Related Books). What do you think Byrd Baylor is trying to tell us about beauty and happiness in her books?

MATH

▶ Here's a chance to play with big numbers. Make your own list of things of real value in your life and attach a monetary value to it.

▶ Compare that list to reality. What are the chemicals that make up the human body worth? Add to that the value of the clothing you wear on a typical school day.

▶ Use your figures and those of others in the class to construct a graph showing the value placed on treasures in your life.

▶ Although the girl in this book is thinking of money at the beginning of the story when she talks about wealth, at the end she thinks of other things as wealth. Thinking monetarily, what do you think of as wealth? How much money or how many things would someone have to have for you to think of them as wealthy?

SOCIAL STUDIES

OCCUPATIONS

▶ The family members in this book like their outdoor jobs and are quick to list the reasons why. Many jobs have so-called perks or rewards besides money. Look first at the jobs or chores you do. Do any of them have perks? For instance, delivering papers is a hard job, but if you like being out of doors, especially early in the morning, that could be extra perks or wealth for you.

▶ What other jobs do you know of that have better rewards than those your family gets?

▶ After you've finished thinking about your perks, ask your family members, neighbors, friends and relatives if their jobs have any extra wealth in them.

▶ When these people talk about their riches, they talk about the sights and sounds of the desert. What would people in your area see, hear and feel that might be thought of as riches?

RELATED BOOKS

NOVELS

Estes, Eleanor. **The Hundred Dresses**.
Harcourt, 1974. ISBN 0-15-642350-2 Grades 3-6
This very brief novel concerns the ridicule visited upon a poor girl in school and the later realization of what the taunters did. As in **The Table Where Rich People Sit,** there is a theme of monetary versus other kinds of values.

Lowry, Lois. **Autumn Street**.
Dell, 1980. ISBN 0-440-40344-8 Grades 4-9
This insightful novel contains characters from the privileged as well as the underprivileged society in the small Pennsylvania town.

PICTURE BOOKS

Baylor, Byrd. **Guess Who My Favorite Person Is.**
Illustrated by Robert Parker. Simon & Schuster, 1985. ISBN 0-689-71052-6
A young man and a girl play a game of choosing their most favorite things.

Baylor, Byrd. **I'm In Charge of Celebrations**.
Simon & Schuster, 1986. ISBN 0-684-18579 2
A young girl describes sights and occasions in the desert that are worth celebrating.

OTHER BOOKS BY BYRD BAYLOR AND PETER PARNALL

The Desert Is Theirs. Simon & Schuster, 1987.
ISBN 0-689-71105-0
This tribute to the Southwest focuses on the Papago people and their adaptation to and appreciation of the desert.

Desert Voices. Simon & Schuster, 1981.
ISBN 0-684-16712-3
Each desert creature tells of its life and special adaptations in prose that approaches poetry.

Everybody Needs a Rock. Simon & Schuster, 1985.
ISBN 0-689-71051-8
The author lists 10 ways to find the perfect rock.

If You Are a Hunter of Fossils. Scribner, 1980.
ISBN 0-684-16419-1
See page 19.

Jigsaw Jackson

by David F. Birchman
Illustrated by Daniel San Souci
Lothrop, 1996
ISBN 0-688-11632-9

SUMMARY

J. Jupiter Jackson is a potato farmer in Maine when he is first introduced to jigsaw puzzles by one Sean McShaker, salesman. His skill at completing them is so great and so fast that Sean talks him into leaving his farm and the animals who had always enjoyed the farmer's songs, stories and games. Soon "Jigsaw Jackson" is wowing audiences everywhere, accomplishing greater and greater feats of jigsaw puzzling set up by Sean McShaker. His animals' efforts to coax him into returning home are disparaged by McShaker, but then, at the White House, a piece of the puzzle is missing and J. Jupiter Jackson returns home, where readers will soon discover the missing piece.

ILLUSTRATION

An inventory of illustration techniques can be found in these fun-filled compositions. Many of the pictures have compositions within compositions. San Souci uses a range of lettering styles with variations in scale. It might be fun to catalog the kinds of lettering type beginning with the book jacket's inside front flap.

CONNECTIONS

NOVEL

This tall tale connects with the books about McBroom written by Sid Fleischman, especially **McBroom Tells the Truth** (Little, 1981. ISBN 0-316-28550-1 Grades 3-6).

THEMES

- Individual talents
- Tall tales

CURRICULUM CONNECTION

- SOCIAL STUDIES – Regional occupations

LANGUAGE ARTS

VOCABULARY DEVELOPMENT

▶ Jigsaw Jackson is an alliterative name. Use the phone book, especially the yellow pages, to find others. Make a list of famous alliterative names.

▶ Jigsaw Jackson's nickname comes from his special skill. Find other nicknames in the sports world that have similar origins.

▶ When the animals try to persuade Jigsaw to return home, Sean McShaker uses a put-down name for them. Make a list of these and add others he could have used.

▶ Why do they call them jigsaw puzzles? How are they made? Have they always been made that way?

NOTICING DETAILS

▶ Jackson's license plate on the old truck is "Spud 1." What would be some good license plates for other characters in real life or in books?

▶ Where is the missing puzzle piece?

▶ Figure out the time of this book.

FANTASY AND REALISM

▶ Which of the events in the story do you believe could have happened? What makes it a tall tale?

EXTENDING THE STORY

▶ Issue and carry out non-dangerous challenges about your special skill. Fill out a form such as the one below:

I'M GOOD AT _____. I CAN _____.
I challenge you to _____.
                        Signed _____

▶ Hold a jigsaw contest in your school. Will you use teams or individuals? Make sure the rules are clear. What would be appropriate prizes?

▶ Make original jigsaw puzzles out of posters or drawings. What makes one puzzle easier than another? More fun? More challenging?

COMPARING SIMILAR LITERATURE

▶ Jigsaw Jackson is a tall tale character. Compare him to **Swamp Angel** (see page 105), **Pecos Bill, Paul Bunyan** and others. See page 106 for other tall tale activities.

SOCIAL STUDIES

▶ The Wild West show run by Bison Bob may be make-believe, but there were real Wild West shows. Find out about them. Does some form of them still exist?

▶ Interview members of three generations about their pastime activities. Have they changed over the years? What leisure time activities are available today that were not available 50 years ago? Has the change had positive and negative effects? What are they?

▶ Completing jigsaw puzzles is one kind of leisure time activity. What do you do with your leisure time? How much leisure time do you have? Make a chart like the one below with each hour of the day listed. First fill in the things you have to do, such as sleep, go to school and do chores. Then add up all the time you are awake and don't have specific things you must do. How do you spend that time? Is that what you'd like to be doing? Do you have choices?

TIME	Mon.	Tues.	Wed.	Thurs.	Fri.	Sat.	Sun.
6:00 a.m.	Sleep	Sleep	Sleep	Sleep	Sleep	Sleep	Sleep
7:00 a.m.	Get ready for school	Get ready for school	Get ready for school	Get ready for school	Get ready for school	Sleep	Sleep
8:00 a.m.	Catch the bus	Catch the bus	Catch the bus	Catch the bus	Catch the bus	Watch cartoons	Sleep
9:00 a.m.	School	School	School	School	School		
10:00 a.m.							

▶ The animals in the book communicate in three ways with Jigsaw while he's on the road. What ways could they have used today? In 1776? In ancient times?

▶ The salesman in this book travels from home to home peddling his wares. How are sales made in today's world?

▶ Investigate advertising. Look at television and magazine ads and evaluate their honesty.

ART

▶ Cut a large sheet of tag or cardboard the size of the bulletin board into enough jigsaw-like pieces for each child to have one good-sized piece. Let each child design his or her piece, sign it and then fit it into place on the bulletin board.

RELATED BOOKS

NOVELS

Fleischman, Sid. **McBroom Tells the Truth**.
Little, 1981. ISBN 0-316-28550-1 Grades 3-6
This is an elongated tall tale of the adventures of McBroom and his 11 children on their super one-acre farm.

Speirs, John. **The Great Carnival Caper**.
Reader's Digest, 1993. ISBN 0-89577-453-4
Grades 3-5
This is a book with a plot and many varied puzzles to solve as three children try to find out why the Thirteen Clown Carnival is in trouble.

PICTURE BOOKS

Baylor, Byrd. **Guess Who My Favorite Person Is**.
Illustrated by Robert Andrew Parker. Aladdin, 1985. ISBN 0-689-71052-6
A little girl and a man wile away a summer afternoon playing a game of choosing their favorites.

NONFICTION

Gryski, Camilla. **Many Stars and More String Games**. Morrow, 1985. ISBN 0-688-05793-4
String games, some of which tell stories, are carefully described and illustrated.

Hankin, Rosie. **What Was It Like Before Television?**
Steck-Vaughn, 1995. ISBN 0-8114-5735-4
An old woman tells some children about the things she did for fun when she was young.

Humphrey, Paul. **What Was It Like Before the Telephone?** Steck-Vaughn, 1995. ISBN 0-8114-5636-2
A museum tour leads to a simplified history of communications.

Lankford, Mary D. **Hopscotch Around the World**.
Morrow, 1992. ISBN 0-688-08419-2
Nineteen forms of hopscotch are described and a world map shows the country of origin.

LaPlaca, Annette. **Are We Almost There?**
Harold Shaw, 1992. ISBN 0-87788-051-4
This book of games that can be played during travel has great variety.

Lyttle, Richard B. **The Games They Played: Sports in History**. Atheneum, 1982. ISBN 0-689-30928-7
Archeological discoveries are the basis of this exploration of the games ancient people played.

Pearson, Susan. **The Green Magician Puzzle**.
Simon & Schuster, 1991. ISBN 0-671-74054-7
Clever riddles are the puzzles in this chapter book in which teams are vying to become Green Magicians in the Earth Day play at school.

Schwartz, Alvin. **Unriddling: All Sorts of Riddles to Puzzle Your Guessary**. Harper Trophy, 1987.
ISBN 0-06-446057-6
This collection of riddles and puzzles from folklore has something for everyone.

Wiswell, Phil. **Kids' Games: Traditional Indoor and Outdoor Activities for Children.** Doubleday, 1987.
ISBN 0-385-23405-8
Rules of games are given and their origins discussed.

A Song of Stars

An Asian legend adapted by Tom Birdseye
Illustrated by Ju-Hong Chen
Holiday House, 1990
ISBN 0-8234-0790-X

SUMMARY

In the night sky lived a beautiful young princess who wove the shimmering threads of the firmament. Newlang was a herdsman, moving with his oxen while singing soft songs. They met and soon their songs were love songs. The princess' father was the Emperor of the Heavens and agreed they should be married, but became angry when they neglected their duties. He condemned them to be separated forever by the Milky Way with Newlang living on the other side. In spite of a dreadful storm the lovers were able to enjoy their first reunion "even if only for a short time." The author's note on the last page explains the celebration of the legend in modern day China and Japan.

ILLUSTRATION

These overlapping shapes give an effect similar to that of stained glass. The still frames of images have a connection with animated film-making. Many of the images are fragmented into various shapes that are then filled in with color from paint medium with color pencil overlays. The isolated shapes of the color create puzzle-like pieces that are bright and spirited on wonderful fields of white.

CONNECTIONS

NOVEL

Traveling through the heavens could make a connection between this book and Madeleine L'Engle's **A Wrinkle in Time** (Dell, 1976. ISBN 0-440-99805-0 Grades 4-7).

THEME

▶ Myths and legends

CURRICULUM CONNECTION

▶ SCIENCE – Astronomy

Language Arts

COMPARE AND CONTRAST

▶ Compare the work of Chouchou and Newlang. Is weaving more important than ox herding? Is weaving a menial job for a princess? Which job was more important? Satisfying? Necessary?

▶ Contrast the pounding storm in the story to a storm here on earth. Examine such elements as

    Waves crashing into an angry tide of stars

    A boat hidden behind the moon

    The gentle flow of the Milky Way

FEELINGS AND ATTITUDES

▶ Imagine and chart the feelings of the three characters during:

	The meeting	The courtship	After the storm
Chouchou			
Newlang			
Emperor			

▶ The emperor thought the love the two shared was strong and sure. When did his feelings change? After he enforced his separation rule did his attitude soften?

CLASSIFICATION

▶ Decide whether the many colorful phrases could be considered to be real or fantasy.

Real	Fantasy
A song of love	Ox nibbling light
Circles on the surface of the river	Fibers of the moonglow

▶ Find others and classify them.

▶ Collect a variety of Asian folk tales. Categorize them as to countries: Japanese, Chinese, Korean, Vietnamese.

EXTENDING THE STORY

▶ Continue the story with a paragraph or two.

    They were satisfied to meet just once a year until old age.

    They found a way to meet secretly more often.

    The emperor changed his mind, married them and allowed them to find happiness remaining together.

Choose one or more of these or create a new scenario.

MORAL OR PROVERB

▶ The Emperor angrily declares that the couple has forsaken duty. In addition they neglected their work. Compose a moral for each, for example "Duty before devotion" or "Happiness is working."

PARTS OF SPEECH

▶ There are some wonderful phrases here. Choose those with colorful adjectives, for example *soft* songs, *starry* current, *gleaming* robes, *rustling* bridge.

▶ Find other phrases with powerful verbs, for example magpies *swooped*, tears *washed*, Newlang *prodded*, you have *forsaken*.

WORD MEANINGS

▶ Determine what the author meant in these phrases:

    threads of the firmament
    sky dwellers
    night thread
    watery rainbow
    swollen Milky Way
    gently rolling bridge

Find other unusual phrases and give meaning to them.

▶ The author uses various words and phrases for the "Milky Way," for example "river of stars," "starry current." Find other words for "Milky Way."

▶ Reread the story to find any words and phrases that need clarification, for example "curtain of a pounding storm."

CHARACTERIZATIONS

▶ Create a positive and negative list for each character. Include personality traits, nature.

Chouchou	Newlang	Emperor
positive negative	positive negative	positive negative

▶ Speculate on why the Emperor did not rescind his decree concerning the separation. Did the couple deserve such punishment?

FIGURATIVE LANGUAGE

▶ Find at least four phrases the author uses in place of the term "Milky Way," such as "river of stars."

▶ Examine the illustrations and create some unique names for the configurations of stars similar to the constellations.

SCIENCE
MILKY WAY

▶ Try to find phrases from the story to finish each sentence.

A *meteor* is a trail of light or _____.
Large and bright *meteoroids* are fireballs or _____.

The smallest ones are *micrometeorites* or _____.

The center of the Milky Way is composed of _____.

▶ The brightest part of the Milky Way extends through some of the signs of the zodiac. The zodiac is divided into 12 sections of 30 degrees each. Name the 12 signs of the zodiac and the identifying symbol.

▶ Constellations are any of 88 imagined groupings of bright stars that appear in the sky. They are named for mythological or religious figures, animals or objects. List a few of the brightest constellations. Name them and sketch them.

▶ Try stargazing on clear, moonless nights. Identify the Milky Way and star groupings.

SOCIAL STUDIES

▶ Locate several Asian countries on a map: China, Japan, Korea, Vietnam, Taiwan. Identify large cities.

▶ Research the government of each country. Are there emperors in any of these countries? If so, are they just figureheads?

▶ The people of China celebrate the Festival of the Milky Way on the seventh day of the seventh month. In Japan it is called the Weaving Loom Festival. (Reread the author's note.) Find out about other holidays in these countries. Research the New Year celebrations.

▶ RELATED BOOKS

NOVELS

L'Engle, Madeleine. **A Wrinkle in Time**.
Dell, 1976. ISBN 0-440-99805-0 Grades 4-7
Meg travels through time and space to locate her father, who is under control of a great brain on the planet Camazotz.

Spinelli, Jerry. **Maniac Magee**.
Little, 1990. ISBN 0-316-80722-2 Grades 4-8
The beginning of this Newbery Award winning book deals with the legends that have sprung up around the deeds of the title character.

PICTURE BOOKS

Ginsburg, Mirra. **The Chinese Mirror**.
Illustrated by Margot Zemach. Harcourt, 1991.
ISBN 0-15-217508-3
This is a Korean folk tale about a mirror. Chaos is created when the people fail to recognize their own images.

Heyer, Marilee. **The Weaving of a Dream**.
Penguin, 1989. ISBN 0-14-050528-8
A poor woman has her tapestry stolen by fairies. Her three sons journey far away to find it. This is the retelling of a traditional Chinese folk tale.

Lee, Jeanne M. **The Legend of the Milky Way**. Henry Holt, 1982. ISBN 0-8050-1361-X
This is a Chinese legend of a flute-playing shepherd. He draws down a weaver princess from the sky.

Lee, Jeanne M. **Toad is the Uncle of Heaven: A Vietnamese Folk Tale**. Henry Holt, 1985.
ISBN 0-8050-1146-3
This folk tale from Vietnam tells the story of Toad. He goes to heaven to end a drought.

Louie, Ai-Ling. **Yeh-Shen: A Cinderella Story from China**. Illustrated by Ed Young. Philomel, 1982.
ISBN 0399-20900-X
A young girl becomes the bride of a prince in spite of a wicked stepmother and stepsister.

NONFICTION

Simon, Seymour. **The Stars**.
Morrow, 1986. ISBN 0-688-05855-8
This informational book provides the reader with facts about a variety of stars from giants and dwarfs to super nova and quasars.

The Banshee Train

by Odds Bodkin
Illustrated by Ted Rose
Clarion, 1995
ISBN 0-395-69426-4

SUMMARY

As the train goes from Troublesome to Steamboat Springs, the fireman and engineer are leery about the trestle over Gore Canyon. Twenty years previously the trestle had collapsed and all aboard a train were killed. Now, however, the new train is giving them trouble: the throttle moves by itself, continually stopping the train. Worse, another train, inexplicably on the same track, is right behind them. Unable to stop to examine the trestle ahead, the men must build up speed. Snow and fog obscure their view and their train refuses to budge. As the pursuing train speeds through them, they glimpse ghostly images and a screaming banshee. Later, they find the trestle gone again, their lives saved by the banshee train.

ILLUSTRATION

A train is a natural subject for perspective and Rose plays with perspective from several interesting angles. The color washes are superb and demonstrate beautifully muted analogous color schemes. Added interest is in the superimposing of objects on one another. The images in the smoke are particularly well done.

CONNECTIONS

NOVEL

In **The Ghost Belonged To Me** (Viking, 1987. ISBN 0-670-33767-6 Grades 3-7) there is a similar incident with a train wreck and a mysterious warning.

THEMES
▶ Ghost Stories
▶ Storytelling

CURRICULUM CONNECTION
▶ HISTORY – Local legends

LANGUAGE ARTS

COMPARING AND CONTRASTING

▶ Find other urban legends and ghost stories from your area. Are they easier to tell than to write? Why do you think this is so?

▶ The appearance of a banshee was a warning of death to some people. What other signs have you heard about? Does anyone you know believe them?

▶ Find out more about banshees. Where do they come from? Is there any scientific basis for their existence?

▶ What are the clues that tell you that a story you are about to hear or read is a ghost story?

▶ One of the definitions of a legend is that either the teller or the listener believes it to be true. Does that make many ghost stories legends?

FINDING SIMILAR LITERATURE

▶ Find and read the novel by Richard Peck entitled **The Ghost Belonged to Me** (see Related Books) in which a different kind of ghostly experience warns of a train wreck.

WRITING

▶ Most families have at least one ghost story. Find someone in your family or neighborhood who has had a ghostly encounter or knows of someone else who did. Get them to tell you the story and then write it up for others to hear.

SCIENCE

▶ Could this story be true? What might a scientist think of it? What explanations could he or she offer for this experience?

▶ Many of the jobs that used to be necessary to run a train are now done by computer. Find out how modern trains operate and which jobs are still done by human beings.

MATH

▶ The trestle in the story crosses Gore Canyon. Calculate the length of the span necessary to cross the largest river or canyon in your area.

▶ Investigate railroad safety and compare it to airline safety. Which method of transportation has the largest number of accidents? The most casualties?

SOCIAL STUDIES

▶ Find the route of this train on a map of Colorado.

▶ Find out about the narrow-gauge railroad that still runs between Silverton and Durango, Colorado, traveling high in the Rockies. Are there other colorful routes for trains in North America today? Find someone who has ridden some of these trains and interview him or her about the trains.

▶ In the book the train must cross a large canyon. Make a list of canyons in the United States. Do roads or railroads cross them? Locate road and railroad maps to find out.

▶ The afterword of the book talks about the Irish immigrants who worked on the railroads. Find out about the use of Chinese, Irish and other immigrant labor in America. Why were these workers desirable? Did life get any better for them after their use as cheap labor?

ART

▶ How successful do you think Ted Rose's illustrations are for this book? Do the trains look real? How does he show the lack of good visibility? Compare his trains in motion to that of Donald Crews in his book Freight Train for much younger viewers and Bart Forbes' **How Many Miles to Jacksonville** (see Related Books).

RELATED BOOKS

NOVELS

Peck, Richard. **The Ghost Belonged to Me**.
Viking, 1987. ISBN 0-670-33767-6 Grades 3-7
This is the first of the Blossom Culp novels by Richard Peck. In this one the clairvoyant child gives warning of a coming train wreck.

PICTURE BOOKS

Ahlberg, Allan. **The Ghost Train**.
Putnam, 1992. ISBN 0-688-11435-0
Various ghosts, ghouls and monsters ride the train and are frightened by a crying baby.

Crews, Donald. **Freight Train**. Greenwillow
This beautifully designed book explains the individual cars on the train.

Fleischman, Paul. **Time Train**.
HarperCollins, 1991. ISBN 0-06-021709-X
Miss Pym takes her class on a train that takes them back to the time of the dinosaurs.

Johnston, Tony. **How Many Miles to Jacksonville?**
Illustrated by Bart Forbes. Putnam, 1996.
ISBN 0-399 22615-X
Based on the childhood memories of the author's father, this nostalgic picture book tells about the mystique of trains in about the same era as **The Banshee Train**.

Lewis, Kim. **The Last Train**.
Candlewick, 1994. ISBN 1-56402-343-5
Sara and James and their parents spend a happy afternoon in a worker's hut near which there used to be a railroad. While there, the father talks about the trains he remembers from his childhood. Suddenly, everyone hears a locomotive and rushes outside to see the train and wave to the driver before it all disappears.

Siebert, Diane. **Train Song**.
Illustrated by Mike Wimmer. HarperCollins, 1990.
ISBN 0-690-04726-6
This is a poetic look at the mystique of trains.

Wyllie, Stephen. **Ghost Train: A Spooky Hologram Book**. Illustrated by Brian Lee. Dial, 1992.
ISBN 0 8037 1163 8
Three ghosts who have been haunting Ravenswick Castle for hundreds of years move to an amusement park and take up residence on the train there.

NONFICTION

Murphy, Jim. **Across America on an Emigrant Train**. Clarion, 1993. ISBN 0-395-63390-7
Murphy uses Robert Louis Stevenson's memoir of crossing America in 1879 by train and combines it with a history of railroading in America and a contrast between the rides offered rich people and poor people.

Goodnight Opus

by Berkeley Breathed
Little, 1993
ISBN 0-316-10853-7

▶ SUMMARY

After hearing his favorite bedtime story for the umpteenth time, Opus "departs from the text" with great exuberance. This humorous take-off on the classic **Good Night Moon** brings the reader around the globe and into the Milky Way.

▶ ILLUSTRATION

The foundation of Breathed's illustrations is classical cartoon. The images are fantastic and surreal at the same time and have the quality of soft sculpture. The strongest drawing evidence is in the images that are limited to the value scale of black and white. Visual references to **Good Night Moon** can be found in certain illustrations.

▶ CONNECTIONS

NOVEL

Allan Ahberg's brief novel **Ten in a Bed** (Viking, 1989. ISBN 0-670-82042 Grades 2-4) has reference to many familiar books.

THEMES

▶ Fairy Tale Extensions
▶ Favorite Early Childhood Books

CURRICULUM CONNECTION

▶ LITERATURE – Parodies & Satires

Language Arts

Understanding Parody

▶ Compare this book to Good Night Moon (see Related Books). How are the two books alike? Where do they differ?

▶ Why is it that the book Good Night Moon does not become dated?

Comparing Literature

▶ Read Where the Wild Things Are (see Related Books). Compare it to Opus' journey. Would Max have wanted to join Opus? Would Opus care to raise a ruckus with Max?

▶ Can you find other characters in stories who "depart from the text"? Can you draw any conclusions about their personalities?

▶ Set up a mini-library of books that rhyme. Have students read through these books in their spare time and nominate a favorite from the selection.

Conducting Surveys

▶ Identify those books that students always wanted to hear when they were younger. Conduct a survey of parents to determine those books that they (the parents) are delighted to never have to read again. Are there any books which the majority of the students preferred?

Getting Meaning From Illustration

▶ Look carefully at the illustrations. Match up the objects in Opus' room with the objects which appear in his trip. Make an illustration of your room, making sure to include all your important "stuff." Write a short story based on the characters drawn from your room.

▶ Note the use of black and white and color in the illustrations. Is there a pattern to their use? Why was one chosen over the other?

Writing

▶ Examine the illustration of Opus in his kitchen after his retreat. Write a narrative of what Opus actually did after Grandma fell asleep reading to him.

Extending Vocabulary

▶ Discuss what Opus means when he says that he "departs from the text." Are there other expressions that mean the same thing?

▶ Look at Malcolm Forbes' name on the title page. What is the play on words in that line?

Math

▶ Examine the copyright date for Good Night Moon. How many years ago was it written? Could your parents have enjoyed that book as a child? Could your grandparents have listened to the story? Are there other books from that same time frame which are still being published? What are they?

▶ Using the copyright date of Good Night Moon, determine how many times a person would have heard or read that story if he or she had he/she read it daily.

Science

▶ Investigate the Milky Way. What is it? Where is it? Does it have anything to do with milk? Where did the name "Milky Way" come from?

▶ Why do we dream? Can you always remember your dreams? Do our dreams sometimes seem real to us?

Social Studies

▶ Opus has brought us to the Lincoln Memorial. What other monuments can be found in Washington, DC? Locate Washington on a map. How far is it from your community to the nation's capital?

▶ Consider writing to the Chamber of Commerce in Washington, DC requesting a city map. Look at how the city is arranged. Why is it designed in that manner? Compare Washington's layout to the design of your community. Which design is more efficient? Why? If you were designing a city, what factors would you need to include to ensure that your city runs smoothly?

RELATED BOOKS

NOVELS

Ahlberg, Allan. **Ten in a Bed**.
Viking, 1989. ISBN 0-670-82042-3 Grades 2-4
Dinah Price finds a different storybook character in her bed each night and each one wants a story about him- or herself.

PICTURE BOOKS

Babbitt, Natalie. **The Something**.
Farrar, 1987. ISBN 0-374-37137-7
A young monster confronts his night-time fears.

Brown, Margaret Wise. **Good-Night Moon**.
HarperCollins, 1947. ISBN 0-06-020706-X
This classic is a comforting approach to the night.

Jacobs, Leland. **Good Night, Mr. Beetle**.
DLM, 1988 . ISBN 0-08505-831-6
Creatures of the barnyard and of the household are bid good night in this charming rhyme.

Lindbergh, Reeve. **Benjamin's Barn**.
Dial, 1990. ISBN 0-8037-0614-6
Benjamin "departs from the text" as he surveys his family's barn.

Sendak, Maurice. **In the Night Kitchen**.
HarperCollins, 1970. ISBN 0-06-025490-4
Mickey explores the night kitchen and the night sky.

Sendak, Maurice. **Where the Wild Things Are**.
HarperCollins, 1988. ISBN 0-06-025493-9
When he and his mother shout with rage at each other, Max propels himself across time and space to where the wild things are.

Armadillo Rodeo

by Jan Brett
Putnam, 1995.
ISBN 0-399-2280-9

SUMMARY

Bo is not like other armadillos. He longs for adventure and he really does get to do all the things he dreams of doing. He mistakes Harmony Jean's cowboy boot for a fellow armadillo. As Bo roams through the countryside enjoying one adventure after another, Ma Armadillo and family are frantically searching for him. This maverick of the family is finally united with his mother and brothers and returns home. He is left with his memories as well as his adventurous spirit. He can always mosey on down to the Curly H for some red hot chili pepper excitement.

ILLUSTRATION

The illustration techniques are so refined in the works of Jan Brett that the pictures seem like photographs rather than renderings. Meticulous detail is evident on every page. Texture is replicated for all manner of surface from the natural shell of the armadillo to the articles of clothing. Texture can also be felt in the rope-like framing of the illustrations that appear on each page. The book is a text of illustration and media methods.

CONNECTIONS

NOVEL

John Erickson's series of books about **Hank the Cowdog** (see Related Books) connect to **Armadillo Rodeo** in that they are also full of Texas lore and customs.

THEME

▶ Mistaken identity

CURRICULUM CONNECTION

▶ SOCIAL STUDIES – Texas

Language Arts

VOCABULARY DEVELOPMENT

▶ Note the adjectives in these descriptions:

pointy-toed, high-heeled, hand-tooled, chili-pepper red boots

rip-roarin', rootin'-tootin', shiny red armadillo

Create some new phrases by filling in these blanks.

_____, _____, _____ Bar-B-Q

_____, _____, _____ jalapeno pepper

_____, _____, _____ camp fire

▶ Make up some other phrases with blanks for other students to fill in.

▶ Find out the meanings of the following words. Decide if there is more than one definition.

cutwork	back forty
tenderfoot	hay chute
rip-roarin'	mosey
rootin'-tootin'	lit off
trundled	

▶ *Harmony Jean* is an unusual name. Create some appropriate names for Bo's two brothers and even his mother.

▶ The pony's name is Spotlight. Compare some good names for the rodeo animals.

▶ *The Curly H* is the name mentioned in the book. Create some good names for cattle ranches along with a matching brand.

COMPARING LITERATURE

▶ Collect other books written about a mother animal and her three children. Are the books humorous or serious? Contrast the plots.

▶ Gather another group of books that depict a mother animal and a lost child. Do they all have happy endings?

ANALYZING AND EXTENDING THE STORY

▶ Extend and fill in the following web:

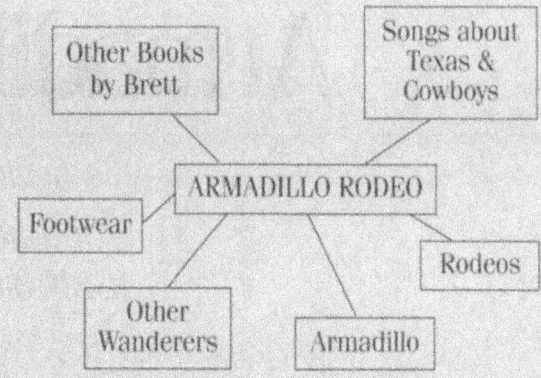

▶ Bo joined the others at a real Texas Bar-B-Q. He enjoyed a red-hot, bright-green jalapeno pepper followed by some lemonade.

▶ Plan a menu for a real Texas Bar-B-Q.

▶ Find a good recipe for barbecue sauce. Adjust the amounts and plan for a crowd.

▶ Restaurants serve a recipe of stuffed jalapeno peppers called Armadillo Eggs. Groups can create a recipe with appropriate ingredients. Choose the best one to prepare in class.

▶ Texas leads the nation in the production of cattle. List the many beef products sold in the United States.

Science

▶ Design a chart of characteristics of armadillos. Add other animals to the list.

Animal	Habitat	Food	Protection	Habits	Relatives
Nine-banded armadillo	North America, thick underbrush	insects, roots	armor/bony plates	nocturnal	sloth, anteater

▶ Research to find other types of armadillos (six-banded, three-banded, giant). Identify the areas of South America in which they are located.

▶ Review characteristics of mammals.

▶ Examine the illustrations and identify the wildlife as well as geographic features in the book. Research to find others indigenous to Texas.

▶ Find out why several varieties of armadillos are becoming endangered species.

Social Studies

▶ The term rodeo comes from the Spanish word rodear, which means "to surround." In the early days of the American cattle industry, the cowboys had to round up the cattle on the ranges and drive them to marketing centers. Present-day rodeos have turned into competitions. Find out what five events are contested and how they relate to the old-time work of the cowboy.

▶ Research the state flag of Texas. Duplicate it and explain its meaning. What do you know about your own state flag?

▶ Find out about the "popular" images of Texas: state tree, flower, bird, motto, song.

Art

▶ Bo mistook Harmony Jean's boot for a shiny red armadillo. Illustrate the two to show similarities.

▶ Find other objects that Bo (who can't see very well) might mistake for an animal, for instance, a rope for a snake, a helmet for a turtle.

▶ Design several backgrounds in which animals could be camouflaged, for example, deer in a forest, snake in leaves, a chameleon in a tree.

▶ Jan Brett used borders of rope in her illustrations. Utilize this type of border to create note paper, wrapping paper, T-shirts.

▶ Look in Jan Brett's other books to see how she uses borders or frames on her pages. Compare this to the way Trina Schart Hyman uses borders in some of her work.

▶ Bluebonnets are found in many of the illustrations. Experiment to duplicate the exact color of blue. Use the flowers in various designs.

▶ Create a "new" Texas state flag featuring armadillos as well as bluebonnets.

▶ Trace Bo's journey with a series of cartoon-like illustrations and quotes. Use a comic book form or strips in correct sequence.

▶ Design appropriate cattle brands for matching names.

Music

▶ Begin a collection of cowboy songs. Include those about real, working cowboys.

▶ Watch some old western movies that feature rodeos.

▶ Learn the Texas two-step and other western line dances.

RELATED BOOKS

NOVELS

Erickson, John. **Hank the Cowdog**.
Gulf, 1988 Grades 3-6
This is a series of very funny books set on a ranch in Texas.

PICTURE BOOKS

Baylor, Byrd. **The Best Town in the World**.
Simon, 1983. ISBN 0-684-18035-9
The narrator's father came from the small Texas town and often extolled its virtues. We'll take it with a grain of salt.

Baylor, Byrd. **The Desert is Theirs**.
Illustrated by Peter Parnall. Aladdin,1987.
ISBN 0-689-71105-0
This is a wonderful description of the relationship between the desert and its children. Here we find the many creatures who inhabit it.

Baylor, Byrd. **I'm In Charge of Celebrations**.
Illustrated by Peter Parnall. Scribner 1986.
ISBN 0-684-185-19-2
There are many reasons to celebrate in the desert. One of them is the many wonders of the wilderness.

Cherry, Lynn. **The Armadillo From Amarillo**.
Harcourt,1994. ISBN 0-15-200359-2
This is a story, told in rhyme, of an armadillo who wanders through Texas. He is able to visit cities, historic sites, and geographic features and to learn about the wildlife of Texas.

Tafuri, Nancy. **Have You Seen My Duckling**
Puffin, 1986. ISBN 0-14-050585-7
A mother duck searches for a missing duckling. She leads her brood around the pond looking for her baby.

NONFICTION

Pearce, Q. L. **Armadillos and Other Unusual Animals**. Silver Burdett, 1989. ISBN 0-671-68528-7
There are 30 animals with bizarre and unusual habits in this book, part of the "Amazing Science Series."

Sowler, Sandie. **Amazing Armored Animals**.
Knopf, 1992. ISBN 0-679-92767-0
This Eyewitness book shows how animal protection varies. There are scales, spikes, spines, bony plates and shells, to name a few. This book explains them all.

OTHER BOOKS BY JAN BRETT

Annie and the Wild Animals. Houghton, 1990.
ISBN 0-395-37800-1
Annie tries to find a new pet by placing corn cakes at the edge of the woods.

Berlioz the Bear. Putnam, 1991.
ISBN 0-399-222480-0
An orchestral performance is nearly spoiled by a bee.

The First Dog. Harcourt, 1988. ISBN 0-15-227651-3
A boy and a wild dog become friends. This animal might be the first domesticated dog.

Goldilocks and the Three Bears. Putnam, 1990.
ISBN 0-399-22004-6
This is a wonderfully illustrated version of the familiar fairy tale.

The Mitten: A Ukrainian Folktale. Putnam, 1990.
ISBN 0-399-21920-X
Niki loses one of the mittens his Grandmother Baba knit for him. It becomes a shelter to accommodate many occupants.

The Trouble With Trolls. Putnam, 1992.
ISBN 0-399-22336-3
A little boy knows the trolls are looking for his dog. He outwits them and brings about a happy ending.

Twelve Days of Christmas. Putnam, 1986.
ISBN 0-399-22037-2
Every word of this traditional Christmas song is beautifully illustrated here. Watch for the more unusual pictures.

Fanny's Dream

by Caralyn Buehner
Illustrated by Mark Buehner
Dial, 1996
ISBN 0-8037-1497-1

SUMMARY

Fanny is sure she is meant to marry a prince (or at least the mayor). True, on the night of the mayor's ball, as she admits to Heber when he finds her in the garden waiting for her fairy godmother, she can't dance, twitter or simper, but she is sure that's her destiny. Heber, short and not at all princely, offers her the hard work sharing his farm and they are married. As the years go by, there's plenty of hard work and not a few disappointments, but the reader is not surprised at her reaction when the fairy godmother does appear.

ILLUSTRATION

The illustrations have a moody quality consistent with the dream sequences. Some of the landscapes look like picture postcards that are inhabited by the story's main characters. Perhaps the more appealing aspect of the illustrations for children is in the imaginative cloud formations.

CONNECTIONS

NOVEL

Joan Lowry Nixon wrote a series of novels about the dreams of three young girls immigrating to America (see Related Books).

THEME

▶ Women's roles in literature

CURRICULUM CONNECTION

▶ HISTORY – Homesteading

LANGUAGE ARTS

COMPARING LITERATURE

▶ Fanny rejects a chance to realize her dream of marrying a prince (or at least a mayor's son). Find other tales such as **The Paper Bag Princess** where something like that happens.

▶ Look at the video *It's the Great Pumpkin, Charlie Brown* and find similarities and differences between it and **Fanny's Dream**.

▶ Fanny is described as "sturdy," but she's strong in more ways than physical ones. Find other strong females in books such as Farethee Well (see **The Cowboy and the Black-Eyed Pea** on page 111), Iva Dunnitt and Shirley (in the Shirley and Claude books by Joan Lowry Nixon).

▶ Fanny and Heber are an interesting couple. Compare and contrast them to Shirley and Claude and **Caleb and Kate** (by William Steig. See Related Books).

EXTENDING THE BOOK

▶ Fanny's dream may be unrealistic, according to her friends and relatives, at least. What are your dreams? Make a list of ambitions you have and prioritize them according to how realistic they are.

▶ Make a list of the events in Fanny's life and compare it to a list of events that might have occurred had Fanny married the mayor's son.

▶ This book is about love, yet the word "love" is never mentioned. Even when Heber asks Fanny to marry him, he doesn't say, "I love you." Yet Fanny and Heber show their love throughout the book. First find the ways in which they do so and then extend that list with other ways people show love for each other.

▶ The fairy godmother, with good reason, apologizes for being late. What might she have been doing? What would life be like for a fairy godmother? What modern conveniences, such as beepers, might make life easier for a fairy godmother?

DEVELOPING VOCABULARY

▶ Fanny's simple home is in great contrast to the mayor's mansion or palace where she once dreamed she was living. Make a list of dwellings from simple to fancy. Use a thesaurus or dictionary to extend your list.

▶ Fanny is described as "sturdy." What are some other words to describe Fanny? Which of them would offend you if they were used to describe you?

▶ Fanny hopes to marry a prince. What if she couldn't get a prince, but could marry a lesser nobleman? Find and list, in order of importance, various names for nobility.

NOTICING DETAILS

▶ Look carefully at the illustrations for things hidden in the clouds and bushes.

▶ Notice the fairy godmother. She is not the usual delicate creature that most of us imagine. Why would the illustrator have portrayed her in this way?

SOCIAL STUDIES

▶ Fanny and Heber might be homesteading. Find out what the rules for homesteading were. What was the Homestead Act? How did that act affect Native Americans?

▶ What skills do you have that would be of use to Heber and Fanny? How are the skills that they needed then different from and the same as the ones farmers need today?

▶ In this book, the man and the woman take on fairly conventional roles, but there are places where those lines seem to blur. Find them and talk about them.

MUSIC

▶ Find songs that would fit various parts of the book: "When You Wish Upon a Star," "Wishin' and Hopin'," and "Side by Side," for instance.

ART

▶ Compare the illustrations in this book to those in **Swamp Angel**. What do you find alike and different in these two books?

RELATED BOOKS

NOVELS

Nixon, Joan Lowry. **Land of Dreams**.
Delacorte, 1994. ISBN 0-385-31170-2 Grades 5-8
Kristin is a young girl emigrating to America with a heart full of dreams. In the rural community in Minnesota that her family joins, the dreams allowed young girls are confined, to say the least.

Nixon, Joan Lowry. **Land of Hope**.
Bantam, 1992. ISBN 0-553-08110-1 Grades 5-8
In 1902, Rebekah Levinsky arrives with her family in New York City, where their dreams are put to many tests and few of them are realized.

Nixon, Joan Lowry. **Land of Promise**.
Bantam, 1993. ISBN 0-553-08111-X Grades 5-8
This third of Nixon's immigration novels centers around the life of Rosie, who settles in Chicago, where she achieves a part of her dream.

PICTURE BOOKS

Keats, Ezra Jack. **Dreams**.
Simon & Schuster, 1992. ISBN 0-689-71599-4
As the people in the apartment building fall asleep and begin to dream, the colors on their window shades change color.

Munsch, Robert. **The Paper Bag Princess**.
Firefly, 1980. ISBN 0-920236-82-0
This tongue-in-cheek fairy tale has traditional roles turned upside down.

Nixon, Joan Lowry. **Beats Me, Claude**.
Viking, 1986. ISBN 0-670-80781-8
This is just one in a series of books about Shirley and Claude, a couple living in the old West.

Nunes, Susan. **Coyote Dreams**.
Illustrated by Ronald Himler Simon, 1988.
ISBN 0-689-31398-5
A boy living on the edge of the desert dreams of joining the coyotes on their nightly prowl.

Spier, Peter. **Dreams**.
Doubleday, 1986. ISBN 0-385-19336-X
A boy and a girl on a hill make shapes of the clouds above them.

Steig, William. **Caleb and Kate**.
Farrar, 1986. ISBN 0-374-31016-5
After a quarrel with his wife, Caleb is changed into a dog.

Yolen, Jane. **Sleeping Ugly**.
Putnam, 1981. ISBN 0-698-20617-7
When this prince comes upon two sleeping princesses, he wisely elects to waken the plain one and let the lying princess sleep or the sleeping princess lie.

Dandelions

by Eve Bunting
Illustrated by Greg Shed
Harcourt, 1995
ISBN 0-15-200050-X

SUMMARY

This is a superb picture book appropriate for a wide range of grade levels. We meet Zoe and her family on their way in an ox-drawn covered wagon from Illinois to their new home. The children and their father are eager, but their mother's sadness is readily apparent. When Papa declares they are "here," there's nothing to see but the endless plain that has surrounded them for weeks. Soon the well is dug, the sod house made, and it begins to feel like home for everyone but Mama. She feels insignificant and lonely and says that the sod house disappears into the terrain almost as soon as they step away from it. Zoe's clump of dandelions that she digs up and brings carefully home from a trip to town are planted on the roof and, in the last scene, we see the brilliant yellow roof they create on the sod house.

ILLUSTRATION

Greg Shed's illustrations serve as visual companions to this story by capturing and reflecting its mood and melancholy. This is accomplished by using softly muted colors and sketchy brush strokes. The essence of the dandelions, the sweeping grassy fields and the open plains is captured with the illustrator's practiced use of texture. Even the texture of the canvas is evident in these full-page and double-page compositions.

CONNECTIONS

NOVEL

Ann Turner's **Grasshopper Summer** (Simon & Schuster, 1989. ISBN 0-02-789511-4 Grades 3-8) has a woman who feels similarly to Mama in **Dandelions**.

THEMES

▶ Home
▶ Loneliness

CURRICULUM CONNECTION

▶ SOCIAL STUDIES – Dwelling places on the plains

LANGUAGE ARTS

EXTENDING THE BOOK

▶ Zoe says that her mother's silences often scared her and that she felt she'd "gone away." What does she mean? How can people's silences be scary?

▶ Zoe says that her mother was often sad. Why would she be any sadder than the rest of the family? They seem happy with their new home. Make a list of the things each might do on a typical day in more settled Illinois and out on the unsettled prairie during that time period. Would the list be different for the mother than for the rest of the family?

▶ When Papa and Zoe are going to town and Mama is worried that they'll get lost, he tells her he'll mark the way with breadcrumbs. What story is he referring to? Would he have known that story?

▶ Why is it that some of this family feel that their simple house is home and the mother does not? What makes a house a home? What things in your house could you remove and still feel that it was home?

COMPARING LITERATURE

▶ Read Ann Turner's **Dakota Dugout** (see page 217) and compare the two books. Obviously the lack of color in one book changes the appearance, but look at the styles of illustration as well as the narration. One book uses very few words. Are they trying to tell the same story? What do you think the author's purpose is for each book? Which book gives you more information about the time, the people, the houses?

▶ Read the novel **Grasshopper Summer** listed below. Would these two families have liked each other?

MATH

ESTIMATION

▶ We don't know exactly where in Illinois or to what place in Nebraska Zoe's family traveled, but assuming both places are in the middle of their states, how far will they have traveled?

▶ They traveled 12 miles a day. How far can you walk in a day? Why would your walk be easier? How long would it take you to walk the distance they traveled?

SCIENCE

▶ Find out about the wildflowers on the prairie and make an illustrated chart or a handbook for identifying them.

▶ There is very little original, unplowed or unaltered prairie left. Find out about the places and people that are attempting to preserve the few areas. Write to the U.S. Department of the Interior or individual prairie states to find out what's being done. Do you want to help?

▶ Read Glen Rounds' book **Sod Houses on the Great Plains** to get more information on how the houses were built. Why would sod make better building material than plain dirt? Cut a slice of thick grass and examine the underside. Would some plants hold the dirt better than others? Why?

SOCIAL STUDIES

▶ Papa says it's free land. Was it free? Who owned it? What did the settlers have to do to keep it?

▶ Zoe and her father go to town to get supplies. If you ran a general store in that time and place, what things would you stock? Where would you get your supplies? What things do you think you would charge the most for?

▶ This book doesn't mention them, but Native Americans paid a heavy price when the Westward Movement took place. Make a list of the tribes that inhabited the areas covered in this book. What happened to them? Compare the numbers of Native Americans then and now. Find out about the Indian Removal Act and the hardships it created. Could they have found a way to share the land? What would you have done?

ART

▶ The illustrations for this book seem to have a golden look to them, which helps with both the story and the title. Use yellow paper or put a yellow watercolor wash on some white paper and then draw or paint what the color makes you think of.

MUSIC

▶ Find the song "Sweet Betsy from Pike." It has many verses. First read them to know the story of Ike and Betsy and their trip to California. Which things in the song do you think might really have happened? Sing the song. Make up new verses based on what you've learned. Could they have settled on the prairie and built a sod house?

RELATED BOOKS

NOVELS

Antle, Nancy. **Beautiful Land: a Story of the Oklahoma Land Rush**. Viking, 1994.
ISBN 0-670-85304-6 Grades 3-6
This brief and very accessible novel is part of the **Once Upon America** series and tells of the trials and tribulations of one family attempting to strike a claim.

Love, D. Anne. **Dakota Spring**.
Holiday, 1995. ISBN 0-8234-1189-3 Grades 4-8
Like **Sarah, Plain and Tall**, this sweet, brief novel gives us a motherless family, but here it's a cold and distant grandmother who comes to help out.

Turner, Ann. **Grasshopper Summer**.
Simon & Schuster, 1989. ISBN 0 02-789511-4
Grades 3-8
The story is great. It includes an excellent description of the grasshopper plague. These are the same kind of people as in **Dandelions.**

PICTURE BOOKS

Ackerman, Karen. **Araminta's Paint Box**.
Simon & Schuster, 1990. ISBN 0-689-31462-0
All right, it isn't believable, but it's fun to follow the trail of the paint box as it and Araminta become separated on the trip west.

Harvey, Brett. **My Prairie Christmas**.
Holiday, 1990. ISBN 0-8234-0827-2
By focusing on one season, the author and illustrator of this book bring the people of that time and place to life.

Turner, Ann and Ronald Himler.
Dakota Dugout See page XXX.

OTHER BOOKS BY EVE BUNTING

See page 52.

NONFICTION

Conrad, Pam. **Prairie Vision: The Life and Times of Solomon Butcher**. HarperCollins, 1991.
ISBN 0-06 021375-2
While the life of the con man-photographer-entrepreneur is interesting (don't miss the story about the white turkey on the roof), it's the photographs that Butcher took that blow your mind. Conrad has included many of them and here we see all the different kinds of dwellings, including but not restricted to the sod houses on the Nebraska prairie in the 1880s and the people who lived in them.

Freedman, Russell. **An Indian Winter**.
Holiday House, 1992. ISBN 0-8234-0930-9
The book focuses on with the Mandan Indians of Dakota territory. Younger audiences can learn a lot from the profuse illustrations in this book, while older students can absorb the splendid informational text.

Goble, Paul. **Death of the Iron Horse**.
Bradbury, 1987. ISBN 0-02-737830-6
The story tells of the one documented time when Indians wrecked a train crossing the prairie.

McNeese, Tim. **Western Wagon Trains**.
Crestwood, 1993. ISBN 0-89686-734-X
The author provides a lot of detail about life on the trek: the food, the amusements, the dangers and the trails themselves.

Rounds, Glen. **Sod Houses on the Great Plains**.
Holiday House, 1995. ISBN 0-8234-1162-1
This is a wonderful source of information about the houses themselves. Rounds also talks about the wild flowers that grew on the roofs of many sod houses

Sneve, Virginia Driving Hawk. **The Sioux**.
Holiday, 1993. ISBN 0-8234-1017-X
This is just one in a wonderful series of picture books about individual Native American tribes.

Red Fox Running

by Eve Bunting
Illustrated by Wendell Minor
Clarion, 1993
ISBN 0-395-58919-3

SUMMARY

This beautifully illustrated book follows the experiences of a red fox as it searches a winter landscape for food. The rhyming text brings us to the killing of a bobcat to bring to the fox's den.

ILLUSTRATION

Mastery of texture is exhibited in the soft, hairy bodies of the animals. The texture in the snow-covered field is equally well represented.

CONNECTIONS

NOVEL

Betsy Byars' **The Midnight Fox**. (Viking, 1968. ISBN 0-670-47473-8 Grades 3-6) concerns a captured fox and a young boy's relationship with that wild animal.

THEME

► Foxes in literature

CURRICULUM CONNECTION

► SCIENCE – Foxes and food chains

Language Arts

▶ Before reading the text, allow students to study the illustrations carefully. Ask them to write a short story using the illustrations as a guide.

▶ Have small groups of students choose one of the double-page illustrations. Ask them to "walk into the setting" and describe what they see, hear, smell and feel. Have groups compare the similarities and differences of their results. Combine the groups' information to create a "Setting Map" for the story.

▶ Chart the animals found in the story. Allow students to add to the chart the names of other animals that might be found in this setting.

▶ How would this story be different if it took place during another season? Challenge students to rewrite the story having it take place in the summer.

▶ Ask students individually or in small groups to rewrite the story in narrative form.

▶ Assign to students one of the other animals in the book. Ask them to tell the story from that animal's perspective.

▶ Look at a variety of fictional stories with foxes in them. Decide what characteristics of foxes in these stories are fact and what are fiction. Discuss why the fox might have the reputation of being sly.

▶ Make a list of "fox" words and expressions such as *foxhole, fox trot, sly as a fox, outfoxed*. What do they mean? Find the origins of as many as you can.

▶ Discuss the concept of "outfoxed." Share a variety of books where a character is outfoxed. Chart the books read as follows:

Title   Author   Who was outfoxed?   How?   By whom?

Science

▶ Find a variety of nonfiction books about foxes. Have students independently research to learn more about this animal.

▶ Use the chart of animals you made above that might be found in this setting. Add to the chart whether each animal would be a meal for the fox or not. What might a fox find to eat in this setting that is not another animal?

▶ Study animal tracks in the snow. Compare the prints of a fox with other "dog-like" tracks such as those of a coyote, dog and wolf. What tracks might you find in your area?

Music

▶ This text is very like the folk song "A Fox Went Out on a Chilly Night." Find and sing the song. Look at Peter Spier's illustrations for that song, listed below.

RELATED BOOKS

NOVELS

Byars, Betsy. **The Midnight Fox**.
Viking, 1968. ISBN 0-670-47473-8 Grades 3-6
Tom befriends and identifies with a black fox while staying at his aunt and uncle's farm for the summer.

PICTURE BOOKS

Bruchac, Joseph. **Fox Song**.
Philomel, 1993. ISBN 0-399-22346-0
An Abenaki child mourns her grandmother but remembers the fox tracks she taught her to read. When she glimpses a fox at their favorite spot, she is reminded that she is not alone.

Spier, Peter. **The Fox Went Out on a Chilly Night**.
Dell, 1961. ISBN 0-440-40829-6
The timeless folk song illustrated by Spier includes music for voice, piano and guitar.

NONFICTION

Ahlstrom, Mark E. **The Foxes**.
Simon, 1983. ISBN 0-89686-220-8
This short book covers much of the animal behavior and food chain of the fox.

Lane, Margaret. **The Fox**.
Illustrated by Kenneth Lilly. Dial, 1982.
ISBN 0-8037-2491-8
We follow one fox from birth to maturity.

Mason, Cherie. **Wild Fox**.
Down East, 1993. ISBN 0-89272-319-X
Ms. Mason befriends a lame fox on Deer Isle, Maine, and, in the process, learns and teaches us a lot about the ecological milieu of the fox.

Train to Somewhere

by Eve Bunting
Illustrated by Ron Himler
Clarion, 1996
ISBN 0-395-71325-0

◢ SUMMARY

From 1850 to the 1920s, trains carried orphans and children whose parents could not or would not care for them to new homes on the Great Plains or in the West. The story of these children is told through one child who boards the train in New York with 14 other children and Miss Randolph, their caretaker, to be taken in by people in the country towns at which they stop. Marianne is older and knows she's not cute or pretty. Those children and the stronger older ones are taken first. At each town the children put on their most cheerful faces and each time there are fewer and fewer to reboard the train. Marianne clings to a chicken feather and the hope that her mother who promised to come back for her before leaving her at the orphanage will be waiting for her at one of the stops. Finally, it is Marianne alone who gets off the train at Somewhere and gives up the chicken feather and her lost hope as she is lovingly embraced by her new family.

◢ ILLUSTRATION

These are well-crafted illustrations using watercolor washes in a variety of ways. In most instances the details are added brush strokes and dry brush applications. The vignettes on the type pages are looser than the framed compositions on the opposite pages.

◢ CONNECTIONS

NOVEL

Joan Lowry Nixon has written a series of novels based on the orphan train experience. See Related Books for the titles.

THEMES

▶ Families
▶ Home
▶ Orphans

CURRICULUM CONNECTION

▶ HISTORY & GEOGRAPHY – Plains States

LANGUAGE ARTS

COMPARING LITERATURE

▶ Read one or all of Joan Lowry Nixon's "Orphan Train" series or Talbot's An Orphan for Nebraska (see Related Books), which are also about the orphan trains.

▶ Read Orphan Train Rider by Andrea Warren to gain more information about the trains and to learn the real life story of one such passenger.

▶ Read other books about orphans such as The Secret Garden and Only Opal. Would any of those orphans have fared better on the orphan trains?

FINDING DETAILS

▶ Do you think Miss Randolph likes her job? What do you know about her from the book?

▶ Why are the gifts that Tillie Book and Marianne exchanged significant?

WRITING

▶ Tell or write the story of what might have happened to Nora? Will you have her see Marianne again in your story?

USING SYMBOLISM

▶ The chicken feather that Marianne treasures is a symbol of her mother and, therefore, it is of great significance when she gives it to the woman who takes her in at Somewhere. Notice the way Bunting uses other symbols in her other books: the dandelions in Dandelions (see page 44) and the sparrow in Fly Away Home.

AUTHOR STUDY

▶ Eve Bunting has written a large number of books. Look at the picture books she has created. What can you learn about Ms Bunting from these books? What kind of subjects does she choose? Read her book Once Upon a Time (see below) for more information about why she chooses the things she writes about.

SOCIAL STUDIES

▶ Bunting has named her imaginary town "Somewhere." Look in the atlas to find strange names of other real towns and cities. Write to their chamber of commerce or their historical society to find out the origin of their names.

▶ Find statistics to back up the story. How many children rode the orphan trains? Why were there so many displaced children during that time period? What was the childbirth death rate during the late 1800s and early 1900s in America? How long did the average person live at that time? Check the census records in your town for that time. How many orphans were recorded? Where were they living? How were they supported?

▶ Would Social Security or welfare have made any difference to the "orphan problem"? Why or why not? Find out about Aid to Dependent Children and Medicaid.

▶ What happens to similar children today? What are the advantages and disadvantages of today's attempts at solutions when you compare them with the orphan trains?

▶ Some of the strong children that were chosen early would probably be used as labor on the farms. Find out more about child labor at the time. Find out about child labor in other countries today.

ART

▶ Fortunately for us, Eve Bunting has written many picture books, and several different artists have illustrated them. Look at them and decide which illustrator's work you like best. Look for details in the illustrations that are not mentioned in the text and decide why the illustrator decided to include them. If David Wiesner had been asked to illustrate Train to Somewhere, how do you think his illustrations would have affected the book?

RELATED BOOKS

NOVELS

Burnett, Frances. **The Secret Garden**.
Dell, 1990. ISBN 0-440-47709-3
This classic has Mary, an orphan child, as the main character.

Nixon, Joan Lowry. **A Family Apart**.
Bantam, 1988. ISBN 0-553-27478-3
This is the first in a series of novels about the six Kelly children who were put on an orphan train in 1860. Each novel follows a different child. Other books in the series are **In the Face of Danger** (ISBN 0-553 05490-2), **Keeping Secrets** (ISBN 0-385-32139-2) and **A Dangerous Promise** (ISBN 0-385-32073-6).

Talbot, Charlene J. **An Orphan for Nebraska**.
Simon, 1979. ISBN 0-689-30698-9
An Irish immigrant child is sent to a farm in Nebraska via the orphan train.

PICTURE BOOKS

Boulton, Jane and Barbara Cooney.
Only Opal: The Diary of a Young Girl.
Putnam, 1994. ISBN 0-399 21990-0
This is a picture book of very poetic excerpts from a real child, orphaned and living in a lumber camp in Oregon near the turn of the century.

OTHER BOOKS BY EVE BUNTING

Dandelions. Illustrated by Greg Shed.
Harcourt, 1995. ISBN 0-15-200050-X See page 44.

Fly Away Home. Illustrated by Ronald Himler.
Clarion, 1993. ISBN 0-395-66415-2
A boy and his father live at the airport while they save money for a real home.

How Many Days to America: A Thanksgiving Story.
Clarion, 1990. ISBN 0-395-54777-6
Modern-day immigrants echo the fears and the hopes of the first Pilgrims.

Man Who Could Call Down Owls. Illustrated by Charles Mikolaycak. Simon & Schuster, 1984.
ISBN 0-02-715380-0
A man who can communicate with owls is met with jealousy on the part of a stranger.

Night of the Gargoyles. Illustrated by David Wiesner. Clarion, 1994. ISBN 0-395-6655-1
Gargoyles who come to life at night grumble about their lot in life.

Stellaluna

by Janell Cannon
Harcourt, 1993
ISBN 0-15-280217-7

SUMMARY

Stellaluna, a baby fruit bat, is separated from her mother and falls headfirst into a bird's nest. The mother bird dutifully raises Stellaluna along with her own nestlings. Stellaluna tries to adapt to bird life: eating insects, sleeping at night and perching head up as her foster mother demands. It's a great relief for all when her own mother is found.

ILLUSTRATION

Clean line drawing is the basic element in creating these "super real" illustrations. The drawings are then filled out or fleshed out by rendering techniques. These techniques produce handsome gradations or value that establish the forms and volumes of these flying creatures and their natural habitat. Muted color is reserved for the background of alternating pages of illustrations. These color fields add drama to the antics of the beautiful flying, resting, feeding, or parenting creatures.

Clearly drawn miniature images are positioned at the top of each page of verse. These images change the square page format by nestling in the arched space or bulging at the top. The drawings are repeated inside the cover jacket, front and back, and serve as a summary of the illustrated bats found at the heading of each set of pages.

CONNECTIONS

NOVEL

Randall Jarrell's short novel **The Bat-Poet** HarperCollins, 1995. ISBN 0-06-205085-0 concerns a bat who tries to convey his feelings through poems that he recites to an unappreciative audience.

THEMES

▶ Being true to oneself
▶ False Identities

CURRICULUM CONNECTION

▶ SCIENCE – Bats, adaptation

LANGUAGE ARTS

COMPARING LIKENESSES AND DIFFERENCES

▶ Create a "Similarities/Differences" chart to document the ways in which birds and bats are the same and different.

COMPARING LITERATURE

▶ Find other stories where a baby animal is separated from its mother and raised by another kind of animal. Start with a version of The Ugly Duckling.

WRITING

▶ Try rewriting the story as a rhyming poem. Perhaps each student could write a couplet to retell a portion of the story.

▶ If possible, leave several copies of the book available with the text pages covered with blank paper. Allow students to write captions for the illustrations in one, to write short stories about the pictures in another, and to write couplets or longer poems in yet another.

IMPROVING VOCABULARY

▶ Bat babies are called "pups." Chart the names of the offspring of other animals.

▶ Generate a list of "bat expressions" such as "bats in his belfry," "going batty," and "as blind as a bat."

▶ Find out what the name "Stellaluna" means in Latin. Discuss why Stellaluna may be a good name for a bat. Make a list of other appropriate names for bats.

EXTENDING THE STORY

▶ In some countries, bats are considered good luck. Brainstorm why this may be true. What other animals have the reputation of being good luck?

▶ Each Chinese New Year is represented by an animal such as a rat, snake, or bull. Find the traits of the animal that represents your birth year. Write a persuasive paragraph telling why those traits do or do not apply to you.

SCIENCE

▶ Learn about some myths about bats. Will they really tangle in your hair? Make a "Fact" and "Fiction" chart.

▶ Sometimes fruit bats are referred to as "flying foxes." Learn more about fruit bats. Are their similarities to foxes only in appearance? How about in other ways such as hunting habits?

▶ Research bats to learn more about them. Start with the back pages of the book where the author gives some interesting bat facts. Find out what kinds of bats inhabit what parts of the world. What do they eat? How big do they grow?

▶ Create food chains that include different kinds of bats. Are bats only predators, or are they prey to other animals?

▶ The scientific name for bats is *Chiroptera*, means "hand-wing." Find and examine illustrations of human hand skeletons and bat wing skeletons. Compare them to discover why this scientific name is appropriate.

▶ Develop a chart titled "Bats Are Mammals." List on the chart the reasons why bats are mammals.

SOCIAL STUDIES

▶ Have students develop a "bat map" of the world. Write about and illustrate different species of bats. Show on a world map where each type lives.

▶ Find out why bats are often associated with witches. Also find out why bats are considered lucky. Set up a debate to determine which group of students is more convincing, the group contending that bats are lucky or the group who claims they are unlucky.

MATH

▶ There are nearly 800 different varieties of bats. Create some group problem-solving challenges starting with this fact. For example, find out how many species of mammals there are on Earth. What percentage of them are bats?

▶ Find out how many insects a single bat eats in a day. How many insects would a single bat eat in a week? A month? A year?

▶ In your research, develop a chart depicting the sizes of the wingspans of different types of bats. Challenge each other to discover how many bats of a certain type would fit wing-to-wing across a wall of your classroom.

▶ Convert the wingspans of bats from inches to centimeters.

RELATED BOOKS

NOVELS

Avi. **Beyond the Western Sea: The Escape from Home**. Orchard, 1996. ISBN 0-531-09513-4
This is the first of a duo of books in which there are several cases of mistaken identity.

Danziger, Paula. **There's a Bat in Bunk Five**. Delacorte, 1980. ISBN 0-440-40098-8
Marcy has been hired as a last-minute replacement camp counselor-in-training, and the bat is only one of the difficulties she must contend with.

Hodgman, Ann. **There's a Batwing in My Lunchbox**. Avon, 1988. ISBN 0-390-75426-6
Danny, with some help from his monster friends, works up a dandy Thanksgiving feast.

Jarrell, Randall. **The Bat-Poet**.
HarperCollins, 1995. ISBN 0-06-205085-0
A bat spends the day composing poems that celebrate life and recites those poems to the other animals.

Peterson, Beth. **No Turning Back**.
Atheneum, 1996. ISBN 0-689-31914-2
In this fantasy, a wolverine and a bat speak to a boy who is trying to find help for a wounded friend. The bat leads Dillon through a dangerous valley where they are pursued by a phantom personifying fear.

PICTURE BOOKS

Dragonwagon, Crescent. **Bat in the Dining Room**. Cavendish, 1997. ISBN 0-761-45007-6
A bat flies into a fancy hotel dining room creating panic in everyone but a shy little girl who sees and understands that the bat is also panicked.

Freeman, Don. **Hattie, the Backstage Bat**.
Viking, 1988. ISBN 0-14-050893-7
A bat who lives in the theater times her entrance just right, and the mystery that is being enacted there is a hit.

NONFICTION

Arnold, Caroline. **Bat**.
Morrow, 1996. ISBN 0-688-13726-1
This is an excellent source of information and photos on bats.

Bash, Barbara. **Shadows of Night: The Hidden World of the Little Brown Bat**. Sierra, 1993. ISBN 0-87156-562-5.
This book takes the reader through the life cycle, physical characteristics and habits of the little brown bat, one of the most widespread bats in North America.

Earle, Ann. **Zipping, Zapping, Zooming Bats**.
HarperCollins, 1995. ISBN 06-023479-2
Full-color photos extend a clear and informative text about all kinds of bats.

Markle, Sandra. **Outside and Inside Bats**.
Atheneum, 1997. ISBN 0-689-81165-9
Fascinating close-ups in full color accompany a text full of wonderful details about the anatomy and physiology of bats.

Milton, Joyce. **Bats, Creatures of the Night**.
Grossett and Dunlap, 1993. ISBN 0-448-40193-2
This easy to read book describes the physical characteristics, behavior and habitats of different kinds of bats.

Selsam, Millicent and Joyce Hunt. **A First Look at Bats**. Walker, 1991. ISBN 0-8027-8135-7
This book offers views of several different species of bats and describes their distinctive characteristics.

The Egyptian Cinderella

by Shirley Climo
Illustrated by Ruth Heller
HarperCollins, 1989
ISBN 0-06-443279-3

SUMMARY

Rhodopis is a slave who, while treated kindly by her master, is treated poorly by the servant girls in the household. A lost golden slipper, a falcon and a pharaoh holding court all make up this Cinderella story set on the banks of the Nile.

ILLUSTRATION

Ruth Heller's illustrations provide an excellent reference guide to ancient Egypt's drawing traditions. Bright and pure colors contained within carefully drawn figures and objects are typical of temple wall decoration. In all but one figure the characters are shown in traditional profile. It might be fun to find the exception to that rule. The figures are shown in scale wearing typical headdress, kilts and necklace as was the usual practice. This is known as the Egyptian "canon" or set of rules.

CONNECTIONS

NOVEL

Mara, Daughter of the Nile (Penguin, 1985. ISBN 0-1-031929-8) is a good mystery novel set in Ancient Egypt.

THEME

▶ Cinderella variants

CURRICULUM CONNECTION

▶ HISTORY – Ancient Egypt

Language Arts

COMPARING LITERATURE

▶ Investigate several versions of the Cinderella story. Design a time line for them. Which one seems to be the oldest? Are any of the versions based on truth? Compare and contrast the versions. Are there traits that each story shares?

▶ There seem to be fewer elements of magic in this story than in other fairy tales. Is this true of all the Cinderella versions? If there is little magic, then is this story really a fairy tale? What elements make a story a fairy tale?

ETIOLOGY

▶ The text informs us that Rhodopis means "rosy cheeked" in Greek. Find the origins of the other names in the book as well as of your own name.

RESEARCH

▶ Read the author's note in the back of the book. Find out about Aesop.

VOCABULARY DEVELOPMENT

▶ Upon meeting Rhodopis, the pharaoh uses a series of similes based on Nature to describe her. Illustrate a classmate and write that person's description based on similes.

GETTING MEANING FROM TEXT

▶ Why was Rhodopis favored by her master? In what ways did he favor her?

▶ If the Cinderella tale were to be set in another culture, what information would the author need to gather about that culture prior to writing the tale? Use this book and its illustrations as well as the other versions of the story to help you to determine the background information (or research) the author had to acquire.

Social Studies

▶ The author's note in the back of the book informs us that Rhodopis was believed to have been born in Greece, sold into slavery, and brought to Samos and then to Egypt. Trace her journey on a world map. How would she have traveled from one place to the next?

▶ Can this story be dated based on clothing, transportation and names of individuals?

▶ The author's note tells us that some of the information is based on fact. Research the factual information to better understand the culture of Egypt at this time.

▶ Find out about the five largest rivers in the world. Investigate their influence on the culture of the areas near those rivers.

▶ In the story, Rhodopis uses the river to wash clothes and to gather reeds on its shore. Later, the river is used for transportation. Investigate the Nile River and learn of its many uses for the people in the region.

Science

▶ Find out about papyrus. How is it made? What are its uses?

▶ Investigate falcons. Jean Craighead George's novel My Side of the Mountain (Dutton, 1959) provides a great deal of information about falconry.

Try your hand at making paper.

Art

▶ Note the style of the illustrations. Investigate Egyptian art of that era and do a self portrait in that style.

RELATED BOOKS

NOVELS

Carter, Dorothy Sharp. **His Majesty, Queen Hatshepsut**. HarperCollins, 1987.
ISBN 0-397-32179-1
This is a fictionalized biography of the only female pharaoh of ancient Egypt.

McGraw, Eloise J. **Mara, Daughter of the Nile**.
Penguin, 1985. ISBN 0-14-031929-8
This is a mystery set in ancient Egypt in which all the action is observed by a slave girl.

PICTURE BOOKS

Clements, Andrew. **Temple Cat**.
Clarion, 1996. ISBN 0-395-69842-1
In the town of Neba, in ancient Egypt, a cat wearies of being lord of the temple and goes in search of love.

San Souci, Robert. **Sootface**.
Doubleday, 1994. ISBN 0-385-31202-4
This is an Ojibwa Indian Cinderella story.

Stolz, Mary. **Zekmet the Stone Carver**.
Harcourt, 1988. ISBN 0-15-299961-2
Zekmet is asked by the Pharaoh's vizier to build the sphinx.

Wynne-Jones, Tim. **Zoom Upstream**.
HarperCollins, 1994. ISBN 0-06-022978-0
Zoom, the cat, and his human friend Maria search through ancient Egypt for Zoom's Uncle Roy.

NONFICTION

Harris, Geraldine. **Ancient Egypt- Cultural Atlas for Young People**. Equinox, 1990. ISBN 0-8160-1971-1
Colored illustrations and photographs combine with straightforward text to take the reader into long-ago Egypt.

Macaulay, David. **Pyramid**.
Houghton, 1975. ISBN 0-395-32121-2
A wonderful, informative look at just how and why pyramids were built.

Stanley, Diane. **Cleopatra**.
Morrow, 1994. ISBN 0-688-10413-4
This picture book biography is beautifully done and offers a great deal of information about ancient Egypt.

Sadako

by Eleanor Coerr
Illustrated by Ed Young
Putnam, 1993
ISBN 0-399-21771-1

SUMMARY

A young girl in Hiroshima is inflicted with the dreaded "atom bomb disease" and is hospitalized. During her hospitalization, she races against time to fold 1,000 paper cranes because legend has it that a crane is supposed to live 1,000 years and if a sick person folds 1,000 paper cranes, the gods will grant her wish and she will become well again. When Sadako dies of the disease after folding only 644 cranes, her friends and classmates work together to fold 356 more so that she can be buried with 1,000 paper cranes. A statue of Sadako now stands in Hiroshima Peace Park. Sadako is standing on the mountain of paradise holding a golden crane. Children gather at the park to hang garlands of paper cranes under the statue each year on Peace Day. The statue base is engraved with the words, "This is our cry, this is our prayer: Peace in the world."

ILLUSTRATION

Young handles chalky drawing tools in subtle yet colorful fashion. In most illustrations, the muted colors run hot and cold. In a few selected illustrations, sepia and limited value scale emphasis can be seen. While the drawing is not like Escher, the images that surface have some of his metamorphosis quality. Multiple objects within the same image exemplify this.

CONNECTIONS

NOVEL

Eleanor Coerr's **Sadako and the Thousand Paper Cranes** (Dell, 1979. ISBN 0-440-47465-5) is a short novel that preceded this picture book version of the story.

THEMES

▶ Courage
▶ Death
▶ Price of War

CURRICULUM CONNECTION

▶ HISTORY – World War II

Language Arts

▶ The story opens with Sadako looking at a blue sky over Hiroshima and thinking it's a good omen. What are omens? Find other examples in the story of signs of good luck. For example, Sadako's mother hangs good luck symbols above the door to protect her family on New Year's Eve. List them on a wall chart and invite students to talk with their families about good luck symbols. Add their ideas to your list.

▶ Do the same for bad omens and bad luck symbols such as a black cat crossing your path, walking under a ladder, or opening an umbrella indoors.

▶ Retell Sadako's story through a series of cause-and-effect statements. Create individual retellings by providing students with small booklets of lined paper stapled together. Label each pair of facing pages with the words "Cause" and "Effect." Challenge students to retell and illustrate the whole story by writing cause and effect statements for each individual event. Allow students then to create a small illustration on each page.

▶ Use the above retellings to play a Cause/Effect game. Divide the class into two teams. One team presents a "cause" statement. The other team must generate an "effect" statement in reply to earn a point.

▶ Revisit the text to find examples of similes. Create your own big book of similes. Each student could generate a simile and illustrate it for a page in the book.

▶ Investigate haiku. Find examples to share with your students. Challenge them to discover what the pattern is that's used in haiku. Then try your hand at writing your own. Students might find that they are so competent at this art, they may wish to create their own book of haiku.

Social Studies

▶ Make a list of holidays and customs mentioned in the book. Small groups of students could investigate these traditions and share their findings with the rest of the class. How are these customs similar or different from customs recognized in our country?

▶ Set aside a special sharing day in your class. Invite your students to share with the class special customs or traditions recognized by their families that have been brought to our country from other places or cultures. Perhaps some parents or grandparents would be willing to come in to share.

▶ Nowhere in the text of the book is the word "Japan" mentioned. Can students say where the story takes place? Can students find out from family or friends where Hiroshima is located?

▶ Find Japan on a map. Locate Hiroshima. Assign small groups of students the responsibility of researching different aspects of the country of Japan such as climate, daily life, natural resources, geography and customs. Plan a "Celebrate Japan" day when groups present their research projects to the rest of the class. Plan on trying some Japanese cuisine and trying your hand at some Japanese crafts such as origami, calligraphy and haiku.

Science

▶ Find out what the "atom bomb disease" is. Obviously, many people have become stricken with leukemia as a result of radioactive fall-out. Do we know what else causes leukemia?

▶ Learn more about cranes. Do they really live to be 1,000 years old?

Art

▶ The book jacket tells us that the book is illustrated with pastels. Discuss why the illustrator's choice of media is effective for this story. Perhaps students could try illustrating some of their examples of haiku with pastels.

▶ Study the art of origami. Provide students with opportunities to try their hand at this Japanese craft.

▶ Give students copies of Japanese symbols. Can they use black paint and large brushes to imitate the art of calligraphy?

RELATED BOOKS

NOVELS

Coerr, Eleanor. **Sadako and the Thousand Paper Cranes**. Dell, 1979. ISBN 0-440-47465-5
Grades 3-6
This longer version of the story is actually the first form it took.

PICTURE BOOKS

Hall, Donald. **Farm Summer, 1942** See page 84.

Uchida, Yoshiko. **The Bracelet**.
Philomel, 1993. ISBN 0-399-22503-X
This is a story of a Japanese-American family living in the United States during World War II.

Hamanaka, Sheila. **Peace Crane**.
Morrow, 1995. ISBN 0-688-13815-2
This poetically told story is narrated by a young inner-city black girl who embraces the legend of the thousand paper cranes to cope and to wish and to dream.

Say, Allen **Grandfather's Journey** See page 184.

NONFICTION

Hamanaka, Sheila. **On the Wings of Peace: In Memory of Hiroshima and Nagasaki**.
Clarion, 1995. ISBN 0-395-72619-0
This is an anthology of stories, essays, poems and illustrations about the dropping of atom bombs on Japan.

Kindersley, Anabel. **Children Just Like Me**
See page 120.

Kodama, Tatsuharu. **Shin's Tricycle**.
Walker, 1995. ISBN 0-8027-8376-7
A teacher who survived the bomb on Hiroshima tells about one of the children who also suffered terribly when the bomb hit.

Maruki, Toshi. **Hiroshima No Pika**.
Lothrop, 1982. ISBN 0-688-02197-3
This is a first-person account of the aftermath of the atom bomb on Hiroshima.

Eleanor

by Barbara Cooney
Viking, 1996
ISBN 0-670-86139-6

▷ SUMMARY

This is a picture book biography of Eleanor Roosevelt. Born to well-to-do but dysfunctional parents, she had few joys in her early years. Although she adored her father, his life had little room for her, and her mother rejected her as ugly and awkward. It wasn't until she entered boarding school in France under the tutelage of a kind teacher that she recognized her own gifts. Cooney's illustrations capture the time and the isolation of the young girl.

▷ ILLUSTRATION

Barbara Cooney's paintings are faithful visual companions to the printed text about Eleanor Roosevelt. The paintings are full-color illustrations that capture the architecture and clothing of that period.

▷ CONNECTIONS

NOVEL

Not a novel but a longer biography is the most logical extension from this book. There are many juvenile biographies of Eleanor Roosevelt, but the best is Russell Freedman's (Clarion, 1993. ISBN 0-89919-862-7).

THEMES

▶ Concept of self
▶ Ugly ducklings

CURRICULUM CONNECTION

▶ HISTORY – First Ladies

LANGUAGE ARTS

WRITING

▶ What did Barbara Cooney have to know to write this book? Read a longer biography of Eleanor Roosevelt (see Related Books) and then consider the decisions Barbara Cooney made about which material to include and which material to illustrate.

▶ The following are quotes by Eleanor Roosevelt. What do they tell you about her? Take one that has meaning for you and write or talk about it.

"Life was meant to be lived and curiosity must be kept alive. One must never, for whatever reason, turn his back on life."

"You gain strength, courage and confidence by every experience in which you really stop to look fear in the face."

"Do what you feel in your heart to be right-for you'll be criticized anyway. You'll be damned if you do and damned if you don't."

"Justice cannot be for one side alone, but must be for both."

"No one can make you feel inferior without your consent."

"You must do the thing which you think you cannot do."

▶ If you were going to do a picture biography similar to this one, whose life would you choose? Which information about that life would you include?

COMPARING LITERATURE

▶ Read a biography of some women whose lives overlapped that of Eleanor Roosevelt (see Related Books). What things about their lives led them toward different roles?

EXTENDING VOCABULARY

▶ Some proverbs might apply to Eleanor's life. "She is the power behind the throne," "Beauty is in the eye of the beholder," and "Handsome is as handsome does" are a few. What other ones can you find that might apply?

▶ One of the things said about Eleanor Roosevelt, which she herself often quoted, was said by a lobsterman in Maine: "She ain't stuck up, she ain't dressed up, and she ain't afeared to talk." Which of the events in her childhood may have helped her develop these qualities?

▶ Investigate other idioms. Interview parents and grandparents to discover well-known adages or sayings such as "a watched pot never boils."

SOCIAL STUDIES

▶ Find out what happened to Eleanor after this book ends.

▶ Make a time line of Eleanor Roosevelt's life. You can find a good beginning time line of her life on the Internet at http://www.academic.marist.edu/fdr/ertime.htm. What else was going on at the time of each of those events? Add that information to the time line. Add photographs and copies of newspaper articles of the time.

▶ Other good Internet sources for information on Eleanor Roosevelt can be found at http://www.dorsai.org/~wbai/eleanor/. (This site pays tribute to her human rights legacy.) Her maternal family tree is outlined at http://www.academic.marist.edu/fdr/ermatern.htm. More information on her life can be found at http://www1.whitehouse.gov/WH/glimpse/firstladies/html/ar32.html.

▶ View the Academy Award winning documentary on her life.

▶ Make a family tree of the Roosevelt family using the information from the book and from other sources.

▶ Many of the areas of New York mentioned in the book still exist. Find out about the current conditions in Hell's Kitchen, the Bowery, Oyster Bay, Hyde Park. Which changes do you think would please Eleanor Roosevelt? Which places would she be concerned about? Can you discover how each section of New York received its name?

▶ When Eleanor Roosevelt became orphaned, relatives took her to live with them. What safety nets exist for orphans today?

▶ Look at the clothing worn by women in this book. How would what they wore affect the things they did? How does the clothing worn by women today affect the things they do?

▶ Make a pictoral time line of styles in women's clothing.

▶ Look at things adults did in Eleanor Roosevelt's youth for fun. Are any of them still practiced? Why have some disappeared or fallen into disuse?

▶ At the boarding school, students wore uniforms. How do you feel about uniforms? Should students at your school have to wear them? What effects would they have?

▶ Divide into teams to hold a debate over the pros and cons of wearing uniforms.

▶ What women are leaders in your area? What qualities do they have that make them effective or ineffective? What buildings, parks and landmarks in your area are named for women? What ones are named for men?

▶ Make a list of all the buildings in your city or area that are named for women.

Art

▶ Look carefully at the buildings in the book. Investigate the styles of these buildings. Does style help to identify the age of the building? Which building styles were popular during Eleanor's lifetime? Photograph buildings in your area that remind you of these.

➤ RELATED BOOKS

NOVELS

Hahn, Mary Downing. **Stepping on the Cracks**. Camelot, 1992. ISBN 0-380-71900-2
Grades 3-6
Margaret and her friend Elizabeth wait and worry about their brothers fighting in World War II while coping with a deserter here at home.

Lowry, Lois. **Autumn Street**
Houghton, 1980. ISBN 0-395-27812-0 Grades 3-8
Elizabeth goes with her mother to stay in a small town in Pennsylvania while her father is in World War II.

NONFICTION

Adler, David. **Our Golda: The Story of Golda Meir**. Viking, 1984. ISBN 0-670-53107-3
This brief biography covers the life of one of Eleanor Roosevelt's contemporaries who also became an effective world leader.

Colman, Penny. **Mother Jones and the March of the Mill Children**. Millbrook, 1994. ISBN 1-56294-402-9
This book tells about the march in 1903 protesting child labor, but it also talks about the life of Mary Harris Jones, the powerful labor leader whose life overlapped that of Eleanor Roosevelt.

Freedman, Russell. **Eleanor Roosevelt: A Life of Discovery**. Clarion, 1993. ISBN 0-89919-862-7
Freedman's biography presents a full-bodied picture of one of the first truly controversial and amazingly effective first ladies.

Freedman, Russell. **Franklin Delano Roosevelt**. Clarion, 1990. ISBN 0-89919-379-X
This photobiography emphasizes the irrepressible Roosevelt and the role he played in transforming America.

Mayo, Edith. **The Smithsonian Book of the First Ladies**. Holt, 1996. ISBN 0-8050-1651-8
This large, informative volume contains information about all the first ladies and uses painting and photographs.

Toor, Rachel. **Eleanor Roosevelt**.
Chelsea House, 1989. ISBN 1-55546-674-5
Grades 5-9
This biography covers her youth, her years as first lady, and her career after her husband's death.

Ziesk, Edra. **Margaret Mead**.
Chelsea House, 1989. ISBN 1-55546-667-2
The anthropologist spent most of her professional life doing research abroad, but her childhood spent in an intellectual family contrasts sharply with Eleanor's.

Island Boy

by Barbara Cooney
Puffin, 1988
ISBN 0-14-050756-6

▶ SUMMARY

A young father brings his still growing family to settle on an island off the coast of Maine in the days of sailing ships. We watch as he first prepares the island for their arrival and then as his family and their holdings grow. Soon the youngest boy, Matthias, has become a man and, eventually, the captain of a large ship. Later, however, he returns to the island to raise his own family and his grandson as well. This quiet story provides a microcosm for the passage of time.

▶ ILLUSTRATION

Pictures and print fit together comfortably on these pages. There is a sense of calm that is achieved both verbally and visually. Visual comfort is achieved by using soft muted colors for scenes and landscapes, by choosing sepia-saturated maps to trigger a sense of nostalgia, and by placing the family in familiar surroundings that assure a feeling of warmth.

▶ CONNECTIONS

NOVEL

Paul Fleischman's **The Borning** (HarperCollins, 1991. ISBN 0-06-023762-7) is set in Ohio and shows the births and deaths of a family within one room. There's a strong corollary to the island of **Island Boy**.

THEME

▶ Family sagas

CURRICULUM CONNECTION

▶ HISTORY – Building communities, invention and discovery

LANGUAGE ARTS

EXTENDING THE BOOK

▶ In the book it says, "Pa taught the boys to plough and to plant, to fell a tree and to build a stone wall. He taught them to cut ice and stone, to hunt and fish. And he taught them how to handle a boat." Imagine that your father is your only teacher. What things should and could he teach you in order to help you survive on your own someday?

▶ Later, Hannah teaches her girls some skills on the island. What skills would be needed? Would they be needed today? What's changed?

▶ When Matthias sits under the apple tree, Cooney says he "thinks about his smallness." What kinds of thoughts might he have had on that subject? What things would he be too small to do? Would you be apt to share any of those thoughts?

▶ These children don't go to school. Many children of today are taught at home instead of school. Make a list of the good and bad things about being taught at home.

BUILDING VOCABULARY

▶ Matthias spends a lot of time sitting under the astrakhan apple tree. We don't hear much about that kind of apple any more. Make a list of every kind of apple you can find out about. Taste as many as possible and take a survey to see what the people in your class think about each apple. Chart the results of your survey.

▶ Matthias' brothers tell him he is too young to leave home when they do. They say he is "wet behind the ears." What do they mean? How could that expression mean that? Find other expressions we use to mean that someone is young or inexperienced. List them and then go on to find other interesting idioms that mean more than they say.

SCIENCE

▶ Matthias brings home a baby seagull and makes it a pet. Find a bird guidebook and decide what kind of seagull this one might have been, considering where the island is and the appearance of the bird as it grows.

SOCIAL STUDIES

▶ If your family decided to go live on an uninhabited island off the coast of Maine, would things be different than they were for Matthias and his family? What technology would help you that they didn't have? What jobs would still be necessary?

▶ Barbara Cooney has drawn a careful map of the area. Why do you think she did so? Is this a real area? Can you locate it on a map of Maine?

ART

▶ Look at the picture in the book that shows young Matthias clutching a lobster as he stands in the water. Now look at the book **Miss Rumphius** (see Related Books) by the same author/illustrator. Can you find an illustration in that book that is similar to this one? Look closely to see the likenesses and differences.

▶ There's another page in **Island Boy** that shows a horse-drawn carriage on a cobblestone street. Compare that picture to the ones in **Ox-Cart Man** (see Related Books) by Barbara Cooney where the farmer gets to town. How are those two illustrations alike and how are they different? Is the mood the same?

▶ Barbara Cooney is especially good at doing land and seascapes that show things far off as well as close up. Use some paints or other media to make your own land- or seascape without trying to copy these.

RELATED BOOKS

NOVELS

Dunlop, Eileen. **Finn's Island**.
Holiday, 1992. ISBN 0-8234-0910-4
Finn, a boy whose Scottish family is in disarray, becomes fascinated with Hirsay, the island where his grandfather grew up.

Fleischman, Paul. **The Borning Room**.
HarperCollins, 1991. ISBN 0-06-023762-7
We center on one room in a house that was built in 1820, and we witness an intergenerational story through the events that took place in that room.

McKenna, Colleen. **Murphy's Island**.
Scholastic, 1990. ISBN 0-590-43552-3
Life on Put-in-Bay Island changes radically after all the summer people leave, and Collette is less sure that she wants to spend the fall there.

O'Dell, Scott. **Island of the Blue Dolphins**.
Dell, 1978. ISBN 0-440-94000-1
This classic novel of survival is set on an island off the coast of California.

Rogers, Jean. **Goodbye, My Island**.
Greenwillow, 1983. ISBN 0-688-01965-X
An island off the coast of Alaska is being slowly deserted as more and more people go to live nearer civilization.

Whelan, Gloria. **Once on This Island**.
HarperCollins, 1995. ISBN 0-06-026248-6
During the War of 1812, Mary and her brother and sister manage the farm on Mackinac Island while their father goes to war.

PICTURE BOOKS

Baron, Kathy. **The Tree of Time**. Yosemite Association, 1994. ISBN 0-939666-73-1
Time in this book is shown through the life and death of a giant sequoia. A time line at the bottom of the page shows contemporaneous world events.

Bunting, Eve. **Dandelions** See page 44.
This family builds their home on the plains at about the same time as **Island Boy**.

Dragonwagon, Crescent. **Home Place**.
Simon & Schuster, 1990. ISBN 0-02-733190-3
A cluster of daffodils growing in the wood leads a hiking family to discovering and speculating on the family that once lived and grew up here.

Johnston, Tony. **Yonder**.
Dial, 1988. ISBN 0-8037-0277-9
A young man and woman marry and settle in a new place. To commemorate every major event in their lives, they plant a tree.

Thaxter, Celia. **Celia's Island Journal**.
Little, 1992. ISBN 0-316-83921-3
This picture book is based on the journal of a 19th century poet living on White Island off the coast of Maine.

NONFICTION

Dean, Julia. **A Year on Monhegan Island**.
Ticknor & Fields, 1995. ISBN 0-395-66476-4
A photographic study of the island off the coast of Maine shows how life changes after the summer tourists leave.

Three Cool Kids

by Rebecca Emberley
Little, Brown, 1995
ISBN 0-316-23666-7

SUMMARY

Here is an urban slant on the traditional tale of the "Three Billy Goats Gruff." These "kids" are "hip" and "cool" and enjoy living on a lot in the middle of the city. But urban blight and construction projects convince the kids that they need a change. They decide to move to another lot, full of sweet greens including delectable weeds. Like their counterparts in the country, they meet a formidable obstacle. A giant rat lives in the sewer under the street and terrifies those who cross. The kids (following the lead of their ancestors) find a way to outwit the rat, cross the street, remain in the city and eat happily ever after.

ILLUSTRATION

Assembling an extraordinary variety of colorful printed and textured papers results in these collage-like compositions that are simultaneously simple and creative. One of the unique aspects of these cocmpositions centers on vantage point. What is the reader's eye-level view of the kids? While the cut shapes are flat, they acheive a sense of space through overlapping and varied texture. The book jacket mentions the authors' efforts to have children mimic sounds of animals. The cut paper technique is one that children can mimic in their own creative expression as well.

CONNECTIONS

NOVEL

Thesman, Jean. **Nothing Grows Here**. HarperCollins, 1994. ISBN 0-06-024457
A family is forced to move to another, less hospitable place, sort of a reverse on this picture book.

THEMES

► Fairy tale extensions
► Proverbs such as "The grass is always greener on the other side of the fence."

CURRICULUM CONNECTION

► SCIENCE & SOCIAL STUDIES - Recycling and waste disposal

Language Arts

DESCRIPTIONS

▶ There are several strong phrases to describe the rat: rude repulsive creature, crusty lips. Reread and list the others. Update the descriptive terms into slang. How would the characters be described in rap? Consider re-telling the story in rap format.

▶ Describe the lot on which the kids lived and the new one across the street and down the block, where they hope to move. Draw and label each lot. Name the surrounding areas.

▶ Draw pictures of each kid. Include every detail.

LETTER WRITING

▶ Brainstorm ideas for a school "clean-up and recycling awareness day." Compose a class letter to the principal and volunteer services. Suggest plans to clean up the school and grounds.

▶ Get involved in a clean-up campaign to improve some area of the city. Write letters to authorities or owners to obtain permission and adult supervision.

VOCABULARY DEVELOPMENT

▶ Separate the class into groups of three or four. Reread and list troublesome or possibly unknown words (dankness, berth, mottled). Later, share the results and target the words that appear on one or more list.

▶ Some words and noises are fun to pronounce. Find them and match them to the character and object, for example, Little's sneakers: *squinka, squinka*.

    Middle's bracelets:_____
    Rat:_____
    Hooves:_____
    Horns on grate:_____
    Horns across bars:_____

Create other nonsense words to match some everyday objects, persons or animals.

PROVERBS AND MORALS

▶ On the last page it is noted "...the grass was very sweet on the other side of the street." Compare to the old proverb: "The grass always looks greener on the other side of the fence." Or try, "The devil you know is better than one you don't know." Would they have moved believing in the last two?

▶ "He or she will tell you what's what!" Explain the meaning of "what's what" or make one up.

▶ Take some familiar proverbs and break them in half, making up a new beginning or ending for each one. For instance, "While the cat's away . . . we don't have to change the litter box." Or "Too much salt . . . spoils the broth."

WRITING

▶ The three kids are Big, Middle and Little Cool. Their names are simple. Remember the name "Gruff." Try to think of some new and different names for the three. The Beauty Salon is "Horns to Hooves." Assign "clever" names for the Recycling Center, certain streets, goat store and sneaker store. Write ads for these stores and their products.

▶ Use the phone book to find names of local businesses. Look at malls and shopping centers. Decide which ones are solid and which are "cutesy."

COMPARE AND CONTRAST

▶ Begin a classroom collection of "Three Billy Goats" books. There are quite a few. Compare their names, personalities, clothing, settings and villains.

▶ Find books that deal with three other animals. There are blind mice, little pigs, little javelinas, kittens, bears and others. Compare these adventures to those of the Cool kids. Locate books that simply deal with the number three-robbers, sillies, musketeers, wishes, sisters, hats. Research the supposed magic behind the number three. Why do so many authors rely on it? Does it add to the essence of the story?

EXTENDING THE STORY

▶ Tell what happens after the Cool kids moved to their new lot. Did Middle enjoy the beauty salon? Did she do a little shopping? How did the recycling center help Big and Little Cool? Describe how they enjoyed their new life.

▶ When the rat floated away with the rest of the debris, he was never heard from again. Suppose he returned to the sewer. Did he want revenge for the way he was treated? Tell how he tried to regain his territory and how he met the Cool kids again.

CHARACTERIZATIONS

▶ List various characteristics of each kid. Deal with personality traits and appearance.

▶ Try to list some "good" traits of the rat along with his evil side.

▶ A rat was chosen to be the "bad guy." Are there other animals that might represent evil? Why are some animals more appropriate for that role than others?

SCIENCE

▶ Research the term *solid waste disposal*.

▶ Decide if the neighborhood plant might recycle decomposable wastes, combustible wastes such as paper, wood, or cloth, and non-combustibles such as metal, glass, ceramics.

▶ What made the recycling plant appealing to the kids?

▶ Investigate other types of waste disposal: industrial, mining and agricultural wastes; garbage; ashes; demolition and construction debris.

▶ Could the construction debris "next door" be taken care of in the recycling plant?

▶ Find out about local recycling programs. Investigate home, school, neighborhood, city and state, attempts at recycling and disposal.

▶ Using the author's cut paper technique, design some posters to be used throughout the school encouraging recycling.

▶ Start a recycling program in the classroom. Begin by using both sides of work papers, separating types of paper and using recycled paper.

ART

▶ Use some recycled paper and other materials to create cut-paper images of a different story.

▶ RELATED BOOKS

NOVELS

Thesman, Jean. **Nothing Grows Here**.
HarperCollins, 1994. ISBN 0-06-024457-7 Grades 4-8
When Maryanne's father dies, she and her mother can no longer afford to live in the pleasant house with the yard. They move instead to a tenement flat where, in spite of herself, Maryanne makes the necessary adjustment.

PICTURE BOOKS

Arnold, Tim. **The Three Billy Goats Gruff**.
McElderry, 1993. ISBN 0-689-50575-2
This version of the fairy tale is set in the mountains of the American West.

Lowell, Susan. **The Three Little Javelinas**.
Illustrated by Jim Harris. Northland Publishing, 1992. ISBN 0-87358-542-9
These lovable wild southwestern cousins of pigs are running away from the hungry coyote. He had hoped to eat them with red chili sauce.

McLerran, Alice. **The Year of the Ranch**.
Viking, 1996. ISBN 0-670-85131-0
A very determined man moves his urban family into the desert to homestead a claim.

Rounds, Glen. **Three Billy Goats Gruff**.
Holiday, 1993. ISBN 0-8234-1015-3
This is a lively retelling of the tale with very funny illustrations.

Scieszka, Jon. **The True Story of the Three Little Pigs**. Illustrated by Lane Smith. Viking, 1989.
ISBN 0-670-82759-2
This time the wolf tells the story his way. The pigs are definitely in the wrong.

Trivizas, Eugene. **The Three Little Wolves and the Big Bad Pig**. Illustrated by Helen Oxenbury; Margaret K. McElderry, 1993. ISBN 0-689-50569-8
The three little wolves build themselves three different shelters. The big bad pig becomes a friend at the last one.

Death of the Iron Horse

by Paul Goble
Simon & Schuster, 1987
ISBN 0-02-737830-6

SUMMARY

According to the author, much fiction has been written about Native American groups attacking the railroads. This particular attack is the only one historically verified. The coming of the railroads to the lands of the western Native Americans fulfilled a great and terrible prophecy. The news that the Iron Horse was getting closer spread panic among the Cheyennes. A group of young men decided to turn it back, interpreting the engine, tracks and headlights in relation to previous experiences, and succeeding in derailing the train and looting it. Some of the items were of use to the Native Americans. These they carried home. The rest, like the money, they spread on the wind.

ILLUSTRATION

Paul Goble uses all design elements selectively to illustrate and clarify this most powerful and prophetic tale of Native Americans. Pen and India ink lines capture shapes and enclose colors of everything from figures to landscapes and skyscapes. All manner of patterns are employed(patterns in the money flying through the air, patterns on printed cloth floating across the desert, patterns of boxcars strewn about as wreckage, and colorful patterns woven into clothing and headdresses. The evolution of the Iron Horse is visually documented in extraordinary detail in these carefully drawn illustrations.

CONNECTIONS

NOVEL

Novels such as Kathryn Lasky's **Bone Wars** (Morrow, 1988. ISBN 0-688-07433-2), which describe further conflict between the Native Americans and the rapidly expanding country, are a suitable connection here.

THEME

▶ Conflicting cultures

CURRICULUM CONNECTION

▶ HISTORY – Westward expansion, Native Americans

LANGUAGE ARTS
USING FIGURATIVE LANGUAGE

▶ Goble uses many metaphors when the Indians react to their first sight of the train: the track is "iron bands binding our Mother, earth"; the headlight is "the eye of the Iron Horse shining." Find other metaphors in the text and decide what Goble is trying to show us by using them.

▶ Use the same metaphors in the above activity and make them into similes by adding "like" or "as": the track was like iron bands binding our Mother, earth; the headlight looked like an eye on an iron horse.

▶ In this story, the Cheyennes left the money behind because it was useless to them. Brainstorm expressions used to state lack of worth such as "I need that like I need a hole in the head," "bringing coals to Newcastle."

COMPARING TO PERSONAL EXPERIENCE

▶ If you had been there at the train wreck, what would you have told the young men to take? The money? The china? How would you have persuaded them to take those things?

SCIENCE

▶ Sweet Medicine's dream is prophetic. What do you think causes dreams? What is your mind doing when you dream? Could a dream predict the future?

SOCIAL STUDIES

▶ Make a chart similar to the one below for the items on the train.

The Item	Worth to Native Americans	Worth to the Travelers
Axes	Tool to open cases	Tool to cut trees or build houses
Pans and kettles	Containers to cook food in	Containers to cook food in
China plates	Might be pretty	Decoration
Dollar Bills		

▶ What if this book were about white settlers attacking an Indian village? What items might the Indians have that would be of great use to them but of little use to the white settlers? Make a similar chart showing those items.

▶ Find out about the building of the Transcontinental Railroad. When did it occur? Who profited from it? Why did it hasten the taking of Indian lands beyond those actually used by the railroad itself?

▶ Make a list of the Indian nations whose land was taken to build the railroad. What happened to each of those nations? Where are their descendants today?

▶ In the foreword to the book Goble tells how, after the Civil War, the armies were used to drive the Indians onto reservations. What laws were passed to make this happen? What treaties were broken? Who was president of the United States at the time? What was his reasoning for doing this? What support did he have?

▶ Find out about one displacement of Native Americans in the West and report its results to the rest of the group.

▶ Notice the flags on the first page of the story. What countries do they represent and why are they there?

ART

▶ Goble's illustrations are stylized: they contain strong elements of design rather than realistic portrayals. Take the illustration you like most and find words to describe what you see. Look at some of the other books by Paul Goble (see Related Books) and find figures and designs in common with this one.

▶ Look at paintings and designs created by the Plains Indians. Find traces of them in Goble's books.

▶ Notice the white line that often appears around people and objects in Goble's illustrations. You can create a similar effect by painting or drawing something like a bowl of fruit. Cut around each object in your painting so that you have separate pieces for everything in it. Paste the objects on a new sheet of white paper leaving a tiny space between the objects so that the white paper shows through. Try it with more complicated pictures. Now try using white paint to outline some objects in a different painting. Which effect do you like better?

RELATED BOOKS

NOVELS

Lasky, Kathryn. **The Bone Wars**.
Morrow, 1988. ISBN 0-688-07433-2 Grades 5-9
In the mid 1870s Thad Longsworth, blood brother to the visionary Black Elk, finds his destiny linked to that of three rival teams of paleontologists searching for dinosaur bones as the conflict between cultures heats up.

Nixon, Joan Lowry. **Orphan Train Series**. Grades 4-8
Circle of Love. Delacorte, 1997. ISBN 0-385-32280-1
Dangerous Promise. Delacorte, 1994.
ISBN 0-385-32073-6
A Family Apart. Bantam, 1996. ISBN 0-440-22676-7
These are just a few titles in the series of books in which we follow various members of a family of children who left New York City on the orphan train.

NONFICTION

Fisher, Leonard E. **Tracks Across America: The Story of the American Railroad**. Holiday, 1992.
ISBN 0-8234-0945-7
With many photographs and drawings, Fisher traces the development of the railroad from its inception in England to the modern trains of today.

Fradin, Dennis. **The Cheyenne**.
Childrens, 1988. ISBN 0-516-01211-8
A brief history of the Cheyenne Indians includes colored photographs.

Fraser, Mary. **Ten Mile Day: And the Building of the Transcontinental Railroad**. Holt, 1993.
ISBN 0-8050-1902-2
This is a short book but the details are fascinating. Among Fraser's key themes are the ways in which the railroad ended the Native American way of life.

Hoig, Stan. **People of the Sacred Arrow**.
Cobblehill, 1992. ISBN 0-525-65088-1
This book tells how the relocated Cheyenne in western Oklahoma are existing today.

MacDonald, Fiona. **A Nineteenth Century Railway Station: Inside Story**. Peter Bedrick Books, 1990.
ISBN 0-87226-341-X
Through this book we get an idea of the kind of travelers on a train such as the one attacked in **Death of the Iron Horse.**

OTHER BOOKS WRITTEN AND ILLUSTRATED BY PAUL GOBLE

Beyond the Ridge. Simon & Schuster, 1989.
ISBN 0-02-736581-6
The topic in this picture book about the Plains Indians is death, and we see it through the eyes of an old woman as her spirit begins her journey beyond the ridge.

Buffalo Woman. Simon & Schuster, 1987.
ISBN 0-689-71109-3
A woman emerges from the buffalo nation to become the wife of a great hunter. However, his people distrust her and she runs back to the buffalo people with her son.

Dream Wolf. Bradbury, 1989. ISBN 0-02-736585-9
This is a reissue of the author's **Friendly Wolf,** in which two lost Indian children are befriended by a wolf who is thereafter honored by their people.

The Girl Who Loved Wild Horses. Bradbury, 1978.
ISBN 0-689-71082-8
This Caldecott award winner tells of a girl's love of a black stallion that leads her to become a wild horse herself.

Her Seven Brothers. Simon & Schuster, 1988.
ISBN 0-02737-960-4
A young woman makes clothing for seven brothers no one else knew she had and then sets off to find them.

I Sing for the Animals. Bradbury, 1991.
ISBN 0-02-737725-3
This picture book gives us a glimpse at Paul Goble as he gives us his thoughts about life.

Red Hawk's Account of Custer's Last Battle.
University of Nebraska, 1992. ISBN 0-8032-7033-X
Here's the battle of Little Big Horn as seen by the victor, Red Hawk.

The Girl Who Loved Wild Horses

by Paul Goble
Simon & Schuster, 1986
ISBN 0-689-71082-8

SUMMARY

In this Caldecott Award-winning book, the illustrations of Plains Indian designs, blending with this dramatic tale, make the young Indian girl seem real. During a storm, she and the tribe's horses become lost after a stampede. Eventually she meets a beautiful spotted stallion, and she and her horses are welcomed into his herd of wild horses. After more than a year, she is returned to her family, but she misses her colt and the wild horses so much that she becomes ill. She so identifies with the horses that the only cure is to allow her to return and ride with the wild horses. It is believed that she eventually became one of them. This is a reason to celebrate, for the tribe is convinced they now have relatives among the horse people.

ILLUSTRATION

Paul Goble's drawing skills are the backbone of these illustrations. Color selections for his horses are rooted in reality yet used dramatically to convey the power and majesty of these animals. Goble employs patterns in multiple ways. Patterns can be found in the illustrations of plant life, sunbursts, native dress and the colorful treatment of teepees. When patterns are used on top of patterns, they add to the story's action. An example can be seen where the pattern of natives is seen against the pattern of horses. The horses, in turn, contrast with the pattern on the teepees and the teepee patterns play against the landscape. An example of repeat pattern can be found in the composition where the horses' reflection creates a mirror image. The concluding illustration of intertwined horse heads linked with the sunburst is a powerfully abstract composition.

CONNECTIONS

NOVEL

Marguerite Henry's **Misty of Chincoteague** (Simon & Schuster, 1990 . ISBN 0-02-743622-5) is one of a series of books about wild horses.

THEME

▶ Transformation

CURRICULUM CONNECTION

▶ SOCIAL STUDIES – Plains Indians

LANGUAGE ARTS

WRITING

▶ Create a new ending for the story. What if the girl returns to her family as a human and tells about her experiences as a horse? What if the horses return to her instead of the other way around?

COMPARING LITERATURE

▶ Paul Goble's book uses themes found in the Plains Indians' lore. Collect books and stories of the other Native American tribes. Compare their designs, story themes and creation tales. How do these compare to African tales?

▶ There are many stories of humans turning into animals and animals becoming human. Find some examples of these and compare them to Native American tales. Try some of the books by Joanne Ryder (see Related Books).

▶ Find other stories about transformation such as the ones in fairy tales where lovers are turned into trees or stars.

▶ Find stories of the Plains Indians that show the importance of the horse and buffalo to their existence.

USING FIGURATIVE LANGUAGE

▶ The poem on the last page contains several similes. Try substituting other ones: *my horse has a hoof like a sharp stone; his fetlock is like a lion's mane.*

▶ There are two similes in the rest of the story: *they gallop away like the wind* and *the hooves struck as fast as lightning.* Can you find other images for these?

▶ Find some of the strong verbs in the story such as *drove* and *snorted.* Try substituting other words. Do they make the sentences stronger or weaker?

SOCIAL STUDIES

▶ Make a list of the tribes that make up the Plains Indians. Make a chart showing their differences and similarities. Did these Native Americans all speak the same language? If not, how did they communicate?

▶ How many members were in these tribes before the Europeans came? How many are in those groups now? Is their population growing or declining?

▶ Compare the illustrations of teepees in this book to photographs and other drawings of the Indians. What designs are prevalent?

▶ Research the coming of the horse to the plains.

▶ On a map locate the areas where the Plains Indians used to be. Where are they now?

▶ What's happening to the wild horses on the plains now?

▶ Investigate the mustang population. Are they still wild?

▶ What was the conflict in cultures that caused the end of the life of the wild horses and the Plains Indians? Could this conflict have been solved any other way? Is there a current conflict? How is it being resolved?

ART

▶ Plains Indians often painted designs based on deeds they were proud of and events from their dreams. Examine the designs in the book and then create some personal designs of your own to represent your hopes and dreams.

▶ Find out about the art produced by other Native Americans. What kind of art is being produced today by Native American artists?

▶ Which colors are prominent in the illustrations of the book? The main figures are shown in the same shades throughout the book. Is anything else pictured with these same colors?

RELATED BOOKS

NOVELS

Campbell, Joanna. **The Wild Mustang**.
Bantam, 1989. ISBN 0-553-15698-5 Grades 4+
Tracy and her brother Colin find an injured mustang and nurse it back to health, hiding its existence from their father.

Farley, Walter. **The Black Stallion**.
Random, 1977. ISBN 0-394-90601-2
This is the first in a series of books about Alec and the wild Arabian horse he is stranded with on a remote island.

Henry, Marguerite. **Misty Of Chincoteague**.
Simon & Schuster, 1990. ISBN 0-02-743622-5
A brother and sister capture two wild ponies on Chincoteague Island.

Laundrie, Amy. **Whinny of the Wild Horses**.
Knopf, 1992. ISBN 0-679-81824-3
A wild colt falls into the hands of a cruel master who uses him on the rodeo circuit.

PICTURE BOOKS

Baker, Olaf. **Where the Buffaloes Begin**.
Puffin, 1981. ISBN 0-670-82760-6
This is an Indian legend of Little Wolf, who becomes one with the buffalo long enough to save his people.

Cohen, Caron Lee. **The Mud Pony**.
Scholastic, 1988. ISBN 0-590-41526-3
A poor boy longs for a pony of his own and constructs one out of mud.

DePaola, Tomie. **The Legend of the Bluebonnet**.
Putnam, 1993. ISBN 0-399-22441-6
"She Who Is Alone" decides to sacrifice her most prized possession to save her people.

Kinsey-Warnock, Natalie. **The Wild Horses of Sweetbriar**. Illustrated by Ted Rand. Dutton, 1990.
ISBN 0-525-65015-6
At the turn of the century, a young girl and her mother spend the year on a remote island off the coast of Massachusetts with a herd of wild horses for company.

Littlechild, George. **This Land Is My Land**.
Children's Book Press, 1993. ISBN 0-892-39119-7
The author tells his own story of the Plains Indians, in which the descendants of the buffalo hunters entered the society of urban America.

Reiser, Lynn. **Night Thunder and the Queen of the Wild Horses**. Greenwillow, 1995.
ISBN 0-688-11791-0
A young girl paints a picture of a wild horse and is awakened one night to ride the horse she created.

Ryder, Joanne. **Winter Whale**.
Mulberry, 1991. ISBN 0-688-13110-7
A girl changes into a gray, humpbacked whale.

San Souci, Robert. **The Legend of Scarface**.
Doubleday, 1978. ISBN 0-385-15874-2
A young boy is marked with a mysterious scar. In order to remove it, he must make a journey to the sun.

NONFICTION

Viola, Herman. **After Columbus: The Horse's Return to America**. Soundprints, 1993.
ISBN 0-924483-74-1
With photos and prints as well as clear, factual text, the author traces the reintroduction of the horse and the spread of its use by the Plains Indians.

The Village of Round and Square Houses

by Ann Grifalconi
Little Brown, 1986
ISBN 0-316-32862-6

SUMMARY

Why do the women in this small African village live in round houses and the men live in square ones? There is a reason; the story is told by a young girl who grew up there. (The village still exists in the remote hills of the Cameroons.) Old Mother Naka, the volcano, had a lot to do with the situation, as it frightened the people. When the red rivers of lava flowed down the sides of the mountain, the villagers "cried out to Naka and prayed where they were lying down." When they realized that they had been spared, they found only two of their houses left standing, one round and one square. Their reason for the future separation of men and women makes a fascinating story.

ILLUSTRATION

These are good color studies in pastel, capturing the mood expressed in the story. In selected illustrations, one can find inspiration from American painters such as John Marin.

CONNECTIONS

NOVEL

Sheila Gordon's **Waiting for Rain** (Dell, 1996. ISBN 0-440-22698-8) is about a different kind of segregation(that of the races in South Africa.

THEME

▶ Pourquoi Tales (stories that explain why something happens).

CURRICULUM CONNECTION

▶ SOCIAL STUDIES – Customs and traditions in other cultures

LANGUAGE ARTS
COMPARING AND CONTRASTING

▶ There is an abundance of folk literature from Africa. Start a collection of various African tales. Instead of "reporting" on a book, begin to classify books in categories, such as:

    Animals – tricksters; storytellers; personified
    Heroes – hunters; tribe members; sorcerers
    Text – repetition; rhythm & rhyme; play on words

▶ As the collection grows, encourage students to create new classifications. This is a good way to compare and contrast this literature.

▶ Compare the appearances of the village as well as the people *after* the volcano erupts to their appearances at the outset. Write a description of each.

▶ Write a schedule for a day in the life of the round houses (women) and do the same for the square houses (men). Compare the two.

▶ List the crops grown in the village. Find examples of the types of meats served. Contrast them with our meals served at home or school.

▶ Investigate private schools that enroll boys or girls only. Gather information on each. Compare them to public schools.

WRITING

▶ Prepare oral weather reports.

▶ Describe the coming volcanic eruption. Predict the time it will occur and how long it will last. Assist the villagers in their survival preparations. Suggest moves to safer ground if necessary. List precautions to take and supplies needed.

▶ Continue with the report after the eruption. Discuss when and if it will be safe for the villagers to return to their homes. What precautions might be necessary? Identify places where families might get help.

▶ Prepare some graphics to be used in the presentation: pictures, maps, labeling.

RECALLING DETAILS

▶ Retell the story changing as many details as possible, such as the shapes of the houses (rectangular, triangular, octagonal. Who would live in each house? Vary the names of the village, people, crops, food.

ATTRIBUTES

▶ List the good and bad traits of a village such as Tos. Include quality of life, education, technology, values.

▶ Do the same for a typical American city or town. Stress transportation, education, entertainment, the arts.

SOCIAL STUDIES
MAP SKILLS

▶ Find the village of Tos on a map of Africa. Use the author's note for directions.

▶ Research and locate the active and inactive volcanoes in the United States.

▶ Find the more famous volcanoes around the world, e.g., Etna, Vesuvius, Krakatoa.

SHELTERS

▶ Collect examples of unusual, simple shelters around the world.

▶ Try to find illustrations of some "round and square houses," e.g., windmills, lighthouses, barns, farmhouses.

▶ Display examples of beautiful and unusual architecture, e.g., Taj Mahal, cathedrals, skyscrapers, Parthenon.

▶ Choose the "best" buildings in your city and state. Explain choice and identify your criteria.

SCIENCE
VOLCANOES

▶ Investigate volcanoes. Explain, illustrate and diagram this geological landform. Include the fissure in the earth's crust above which is a cone of volcanic material.

▶ Build a class volcano (use chemicals necessary for "an explosion").

▶ Research volcanic activity. Locate and identify volcanoes for each of these categories:

  constantly active
  moderate activity
  dormant (quiescent)

▶ Research the history of Mount St. Helens in the state of Washington. Create a time line for eruptions there.

▶ Were the villagers of Tos prepared for the eruption of Naka Mountain? What type of volcano was this mountain?

▶ Write a short description of the cause and effect of lava explosions. Describe the resulting ashes. Explain the appearance of the village people after examining the book's illustrations.

▶ Research inactive periods:

  After the cooling stage, what happens to the volcano?

  The people rebuilt the village of Tos. Why? Did they know something about inactive volcanoes?

  Examine the last page. Explain the words, "Til Naka speaks again!"

WEATHER

▶ Notice the illustrations. What happens to the colors and shades from the pre-eruption period to the eruption itself? Examine the appearance of the village and the people immediately after to the gradual rebuilding. Explain this section of the book as a weather report.

▶ Research the Richter scale. How is it used? What is its value?

▶ The eruption of Mount St. Helens was blamed for weather conditions across the country. Is that possible?

▶ How did the eruption of Montserrat compare to this one? What effect did it have on life there?

RELATED BOOKS

NOVEL

Gordon, Sheila. **Waiting for the Rain**.
Dell, 1996. ISBN 0-440-22698-8 Grades 5-9
Frikkie and Tengo, two friends since childhood, are torn apart by the dictates of apartheid in South Africa.

PICTURE BOOKS

Christiansen, C. B. **My Mother's House, My Father's House**. Simon & Schuster, 1990.
ISBN 0-689 313942
A little girl lives in two houses. She must travel to both to visit her mother and father.

Dragonwagon, Crescent. **Home Place**.
Illustrated by Jerry Pinkney. Simon & Schuster, 1990. ISBN 0-02 733190
Family members on an outing find clues to another family from long ago. Who lived there? What secrets are hidden in the area?

NONFICTION

Isaacson, Philip M. **Round Buildings, Square Buildings & Buildings That Wiggle Like a Fish**.
Alfred A. Knopf, 1988. ISBN 0-394-89382-4
This book contains photographs of architectural styles around the world. Among other structures, it explores churches, bridges, cliff dwellings, fortresses, mills and lighthouses.

Turner, Ann. **Dakota Dugout**.
Illustrated by Ronald Himler, Simon & Schuster, 1985. ISBN 0-02-789700-1 See page 217.
A young couple become early settlers in the great plains of the West. Their sod house becomes a home.

OTHER BOOKS WRITTEN BY ANN GRIFALCONI

Darkness and the Butterfly. Little, Brown, 1987.
ISBN 0-316-32863-4
Anna gets lost in the woods. A wise old woman and a yellow butterfly help her find the way home.

Fly Away Girl. Little, Brown, 1992.
ISBN 0-316-32866-9
A little girl is sent to the edge of the Niger River, where she must collect rushes for the New Year's celebration. She is able to complete her tasks in spite of distractions.

Kinda Blue. Little, Brown, 1993.
ISBN 0-316-32869-3
Young Sissy has the blues. She describes the loving answers to her problems that turn her doubts away.

OTHER BOOKS ILLUSTRATED BY ANN GRIFALCONI

Don't You Turn Back by Langston Hughes, edited by Lee Bennett Hopkins. Knopf, 1969.
ISBN 0-394-90846-5 Out of print.
Outstanding variety marks this collection of poems that portray a harsh world in which some children live.

Everett Anderson's Goodbye by Lucille Clifton.
Henry Holt, 1983. ISBN 0-8050-0800-4
A little boy struggles through five stages of grief after his father's death.

Georgia Music

by Helen V. Griffith
Illustrated by James Stevenson
Greenwillow, 1986
ISBN 0-688-06071 4

▶ SUMMARY

A little girl comes to spend the summer with her grandfather, and together they enjoy the life on his small Georgia farm: working in the garden and listening to the birds and insects. In the evening the old man plays tunes on his harmonica, which he says is a return favor for the birds and insects who played their music for him. The next summer, the little girl and her mother find that the old man is too sick to remain on the farm and they take him to live with them in Baltimore. There, he says nothing and obviously misses his farm and the Georgia music. When the little girl makes music on the harmonica it brings back the good times for both of them.

▶ ILLUSTRATION

The watercolor washes that fill the background in these compositions and the quick, sure lines of the images drawn over those washes convey a sense of freshness and spontaneity. These are characteristic traits of a practiced and highly skilled commercial illustrator. The gestures of the main characters are captured by the crisp pen and ink lines.

▶ CONNECTIONS

NOVEL

In Bruce Brooks' **Everywhere** (HarperCollins, 1990. ISBN 0-06-020728-0) a boy works hard to keep the strong connection between him and his grandfather even though the man appears to be dying.

THEMES

▶ Power of music
▶ Problems of the elderly
▶ Displaced persons

CURRICULUM CONNECTION

▶ SOCIAL STUDIES – Rural Georgia contrasted with urban Baltimore
▶ MUSIC – Country music, making music

LANGUAGE ARTS

FINDING DETAILS

▶ In all three of Griffith's "Granddaddy" books (listed below), the old man is shown to have a sense of humor. What lines in the books show his sense of humor? Read them aloud in the tone in which you think he said them.

MAKING INFERENCES

▶ Read How Does It Feel to Be Old (see Related Books). Which of the many moods and feelings of the elderly do you think the grandfather in Georgia Music shares at the beginning of the book? Which ones for the end?

COMPARING LITERATURE

▶ Read Granddaddy's Place and Granddaddy and Janetta (see Related Books). Decide which book tells you the most about Granddaddy and which one tells the most about Janetta. Which one tells you most about Georgia?

▶ Compare this fictional grandfather with some of the others in literature, such as Song and Dance Man by Karen Ackerman (see page XXX). Which of these men do you think would like each other? What might they like to do together?

▶ Look at other books that portray old people. What impression do they leave about old age? How do these impressions compare with the manner aging is depicted in advertisements and on TV. You may find that your information will be best shown in a chart similar to the following:

Character & Book	What Character is Shown Doing	Impression of Age
Grandpa in Georgia Music	working in garden playing harmonica sitting in chair	First part of book: productive, happy Second part of book: Lonely, sick

INVESTIGATING LANGUAGE

▶ In Georgia Music Granddaddy says the bird is "sassy." Later he calls Janetta a "sassy" bird. What are some synonyms for sassy? What do you think the old man meant?

MATH

▶ Many people have retirement funds and Social Security to help pay for their old age. If you started saving for your old age at $10 a month starting now, how much money would you have by the time you were 65? Don't forget to compound the interest. Would you have more if the money were invested in a bank or in some other kind of fund?

▶ Find out how much it costs for daily care in a nursing home, in the hospital, in a retirement home. How long would $40,000 dollars last? Add in medical care. Now how long would it last?

SCIENCE

▶ Find out what happens to the human body during the aging process. When does the body start to age? Do diet and exercise have any effect on the aging process? Interview fitness experts and nutritionists or read what they have written on the subject.

▶ Look at advertisements directed toward middle-aged readers. What types of products claim to halt or change the aging process? Which ones do you believe? Why or why not?

▶ There are many birds and insects mentioned in this book. Find pictures of each of them. How can you find out about the sounds they make?

SOCIAL STUDIES

▶ Find out your family statistics. How old did your mother and father's grandparents live to be? How about your grandparents? Can you find out more about the ages on your family tree?

▶ Is life expectancy in general getting longer or shorter? What do you think might account for this? What changes does it make in society?

▶ This grandfather has a family to care for him when he is no longer able to live alone. What happens to elderly people for whom this is not possible? What alternatives do they have? Does the government help? Should it?

▶ Contact the AARP to see what senior citizens are doing politically and socially.

MUSIC

▶ Locate and play some of the following instruments: harmonica, ocarina, penny whistle, recorder and ukelele. On which can you easily pick out a tune? How many can you learn to play? Can you make any of them sound like "Georgia music"?

▶ In this book the music was used to entertain and to soothe. What music suits your various moods? What instrument do you find most soothing? Most exciting? Most energizing? What musician would you listen to if you had had a hard day and needed to calm down? What musician would you listen to if you were trying to study for a test? What musician would you listen to if you were about to play in a tournament?

▶ RELATED BOOKS

NOVELS

Barron, T. A. **Heartlight**.
Philomel, 1990. ISBN 0-399-22180-8 Grades 6-9
This science fiction novel is a good read-aloud, although it's probably too difficult for most children in these grades to read independently. This grandfather and his granddaughter Kate are the best of friends and, when he succeeds in making a small amount of Pure Concentrated Light, they use it to travel into space.

Brooks, Bruce. **Everywhere**.
HarperCollins, 1990. ISBN 0-06-020728-0
Grades 4-9
This brief novel packs a big wallop. Grandfather is dying or, at least, has suffered a heart attack. His grandson and a new friend try magic to keep him alive. Read this aloud and be sure to allow plenty of time for discussion during and after it.

Jukes, Mavis. **Blackberries in the Dark**.
Random, 1985. ISBN 0-679-86570 Grades 3-6
This is the first visit Austin has made to his grandparents' home since the death of his grandfather. Together he and his grandmother grieve and find new traditions.

PICTURE BOOKS

Ackerman, Karen. **Song and Dance Man**.
Illustrated by Stephen Gammell. Knopf, 1988.
ISBN 0-394 99330-6
The grandfather in this Caldecott Award winner is a former vaudeville performer who revives his act for his grandchildren.

DeFelice, Cynthia. **When Grandpa Kissed His Elbow**. Simon & Schuster, 1992.
ISBN 0-02-726455-6
This grandfather loves to stretch the truth a bit, but he shows the little girl the magic that surrounds them.

DePaola, Tomie. **Tom**.
Putnam, 1993. ISBN 0-399-22417-3
Tommy and his grandfather, whom he calls Tom, are good friends, delighting in each other's company and the tricks they play.

Ernst, Lisa Campbell. **The Luckiest Kid on the Planet**. Bradbury, 1994. ISBN 0-027-33566-6
Grandfather is a big part of Lucky's life. When Lucky finds out his real name is Herbert, he undergoes an identity crisis and it's Grandfather who helps him through it.

Farber, Norma. **How Does It Feel to Be Old**.
Dutton, 1988. ISBN 0-525-32414-3
This series of vignettes has elderly people giving many sides of the picture. Trina Schart Hyman's illustrations are perfect.

Fox, Mem. **Wilfrid Gordon MacDonald Partridge**.
Kane/Miller, 1989. ISBN 0-916-291-26-X
A little boy is best friends with the people in a nearby "old folks" home.

Johnston, Tony. **Grandpa's Song**.
Dial, 1991. ISBN 0-8037-0801-7
This grandfather loves to sing and has a favorite number he renders at all occasions. When he begins to lose his memory, the song helps him refocus.

Keller, Holly. **Grandfather's Dream**.
Greenwillow, 1994. ISBN 0-688-12339-2
This Asian grandfather's dream is to restore his native land and bring back the cranes that once nested there.

Strangis, Joel. **Grandfather's Rock**.
Houghton, 1993. ISBN 0-395-65367-3
In this variant of an Italian folk tale, a family is taking the grandfather to the old age home and the parents get a lesson from the younger generation.

OTHER BOOKS BY HELEN V. GRIFFITH

Alex and the Cat. Greenwillow, 1982.
ISBN 0-688-00420-2
The dog and cat are friends, but each reacts differently to everything.

Emily and the Enchanted Frog. Greenwillow, 1989.
ISBN 0-688-08483-4
This picture book has several short stories in it. "Emily and the Mermaid" is especially good.

Grandaddy and Janetta. Greenwillow, 1993.
ISBN 0-688-11226-9
This is the same grandfather and little girl as in **Georgia Music** in a longer and funnier book of their earlier days together in Georgia.

Grandaddy's Place. Morrow, 1991.
ISBN 0-688-10491-6
Again, it's the same pair as in **Georgia Music**, but this is Janetta's first visit to the farm.

The Farm Summer 1942

by Donald Hall
Illustrated by Barry Moser
Dial, 1994
ISBN 0-8037-1501-3

SUMMARY

In this story, the author and illustrator paint a brilliant picture of life on a New England farm during the summer of 1942. A young boy, Peter, leaves his home in San Francisco to spend the summer in New Hampshire with his grandparents on the farm where his father grew up. While he is learning about farm life and learning to love the peacefulness of it, he is also missing his parents. His mother has gone to New York City to work in the war effort, while his father is serving on a destroyer in the South Pacific.

ILLUSTRATION

Moser's illustrations are carefully crafted watercolor paintings. The watercolor washes are crisp and clean, the work of a master draftsman and versatile designer. Pictures fill the pages and faithfully mirror the words of the story.

CONNECTIONS

NOVEL

Gary Paulsen's book **Harris and Me** (Harcourt, 1993. ISBN 0-15-292877-4) is set on a farm where the two boys get into hilarious troubles.

THEMES

▶ Farm life
▶ Memories

CURRICULUM CONNECTION

▶ SOCIAL STUDIES – Farming today vs. yesterday
▶ HISTORY – 1940s

LANGUAGE ARTS

WRITING
▶ Divide the class into four or more groups. Make each group responsible for one kind of farm (dairy, vegetable, cattle, fruit, tree farm. Find a creative way to show others what you've learned.

INTERVIEWING
▶ Interview parents and grandparents about what they remember about their lives in 1942. Have a roundtable discussion sharing the results of the interviews. How do these memories coincide with what we've learned about 1942 in the book?

COMPARING LITERATURE
▶ Find other books about characters who visit farms. Include some short novels such as **Harris and Me** by Gary Paulson (see Related Books).

GETTING MEANING FROM TEXT
▶ Compare and contrast Peter's life in San Francisco with his life on the farm in the summer of 1942.

SOCIAL STUDIES

▶ Generate a "Now" and "Then" wall chart. From the story and illustrations compare how life in 1942 was different from life now. For example: (Then) Families sat around and listened to a radio show in the evening. (Now) Families watch television. Make a third column called "Therefore" in which to place some results of those changes.

▶ What war was being fought in 1942? Why was it fought? What countries were involved? When did it end? Why was Peter's mother called away to New York to work on a secret project? What might that project have been?

▶ As a result of the war, what countries ceased to exist? What countries' borders changed?

▶ Ask parents and grandparents about rationing, bomb shelters, blackout curtains, volunteer work, victory gardens, or anything else they might remember about the war years in this country.

▶ Find out who "Rosie the Riveter" was and what she represented in our country. Read the book **Rosie the Riveter** to find out what impact the war had on changes in family life (see Related Books). How did the stereotypical role of women change during this period and why?

▶ List the modes of transportation Peter used to get to New Hampshire. How many of them are still in use today?

▶ Find New Hampshire on a United States map. Also locate San Francisco and New York City. Map Peter's route to his grandparents' farm and determine how many miles he traveled to get there.

▶ Peter's father was on a destroyer in the South Pacific. Make a display of warships using models, drawings and pictures. What islands and countries are found there? What was their involvement in the war?

▶ Write to the tourist boards of each of the New England states requesting information about natural resources, dominant industries, climate. How has New England changed since 1942? Are there any communities whose main source of livelihood is still agriculture?

▶ Find a tape of an old-time radio show. Like Peter did, enjoy a snack of Moxie and ginger snaps while you listen.

▶ Try to find an old Sears and Roebuck catalog. Examine the types of items besides bathroom fixtures that were then available through mail order catalogs.

MATH

▶ Determine how many miles Peter flew to get to New York City from San Francisco. If it took him 16 hours to get there, how fast did the plane travel?

▶ Find out how fast today's jetliners travel. Determine how long it would take for Peter to make his trip today. Also figure out how much farther Peter could go today in 16 hours and where his final destination might be.

SCIENCE

▶ Peter drinks fresh milk from his grandfather's cow. His grandfather tells him that it tastes different from San Francisco milk because it is not pasteurized. How and why is milk pasteurized?

▶ What decisions must farmers make today about pesticides? How do their decisions affect consumers?

MUSIC

▶ Try to find a copy of Peter's favorite song, "Life is Like a Mountain Railroad." Then come up with as many railroad songs as you and your class can think of to sing.

▶ Play records by the Andrews Sisters, Kate Smith, Bing Crosby, Benny Goodman and other recording artists popular at that time.

RELATED BOOKS

NOVELS

Coerr, Eleanor. **Sadako and the Thousand Paper Cranes**. Dell, 1986. ISBN 0-440-47465-5
Grades 3-6
Sadako is dying of leukemia as a result of being in Hiroshima when the atom bomb was dropped.

Hahn, Mary Downing. **Stepping on the Cracks**.
Camelot, 1992. ISBN 0-380-71900-2 Grades 3-6
This novel is set in the same time as **Farm Summer 1942** and concerns life on the home front.

Lowry, Lois. **Autumn Street**.
Houghton, 1980. 0-395-27812-0 Grades 3-6
This novel is also set in small-town 1940s in America.

Paulson, Gary. **Harris and Me**.
Harcourt, 1993. ISBN 0-15 292877-4 Grades 3-8
The narrator is a city boy who spends a summer on a relative's farm in the same era as **Farm Summer 1942**.

Taylor, Theodore. **The Cay**.
Flare, 1995. ISBN 0-380-01003-8 Grades 3-6
When their ship is torpedoed, a spoiled, prejudiced young boy and a black man are stranded on a deserted island in the Caribbean.

PICTURE BOOKS

Yolen, Jane. **Honkers** See page 248.
A young girl spends the summer on her grandparents' farm while she awaits the birth of a new sibling.

NONFICTION

Rosie the Riveter: Women Working on the Home Front in World War II. Crown, 1995.
ISBN 0-517-59790-X
This book is replete with photographs and drawings from the World War II era and concentrates on women's roles on the homefront workplace.

OTHER WORLD WAR II BOOKS

See page 61.

I Am the Dog; I Am the Cat

by Donald Hall
Illustrated by Barry Moser
Dial, 1994
ISBN 0-8037-1504-8

SUMMARY

A cat and a dog take turns explaining the world as they know it. The emphasis here is on perspective. Any animal owner or animal lover can certainly appreciate the humor of these two animals' perspectives of the things around them.

ILLUSTRATION

These are strong, powerful watercolors that are obviously linked to good drawing skills and closely mirror the written word. In many cases we get the animal's-eye view of the action. Technically, it doesn't get any better than this.

CONNECTIONS

NOVEL

The novel **Incredible Journey** (Bantam, 1990. ISBN 0-553-05874-6) emphasizes the unique characteristics of each of two dogs and a cat.

THEMES

▶ Perspectives and perception

CURRICULUM CONNECTION

▶ SCIENCE – Attributes of various species

LANGUAGE ARTS

MAKING PREDICTIONS

▶ Prior to sharing the book, choose several of the quotes from the story, print them on chart paper and have students decide what type of animal would say each quote. Read the book to confirm the predictions.

WRITING

▶ Generate your own "quotes" from other animals that provide clues to their identity. Have others try to guess the animals by these quotes.

▶ Bring in photographs of pets and write speech bubbles that provide information about the pet. For example, "I am Montgomery. I like to sit on top of the fridge to get a bird's eye view of the world."

▶ Name the cat and dog from the story. Choose names that seem to fit their quirks.

▶ Choose any other pet and have the animal narrate a day in its life.

▶ The pampered lives the cat and dog in this story live are certainly far different from the lives of stray animals. Write or tell about a day in the life of a stray animal.

▶ Make lists of adjectives to describe dogs and to describe cats. Compare these lists. Is there any overlap of traits? How are cats and dogs the same? How are they different?

ORAL EXPRESSION

▶ Stage a debate. Some people feel pretty strongly about the virtues of cats or the virtues of dogs. Which make better pets? Prepare arguments to defend your point of view.

VOCABULARY DEVELOPMENT

▶ Create semantic maps for dogs and for cats. Add to the maps as more information about each is learned. For instance, the topic *dogs* goes in the center with spokes going out which are labeled roles or jobs, types or breeds, and so on.

▶ Play a category game based on dog and cat information. Divide the class into small groups and have the groups give their answers in a round-robin fashion. The last correct answer generated wins the point. Categories might include things such as famous cats, dog breeds, expressions (idioms) with either the word *cat* or *dog* in them, dogs in literature, roles dogs can have, members of the feline family.

▶ Assemble large color photographs of cats and dogs such as those from old calendars. Post as many as you are able to gather. Take turns asking "yes/no" questions to determine which animal is "it." For example, Is it a long-haired animal? Is it a feline? Is its coat more than one color? Is it shown out-of-doors? The more pictures shown, the more challenging the game will be.

SCIENCE

▶ Investigate breeds of cats and dogs. Are some more suited for particular areas of the world? Look at the American Kennel Club's division of dogs into categories. Do these categories still make sense? Consider writing to the Kennel Club to discover how rules and regulations regarding breeds of dogs are determined and enforced.

▶ Find out about wild members of the dog and cat family. Present the information learned in the format of the book. Combine these individual "I Am _____" stories into class books with titles such as *We are the Cat Family* and *We are the Dog Family*. Consider sharing these illustrated books with other classrooms in the school.

RELATED BOOKS

NOVELS

Burnford, Sheila. **The Incredible Journey**.
Bantam, 1990. ISBN 0-553-05874-6 Grades 3-8
Two dogs and a cat travel 250 miles through the Canadian wilderness together in this book, which has been made into a movie.

Lowry, Lois. **Stay: Keeper's Story**.
Houghton, 1997. ISBN 0-395-87048-8 Grades 3 - 6
This is a dog's story, told in first person, by a very talented mutt.

PICTURE BOOKS

Brett, Jan. **The First Dog**.
Harcourt, 1992. ISBN 0-15227650-5
This represents an explanation of how the domestication of wild animals could have begun.

Griffith, Helen. **Alex and the Cat**.
Greenwillow, 1982. ISBN 0-688-00421-0
More Alex and the Cat. Greenwillow, 1983.
ISBN 0-688-02292-8
Both of these clever and funny books tell the story of Alex, a shaggy dog, and Cat, who doesn't seem to have a name.

Kipling, Rudyard. **"The Cat That Walks by Itself"** from the **Just So** stories (available in many editions) tells the classic tale of how the various animals came to work for humans.

Lindenbaum, Pija. **Boodil, My Dog**.
Holt, 1992. ISBN 0-8050-2444-1
Boodil is a bull terrier with a style and mind of her own. Her young owner's perception of her great abilities just doesn't seem to match the reality of the dog's quirks, as is humorously shown in the illustrations.

Singer, Marilyn. **It's Hard to Read a Map with a Beagle on Your Lap**. Holt, 1993. ISBN 0-8050-2201-5
Here's a collection of silly poems about different breeds of dogs.

Wagner, Jenny. **John Brown, Rose, and the Midnight Cat**. Puffin, 1980. ISBN 0-14-050306-4
John Brown, a sheep dog, loves Rose, the old lady who shares the house.

OTHER BOOKS BY DONALD HALL

Ox-Cart Man. Illustrated by Barbara Cooney.
Penguin USA 1979. ISBN 0-670-53328-9.
This is a story of rural nineteenth century life in New England. Also see page 92.

Old Home Day

by Donald Hall
Illustrated by Barry Moser
Browndeer Press, 1996
ISBN 0-15-276896-3

▣ SUMMARY

This book tells the long history of a small section of New Hampshire. Starting with the formation of the land, and ending with a contemporary young couple, Mr. Hall chronicles the many changes that have occurred over time in such a way as to make this far more than the study of one small town.

▣ ILLUSTRATION

Soft watercolor washes are the backbone of these illustrations. Compositions of various landscapes and small town settings are filled with soft, muted colors. The illustrations in many picture books are arranged like family albums. In this book the text is well served by this choice of format.

▣ CONNECTIONS

NOVEL

Paul Fleischman's **Borning Room** (HarperCollins, 1991. ISBN 0-06-023762-7) also tells an inter-generational story.

THEME

▶ Changes

CURRICULUM CONNECTION

▶ SCIENCE – Geology of an area
▶ SOCIAL STUDIES – Development of an area

LANGUAGE ARTS

CAUSE AND EFFECT

▶ Retell this story as a series of cause-and-effect statements. For example, because of the clear, fresh water, Enoch Boswell decided to settle beside Blackwater Pond.

COMPARING LITERATURE

▶ There are strong similarities between this book and Lynne Cherry's **A River Ran Wild** (see Related Books). How many can you find? Make a flow chart for each book with the similar events highlighted.

EXTENDING THE STORY

▶ Skim the book and make a list of general time periods included. Go on a treasure hunt in the library and find picture books that take place in each of those time periods.

▶ Create a time line of your life based on important events beginning with your birth. Write short paragraphs on index cards depicting each event and attach them to a class time line. What events were common to most if not all students? Make statements of comparison and contrast relating your life to other students' lives.

SCIENCE

▶ The first sentence in the book says, "When the ice mountain melted north, it scraped trenches and dents in the valleys between the hills." What is the author referring to when he talks of the "ice mountain"? Find out what part glaciers played in the formation of the land in your area.

▶ Identify the bodies of water within your area. How many are natural? How many are man-made? Investigate the origins of all of them and determine what existed where any man-made bodies of water currently exist. For those natural bodies of water, try to discover if they have been altered over time by activities like the creation of dams, floods or the re-channeling of water.

SOCIAL STUDIES

▶ Read **Heron Street** by Ann Turner. See page 220. Discuss how the two books are similar. Have similar changes occurred in your community? Interview family and friends to determine what your neighborhood looked like 10 years ago. What did it look like 20 or 30 years ago? Have all the changes been "progress"?

▶ The town in the book can trace its founding families. What families helped to found your community? Do members of those families still reside in the community? Are buildings or streets named for them?

▶ Does your community celebrate anything like "Old Home Day"? If so, how do they celebrate? Find out when your community became a town or city. How many years ago was that? What was the area like when the founding families first arrived in the area?

▶ Generate a list of holidays that your community celebrates such as the Fourth of July and Memorial Day. Discuss what special events are planned for those celebrations. Interview parents and grandparents to learn how they celebrated those events as children. This book tells us that one Old Home Day celebration served red flannel hash. Find out what it is and try some! What foods are commonly served during celebrations in your community? If your family has not lived in your current community for generations, discover what holidays parents and grandparents celebrated as children which are part of your cultural heritage.

▶ Investigate your own family trees to discover how far back you are able to find names of ancestors and their birth dates. Do any family given names recur in several generations?

▶ The inside title page shows a group of people exploring an old cemetery. Predict why these people may be doing that. What could they learn? If possible, visit an old cemetery. Gather names and dates from gravestones. How does this information help us to learn something about our community and the lives of its former inhabitants? While at the cemetery, try your hand at gravestone rubbings. Note interesting epitaphs.

▶ The book refers to a number of important events in America's history. Use these as a base for a time line. Investigate other important national or local events and place index cards about those events on the time line.

ART

▶ Create a collage of magazine pictures that could represent the faces, places and events of your community.

▶ RELATED BOOKS

NOVEL

Fleischman, Paul. **The Borning Room**.
HarperCollins, 1991. ISBN 0-06-023762-7
Grades 3-9
We see a series of generations through the occurrences in one room in an Ohio farmhouse starting with 1851.

PICTURE BOOKS

Anno. **Anno's USA**.
Putnam, 1983. ISBN 0-399-20974-3
A traveler walks and rides through the countryside surrounded by vignettes of our country's culture and history.

Cherry, Lynne. **A River Ran Wild: An Environmental History**. Harcourt, 1992.
ISBN 0-15-200542-0
What Hall does for a New Hampshire town, Lynne Cherry does for the Nashua River, which runs through New Hampshire.

Turner, Ann. **Heron Street** See page 220.

Wells, Rosemary. **Waiting for the Evening Star** See page 238.

Yolen, Jane. **Letting Swift River** See page 245.

OTHER BOOKS BY DONALD HALL

I am the Dog: I am the Cat. Illustrated by Barry Moser. See page 87.

Lucy's Summer. Illustrated by Michael McCurdy, Browndeer Press, 1995. ISBN 0-15-276873-4
This realistic story, set in New Hampshire in 1910, tells the story of a young girl's summer.

Ox-Cart Man. Illustrated by Barbara Cooney.
Penguin USA, 1979. ISBN 0-670-53328-9
Rural life in 19th century New England is depicted as the father of a family makes the long journey to the Portsmouth market.

Sami and the Time of Troubles

by Florence Parry Heide & Judith Heide Gilliland
Illustrated by Ted Lewin
Clarion, 1992
ISBN 0-395-55964-2

SUMMARY

The trouble is the war and it's been going on for Sami's entire life in Lebanon. An adjustment of a sort has been made: When the fighting is going on, the family lives in the basement of his uncle's house; when it is calm, they can go outside to play and to shop, even to work. There is apparent love and caring among the family members, who work hard at keeping their dreams alive.

ILLUSTRATION

Contrasting dark and light color washes mirror the juxtaposition of sound and silence or night and day. The medium of watercolor is usually associated with things bright, soft and lyrical. While these illustrations represent an unusual use of the medium, they are very powerful images. On pages where the background areas are dark, the type of lettering retains the whiteness of the paper.

CONNECTIONS

NOVEL
Laird's novel **Kiss the Dust** (Dutton, 1991. ISBN 0-525-44893-4) is set in nearby Iraq and concerns the plight of refugees from war.

THEME
► Effects of war on the innocent

CURRICULUM CONNECTION
► SOCIAL STUDIES – Lebanon, current conflicts

LANGUAGE ARTS

EXTENDING THE TEXT

▶ When Sami's uncle complains about keeping the large vase in the basement, he asks why they must have it and Sami's mother gives no answer. Why do you think she wants it there?

FINDING DETAILS

▶ Make a list of the things the family uses to help lift their spirits. Which of them would make you feel better?

▶ What things in the text or pictures tell you when people are frightened?

COMPARING PERSONAL EXPERIENCE

▶ The family uses many memories to help them get through the bad times. What memories would help you in such times?

▶ How do you think your family would react to these living conditions? Who would be the storyteller? Who would be the most likely to be upset? Who would keep the family's spirits high?

▶ When they can go outside, they see people doing all sorts of things. What would you do first if you had to stay in a basement, frightened and bored for a long period of time?

▶ The people suffer greatly because of the war, yet when the children get outside, they play at war. Why? Would you?

SOCIAL STUDIES

LEBANON

▶ Locate Lebanon on the map. Notice the countries that surround it. What body of water might have been at the beach where Sami and his family build a sand castle?

▶ Find out about the war in Lebanon. How did it start? Is it still going on? What part did or does the United States play in that war?

WAR

▶ Read other books that show the effect war has on children (see Related Books). Which ones do you think are most effective?

▶ The grandfather tells about "the day of the children." What effect did it have? Did it end the war? Could it have? What can children do to stop a war?

▶ Find out about organizations that try to stop wars. Are they ever successful? Find out about the Children's Crusade and the Children's March.

COMMUNICATION

▶ The family gathers around the radio when the fighting is heard. What information might they get that would help? What if there were no radio? How did people hear about battles and catastrophes before the invention of radios and TV?

ART

▶ The walls of the basement are hung with carpets. Look at carpet patterns in catalogues or stores and sketch the patterns you like. Use the designs you like in your own artwork.

RELATED BOOKS

NOVELS

Gauch, Patricia Lee. **Thunder at Gettysburg**.
Putnam, 1990. ISBN 0-399-22201-4 Grades 3-5
This brief novel is based on an account of the battle of Gettysburg as witnessed and experienced by a 14-year-old girl who finds herself unexpectedly surrounded by the fierce conflict.

Laird, Elizabeth. **Kiss the Dust**.
Dutton, 1991. ISBN 0-525-44893-4 Grades 5-9
The harried life of refugees is seen through the eyes of a 12-year-old girl in Iraq whose family must move from their home to increasingly less habitable places.

PICTURE BOOKS

Lyon, George Ella. **Cecil's Story**.
Orchard, 1991. ISBN 0-531-05912-X
Cecil, a boy about Sami's age, waits for his mother to bring his wounded father home from the Civil War. Cecil is more physically distant from war than Sami is but also has fears and worries caused by it.

Polacco, Patricia. **Pink and Say**.
Putnam, 1994. ISBN 0-399-22671-0
The Civil War is personalized in this tragic story of the friendship between two soldiers.

NONFICTION

Carter, Jimmy. **Talking Peace: A Vision for the Next Generation**. Dutton, 1993. ISBN 0-525-44959-0
In a book aimed at fairly mature readers, ex-President Carter discusses the forces that work against peace and various ways to address them, including some of the ways his peace-making efforts have worked in the past.

Children of Former Yugoslavia. **I Dream of Peace: Images of War by Children of Former Yugoslavia**.
HarperCollins, 1994. ISBN 0-06-251128-9
Testimony of the effects of war on children who witness the brutality and cruelty of war is the focus of this book with many violent images.

Ousseimi, Marta. **Caught in the Crossfire: Growing Up in a War Zone**. Walker, 1995.
ISBN 0-8027 8363-5
This is a nonfictional account which starts with the same area as that in **Sami** but goes on to examine the effects of war on the innocent elsewhere.

Scholes, Katherine. **Peace Begins With You**.
Sierra, Little Brown, 1990. ISBN 0-316-77436-7
The focus here is on the courage it takes to make peace with yourself, your friends and in larger conflicts. The author also talks about the need for peace with the environment. This is a gentle, thought-provoking picture book.

OTHER BOOKS BY FLORENCE PARRY HEIDE AND JUDITH HEIDE GILLILAND

The Day of Ahmed's Secret. Illustrated by Ted Lewin. Lothrop, 1990. ISBN 0-688-08895-3
A boy in Cairo delivers bottled gas. He tells us about his routine and about his secret that he intends to share with his family that evening. The secret is that he now knows how to read.

OTHER BOOKS ILLUSTRATED BY TED LEWIN

Lewin, Ted. **When the Rivers Go Home**.
Simon & Schuster, 1992. ISBN 0-0- 757382-6
We see a swamp in central Brazil through Lewin's eyes as he examines the wildlife and the ecosystem.

McDonald, Megan. **The Potato Man**.
Orchard, 1991. ISBN 0-531-05914-6
Grampa tells about a time of peddlers with horse-drawn carts and of Mr. Angelo, the potato peddler, who looked rather like a potato and was taunted by children.

McDonald, Megan. **The Great Pumpkin Switch**.
Orchard, 1992. ISBN 0-53- 05450-0
This is the sequel to **The Potato Man** in which Grampa tells of a time he and a friend accidentally ruined his sister's prized pumpkin and needed the quick thinking of the Potato Man to pull a switch.

Yolen, Jane. **Birdwatch**.
Putnam, 1990. ISBN 0-399-21612-X
This delightful book of short bird poems is imaginatively and beautifully illustrated by Ted Lewin.

Sweet Clara and the Freedom Quilt

by Deborah Hopkinson
Illustrated by James Ransome
Random House, 1993
ISBN 0-679-87472-0

SUMMARY

Clara is taught to sew by another slave on the plantation so that she can work in the big house instead of in the cotton fields. Soon after, Clara learns about maps and the Underground Railroad to freedom. She constructs a quilt with a map in the pattern so that she'll remember the way to the Ohio River. Other slaves, realizing what Clara is making, add details to her map. When she is ready, she leaves the quilt map behind for others to follow; she has the map memorized.

ILLUSTRATION

The quilted patterns that introduce and conclude the series of illustrations represent an emphasis on pattern, and that happens in many of the intervening illustrations as well(the portrayal of the cotton field, the farm land in the landscapes, the flower bed under the trees, and the costumes of the characters. Ransome uses the full-color palette and a facile brush.

CONNECTIONS

NOVEL

Jennifer Armstrong's **Steal Away** (Orchard, 1992. ISBN 0-531-05983-9) tells of a slave girl, Bethlehem, and her flight with a white girl via the Underground Railroad.

THEMES

► Slavery
► Quilts

CURRICULUM CONNECTION

► SOCIAL STUDIES – Maps, slavery, Underground Railroad

LANGUAGE ARTS

MAKING INFERENCES

▶ Do you think Clara can read? Can the other slaves she knows? If they all could read, what might have been different about this book?

FINDING DETAILS

▶ Reread the parts of the book where Clara learns something about the geography of the area. Look at the large picture of the quilt on the endpapers of the book. Find the place in the pattern of the quilt where those details are stitched.

SCIENCE

▶ Clara works for a while in the cotton fields, but Aunt Rachel is afraid that she won't be able to do the work. Find out what work needs to be done to produce cotton. Is it different today? What work is now done by machines that used to be done by slaves?

SOCIAL STUDIES

SLAVERY

▶ How did the Underground Railroad work? How many slaves escaped using it? Was your area of the country involved? If so, how?

▶ Why did the slaves have to get to Canada? Wouldn't just getting to the northern United States be safe? Investigate the Fugitive Slave Law. Why was it passed? What effect did it have?

▶ Make a map showing the states and territories of the United States in 1861, coloring the slave states and free states differently. On the map, locate and mark with a symbol the sites of the major battles of the war.

▶ If you were going to help a slave escape from where you live now and get to the Canadian border, what directions would you give him or her?

▶ What stand, if any, did people in your area take on slavery? Were they slave owners? Slaves? Abolitionists? Find some of their arguments justifying or protesting their role.

▶ Find the names of as many well-known historic figures as possible, especially U.S. presidents, who were slave owners. Find portraits of them and make a bulletin board display. Under each portrait, list the person's accomplishments as well as his or her role in slavery.

▶ Find out about the role of the role of the North in slavery. For instance, what happened to that cotton produced by slave labor? Where did it go? Where was it made into cloth?

ART

▶ Look through books on quilting or visit a quilt display to see the different patterns used in quilts.

▶ Design a quilt, using squares of paper that would show your area and the way to some special place for you. Think about colors and patterns you would use to make a real quilt.

▶ Select the best design produced in class and make a real quilt. Invite parents to help with the quilt construction. Get a quilter to show you how and help you along the way. Raffle off the quilt as a fund raiser for a worthy cause.

MUSIC

▶ Songs like "The Drinking Gourd" were used by the slaves to help each other find the way to freedom. Find and sing other slave songs.

RELATED BOOKS

NOVELS

Armstrong, Jennifer. **Steal Away**.
Orchard, 1992. ISBN 0-53- 05983-9 Grades 3-6
When the young orphan, Susannah, moves in with relatives in Virginia in 1855, she is presented with a personal slave, Bethlehem. Slave life from either black or white perspectives seemes wrong to Susannah, so she makes plans to escape. When Bethlehem decides to join her, their only escape is through the Underground Railroad.

Fox, Paula. **The Slave Dancer**.
Dell, 1973. ISBN 0-440-40402-9 Grades 4-9
Jessie, a 13-year-old New Orleans child, is kidnapped by a slaving crew to play his flute for the slaves being transported back from Africa. The book details the horrors of the slave trade and slave passage which continued after the transportation and importation of slaves was forbidden by U.S. law.

Paulsen, Gary. **Nightjohn**.
Laurel Leaf, 1995. ISBN 0-440-21936-1 Grades 4-9
Nightjohn teaches the other slaves to read, knowing that knowledge is power. This is a graphic and compelling book about the evils of slavery.

Sanfield, Steve. **The Adventures of High John the Conqueror**. Illustrated by John Ward. Dell, 1989. ISBN 0-440-40556-4 Grades 4-9
This is a collection of short stories about a trickster folk character, High John. Closely related to Br'er Rabbit, High John was first a slave and later a sharecropper who used his wit and wiles to get the best of the white masters. Within the tales themselves and in the explanatory material, the author has included a good deal of information about slave life.

PICTURE BOOKS

Lawrence, Jacob. **Harriet and the Promised Land**.
Simon, 1968. ISBN 0-671-86673-7
Poster-like illustrations and a brief rhythmic text combine to make this a powerful book about Harriet Tubman.

Marie, D. **Tears for Ashan**.
Creative Press Works, 1989. ISBN 0-9621681-0-6
A picture book tells of an African boy witnessing the capture of his friend by European slavers.

McKissack, Patricia. **Christmas in the Big House, Christmas in the Quarters**. Illustrated by John Thompson. Scholastic, 1994. ISBN 0-590-43027-0
This book contrasts the life between the slaves and their owners.

Turner, Ann. **Nettie's Trip South**.
Illustrated by Ronald Himler. Simon & Schuster, 1987. ISBN 0-02 789240-9 See page 223.

NONFICTION

Bryan, Ashley. **Walk Together Children: Black American Spirituals**. Atheneum, 1974.
ISBN 0-689-70485-2
Twenty-four spirituals provide a musical story of the American slaves.

Lester, Julius. **To Be a Slave**.
Dial, 1968. ISBN 0-8037-8955-6
Using writings and interviews of slaves, this book chronicles their capture, transport and enslavement in the South as well as the time directly after the Civil War, giving us a terrible and intimate portrait of slavery.

Levine, Ellen. **If You Traveled on the Underground Railroad**. Illustrated by Richard Williams. Scholastic, 1988. ISBN 0-590-40556-X
Like the other books in this series, this volume uses a question-and-answer format to provide information about its subject.

Rappaport, Doreen. **Escape from Slavery: Five Journeys to Freedom**. HarperCollins, 1991.
ISBN 0-06 021631-X
Rappaport gives a brief history of the Fugitive Slave Act of 1793 and then goes about telling fascinating tales of real life heroism and daring.

My Great-Aunt Arizona

by Gloria Houston
Illustrated by Susan Condie Lamb
HarperCollins, 1992
ISBN 0-06-022606-4

SUMMARY

This picture book biography chronicles the life of the author's great-aunt, who was born in Henson Creek in the Blue Ridge Mountains. She loved to grow flowers, sing, and square dance, but most of all to read about faraway places and people she hoped to visit someday. Great-Aunt Arizona never did get to visit all the places she dreamed about. Instead she spent her life in the Blue Ridge Mountains teaching children to read and write and about faraway places she had visited in her mind. When her students asked her if she had been to these faraway places, she always responded, "Only in my mind, but someday you will go." Great-Aunt Arizona taught for 57 years and died on her 93rd birthday, having never left the mountains.

ILLUSTRATION

These are lighthearted rather airy illustrations that contrast with the more somber theme of unfulfilled dreams. They are conventional illustrations using a variety of media.

CONNECTIONS

NOVEL

The brief novel, **Sarah Plain and Tall** (HarperCollins, 1985. ISBN 0-06-024101-2) might work here as a novel connection. Sarah travels, which, of course, Arizona never got to do, but Sarah also travels in her mind back to Maine when she is on the prairie.

THEMES:

▶ Teachers
▶ Travel

CURRICULUM CONNECTION

▶ SOCIAL STUDIES – Appalachia

LANGUAGE ARTS

VOCABULARY DEVELOPMENT

▶ Review terms for relatives. Have students design "brain-teasers" using terms for relatives. For example, "If I am your nephew's sister, who am I?"

▶ Ask students to create family trees that include as many extended relatives as possible. Demonstrate to students how family trees will differ depending on the make-up of each student's family. For example, some students may have more than two parents they wish to include in their project.

▶ Read the dedication of the book, which tells us that teaching is the most "influential" profession in the world. Discuss the meaning of the word and why the author might say that. Write a short paper nominating a former teacher, the one who has had the most influence on you, for an award.

COMPARING LITERATURE

▶ Read **Miss Rumphius** by Barbara Cooney (see Related Books). Create a Venn diagram to compare and contrast how Miss Rumphius and Arizona are alike and different. Write short essays explaining which you would prefer to have as a great-aunt and why.

▶ Find other picture books that are about strong and determined girls and women. Include **Miss Rumphius**, **Emma**, **Miss Tizzy**, and **Only Opal** (see Related Books). Develop a "Women in Literature" awards ceremony. Make nominations for awards (for example, nominate Miss Tizzy for the "Most Entertaining Neighbor Award"), write and present nominating speeches to the rest of the class with props and costumes, have an actual awards ceremony, and write and present acceptance speeches.

WRITING

▶ Design postcards from all the faraway places Arizona's students might have learned about. Write notes on the postcards to Arizona from her students telling her what they like best about the place they are visiting.

SOCIAL STUDIES

Gather together as many picture books as you can find that depict American life throughout history. Include **Island Boy**, **Miss Rumphius**, **The Potato Man**, **The Ox-Cart Man** and **When I Was Young in the Mountains** (see Related Books). Study the stories and illustrations for clues about when in American history the stories probably took place. Create a time line using the book titles. Find other stories to add to the timeline as your school year progresses. Can you find a picture book that would fit into each decade of the last two centuries or more?

▶ Arizona loved reading because she loved to learn about and dream about faraway places. Choose faraway places to read and learn about. Then design travel brochures advertising each place.

▶ Create a graph depicting the distances from your school to each of the advertised places in the above activity.

▶ On a world map chart an-around-the-world journey, stopping at each of the above places. Using the itinerary, determine the total distance traveled, what modes of transportation might be involved, and how long it might take to complete the trip.

▶ Find the Blue Ridge Mountains on a map. What state or states are they in? Can you find a place called Henson Creek?

SCIENCE

▶ Discuss why Great-Aunt Arizona grew flowers on the window sills of her classrooms. Research the advantages of having indoor plants and make lists of plants and flowers that would be likely to survive in your classroom windows. Collect plants for individual window-sill terrariums.

▶ Try to identify some of the flowers growing on Great-Aunt Arizona's window sills. Use flower identification guides or seed catalogs.

▶ Arizona and her class planted a tree at the edge of their schoolyard year after year. Plant a tree somewhere in your community.

MUSIC

▶ Find and sing the 1950s song "Faraway Places."

RELATED BOOKS

NOVELS

Maclachlan, Patricia. **Sarah, Plain & Tall**.
HarperCollins, 1985. ISBN 0-06-024101-2
Grades 3-6
Sarah answers an ad to become a farmer's wife on the prairie and mother to his children.

Reeder, Carolyn. **Grandpa's Mountain**.
Camelot, 1993. ISBN 0-380-71914-2 Grades 3-6
This novel is set in Appalachia and concerns the efforts of a farmer to keep his land from being confiscated by the government.

PICTURE BOOKS

Cooney, Barbara. **Miss Rumphius**.
Penguin USA, 1982. ISBN 0-670-47958-6
Miss Rumphius promises she will do three things: She will travel to faraway places, live by the sea when she is old and do something to make the world a more beautiful place. The story is told by Miss Rumphius' grand-niece.

Kesselman, Wendy. **Emma**.
HarperCollins, 1985. ISBN 0-440-40847-4
Usually Emma is alone and lonely. When she discovers painting pictures as a hobby, her life changes for the better.

Cooney, Barbara. **Island Boy**.
Penguin USA, 1988. ISBN 0-670-811749-X
This story shows generations of a family on a small island off the coast of Maine.

Cooney, Barbara. **Only Opal**.
Philomel, 1994. ISBN 0-399-21990-0
This picture book is based on a diary kept by a five-year-old child in turn-of-the-century Oregon.

Hall, Donald. **Ox-Cart Man**.
Penguin USA, 1979. ISBN 0-670-5332- 9
This book depicts rural life in nineteenth century New England.

Gray, Libba Moore. **Miss Tizzy**.
Simon and Schuster, 1993. ISBN 0-671-77590-1
The children love Miss Tizzy and visit her every day even though the adults in the neighborhood think she's a bit eccentric.

McDonald, Megan. **The Potato Man**.
Orchard, 1991. ISBN 0-531-05914-6
A grandfather remembers his childhood, especially the man who delivered potatoes, Mr. Angelo.

Rylant, Cynthia. **When I Was Young in the Mountains**. Penguin USA, 1982. ISBN 0-525-42525-X.
In this gentle story, the author shares memories of her childhood with her grandparents in the mountains.

The Log Cabin Quilt

by Ellen Howard
Illustrated by Ronald Himler
Holiday House, 1996
ISBN 0823412474

SUMMARY

Elvirey tells the story of her family's trip to the woods of Michigan. They left Mam "buried in Carolina along with all her personal things" because Pap said "There ain't no room for suchlike." However, Granny heaved a sack of quilting scraps up on the wagon and declared she would sit on it. It was nearly winter when they found the place Pap said was home. As the days grew colder, Pap and brother Bub worked to build the cabin. Granny "pieced on her quilts," while Sis and Elvirey chinked the walls with mud, grass and moss, but the cabin never felt like home. One morning Pap went hunting and didn't get home by evening. The snow and icy wind blew in through the chinks in the walls. The mud, grass and moss had frozen and were falling out of the cracks. How Granny's scraps of memory, the pieces of their family's life, helped them through the winter is poignant and touching. It gives the "log cabin quilt" a new meaning.

ILLUSTRATION

This is a different palette and illustrative approach for Ronald Himler. The images are appropriately somber, but color is introduced in the form of a quilt that threads its way through the images from beginning to end. Each framed illustration is placed opposite the text and has the feeling of a painting that might have been found on the walls of the home the family left. The objects selected for the vignettes on the print page are delightful. They make the connections for us between the framed pictures and the focus of the text.

CONNECTIONS

NOVEL

There's an obvious connection here with any quilt books, some of which are listed below. **The Canada Geese Quilt** (Yearling, 1992. ISBN 0-440-407192) is a short novel about quilting.

THEMES

▶ Quilting

▶ Children on their own

CURRICULUM CONNECTION

▶ SOCIAL STUDIES – Westward expansion

LANGUAGE ARTS

WRITING

▶ Here are some descriptive phrases for objects in the story. Reread to find others to add.

   trees – black and naked
   wind – made ears ache
   trip – bones rattled
   cold – "shivered my back"

▶ Snow was described as something fine and white that sifted like sugar. How might you write to your friends back home about the first time you saw snow? What about the bone-chilling cold or the teeth-rattling trip in the wagon.?

▶ If you could make a quilt of the important pieces of cloth in your life, what would they be? Your christening dress? Your father's tie? Your security blanket?

EXTENDING THE BOOK

▶ Use this web as a starting place to extend the book into areas you'd like to investigate:

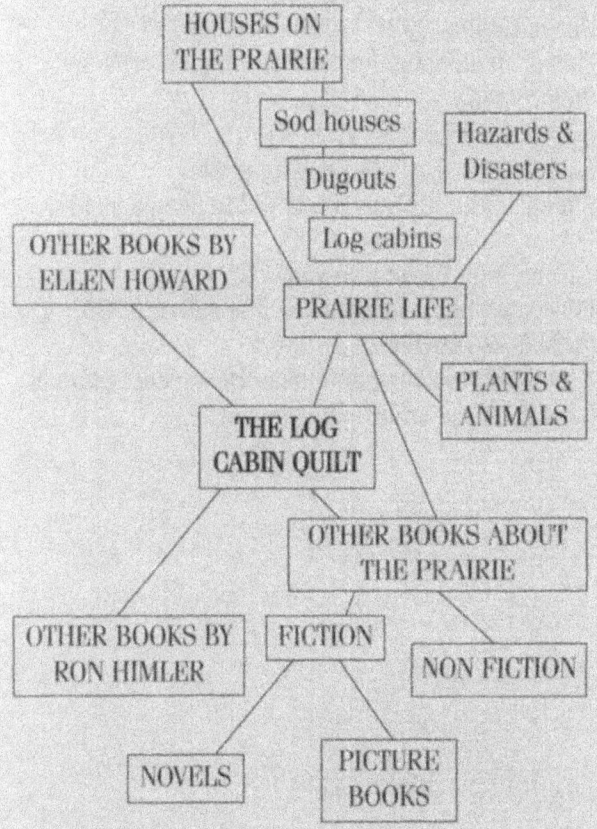

MAKING INFERENCES

▶ What personal things of Mam's were left behind in Carolina?

▶ Predict what the cabin would look like in spring. Did Elvirey think of a way to make it look cheerful?

CAUSE AND EFFECT

▶ What things in the story would have changed if:

   Mam had lived?
   Granny refused to move to Michigan?
   Pap had chosen a warmer state?
   Pap had lost his way in the storm?
   There were no quilting scraps?

EXTENDING VOCABULARY

▶ Reread the text and find "different" ways of speaking, such as "I reckon," "I aim to," "of a sudden," "suchlike," "mite," "afore," "pears," and "downright," as well as "What in thunderation?" and "Set you down."

▶ Look up the meaning of *travois poles, calico, chinked, petticoat, piecing, jubilee*. Read the book again and find any other words that need defining.

EXPLORING FEELINGS AND ATTITUDES

▶ Speculate on the feelings of Pap, Granny, Sis, Bub and Elvirey on leaving their home after the death of Mam.

   Did this attitude change with the coming of spring and their new home?

   What changed when Pap finally said Mam's name aloud?

   When Pap said "The place is downright homey" how did everyone feel?

COMPARING LITERATURE

▶ Begin a collection of "quilt" stories. Volunteers choose one to share. Explain the type of quilt in each one.

▶ Find and read a few "prairie" books. Explain the hardships faced in each story.

SOCIAL STUDIES

▶ Why were they moving west? Did any groups give up and return home? What were some of the destinations?

▶ On a map of the United States trace the journey from the Carolina area to Michigan.

▶ Find a map of the United States in the 1860s. Which were states and which were territories?

▶ The Homestead Law was enacted in 1862 to allow men like Pap to acquire land in the public domain. Research to find out why the government conducted such a giveaway program. What were the stipulations of the Homestead Act?

▶ Why did the father choose to go to the woods of Michigan?

▶ Decide how long the journey would take in a covered wagon. What about a car? A train? A plane?

▶ Choose another state for the family. Find out about the climate, flora and fauna, natural resources, and animal life and decide on the one that would be "user friendly."

ART

▶ Design a "memory quilt." Create photo-like pictures to depict the family and the important events of your life. Arrange them in sequential order. Put the "photographs" together with yarn. This "for display only" quilt makes an effective bulletin board.

▶ Make individual mini-quilts with photographs. Students can design a picture biography.

RELATED BOOKS

NOVELS

Kinsey-Warnock, Natalie. **Canada Goose Quilt**.
Yearling, 1992. ISBN 0-440-407192 Grades 3-6
A 10-year-old girl must finish a quilt started by her grandmother in this brief intergenerational novel.

Love, D. Anne. **Bess's Log Cabin Quilt**.
Illustrated by Ronald Himler. Holiday, 1995.
ISBN 0-8234-1178 8 Grades 3-6
In this short novel, Bess Morgan becomes a heroine by winning a quilt contest, caring for the family and frightening away Indians.

PICTURE BOOKS

Bunting, Eve. **Dandelions** See page 44.

Hopkinson, Deborah. **Sweet Clara & the Freedom Quilt** See page 96.

Paul, Ann. **Eight Hands Round**.
HarperCollins, 1991. ISBN 0-06-024704-5
This is an alphabet book of quilting patterns and their history.

Polacco, Patricia. **The Keeping Quilt**.
Simon, 1988. ISBN 0-671-64963-9 See page 163.

Turner, Ann. **Dakota Dugout**.
Illustrated by Ronald Himler. Macmillan, 1985.
ISBN 0-02-789-700-1
A woman's touching and memorable description of her life on the prairie in a sod house.

Swamp Angel

by Anne Isaacs
Illustrated by Paul O. Zelinsky
Dutton, 1994
ISBN 0-525 45271-0

SUMMARY

This is an original tall tale depicting the life of a super-woodswoman, a sort of female Paul Bunyan. Born in 1815, Angelica Longrider quickly reached fame in the woods of Tennessee by saving the settlers from a ferocious bear and creating the Smoky Mountains in the wrestling match that ensued. When she unrolled the bear skin, she created the Shortgrass Prairie. Able to lasso a tornado like Pecos Bill and drink a lake dry like Babe, the blue ox, Swamp Angel is a hero in the folktale tradition.

ILLUSTRATION

The most obvious characteristic of these illustrations is the successful simulation of varying wood grains. The storytelling images are captured in a variety of geometric shapes such as squares, ovals, rectangles and lunettes that appear to be paste-ups on the wood grain backgrounds. The reference is probably best described as decoupage. Of special note is Zelinsky's treatment of figure and landscape in contrasting scale.

CONNECTIONS

NOVEL

Gary Paulsen's **Cookcamp** (Yearling, 1992. ISBN 0-440-40704-4) is far from a tall tale, since it's based on real incidents in the author's life, but it is set in a lumber camp and is rich in the portrayal of that setting.

THEMES

▶ Strong women
▶ Tall tales

CURRICULUM CONNECTION

▶ GEOGRAPHY – Landmarks, occupations

Language Arts

Exploring a Genre

▶ There are many tall-tale characters in American folklore. Find and read as many as possible and then chart them in the following manner:

Character	Location	Occupation	Characteristics
Paul Bunyan	North Woods	Lumberman	Huge Strong
John Henry	South	Steel Driver	Strong Tireless
Mike Fink	Mississippi River	Boatman	Strong Aggressive
Casey Jones	Midwest	Railroad Engineer	Brave Determined
Pecos Bill	West	Cowboy	Strong Funny Clever

▶ Look at the occupations column and decide what qualities people who have that job should have. Exaggerate those qualities and you have the makings of a tall tale. Try it with a job that is not listed. What would a super teacher be like? How about a super parent? A super student? Usually tall tales are not meant to be believable, but many are written about people who actually lived: Davy Crockett, Johnny Appleseed, Casey Jones. What has been added to make them into super heroes?

▶ Make some exaggerated statements such as "It was so hot today that bird's eggs cooked in their nests"; "It was so windy that several buildings in town moved to the next county." Now write a story based on your statement.

▶ What do the heroes of tall tales have in common with comic book heroes such as Batman and Superman?

Extending the Text

▶ Put another fierce animal in the story such as a wolf or snake. How would Swamp Angel have reacted? What would be the result?

▶ Suppose Thundering Tarnation had a son or a daughter who followed Swamp Angel. What could have happened in Montana?

▶ Add years to the story. What would Swamp Angel accomplish in her old age?

Using Figurative Language

▶ Find and list examples of some of these kinds of figurative language:

Exaggeration: "To get a breath of air, she had to drink the whole lake dry."

Irony: "Quiltin' is men's work!"

Simile: "As plentiful as dewdrops on corn."

Alliteration: "pile of pelts," "mountain of mange."

Humor: "The first hunter was found wearing an empty molasses bucket, a silly grin on his face."

Using Comparison and Contrast

▶ Chart the possible and impossible situations in the story.

▶ Compare the special qualities of Swamp Angel and Thundering Tarnation.

Math

▶ Create recipes for the "bear food." Decide how much is enough for the class. Estimate the proportions for a family and a single person. Choose from bear steaks, bear roasts, bear muffins, bear stuffing and bear cake.

▶ Look at the illustrations and estimate the size of Swamp Angel as compared to the humans and other objects in the book.

▶ Find out how big Tennessee is and then estimate the size of the pelt.

Social Studies

Maps

▶ List the areas of the United States named in the book. Retell the story of Swamp Angel pointing out the locations on a map of the United States and Canada.

▶ Locate other tall-tale hero locations on the map.

▶ This tale begins in 1815. Examine the illustrations to see how Zelinsky showed the period.

Music

▶ Find and sing the tall-tale song "Logger Lover."

RELATED BOOKS

NOVELS

Fleischman, Sid. **Here Comes McBroom: hree More Tall Tales**. Greenwillow, 1992. ISBN 0-688 11160-2 Grades 3-6
This is an anthology of three McBroom tales: "McBroom the Rainmaker," "McBroom's Zoo," and "McBroom's Ghost."

Paulsen, Gary. **Cookcamp**.
Yearling, 1992. ISBN 0-440-40704-4 Grades 4-8
A boy is sent to stay with his grandmother, who runs a cookcamp for lumber workers.

PICTURE BOOKS

Kellogg, Steven. **Mike Fink**.
Morrow, 1992. ISBN 0-688-07003-5
The King of the Keelboatmen gets the Kellogg treatment in this rollicking tall tale.

Kellogg, Steven. **I Was Born about 10,000 Years Ago**. Morrow, 1996. ISBN 0-688-13411-4
This is a picture book of an old tall-tale folk song.

Lester, Julius. **John Henry**.
Illustrated by Jerry Pinkney. Dial, 1994.
ISBN 0-8037-1606-0
This powerful, witty and boisterous version of the black folk ballad is a worthy addition to the tall tale library.

Blow Away Soon

by Betsy James
Illustrated by Anna Vojtech
Putnam, 1995
ISBN 0-399-22648-6

SUMMARY

A little girl dislikes the desert wind, but her grandmother shows her the place of the wind in the cycle of life. Together they walk through the desert and Sophie collects sand, grass, a feather and a fossil shell which they place on an altar for the wind to blow away. She learns from her grandmother that some things must be let go, and some things are to hold on to for a very long time.

ILLUSTRATION

Each illustration appears to have been composed on a textured surface that simulates the feel of linen. The selective use of texture and soft pastel color tones adds to the gentle mood of the story. Muted colors blend so softly into one another as to create a sense of the surreal. Elements of nature, such as the wind and the atmosphere, are revealed through their effects on carefully drawn characters, landscapes and objects. There is a feeling of harmony in the compositions and in the relationship between the story's characters and nature.

CONNECTIONS

NOVEL

Tuck Everlasting (Farrar, 1975. ISBN 0-374-37848-7) is a novel that also accents the cycle of life and the tragedy that can result when it is interrupted.

THEMES

► Cycles of life
► Life and death

CURRICULUM CONNECTION

► Science – Life cycles, change

LANGUAGE ARTS

FIGURES OF SPEECH

▶ Make a list of the many examples of personification in the book. Find more examples in other stories and poems.

WRITING

▶ Write your own "personification poetry." Start with the line "I am the wind..." or some other element of nature.

▶ Discuss and list the many jobs of the wind in the story. Add to your list other tasks the wind accomplishes. Write job descriptions for other elements of nature. For example, what would be the skills listed on a job description for a rainstorm? The sunshine? Snow or hail or sleet?

COMPARING LITERATURE

▶ Read aloud **Thunder Cake** by Patricia Polacco (see Related Books). Chart the similarities and differences between the stories. Can you find other stories about being afraid of elements of weather? How do the two grandmothers in the two stories address their granddaughters' fears? Which grandmother would you like for your own?

▶ Read other stories about relationships between children and grandparents. Design a classroom big book titled *Grandparents are Grand*. Contribute a page with an illustration or photograph of a special grandparent and a short story about a special time spent with that person.

INTERPRETING THE STORY

▶ Discuss the first line of the story. What could it mean? What is the relevance of this line to the story?

SCIENCE

▶ The narrator was surprised to find a seashell on the top of a stony hill so far from the sea. Read Byrd Baylor's **Hunter of Fossils**. Are there any indications that your community was once under water? Examine some fossils and discuss what fossils tell us about the history of a particular place.

▶ The characters' shoes leave footprints in the sand. What will the wind do to these footprints? In what other ways might the wind impact the environment? Take a walk and look for some effects of wind and other elements of nature.

▶ Develop charts depicting the positive and negative aspects of weather conditions such as wind, rain, sunshine and snow. Which of these things are positive in moderation, but sometimes negative in excess?

SOCIAL STUDIES

▶ Do a little research to discover where the setting of this story is. Draw state names from a hat. Compare the state drawn to the illustrations in the book. Then write a brief argument about whether or not the story could be in that state.

▶ Some of the houses in the story are built of adobe. Find out what adobe is and why it is used. What building materials have been traditionally used in your community? Why?

MATH

▶ Form groups to fly a kite as high as possible. Measure the string released to determine how far the kite has flown. Graph the distances that each group comes up with to compare and contrast. Then convert measurements into inches, feet, yards and meters.

▶ Set up a weather center at school. Choose a weather person each day to measure and graph the temperature and wind direction.

ART

▶ Examine the illustrations and text pages. Why did the illustrator choose such a texture for the pages of the book?

▶ Study each illustration and chart the evidence that there is movement in the air in each one.

➤ RELATED BOOKS

NOVEL

Babbitt, Natalie. **Tuck Everlasting**.
Farrar, 1975. ISBN 0-374-37848-7 Grades 4-9
The Tucks have stepped off the wheel of life by drinking from a spring that makes them live on unchanged forever.

PICTURE BOOKS

Baylor, Byrd. **If You Are a Hunter of Fossils**
See page 19.

Lasky, Kathryn. **The Gates of the Wind**.
Harcourt, 1995. ISBN 0-15-204264-4
Gamma Lee leaves the security of her village to journey to the Gates of the Wind, where she is finally accepted as one of the wind's own.

Orie, Sandra De Coteau. **Did You Hear the Wind Sing Your Name?** Walker, 1995.
ISBN 0-8027-8350-3
This song in praise of spring and the cycles of life is taken from an Oneida song of spring.

Polacco, Patricia. **Thunder Cake**.
Philomel, 1990. ISBN 0-399-22231-6
A young girl is helped by her grandmother to overcome her fear of thunder.

Ryder, Joanne. **Catching the Wind**.
Morrow, 1989. ISBN 0-688-07171-6
This imaginative book lets the wind carry you over the earth to see everything from a new perspective.

Yolen, Jane. **The Girl Who Loved the Wind**.
HarperCollins, 1992. ISBN 0-690-33101-0
A much loved but overprotected princess relies upon the wind to bring her news of the world outside her walls. Eventually, she breaks out of her prison to be with the wind and see it all.

Zolotow, Charlotte. **When the Wind Stops**.
HarperCollins, 1995. ISBN 0-06-025425-4
A little boy is reassured by his mother about endings and how each one is also a beginning.

NONFICTION

Dodd, Anne Wescott. **Footprints and Shadows**.
Simon and Schuster, 1992.. ISBN 0-671-78716-0
The rhythmic and lyrical text of this book explains where footprints and shadows go.

Dorros, Arthur. **Feel the Wind**.
HarperCollins, 1989. ISBN 0-690-04739-8
This is a sensory approach to the effects of the wind on our lives.

Simon, Seymour. **Wildfires**.
Morrow, 1996. ISBN 0-688-13935-3
Dramatic photos and clear text combine to show how the fire, while often disastrous to some life, is also part of the cycle of life in the forest.

The Cowboy and the Black-Eyed Pea

by Tony Johnston
Illustrated by Warren Ludwig
Putnam, 1992
ISBN 0-698-11356-X

SUMMARY

In this take-off of "The Princess and the Pea," Farethee Well has inherited a large ranch and now has many suitors. Wanting a sensitive, true cowboy, she places an itty-bitty black-eyed-pea under the saddle blanket of each man who shows up. No one notices the pea and so is rejected until, on a rainy night, one man is so bothered by the pea, he asks for more and more saddle blankets to cushion himself. There's the one she wants!

ILLUSTRATION

These illustrations are filled with information about the people, costumes and landscapes. In most instances, the figures have cartoon-like characteristics. The color seems to have been added to the drawings.

CONNECTIONS

NOVEL

For life on a Texas ranch, you can't beat the books about the cowdog named Hank written by John Erickson, such as **The Case of the Hooking Bull** (Gulf Publishing, 1992. ISBN 0-87719-213-8).

THEMES

▶ Impossible tasks
▶ Fairy tale extensions

CURRICULUM CONNECTION

▶ SOCIAL STUDIES – Regional studies: dialects & customs

LANGUAGE ARTS

COMPARING LITERATURE

▶ Find and read other versions of "The Princess and the Pea" and compare them to this story.

▶ Farethee Well is a very capable cowperson herself, as she proves when she stops the stampede. Find some other strong female characters in books and compare them to Farethee Well. What are the capabilities of each character? How are they used?

▶ In some respects this is a tall tale. Read Steven Kellogg's **Pecos Bill** and **Paul Bunyan**. Read **Swamp Angel** (see page 105). Find the elements in **The Cowboy and the Black-Eyed Pea** that make it a tall tale and compare to the others.

VOCABULARY DEVELOPMENT

▶ There are some delicious words and phrases in this book. Decide, without looking them up, synonyms for such words as "bodacious" and "itty-bitty."

▶ The name "Farethee Well" is a pun. We once heard of a collie whose name was Melon (melancholy). An exterminator company is named "Insect-Aside." Find other puns in names both in fiction and in real life. Look through the yellow pages for other company names that are puns.

EXTENDING THE BOOK

▶ If this story were set in coal-mining instead of ranching country, what changes would be made? Would Farethee Well put coal dust in his shoe? What if it took place in logging country?

▶ Find and read aloud some cowboy poems and song lyrics.

SCIENCE

▶ Find out why there are so few longhorn cattle in the United States today. Why were they once so prevalent? Make a list of cattle breeds and the strong points of each.

▶ How sensitive are you? Devise some experiments using tiny articles such as dried peas and various layers of material to see who can best detect it. Collect your data and tabulate your results scientifically.

SOCIAL STUDIES

▶ Are there still cowboys? Are there still cattle drives? If not, why not?

▶ Find out about the role of cowboys on ranches today. Where are most cattle raised? Make a list of names that were used in the cowboy culture: *drover, trail boss, cook, cook's louse, trail scout, greenhorn.* Define their jobs. Who does them now? Have such jobs been eliminated?

▶ Look at the various items on the traditional cowboy costume. What is the function of each? How many are still useful?

MUSIC

▶ Find and sing cowboy songs, songs about Texas, and "Logger Lover," a folk song about a superman logger.

ART

▶ Look at the illustrations that Warren Ludwig did for this book. Then imagine that some other illustrator was assigned to do the book. How would it look if Steven Kellogg or Glen Rounds did it? If you were editor, which illustrator would you ask to do it?

RELATED BOOKS

NOVELS

Erickson, John. **Hank the Cowdog: The Case of the Hooking Bull**. Gulf Publishing, 1992. ISBN 0-87719-213-8 Grades 3-7
This is just one in a series of books about Hank and they're all very funny and not difficult to read. Hank considers himself the official watchdog of the ranch and, aided by his slow but faithful assistant Drover, he attempts to fulfill his arduous task.

Paulsen, Gary. **Call Me Francis Tucket**. Delacorte, 1995. ISBN 0-385-32116-3 Grades 3-7
This fairly easy-to-read novel is a sequel to **Mr. Tucket** and tells the frontier adventures of a young boy who is separated from his wagon train, survives a stampede and outwits a pair of outlaws.

PICTURE BOOKS

Kellogg, Steven. **Paul Bunyan**. Morrow, 1992. ISBN 0-688-03849-2
This is one of Kellogg's tall tale series depicting some of the events in the life of the super-lumberman.

Kellogg, Steven. **Pecos Bill** Morrow, 1986. ISBN 0-688-05871-X
The super cowboy who fell out of the wagon and was raised by coyotes is the hero of this tall tale.

Kimmel, Eric. **Four Dollars and Fifty Cents**. Holiday, 1990. ISBN 0-8234-0817-5
Shorty, the cowboy, owes the Widow Macrae $4.50 and he tries every trick in the book to avoid paying his debt.

Rounds, Glen. **Charlie Drives the Stage**. Holiday, 1989. ISBN 0-8234-0738-1
Charlie is the only stagecoach driver who could possibly get the very important passenger to the next city on time, and he does. It's not until the end of the book that we discover Charlie's identity.

Sharmat, Marjorie. **Gila Monsters Meet You at the Airport**. Puffin, 1983. ISBN 0-14-050430-3
Our narrator, who has been brought up in New York City, is moving out West, and he has all sorts of fears and stereotypical information.

Stevenson, Janet. **The Princess and the Pea**. Holiday, 1982. ISBN 0-8234-0442-0
This is a more or less straightforward adaptation of the Hans Christian Andersen tale.

NONFICTION

Rounds, Glen. **Cowboys**. Holiday, 1991. ISBN 0-8234-0867-1
Within this simple narrative of a day in the life of a cowboy, Rounds packs a great deal of information.

How Pizza Came to Queens

by Dayal Kaur Khalsa
Crown Books - Potter, 1989
ISBN 0-517-57126-9

SUMMARY

It's hard to believe that there was a time when few Americans had ever tasted pizza. Mrs. Pelligrino, who arrived to visit the Pennys, had traveled all the way from Italy clutching an oddly shaped package that she wouldn't allow anyone to touch. The family, along with May, who was also visiting, began to realize that the lady from Italy was not happy. She sniffed the kitchen and sighed sadly, "No pizza." No one had any idea what she meant. As she became sadder, the girls tried everything to cheer her up. They put on plays, took her out to eat, and generally entertained her, but the "old sadness" was always on her. They finally decided to learn about this "pizza thing." A trip to the library followed by one to the market brought out the mysterious package. What took place turns into a delicious surprise!

ILLUSTRATION

Each illustration holds references to the 1950s (automobiles and buses, favorite paintings and furniture styles. The figures in each illustration have an independence from the settings, as though all the parts were brought together from elsewhere to make a new composition. Strong colors are used throughout.

CONNECTIONS

NOVEL

Kathryn Lasky's novel, **Night Journey** (ISBN 0-140-32048-2), concerns the relationship between a young girl and her great-grandmother, who fled from Russia bringing the memories and the traditions of the family.

THEMES

▶ Food
▶ Communication breakdowns

CURRICULUM CONNECTION

▶ SOCIAL STUDIES – Immigrants, food and customs, language

LANGUAGE ARTS

COMMUNICATION

▶ Even though Mrs. Pelligrino knew some English, May and the Penny family spoke no Italian. How did they communicate?

▶ Ask someone who speaks another language that you do not speak to spend the day with your class using that language. Ask that everyone in class establish some sort of communication with that person in the course of the day. At the end of the day, talk about your discoveries.

▶ What could the children have done to help Mrs. Pelligrino understand them?

▶ How did she learn the little English she used that summer?

▶ Make an English/Italian dictionary.

▶ Think of occasions when food seems to bring people together or serves as the center for a celebration.

MAKING COMPARISONS

▶ Compare the way of life in the book era of the 1950s and that of today. Fill in a chart.

	Past	Present
snacks	milk and pretzels	Doritos
meals		
games		
clothes		
restaurants		
cars		
role of mother		

If possible add other categories.

▶ Find some old cookbooks and recipes. Talk about Jello molds, tuna casserole (with potato chips), meat loaf, Lady Baltimore cake.

▶ Compare the food mentioned in the book with meals of today. (Have some new cookbooks handy.)

▶ How did the restaurant's menu contrast with one at a fast-food place?

▶ Investigate nutrition labels on today's food. Exactly what does the information tell us?

▶ There are various kinds of frozen pizza today. Compare them to the TV dinners of the past. Which are most nutritious? Which contain the most fat?

▶ There is a clear definition of pizza in the book. Another is "an Italian food comprising a doughy crust overlaid with a mixture of cheese, tomatoes, spices, etc. and baked." Find and contrast other definitions. Locate a variety of dictionaries.

▶ All kinds of pizza are sold in the United States. List, compare and vote on the best in each category:

  frozen pizza
  pizza delivery stores

If there is any debate, volunteers can give a "commercial" for their favorite.

WRITING

▶ Describe the moment in the kitchen when Mrs. Pelligrino unwrapped her mysterious package.

▶ How did Mrs. Pelligrino use her rolling pin? And what did she do with the circles of dough?

▶ Describe the day Mrs. Pelligrino went home to Italy. What kind of a day was it for everyone? (Mrs. Pelligrino, Mrs. Penny, May, the girls.)

▶ In groups plan a TV commercial for "Mrs. Pelligrino's Pizza." Choose an appropriate name, e.g., Sarah Lee, Mrs. Paul's, Mrs. Smith's. Explain the loving care that goes into the preparation and baking of each one. Extol the virtues of the fresh ingredients. Elaborate on these items. Practice in the groups and present to the class.

EXAMINING THE ILLUSTRATIONS

▶ Mrs. Pelligrino always wears a black dress. Describe the different aprons she wears over it. Does anyone you know wear aprons? When and why?

▶ Most of Mrs. Penny's dresses (except for the "sailor dress" to wear shopping) have a variety of prints. Describe them.

▶ In the cheese store find ways to describe the many different cheeses there.

▶ The library illustration has both children and adult books. Examine the titles and list some of each. Name those that are still classics today.

▶ The children had a "play store" in the yard. Notice the stock for sale. Find those items that are still being sold.

▶ Look at the illustrations of the play the girls staged for Mrs. Pelligrino. What do the costumes tell?

ART

▶ Design an eye-catching container for Mrs. Pelligrino's pizza. Practice with crayons or markers. Use eye-catching colors. Prominently display the name of the pizza. Leave room for the ingredients and the nutrition facts.

SOCIAL STUDIES

▶ On a map of the New York City area find Queens. (It is the city's largest borough.)

▶ List some of the larger communities found there (Astoria, Jamaica, Long Island City).

▶ Find and name two of the large airports in the New York area.

▶ Locate sports venues. What sports are played at Shea Stadium, Forest Hills, Madison Square Garden and The Meadows?

▶ Find the country of Italy on a world map. Locate some of the familiar countries and name the foods linked with them, e.g., Spain, Poland, Portugal.

▶ On the same map find the continent of Asia. Look for various Asian countries and identify some foods connected with them, e.g., China, Japan, Thailand, Vietnam, India.

▶ Examine the other continents and find other countries and their related foods.

▶ Choose a city in Italy for Mrs. Pelligrino. Trace her route to Queens, NY, USA (by ship, plane).

TIME PERIOD

▶ Decide on the approximate time period in which this book takes place. List the hints found in the illustrations and text.

MATH

▶ Survey the class for preferences for pizza toppings. Create a bar graph, line graph, pictograph and a pie chart to show the results.

▶ Plan to cook or order pizza. Students' preferences for toppings and the number of slices in each one will determine how many to order.

▶ Read the recipes on the front and back covers. Decide the exact amount of ingredients needed if the recipe has to be doubled or tripled.

▶ RELATED BOOKS

NOVELS

Byars, Betsy. **Trouble River**.
Viking, 1969. ISBN 0-670-73257-5 Grades 3-6
The grandmother in this novel is difficult and feisty, but Dewey gets her down the river on a homemade raft to escape the Indian attacks.

Lasky, Kathryn. **Night Journey**.
Puffin, 1986. ISBN 0-140-32048-2 Grades 3-8
A young girl, forced to spend time with her great-grandmother, slowly learns what a remarkable woman she is.

PICTURE BOOKS

Aliki. **A Medieval Feast**.
HarperCollins, 1986. ISBN 0-690-04245-0
This book explains life in a manor house. The customs, clothing and food of the Middle Ages are featured.

DePaola, Tomie. **Tony's Bread**.
Putnam, 1989. ISBN 0-399-21693-6
Tony dreams of becoming the best and most famous baker in northern Italy.

DePaola, Tomie. **Watch Out for the Chicken Feet in Your Soup**. Simon, 1985. ISBN 0-671-66745-9
Joey's Italian grandmother entertains his friend, who gains an understanding of another culture.

Say, Allen. **Grandfather's Journey** See page 184.

Watson, Mary. **Butterfly Seeds** See page 235.

Almost Famous Daisy

by Richard Kidd
Simon & Schuster, 1996
ISBN 0-689-80390-7

SUMMARY

A painting competition inspires Daisy to become a famous painter. She and her pet dog, Duggie, travel the world so she can paint her favorite things in the places they visit. We learn of the progress of their travels via the many postcards she sends to her parents. Included in those postcards are introductions to famous paintings by well-known artists. Finally, Daisy realizes that her favorite things were at home all the time.

ILLUSTRATION

The illustrations by Kidd do a fine job of breaking down the traditional barriers that sometimes exist between fine and commercial art. This book would probably be most enjoyed if seen simultaneously with a good art history text.

CONNECTIONS

NOVEL

Zibby Oneal's **In Summer Light** (Viking, 1985. ISBN 0-670-80784-2) is a story about an artist consumed by his need to paint.

THEMES

▶ Artists
▶ Travel

CURRICULUM CONNECTION

▶ ART - Masterpieces

Language Arts

▶ Examine each of the postcards Daisy sends. Label each part of the postcard. Take a close look at the closing in each of the postcards. How do those words illustrate Daisy's feelings? Might other closings have been used?

▶ Try to translate the foreign words found in the book.

▶ Carefully look at Duggie in the illustrations. Is it possible to predict where he and Daisy are headed next by finding the clues next to the dog?

▶ Find prints of famous paintings. Make these into postcards and use them to write to classmates describing the artists or the paintings themselves.

Social Studies

▶ Examine Daisy's itinerary and map it. Using a world map, plot her journey as well as any side trips she should have taken. By researching the countries Daisy visited, you will think of other interesting sites.

▶ Write an itinerary for Daisy's next trip including points of interest missed in this first journey. Given these new stops along the way, write postcards home to detail her travels.

▶ Each student chooses a state in the United States, researches art and artists within that state and writes an itinerary for traveling across that state with illustrations of notable art "hot spots." Combine students' work to create a cultural journey across America.

Math

▶ Note that in packing for the trip, Daisy packs five cans of "Duggie's Favorite." The postcards tell us that Daisy and Duggie were gone from Monday until Sunday. Looking at the illustrations, we can see that cans of food are being consumed. How much food did Duggie eat each day? Do we report Daisy to the SPCA?

▶ Find out when each artist painted the illustrated painting by looking at the postcards. Use math computations to determine how many years ago each painting was completed. Create a time line showing the years these and other works of art were painted.

▶ Find out the years each of the artists lived. Were any of the featured artists contemporaries?

▶ Study the book to find indicators for the passage of time. How many different ways is the concept of time shown? (Hint: newspapers with dates, calendars, dates on postcards.)

Art

▶ Where's the artist? Find well-known artists throughout the book. Research them to learn about their lives and their works of art.

▶ Carefully look at the pages that contain the postcards. See if you can discover other glimpses of the featured artists' works. Look at the pages that depict Daisy painting. Note that the background detail resembles the style used by the featured artist. What characteristics combine to make the distinctive style of each artist?

▶ This journey introduces Daisy to the styles of some French, Russian, Dutch and American artists. Did the artists featured paint in their countries of birth? Choose five other well-known artists for Daisy to learn about next. Chart her journey to explore those artists and their works.

▶ Visit a museum to compare and contrast the styles of artists featured there. If a museum is not handy to you, surf the Internet to bring a museum into the classroom.

▶ Examine the postage stamps on the postcards that commemorate each artist. Design appropriate stamps for other well-known artists.

RELATED BOOKS

PICTURE BOOKS

Biork, Christina. **Linnea in Monet's Garden**.
Farrar, 1987. ISBN 912958314-4
A little girl visits Claude Monet's garden and sees his famous paintings.

James, Simon. **Dear Mr. Blueberry**.
Simon and Schuster, 1991. ISBN 0-689-50529-9
The text of this story is a series of letters between Emily and her teacher, Mr. Blueberry, over the course of a summer vacation.

Kesselman, Wendy. **Emma**.
HarperCollins, 1985. ISBN 0-440-40847-4
An old woman discovers herself as an artist, much to her family's amazement.

Rylant, Cynthia. **All I See**.
Orchard, 1988. ISBN 0-531-08377-2
A painter and a young boy establish a friendship while each creates his own works of art.

Waber, Bernard. **Dear Hildegarde**.
Houghton, 1980. ISBN 0-395-29745-1
An owl writes a "Dear Abby" type of column for animals who write him very funny letters asking for advice.

Williams, Vera. **Stringbean's Trip to the Shining Sea**. Greenwillow, 1988
This book focuses on postcards and snapshots from Kansas and the Pacific Ocean that two bothers sent home to their family.

NONFICTION

Muhlberger, Richard. **What Makes a Monet a Monet?** Penguin, 1993. ISBN 0-670-85200-7
This is one of a series of books that explains what each artist was trying to help us see.

Venezia, Mike. **Da Vinci**. Children's, 1989.
ISBN 0-516-02275-X
This is one of a series of books on great artists by this author.

NOVELS

Oneal, Zibby. **In Summer Light**.
Viking, 1992. ISBN 0-99928975-1 Grades 5-9
A young teenager spends her summer with her often distant artist father and tries to understand his need to paint.

Children Just Like Me

by Barnabas and Anabel Kindersley
Dorling Kindersley, 1995
ISBN 0-7894-0201-7

SUMMARY

Photographs and text explore the lives of children around the world. Children from many cultures tell of their families, homes, schools, friends, foods and dreams in a fascinating journey around the world through the eyes of children. As most of the children in this book are between 7 and 11 years old, third and fourth grade readers should have little difficulty relating to them. UNICEF receives a royalty for each book sold.

ILLUSTRATION

These are literally pictures in the photographic sense as opposed to illustration. The pictures constitute a visual dictionary of colorful and straightforward information about the children and the people, places and objects in their world. Anabel and Barnabas Kindersley have produced a "Family of Man" album with children as the center of interest.

CONNECTIONS

NOVEL

The best connection might well be to a nonfiction narrative, **The Land I Lost: Adventures of a Boy in Vietnam** (HarperCollins, 1986. ISBN 0-06-440183-9) by Huynh Quang Nhuong.

THEMES
- Home
- Customs

CURRICULUM CONNECTION
- SOCIAL STUDIES – Maps, customs around the world, lives of children in other lands

LANGUAGE ARTS
MAKING COMPARISONS
▶ Find similarities among the children shown. Generate statements about these traits.

▶ Look through the photographs of objects throughout the book. Which of those objects can be found in your home.

▶ Choose a child from the book. Make a Venn diagram comparing yourself and that child.

QUESTIONING
▶ Draft questions you would choose to ask if you could interview any of the depicted children. Consider joining the "Make a Friend Penpal Club" listed at the end of the book and put those questions to good use.

ORAL PRESENTATIONS
▶ Bring in and talk about something unique to your heritage.

WRITING
▶ Design a poster of yourself. Include photographs and illustrations to show all about you in the same format as was used in the book.

▶ Each child has written his or her own name. How many of them use the same alphabet that we do? What countries are they from? How many use a different writing system? Are there people in your community who would be able to teach the class something about a different alphabet?

DEVELOPING VOCABULARY
▶ In some cases, the meaning of a child's name is given. Does your name have a particular meaning?

▶ How many names are there for *mother*, *father*, *grandmother* and *grandfather*? Are those same names used by students in your class?

SOCIAL STUDIES
▶ Locate these children on a world map. Use one color push-pin or marker for the children in the book. Poll the students in the classroom. To what countries do they trace their roots? Use a different color to indicate students' ethnic roots.

▶ Consider launching week-long themes. Choose a child per week and take a trip around the world through literature, folk songs and foods.

▶ Discuss different ways of building families: adoption, remarriage, birth, foster homes, joining two households together.

▶ Compare shelters in the book. Are there any ways that all the shelters are alike? How can the shelters provide information about the climate of the area?

▶ Investigate the occupations of the families depicted in the book. Divide those occupations according to goods versus services. Do most of the families provide goods? Design a flow chart showing the raw goods evolving to products.

▶ Choose one child and investigate that child's life and country. Dress as that child and have classmates interview you to learn about that child.

▶ After reading this book, plan a dream vacation. Which country would you choose to visit and why? After learning about that country, write a travelog or send a postcard home telling what you've seen and done.

▶ Look at the type of things each child is learning in school. Are their school days like yours? How many of them learn English in school? What languages can you learn at your school?

▶ Use the index to get a listing of the languages spoken by the children in this book. Match the languages to the countries.

▶ Notice the number of children wearing sneakers! Where were sneakers invented? Find out.

MATH
▶ Convert United States money into the "currency of the day." Determine the cost of school lunch in each day's currency.

▶ Make math word problems based on the distance children in the book are from one another or from your class.

RELATED BOOKS

NOVELS

Gilson, Jamie. **Hello, My Name is Scrambled Eggs**. Lothrop, 1985. ISBN 0-688-04095-0 Grades 3-6
A young boy teaches a Vietnamese girl English, and they often compare cultures.

Hicyilmaz, Gaye. **Against the Storm**. Little, 1992. ISBN 0-316-36078-3 Grades 6-9
This novel is set in modern Turkey and some of the culture of rural and urban Turkey comes through with the plot.

Neville, Emily. **The China Year**. HarperCollins, 1991. ISBN 0-06-024384-8 Grades 5-9
Henrietta and her family spend a year in Beijing, China and undergo a strong culture clash.

PICTURE BOOKS

McDonald, Megan. **My House Has Stars**. Orchard, 1996. ISBN 0-531-09529-0
The accent is on homes here. Each page presents a home from a different culture.

Pomerantz, Charlotte. **The Chalk Doll**. HarperCollins, 1989. ISBN 0-397-32319-0
A Jamaican mother makes the homemade toy she played with as a child sound so good her daughter wants one like it.

Sanders, Eve. **What's Your Name? From Ariel to Zoe**. Holiday, 1995. ISBN 0-8234-1209-1
This is an alphabet book featuring children from several different cultures.

Say, Allen. **Tree of Cranes**. Houghton, 1991. ISBN 0-395-52024-X
A Japanese child watches his mother combine customs from America with those of classical Japan.

NONFICTION

Huynh Quang Nhuong. **The Land I Lost: Adventures of a Boy in Vietnam**. HarperCollins, 1986. ISBN 0-06-440183-9
Based on the author's memories, these are short stories about his life in Vietnam before the war.

Sneve, Virginia Driving Hawk. **The Iroquois**. Holiday, 1994. ISBN 0-8234-1163-X
This is one of a series of book by Sneve that briefly explore the customs of modern Native American people.

The Million-Dollar Bear

by William Kotzwinkle
Illustrated by David Catrow
Knopf, 1995
ISBN 0-679-85295-6

SUMMARY

Argyle Oldhouse owns the Million-Dollar Bear along with many other rare and expensive teddy bears. The Million-Dollar Bear is so valuable that he is kept in a vault and separated from the others and so is very lonely. Then, through a series of mistakes and mishaps, the Million-Dollar Bear is first lost and then found by a wonderful family who does not consider his value a monetary one.

ILLUSTRATION

David Catrow's portrayal of the key personalities in this story is closely related to the way he illustrates political cartoon characters. His satirical depiction of the millionaires is in stark contrast to the soft imagery reserved for all the bears. This is most apparent when we see the warm, cuddly texture of the central bear character. Exaggeration, the standard tool of cartoonists, captures the menacing face and body features of the human personalities, which contrast strongly with the inviting tactile qualities of the bears.

CONNECTIONS

NOVEL

Get Rich Mitch by Marjorie Sharmat (Morrow, 1985. ISBN 0-688-05790-X) is a light novel that revolves around the troubles of a boy who wins $250,000.

THEMES

- ▶ Values
- ▶ Wealth
- ▶ Collections

CURRICULUM CONNECTION

- ▶ HISTORY – Philanthropists

LANGUAGE ARTS

FINDING DETAILS

▶ Look carefully at the illustrations to find other bear-related references: the Bearair hairdryer, for instance. What other bear things could they have used?

COMPARING LITERATURE

▶ Read The Velveteen Rabbit, Winnie the Pooh, Among the Dolls, Paddington, Corduroy, The Hidden House, Alexander and the Wind-Up Mouse (see Related Books) or other books about toys. Which one would you recommend for reading by J. P. Plumpgarden or Argyle Oldhouse?

BUILDING VOCABULARY

▶ Why are stuffed bears called "Teddy Bears"?

▶ The two rich men in this book have stuffy sounding names: Argyle Oldhouse and J. P. Plumpgarden. Invent some similar names for their friends, if they had any, and the rest of their families. Make an illustrated family tree for one of them.

▶ The cleaning company in the book is called "The Squeegy Cleaning Company." Use the yellow pages of the phone book to find other companies that use clever names or names with puns such as Upper Crust Bakery, Final Cut Hairdressers and the Dew Drop Inn.

EXTENDING THE BOOK

▶ Is there really a very expensive teddy bear? List possible places or books you could reference to find out.

▶ What gives a thing monetary value? What other kinds of value are there? What thing or things do you most value?

USING LITERARY DEVICES

▶ Everything the bears think or say is written in italics. Why do you think the author or editor made that choice? Find out about different kinds of fonts or typefaces. Use a computer and experiment with different styles of print. Type in one of your favorite sayings or poems and print it out in different fonts. What effect does the style of print have on the words or the feeling you get from them? Examine other books to see how they use various fonts in different sizes.

MATHEMATICS

▶ Examine the concept of a million. Is it possible for you to have a million of anything that you can see and count? How long does it take you to breathe a million times? To walk a million steps?

▶ Read How Much Is a Million and Anno's Mysterious Multiplying Jar (see Related Books).

SCIENCE

▶ How have safety and health concerns changed the kinds of toys available for young children? Could any part of a teddy bear or similar toy be hazardous?

SOCIAL STUDIES

▶ Ask people of three different generations to list the toys they can remember loving when they were young. Do the lists have anything in common?

▶ How has technology changed the kinds of toys kids play with?

▶ Research the history of teddy bears and other stuffed toys. Visit an antique shop that specializes in toys and compare those toys to more familiar ones.

▶ Get involved with Toys for Tots or some other charity that distributes toys to children who could not otherwise afford them.

▶ Examine a stuffed animal. What is it made of? Where might each of the materials come from? Where was it made?

ART

▶ Make a stuffed animal for a younger child. Be sure that it is not hazardous.

▶ RELATED BOOKS

NOVELS

Bond, Michael. **A Bear Called Paddington**.
Dell, 1968. ISBN 0-440-40483-5 Grades 3-5
Paddington is not a toy, but these adventures of a simple but lovable bear and his relationship with the Brown family is a wonderful read-aloud.

Sharmat, Marjorie. **Get Rich Mitch**.
Morrow, 1985. ISBN 0-688-05790-X Grades 3-6
This is a sequel to **Rich Mitch** in which Mitch has spent most of his $250,000, but his materialistic family can never have enough.

Sleator, William. **Among the Dolls**.
Dutton, 1975. ISBN 0-525-25563-X Grades 4-9
This rather lengthy novel involves the revenge exacted by some dolls on their abusive owner.

Williams, Margery. **The Velveteen Rabbit**.
Avon, 1982. ISBN 0-380-58156-6 Grades 3-5
This brief novel of what it means to be loved and to be real is a classic toy story.

PICTURE BOOKS

Anno, Mitsumasa. **Anno's Mysterious Multiplying Jar**. Putnam, 1983. ISBN 0-399-20951-4
We start with a single magic jar inside of which is an island. From there we move by factorials into greater and greater numbers.

Baylor, Byrd. **Table Where Rich People Sit**
See page 22.

Freeman, Don. **Corduroy**.
Puffin, 1976. ISBN 0-14-050173-8
In this classic picture book, a teddy bear yearns to be purchased from the department store.

Lionni, Leo. **Alexander and the Wind-Up Mouse**.
Knopf, 1974. ISBN 0-394-82911-5
This simple picture book contrasts a toy's life with that of a real mouse.

Schwartz, David. **If You Made a Million**.
Lothrop, 1989. ISBN 0-688-07017-5
If your investments really paid off, this character will show you what a million dollars looks like.

Schwartz, David. **How Much Is a Million**
Lothrop, 1985. ISBN 0-688-04050-0
A million is shown in relationship to things kids know about.

Waddell, Martin. **The Hidden House**.
Illustrated by Angela Barrett. Philomel, 1990.
ISBN 0-399-22228-6
An old man in an isolated cottage makes three wooden dolls to keep himself company. When he leaves, the dolls remain undiscovered and unloved until a new little girl moves in.

NONFICTION

Lohf, Sabine. **Building Your Own Toys**.
Childrens, 1989. ISBN 0-516-9251-9
Each toy is explained and shown in a full color photograph and the brief instructions are given on the opposing page.

Fables

by Arnold Lobel
HarperCollins, 1983
ISBN 0-06-443046-4

SUMMARY

This Caldecott Award-winning book is one of this author's many classics for children. There are 20 original fables in this collection and, although contemporary in nature, they give the reader a new and exciting view of the genre. Each animal character is as unique as its situation. This is definitely not your ordinary fable collection.

ILLUSTRATION

An independent picture accompanies each fable and occupies the page that faces it. The story and its visual counterpart are each framed within their own vertically positioned rectangle. The illustrations are additionally double-matted or framed, focusing attention on the illustrated characters. In selected compositions, the main characters break out of the box-like compositional space. Alternative lettering type is used to create a contrast between the story and summary phrase.

CONNECTIONS

NOVEL

Brooke's **Untold Tales** (HarperCollins, 1992. ISBN 0-06-020271-8) twists familiar fairy tales in a way similar to Lobel's handling of the fables.

THEMES
▶ Fables
▶ Parodies

CURRICULUM CONNECTION
▶ LITERATURE – Fables

LANGUAGE ARTS
INVESTIGATING THE GENRE

▶ Compare this book to other books of fables (see Related Books). How are these stories like them and how are they different? Write a definition of "fable" which applies to all of those you read.

▶ Find out about Aesop and the fables he wrote.

▶ Read fables from other cultures.

▶ Read some of the fairy tales by Hans Christian Anderson. Why do you think some people consider these to be fables?

WRITING

▶ Before he wrote **Fables**, Arnold Lobel tried to write a new version of Aesop's fables. He found he disliked fables as a genre and couldn't do it. However, how to construct a fable stayed in his head. He found that other things he tried to write turned into fables, including these tongue-in-cheek stories. Now that you've read a lot of fables, try your own hand at composing one.

▶ Create a newspaper article about one of the incidents you read about in your fable research.

DRAMATICS

▶ Form cooperative entertainment groups. Each will decide on a presentation based on a fable. Choose pantomime, musicals, monologues, skits or puppet shows for your presentation.

VOCABULARY DEVELOPMENT

▶ Design acrostics about various fable animals. Create each one exclusively for synonyms or antonyms.

▶ Make up similes based on the fables: The rhinoceros was as gullible as a _____. The camel dances like a _____.

▶ Prepare a detailed description of one animal character. Emphasize adjectives. Let others guess what fable animal you are talking about.

▶ Repeat a moral from one of the fables. Using only the table of contents, let others decide which tale is the correct source of that moral.

SCIENCE

▶ Find specific fables in which animals are natural enemies. Are they enemies in the fable?

▶ Design a chart with headings such as color, size, mobility, food, sound. Chart each animal twice: the way it appears in nature and the way it appears in a fable.

▶ Display a world map. Place symbols for the various animals in their habitats throughout the world. Now look at the fables. Does that fable come from a country where those animals can be found?

▶ Discuss animal stereotypes: wise owl, quiet mouse, hungry bear. List the fable animals that follow the conventional wisdom: a fat and hungry pig, a fish-loving cat. Identify animals in fables that do not act typically.

ART

▶ Using paint, crayons, and cut paper, design a backdrop for a fable. Place animals on or in the picture. Try unusual habitats for common fables. Will it change the fable?

RELATED BOOKS

NOVELS

Brooke, William. **Teller of Tales**.
HarperCollins, 1994. ISBN 0-06-023399-0
Grades 3-6
Here a cranky old man and a little girl rewrite some tales, including "Goldilocks," "The Emperor's New Clothes," "Rumplestiltskin," and "Little Red Riding Hood," with satire and satisfying twists.

Brooke, William. **Untold Tales**.
HarperCollins, 1992. ISBN 0-06-020271-8
Grades 3-6
Three tales are twisted and given new, humorous insight: "Beauty and the Beast," "The Frog Prince" and "Sleeping Beauty."

PICTURE BOOKS

Anno, Mitsumasa. **Anno's Aesop: A Book of Fables by Aesop & Mr. Fox**. Orchard, 1989. ISBN 0-531 05774-7
Mr. Fox can't read and so he uses the pictures to make up his own fables for his son which are juxtaposed with Aesop's version. Amazingly, the moral is often similar.

Rice, Eve. **Once in a Wood: Ten Tales from Aesop**.
Greenwillow, 1979. ISBN 0-688-80191-9
Whimsical black and white drawings illustrate the simply told conventional tales.

Zwerger, Lisbeth. **Aesop's Fables**.
Picture Book, 1991. ISBN 0-88708-108-8
A dozen fables from Aesop are illustrated with delicate full-page illustrations.

Young, Ed. **Seven Blind Mice**
Putnam, 1992. ISBN 0-399-22261-8
The ancient fable "The Blind Men and the Elephant" is given new life and dimension in this striking book.

OTHER BOOKS WRITTEN AND ILLUSTRATED BY ARNOLD LOBEL

The Book of Pigericks. HarperCollins, 1983.
ISBN 0-06-023982-4
This delightful collection of limericks all concern pigs.

Grasshopper on the Road. HarperCollins, 1986.
ISBN 0-06-444094-X
Although the morals in these short fables are unstated, they are evident in this easy-to-read book.

Ming Lo Moves the Mountain

by Arnold Lobel
Greenwillow, 1982
ISBN 0-688-00610-8

SUMMARY

Ming Lo and his wife are most unhappy with the mountain that looms over their house. They are quite content with the house itself; it is that mountain which must go! Advice is sought from the village wise man who, eventually, supplies the perfect strategy.

ILLUSTRATION

The soft and subtle color scheme employed in these illustrations reflects the text's calm mood. Figures, buildings and landscapes are all represented in seemingly simple but sophisticated drawings. The author/illustrator successfully combines simple lines, muted colors and fresh watercolor washes.

CONNECTIONS

NOVEL

In Natalie Babbitt's **Kneeknock Rise** (Farrar, 1970. ISBN 0-374-34257-1) the people of the village are sure that a monster they call the Megrimum lives on top of their mountain.

THEMES

▶ Trickster tales
▶ Wise elders
▶ Impossible tasks

CURRICULUM CONNECTION

▶ HISTORY – Moving mountains, overcoming odds, changing environments

LANGUAGE ARTS

▶ Read only the first page and predict why Ming Lo and his wife did not love the mountain. Read to confirm your answers.

▶ Each technique given by the wise man to move the mountain would work for something else. What is each technique more appropriate for? Each of the techniques has a negative effect. When they attempted to bribe the mountain with food, they apparently used up their food supply. Write each of the other techniques as cause/effect statements.

▶ Try rewriting the story in rhyme or presenting it as a play.

▶ Look at the illustrations of the wise man. How is his anger depicted? Would the text alone give any clues to his increasing anger? Brainstorm words that indicate anger. List these on chart paper and post the list as a reference to use during creative writing times.

▶ The concept of "outfoxed" can be difficult for some children to understand. Try introducing some of the books listed in Related Books and charting just who was fooled, by whom, and for what purpose. Identify character traits and situations that allow characters to be outfoxed. Would the stories be the same without this trickery? Does the character ever realize that he or she was tricked? Add to the outfoxed chart throughout the year as other books whose plots are based on trickery are introduced.

▶ Ming Lo consulted a wise man in this story. Why? How would someone earn the reputation of "wise"? Is the wise man in this book indeed wise? Now compare him to the fortune teller in **Fortune Tellers** (see page 7) Who is wiser? Who is Trickier?

▶ Were there other solutions to Ming Lo's problem other than moving the house?

▶ Ming Lo's home certainly left a great deal to be desired. If you were a real estate agent, how would you write an ad to sell his house? Take a look at classified ads in your local newspaper to get some ideas. You might also try your hand at translating some of the ads you read in the paper. What does, "just needs a little TLC" *really* mean? How about "handyman special"?

▶ We sometimes refer to a difficult task as "moving mountains." Find examples in your own family or in your society where a figurative mountain was moved.

SOCIAL STUDIES

▶ Note that the "wife of Ming Lo" has no name. Why not? Does this lack of a name reflect the author's sexist attitude? Is it culturally based?

▶ Does that name in and of itself have any meaning?

▶ Assume that this book is set somewhere in Asia. Choose an Asian country and investigate the naming of babies there. Try to write your name based on the principles of naming in that country.

▶ Review the illustrations. What country is meant to be depicted? Compare these illustrations with photographs of the real thing. Did Lobel employ stereotypes or, perhaps, are these illustrations meant to be historical in nature?

▶ Use the clues from the illustrations to pick out a possible location. If the story is set in that place, of what mountain range could this be a part?

▶ Investigate types of shelters. Was Ming Lo's home appropriate to its location? Are there any advantages to building one's home close to a mountain? Make a list of the various types of shelters. Choose a type of dwelling and find out all you can about it. Then mark on a map places where that style of abode is likely to be found. What is the relationship between climate and type of dwelling?

SCIENCE

▶ Look again at the illustrations. Note that the trees seem to look like bonsai trees. Why? What would you guess weather is like, based on the trees' appearance? Find out about bonsai.

▶ How does elevation impact weather? Is the weather near and on mountains different from the weather on flat land?

RELATED BOOKS

NOVELS

Babbitt, Natalie. **Kneeknock Rise**.
Farrar, 1970. ISBN 0-374-34257-1 Grades 4-8
This novel has a mountain that the villagers both fear and love.

Buck, Pearl. **The Wave**
HarperTropher, 1986. ISBN 0 06-440171-5
Grades 4-9
A boy in Japan goes to his friend's house on a mountaintop, from which point he watches a tidal wave destroy the village.

PICTURE BOOKS

Aesop. **The Fox and the Crow**
Many versions available. Using flattery, a fox tricks crow out of a piece of cheese.

Alexander, Lloyd. **The Fortune Tellers**
See page 7.
This humorous story also revolves around a wise person.

McKissack, Patricia. **Flossie and the Fox**.
Penguin, 1986. ISBN 0-8037-0251-5
When Flossie is sent to deliver eggs to a neighbor, Big Mama warns her about the fox. Flossie has never seen a fox, so she isn't quite sure just what to expect. When the fox does, indeed, appear, Flossie refuses to believe it's really a fox until it can prove it. The poor fox is desperate to prove to this little girl that he most certainly is a fox. At the end of the story, we learn that Flossie has managed to "out-fox" the fox!

Ross, Tony. **Stone Soup**. Penguin USA, 1990. ISBN 0-8037-0890-4
A wolf is tricked into doing many tasks instead of eating the chicken as he had planned.

OTHER BOOKS BY ARNOLD LOBEL

Fables. HarperCollins, 1980. ISBN 0-06-023974-3
Here is a collection of tongue-in-cheek fables.

The Rose in my Garden. Morrow, 1984.
ISBN 0-688-02587-0
This cumulative story follows the slow development of a beautiful garden and the arrival of the creatures that will inhabit it.

Small Pig. HarperCollins, 1969. ISBN 0-06-444120-2
The pig is happy on the farm until the farmer's wife has a cleaning fit and cleans up the mud the pig enjoyed most.

A Treeful of Pigs. Morrow, 1979.
ISBN 0-688-84177-5
A very lazy farmer spends his time in bed instead of helping his wife take care of their herd of pigs. His poor wife tries lots of tricks to get the farmer to help her.

Voices of the Wild

by Jonathan London
Illustrated by Wayne McLoughlin
Crown, 1993
ISBN 0 517 59217 7

SUMMARY

A series of northern animals tell of their lives and their impression of man. The illustrations nicely combine the presence of man with the animals in their habitat, and we see the human presence through the eyes of the animals. The human goes about his canoe trip, unaware of all who watch him, but loving the wilderness.

ILLUSTRATION

Double-page spreads give a panoramic sense. With a few exceptions, the colors are dark and night-like. One such exception is the introductory page, which gives a full-lighted, warm sky and an image of the otter that is upbeat and light-filled. McLoughlin also uses print for contrast: sometimes black on light colors and then white print on fields of dark color. Perhaps the most unique illustration is the one with the bear in which we see the bear acting almost like a bridge. The technical skill is outstanding.

CONNECTIONS

NOVEL

Gary Paulsen's **Woodsong** (Simon, 1990. ISBN 0-02-770221-9) contains one man's perception of the wilderness world with which he has intimately been involved.

THEME

▶ Varying perspectives and perceptions

CURRICULUM CONNECTION

▶ SCIENCE – Human role in environment

LANGUAGE ARTS

WRITING

▶ Each of the animals' statements provides a brief description of the animal and of its action. Identify the verbs and list them on chart paper. Brainstorm synonyms for these verbs. Substitute some of the brainstormed words for the original words in the text. Which sound better?

▶ Now go back and identify the adjectives. Again, brainstorm synonyms and substitute them for the original words. If both the verbs and the adjectives in the text are replaced by synonyms, does the meaning of the verse change?

▶ Choose other animals (perhaps those native to your area) and write in those animals' "voices."

▶ Retell the story from the man's perspective. What does the man see and what does he not see while in the animals' habitat? Why would man "miss" some of the animals?

▶ Consider taking a closer look at the concept of perspective. How can perspective affect the way a story is told? Clip newspaper and magazine ads and rewrite them from a different perspective. Instead of trying to sell the products, write your "ads" to keep people from using the products. Investigate other books, including those listed under Related Books, in which perspective plays an important role.

COMPARING AND CONTRASTING

▶ On the next to the last page (the page with the footprints), the text seems to indicate a similarity between animals and nature and man. List ways man and the animals in the book are alike.

VOCABULARY

▶ *Voice* is a multiple meaning word. Investigate other multiple meaning words, especially those found in nature, such as *branch*, *limb* or *bank*.

SCIENCE

▶ List the animals in the book. Based on what you already know about them, where is this book's setting? What other animals would have been in that environment and might have seen the man?

▶ Looking at that list of animals, which, if any, should humans fear? Why? Which animal(s) should fear humans and why?

▶ Again, use the list of animals to classify them in various ways such as predator and prey, by animal families, or by carnivore and herbivore.

▶ On the next to the last page of the book are found a series of footprints. Match the tracks to the animal.

▶ The man in this book is using his sense of sight to discover the animals. What senses are the animals using to discover the presence of the man?

▶ Are any of the animals in this book on the endangered species list? What exactly is that list? Who makes it and what, if any, protection does it afford the animals on the list? What requirements must be met for an animal to be placed on the list?

▶ Choose one of the 12 animals in this book and learn more about it.

SOCIAL STUDIES

▶ Why is a kayak an ideal mode of transportation for this journey? How would the book have been different if a motor boat had been used? List other forms of water transportation.

▶ What sorts of jobs are available for people who prefer to spend time in the out-of-doors in various animal habitats?

▶ The last page of the book shows totem poles. Who made them and why? Do those totem poles help to narrow down the setting for this book?

RELATED BOOKS

NOVELS

Paulsen, Gary. **Brian's Winter**.
Delacorte, 1996. ISBN 0-385-32198-8 Grades 3-6
This sequel to **Hatchet** is really an alternative to it. What would have happened had Brian had to spend the winter alone in the wild?

Paulsen, Gary. **Hatchet**.
Bradbury, 1987. ISBN 0-14-032724-X Grades 3-6
This popular and very accessible novel concerns the survival of a young and previously pampered boy in the wilderness of northern Canada.

Paulsen, Gary. **The River**.
Dell, 1993. ISBN 0-440-40753-2 Grades 3-6
This sequel to **Hatchet** has Brian attempting to re-enact his survival experience, this time with witnesses.

Paulsen, Gary. **Woodsong**.
Simon, 1990. ISBN 0-02-770221-9 Grades 3-9
In short stories, Paulsen relates his own wilderness experiences.

PICTURE BOOKS

Arnosky, Jim. **Every Autumn Comes the Bear**.
Putnam, 1993. ISBN 0-399-22508-0
Just before winter, a bear appears on a farm in search of a place to sleep during the cold months ahead. This is a realistic depiction of a bear and its woodland environment.

Arnosky, Jim. **Crinkleroot's Guide to Walking in Wild Places**. Aladdin, 1993. ISBN 0-689-71753-9
Here is a nonfiction guide for walking in and appreciating nature.

Cochran, Oren. **Great Grey Owl**.
Whole Language, 1986. ISBN 0-92200739-11-3
Written in verse, the book accurately and poetically describes the activities of a great grey owl during a 24-hour period.

BOOKS ABOUT PERSPECTIVE

Hall, Donald. **I Am the Dog; I Am the Cat**.
Dial, 1994. ISBN 0-8037-1504-8
A dog and a cat each tell their impressions of the world. See page 87.

Heide, Florence Parry. **The Shrinking of Treehorn**.
Holiday, 1971. ISBN 0-823-40975-9
Treehorn is shrinking and on one will listen or help. Things that were once quite easy become difficult when you're suddenly small.

McMillan, Bruce. **Mouse Views: What the Class Pet Saw**. Holiday House, 1993. ISBN 0-8234-1008-0
Color photographs show classroom objects from a mouse's perspective.

Van Allsburg, Chris. **Two Bad Ants**.
Houghton, 1988. ISBN 0-395-48668-8
A troop of ants is off to retrieve the crystals that the ant scouts have discovered. Two of the ants decide to remain behind with the crystals when the rest of the troop returns to the colony. The adventures that await these two ants give the reader an ant's perspective of a modern kitchen.

NONFICTION

Paulsen, Gary. **Father Water, Mother Woods**.
Delacorte, 1994. ISBN 0-385-32053-1
These short essays recount many of Paulsen's experiences fishing and hunting in childhood and adulthood. They obviously provide much of the background for his fiction writing.

Cecil's Story

by George Ella Lyon
Illustrated by Peter Catalanotto
Orchard, 1991
ISBN 0531-08512-0

► SUMMARY

In this sensitive story a boy, apparently Cecil, tells us what happens when a father goes to war. The story begins on the cover as we see a 19th century family peacefully occupied on their farm. The title page shows the father and boy returning from a successful fishing trip. The dedication page shows soldiers marching off. As the narration begins, we find that Cecil's father has gone off to war and has been hurt. His mother has gone to get him, and Cecil is staying with neighbors. He tells us of his loneliness, his worry, and his fear that his father will not come back. Illustrations pick up the story and show us the father and mother on their return, the father with just one arm. The book makes an eloquent statement about the price of war.

► ILLUSTRATION

When watercolors are allowed to mix and meld together, new images are created. Superimposed images seem dream-like; various characters and thoughts fuse together. Peter Catalanotto's watercolor paintings' dreamy quality is the result of his exceptional skill with the medium.

One composition shows a single figure in multiple situations. With this technique, the illustrator succeeds in capturing a lapse in time. The metamorphosis of embryo to chick spans two pages and validates the time lapse referenced by the text. These are carefully applied watercolor washes over which the text has been printed.

► CONNECTIONS

NOVEL
Another Civil War book that deals with a child's relationship with his father is **Shades of Gray** (Avon, 1991. ISBN 0-380-71232-6).

THEMES
► The passage of time
► Effect of war on the innocent

CURRICULUM CONNECTION
► HISTORY – Civil War

LANGUAGE ARTS

GRAMMAR

▶ The story is told in the second person. Try telling it in the first or third person. What does that do to the story? Why do you think the author chose the second person?

COMPARING LITERATURE

▶ Compare this book with **Sami and the Time of Troubles** (see page 93). Are the authors and illustrators of these books trying to give us the same message? Find other books with similar messages.

MATH

▶ The statistics of the many wars in which the United States participated can be interesting. Find as many statistics as you can for the war in Vietnam, the Gulf War, World War II, World War I, the Civil War and the Revolutionary War. Which was the bloodiest, the longest? Which had the most civilian casualties?

SCIENCE

▶ Looking at the pictures where there are many moons and the one where the egg and chick are shown in the book can give you some sense of how much time went by while Cecil stayed with the neighbors. Find out how long it takes for a chick to hatch and how much time elapses between full moons.

▶ The plow that Cecil worries about being able to handle is different from the plows modern farmers use, but it's also different than the earliest plows. Find illustrations of as many different stages of technology in the development of the plow as possible. Can you figure out what each improvement did to the ease of plowing?

SOCIAL STUDIES

▶ On a blank map of the United States, color in the states of the Confederacy in gray and the states of the Union in blue. Color free states and territories a different color. Locate the major battles of the Civil War and place a star at those sites. Where might Cecil's father have been hurt? Where might Cecil have lived? What makes you think so?

▶ Look in your local history books or on family trees for the name of one Civil War soldier. Write to the National Archives and Records Service in Washington, DC, to request application NATF Form 26 to ask for his war record. What does it tell you? Find more information on the battles in which he was involved.

▶ Find out what weapons were used in the Civil War, cannons as well as rifles. How far could each of them fire? Stand that far from another class member. What can you tell about each other from this distance? How far will today's war weapons fire? Stand that far from each other. What can you tell about each other from this distance? Would it be easier to fire at someone with the first weapon or the second? Why?

▶ What other countries have had civil wars? How did they turn out?

ART

ARTIST'S TECHNIQUES

▶ Look carefully at the cover, the title page and the dedication page of the book. What do they tell you that the words do not?

▶ Look at the picture of Cecil looking after the cows. What do the blurred images of the moon tell you? Look on the next page where Peter Catalanotto does the same thing to an egg. How else might he have chosen to show the passage of time?

▶ Look at the picture of the soldiers marching off to war on the dedication page of the book and then look at the page where Civil War soldiers are sitting in front of a fire. In the background you can see the same image of soldiers marching as on the dedication page. What's Peter Catalanotto trying to tell us?

▶ On that same page, look at those soldiers. Are they wearing blue or gray? What does that tell us?

▶ Look at the page where Cecil is shown with the mule and the plow. Again, what is Mr. Catalanotto saying? How else could he have said it? What could the text have said to make the same statement?

▶ On the next page, we see Cecil's mother holding him, but the images are transparent. What choices did the artist have here?

➤ RELATED BOOKS

NOVELS

Gauch, Patricia Lee. **Thunder at Gettysburg**.
Illustrated by Stephen Gammell, Bantam, 1975.
ISBN 0-553-15951-8 Grades 3-5
Tillie, a young girl living near the battle of Gettysburg, tells us in this brief novel what she could see from her own attic and then from two other nearby houses.

Lunn, Janet. **The Root Cellar**.
Puffin, 1985. ISBN 0-14-031835-6 Grades 4-8
This is a wonderful time fantasy in which a young girl is transported to the Civil War era and must go to the front lines to bring back a wounded soldier.

Reeder, Carolyn. **Shades of Gray**.
Avon, 1991. ISBN 0-380-71232-6 Grades 4-9
This is a reach for most third-and fourth-graders, but a good read-aloud. It deals with the aftermath of the war. Will has lost his whole family during the Civil War and is sent to live with a man he considers a coward because he refused to fight.

PICTURE BOOKS

Ackerman, Karen. **The Tin Heart**.
Atheneum, 1990. ISBN 0-689-31461-2
Two girls living on opposite sides of the Ohio River are friends until the Civil War breaks out, whereupon they can no longer visit each other. Each wears half of a heart as a reminder of their friendship.

Polacco, Patricia. **Pink and Say**.
Putnam, 1994. ISBN 0-399-22671-0
This heart-wrenching story tells of the friendship between two soldiers, one black and one white. See page 167.

Turner, Ann. **Nettie's Trip South**.
Illustrated by Ronald Himler, Simon & Schuster, 1987. ISBN 0-02 789240-9
This picture book takes place before the Civil War and tells of the horrors of slavery. See page 223.

NONFICTION

One of the best sources of information on the Civil War is **Cobblestone Magazine**. Many issues have been devoted to the period, covering many aspects of the conflict. Back issues of the magazine as well as current subscriptions can be obtained from Cobblestone Publishing, 30 Grove St., Peterborough, NH 03458.

Fritz, Jean. **Stonewall**.
Illustrated by Stephen Gammell, Putnam, 1979.
ISBN 0-399-20698-1
This lengthy biography of the legendary Confederate General Stonewall Jackson shows his obsession with rules and his neurotic behavior, but also why the strange man was so adored by his troops that he became the epitome of Southern gallantry. The narration deals with the battles of Chancellorville, Manassas, and many other skirmishes.

Kent, Zachary. **The Story of the Battle of Shiloh**.
Childrens Press, 1991. ISBN 0-516-44754-8
This book deals in an accessible manner with General Grant and his decisions in one of the bloodiest battles in the Civil War.

Murphy, Jim. **The Boys' War**.
Clarion, 1989. ISBN 0-89919-893-7
Many boys not much older than Cecil were part of the action of the war itself. Actual letters and diaries detail the experiences of boys under the age of 16 who fought in the Civil War and combine a visual with a written history of the wars as seen through the perspectives of the youngest participants.

Black and White

by David Macaulay
Houghton, 1990
ISBN 0-395-52151-3

◢ SUMMARY

What appear to be four separate stories, one installment of each appearing on each spread of the book, turn out to intermingle and, in time, become one story. Always Macaulay is playing with our perceptions and making allusions and illusions. A robber hides out in a herd of cattle who, in turn, disrupt the passage of a train. At the train station, passengers at first are absorbed in the newspapers they are reading, but as the wait lengthens, they start playing with the newspapers and with each other. A boy, a passenger on the train, witnesses some of the events, but not all of them. Parents, previously staid and distant, have apparently changed, at least temporarily, because of their time spent waiting for the train that day. The book can be frustrating, confusing or, in the proper hands and minds, a challenge and a source of fascination.

◢ ILLUSTRATION

Sorting out the myriad images in this book is a bit like watching the multiple pictures on a split screen TV. It's essential to revisit these pictures again and again in order to appreciate or calculate the variety of illustration styles. One way to observe how David Macauley manages a time sequence is to flip through the book quickly and observe the change in the crowd at the train station. Inventiveness is the key word for this publication.

◢ CONNECTIONS

NOVEL

Although totally different in mood, Paul Fleischman's **Bull Run** (HarperCollins, 1993. ISBN 0-06-440588-5) presents many points of view of events. In this case it's the brutal battle of Bull Run during the Civil War.

THEMES

▶ Varying perceptions of same event
▶ Differing points of view

CURRICULUM CONNECTION

▶ SCIENCE – Ecosystems in which every life affects other lives

LANGUAGE ARTS

FINDING DETAILS

▶ Look at the back cover of the book. There appears to be a cow. But look closer and you will see a human figure in the pattern. Where is the figure pointing? Is there a title in the book he may be referring to? If he is, what might he be telling you about reading this book? Can you find the same figure elsewhere in the book? Who is he? What does he tell you at various points?

BUILDING VOCABULARY

▶ The title of one story, "Udder Chaos," is a pun. Find other examples of puns in jokes, riddles and story titles. Put them on a bulletin board.

EXTENDING THE TEXT

▶ The title of the book is not printed in black and white on the cover, although that might be a logical thing to do. Notice the way it is printed there and on the spine of the book, and notice the colors Macaulay uses. What do you think is meant?

▶ Find and tell many answers to the riddle question, "What's black and white and red all over?" Take a poll about the answers to this question and find out the most commonly known answer. Macaulay never mentions that riddle, but you can find the ways he uses it throughout the book.

▶ Notice where and how the robber hides. Often it is among black and white things: the cows and the choir. What else could he have hidden among if they were in the book? Penguins? Draw pictures with other such places to hide the robber.

▶ Sometimes the words in the book help explain the illustration; sometimes they contradict the illustration. Make a chart similar to the one below and find an instance of each.

Text and Illustrations Match	Text and Illustrations Don't Match
"An old woman enters the compartment"	"The worst thing about Holstein cows is that if they ever get out of the field, they're almost impossible to find."
"Every morning at seven o'clock they leave for their offices in the city."	"The boulders are moving."
"The man is shouting and waving his fists."	"He sticks out his hand to catch a few flakes."

▶ Look at the author's picture on the flap of the book. Why do you think he is pictured in a make-believe train?

▶ Make a time line of the events in the story. What do you think happened first?

▶ Read the author's warning on the title page of the book. Did you heed it? What difference would it make?

▶ Look carefully at the first and last pictures in the book. Do you know where the train station came from?

▶ The dog in the story "Problem Parents" may remind you of the dog in the books by Chris Van Allsburg. Find out if the two authors know each other and, if so, how they met.

▶ You could say that the newspapers are a symbol in this book from beginning to end. List all the things you think of about newspapers: What are they for? What do we do with them? Then think of ways Macaulay used these ideas in his book.

AUTHOR STUDY

▶ Find and read all or parts of David Macaulay's acceptance speech for the Caldecott Award he received for **Black and White**. In it he explains a little of what he was trying to do in the book. He also has four parts to his speech, and they are the titles of each of the stories in his book, but with different meanings.

COMPARING LITERATURE

▶ Look at Macaulay's book **Why the Chicken Crossed the Road**. Could that book have come before or after this one? Is it the same robber? The same cows?

▶ Find other books where the artists play with our perspective such as **Zoom** and **Bad Day at Riverbend** (see page 226).

SCIENCE

▶ Almost everything that happens in this book affects something or someone else. Make a list of every action in the story and beside it put the things that action caused to happen. Then, take any ecosystem such as a pond, a field or a woods. List a series of events that might take place within that ecosystem during a day or a season and show how it affects other things in the system.

ART

▶ Both the art and the text of this book use positive and negative space. (There's as much in what the words don't say as there is in what they do say.) Do some art activities using negative and positive images. Start by cutting a shape from a piece of construction paper and then pasting both the shape and the piece it's cut out of on another paper in a pleasing manner. Go on from this start to create your own work of art.

➤ RELATED BOOKS

NOVEL

Fleischman, Paul. **Bull Run**.
HarperCollins, 1993. ISBN 0-06-440588-5
Grades 4-9
Each chapter presents a different viewpoint as various people head to the battle of Bull Run.

PICTURE BOOKS

Banyai, Istvan. **Zoom**.
Viking, 1995. ISBN 0-670-85804-8
We play with perspective zooming out from a small detail into a series of ever widening views.

Van Allsburg, Chris. **Bad Day at Riverbend**
See page 226.

OTHER BOOKS BY DAVID MACAULAY

Baaa. Houghton, 1985. ISBN 0-395-38948-8
Humans disappear from the earth, which is then taken over by sheep who ultimately become as bad as the humans they replaced.

Castle. Houghton, 1982. ISBN 0-395-25784-0
Not only do we see the careful details and planning of the inside and outside of a 13th century Welsh castle, but we see the walled town surrounding it in equal detail.

Cathedral. Houghton, 1981. ISBN 0-394-31668-5
This is an architectural study of the planning and building of a Gothic cathedral.

City: A Story of Roman Planning and Construction.
Houghton, 1974. ISBN 0-394-19492-X
The title says it all, but the illustrations are so detailed that interested viewers can be lost in them for days.

Mill. Houghton, 1989. ISBN 0-395-52019-3
Four different cotton mills of 19th century New England are diagrammed.

Pyramid. Houghton, 1975. ISBN 0-395-21407-6
On a site high above the Nile, a pyramid is planned and built for a mythical pharaoh.

Ship. Houghton, 1993. ISBN 0-395-52439-3
First we see the way the Spanish caravel was built and how she sailed. Then, four centuries later, we go with the marine archeologists exploring its ruins.

Unbuilding. Houghton, 1987. ISBN 0-395-45360-7
This time it's the Empire State Building that we're investigating, and this time we do it through its deconstruction.

Underground. Houghton, 1976.
ISBN 0-3945-34065-9
The city is as fascinating beneath the surface as it is above. We look at sewers, subways and electrical systems.

The Way Things Work. Houghton, 1988.
ISBN 0-395-42857-2
In this exhaustive book, Macaulay shows us (often through the antics of woolly mammoths) how a multitude of things work.

Why the Chicken Crossed the Road.
Houghton, 1987. ISBN 0-395-44241-9
The riddle in this book is more obvious than in **Black and White**, but it is the cause of a whole series of events and hilarity.

Rome Antics

by David Macaulay
Houghton, 1997
ISBN 0-395-82279-3

▶ SUMMARY

Macaulay gives us a chance to play in and among the monuments and ancient buildings of Rome in this delightful book that shows his love and knowledge of the city. Before the title page, a woman releases a homing pigeon and we follow that pigeon's flight as a red line through the city, getting a pigeon's-eye view of the juxtaposition of things mundane and glorious. Eventually the pigeon flies into an artist's garret where we read the message at last: "Yes." The landmarks are identified and briefly described in an afterword.

▶ ILLUSTRATION

This is a wonderful historical record of the monuments, buildings and people of Rome. Macauley's understanding of engineering and architecture is obvious and easily transferred into information for any reader. He captures some of the trivia for tourists in Rome (the pigeons and the cats, for instance) without letting them overpower the beauty of the city. His use of a pigeon's flight enables him to play with the perspective while teaching us about the architectural patterns, the buildings and the monuments. His cartoon-like people give us size references and the knowledge that the city is alive and in constant use and has been so for centuries.

▶ CONNECTIONS

NOVEL

Joan Goodman's **Songs from Home** (Harcourt, 1994. ISBN 0-152-03591-5) is set in modern Rome, and many of the buildings and monuments in **Rome Antics** are mentioned in the story.

THEMES

▶ Differing perspectives
▶ Ancient buildings
▶ Letters and messages

CURRICULUM CONNECTION

▶ HISTORY – Ancient Rome
▶ ART – Architecture, famous buildings

LANGUAGE ARTS

WORD PLAY

▶ The title **Rome Antics** is a pun. Find other book titles that involve word play, such as most of the books by James Howe (**The Celery Stalks at Midnight**) and Fred Gwynne (**The King Who Rained**).

WRITING

▶ We know that the answer is "yes." We suspect but we don't know what the question was. Have a contest for the most interesting question that the woman could be answering.

FINDING DETAILS

▶ Find the reasons for the pigeon's actions in the book. For instance, we can tell that it lands several times and usually we can see why.

▶ Look for modern actions in the ancient city. Make a list of them and categorize them under technology, human nature, accidents and similar categories.

MAIN IDEA

▶ What do you think David Macaulay is trying to tell us in this book?

COMPARING LITERATURE

▶ Although David Macaulay's books differ widely in subject and style, there are elements in common among them. Read and categorize his books listed below.

SOCIAL STUDIES

▶ Make a list of the shakers and movers of Ancient Rome. Start with Julius Caesar, Augustus Caesar, Cicero, Constantine, Diocletian, Hadrian, Horace, Marcus Aurelius, Marc Antony, Nero, Seneca and Virgil. Choose one of them to research and then conduct an Ancient Rome day in which students come dressed as one of the characters and act out the roles.

▶ Most old cities have a market square quite like the one in Rome. Find pictures of those squares and compare them. What purpose did they and do they serve?

▶ Go to website: http://www.roma2000.it/zmonum2.html#Monumenti for a list of many of the buildings of Rome in Italian with information on them in English. See if you can translate the names before you click on them. Compare the information there with the information in **Rome Antics**.

ART

▶ Things to Notice in **Rome Antics**:

the way Macauley's drawings of sculpture differs from the drawings of people

the repeated patterns in the buildings

the way the structure of the open umbrella is contrasted with the ancient structures.

the views of the interior and exterior of the same buildings such as the Pantheon

the way the floor in the Pantheon echoes but does not duplicate the one in the ceiling

the pigeon's flight, which often echoes the building's shape

the symmetry on the double-page spread looking up at the sky

the effect of the red line against the black and white images

the lines created by the shaken mop

▶ **Rome Antics** offers a pigeon's eye view of Rome. Using a camera or drawing, construct a similar view of any object in your classroom, school or city.

▶ Many times the windows on each level of a building have a different style (usually Ionic, then Doric, then Corinthean.) Find examples of each of the styles in books on architecture (see Related Books) or in David Macaulay's other books.

▶ List 10 items or images from **Rome Antic** such as columns or cornices. Sketch them and then find replications of them in local buildings such as town halls, schools and churches.

▶ Take cameras and sketchbooks and take a walk around the center of your nearest town or city. Capture images of the buildings from as many angles as a pigeon would. Compare your images with those of Macaulay.

RELATED BOOKS

NOVELS

Brown, Brian. **Breakout!**
Zondervan, 1996. ISBN 0-310-20213-2 Grades 4-7
A baker rescues a young juggler from the Roman Coliseum.

Doyle, Peter Reese. **Kidnapped in Rome**.
Focus on the Family, 1996. ISBN 1-561-79480-5
Grades 4-8
Three kids in Rome get mixed up with terrorists who are using counterfeit money to frame some government officials.

Goodman, Joan Elizabeth. **Songs from Home**.
Harcourt, 1994. ISBN 0-152-03591-5 Grades 5-8
Anna and her father, Stephen, are street entertainers in Rome. Her mother died when she was a baby, and her father refuses to tell her anything about her mother. When they meet an old family friend, Anna learns the truth about her parents.

Langley, Andrew. **The Roman News**.
Candlewick, 1996. ISBN 0-7636-0055-5 Grades 4-8
This is not truly a novel but a different and interesting look at the facts. Subtitled "The Greatest Newspaper in Civilization," the book offers what would have been headline stories in ancient Rome if newspapers had existed at the time. The articles and headlines present history with a current look.

Spinelli, Jerry. **Wringer**.
HarperCollins, 1997. ISBN 0-06-024913-7
Grades 4-8
This excellent novel is not about Rome, but it is about a pigeon and a boy who risks his standing in the community by befriending it.

NONFICTION

Clare, John D. **Classical Rome: Living History**.
Harcourt, 1993. ISBN 0-152-00513-7
This 64-page book chronicles the development of the Roman Empire from establishment to collapse.

James, Simon **Ancient Rome: Eyewitness Book No. 24** Knopf, 1990. ISBN 0-679-80741-1
Like the other Eyewitness Books, this photo essay offers clear information about the subject, this time with illustrations revealing the inside and outside of a Roman house, theater, fort and baths.

Macaulay, David. **City: A Story of Roman Planning and Construction**. Houghton, 1983.
ISBN 0-395-34922-2
This is an excellent study of Roman civil engineering. One section is devoted to tools and materials, while Macaulay's usual careful drawings show great understanding and appreciation of the principles of architecture.

Watkin, Richard. **Gladiator**.
Houghton, 1997. ISBN 0-395-82656-X
Black and white drawings and well-researched text tell the story of the cruelty and violence of the Colisseum from first combat in 264 to the fully developed games held there.

OTHER BOOKS BY DAVID MACAULAY

City. See above.

Baa. Houghton, 1985. ISBN 0-395-38948-8
This is Macaulay's most didactic and pessimistic book about a civilization of sheep that arises after the last person disappears.

Black and White. Houghton, 1990.
ISBN 0-395-52151-3 See page 138.

Castle. Houghton, 1977. ISBN 0-395-25784-0
One of Macaulay's architectural books, this one details the building of a castle.

Cathedral: The Story of Its Construction.
Houghton, 1973. ISBN 0-395-17513-5
An imaginary cathedral in an imaginary medieval city of France is planned and constructed.

Mill. Houghton, 1983. ISBN 0-395-34830-7
Construction of a spinning mill offers a first-rate history lesson.

Motel of the Mysteries. Houghton, 1979.
ISBN 0-395-28425-2
Another of Macaulay's satiric looks at our civilization, this book imagines the artifacts of our society discovered by archeologists of the future.

Pyramid. Houghton, 1975. ISBN 0-395-21407-6
We are witness to each stage in the conception, planning and construction of a generic pyramid.

Ship. Houghton, 1993. ISBN 0-395-52439-3
A 15th century caravel is discovered and recovered from the depths of the Caribbean, and we go back with Macaulay to its construction in Seville.

Shortcut. Houghton, 1995. ISBN 0-395-52436-9
In an art style similar to that in **Why the Chicken Crossed the Road**, Macaulay ties together disparate events with a slapstick climax.

Unbuilding. Houghton, 1980. ISBN 0-395-29457-6
If they decided to dismantle the Empire State Building, this might be the process. In a process opposite from his building books, Macaulay shows us just as much architecturally.

Underground. Houghton, 1976. ISBN 0-395-24739-X
This time we look at an underground city: its building foundations, subways and sewers.

The Way Things Work. Houghton, 1988. ISBN 0-395-42857-2
The principles of physics, invention and machinery are playfully examined through the actions and reactions of mythical woolly mammoths.

Why the Chicken Crossed the Road. Houghton, 1987. ISBN 0-395-44241-9
A chain of madcap events starts and ends at the same point.

Washing the Willow Tree Loon

by Jacqueline Briggs Martin
Illustrated by Nancy Carpenter
Simon and Schuster, 1995
ISBN 0-689-80415-6

SUMMARY

Oil spills unfortunately occur thousands of times each year. This particular one happened when a barge hit a bridge in Turtle Bay. All the birds in this bay—the diving, floating and swimming birds—were covered with oil. One bird, the willow tree loon, tried to clean herself, but the oil-matted birds need a special kind of treatment. The loon was powerless to help herself. This book follows the rescue of the loon and the effort of many people to rehabilitate it. These generous people made it possible for the loon to live and to swim and fly again. Each step of the rescue is explained clearly and sequentially. From the capture through the cleaning to the release, the book eloquently alerts the reader to the importance of all conservation and its many rewards.

ILLUSTRATION

All of the techniques and technical know-how of an accomplished illustrator can be found in these painterly compositions. The pictures could be used as a handbook for understanding mixed media. Colorful washes, spattered paint and resists are a few of the methods that are at work in these renderings.

CONNECTIONS

NOVEL

A novel that presents human responsibility for the care of the earth is Jean George's **The Talking Earth** (HarperTrophy, 1987. ISBN 0-06-440212-6).

THEMES

▶ Working together
▶ Communities

CURRICULUM CONNECTION

▶ SCIENCE – Pollution and its effects on wildlife

LANGUAGE ARTS

USING SEQUENCE

▶ List the volunteers and their jobs in the rehabilitation process from the capture of the loon to the release. Explain the very special care that must be taken for each task.

▶ Choose a task and interpret each step sequentially.

WRITING

▶ Tell the story from an animal's point of view. Choose one animal to tell the story of the devastation.

EXTENDING THE STORY

▶ Change the story by unfolding the tale so that not only did the first person pass her by, but no one else ever stopped to save the loon.

▶ What could have happened after the artist released the loon and watched her swim away? Where did she go? What happened to her?

▶ Reverse the story as if the oil spill never occurred. Describe the beauty of the bay and the life of the many animals.

INCREASING VOCABULARY

▶ Loons have a haunting cry. Collect tapes of bird sounds or record and collect bird calls of your area. Identify each one. Recall bird similes: proud as a peacock, crazy as a loon. Find other bird similies and create new ones.

▶ Take turns describing each bird call. Are words such as *quack*, *tweet*, *chirp*, *caw* and *peep* necessary?

▶ Loons *swim*, *dive*, *eat* and *preen*. Choose other verbs for various birds and their young.

ATTRIBUTES AND CHARACTERISTICS

▶ Volunteers who catch and treat birds must have hours of training and a permit from the government. List the characteristics of this type of person.

▶ Some volunteers expect a reward, e.g., a model for paintings, an early morning song. What gifts might others expect?

SCIENCE

▶ Research one of the largest oil spills ever to occur. It involved the *Exxon Valdez* in Alaska. Report the story as a newsperson. You may choose to write it as a newspaper article or for a reporter on radio or TV.

▶ Choose an ecosystem (desert, forest or pond) and list the best ways to preserve it. Compare notes with those who worked with other ecosystems and look for similarities and differences.

▶ List all animals found in wetlands under the correct heading: mammal, bird, insect or amphibian. Find out if any are listed as endangered species.

▶ Work with the name waterfowl. Categorize the birds as swimming, diving or floating.

▶ Brainstorm "children-friendly" conservation activities. Classify them into groups: home or school; easy or difficult; materials needed or not; animals involved or not.

▶ Share a copy of **50 Simple Things Kids Can Do to Save the Earth** (see Related Books). Classify the activities. Several groups can choose a category as a project. Decide on how to report on the accomplished work.

▶ All life depends on clean water. Here are four areas where pollution can be mitigated and clean water can emerge. Choose one of these areas and decide on small ways to save our water:

    kitchen, bathroom (household chores)
    garage
    gardening
    recreation

▶ Oil spills occur as the result of the world's demand for oil. Research substitutes for this fuel. How can the world depend less on oil and more on renewable energy? List other energy sources.

▶ Oil spills are not the only cause of pollution to our water. Find out about other dangers to our water, such as junk-filled streams and run-off from agriculture.

▶ Wetlands are pollution filters, protection from storm surges, flood control and wildlife refuges. Find out about other filters.

▶ In the United States there are 90 million acres of land in the National Wildlife Refuge Systems that contain recreational areas and many forms of wildlife. Find these in your area.

▶ Many newspapers publish recent bird sightings as reported to the Audubon Society. Check your own newspaper or call the Audubon Society environmental help line in your state.

RELATED BOOKS

NOVELS

George, Jean Craighead. **The Talking Earth**.
HarperTrophy, 1987. ISBN 0-06-440212-6
Grades 4–9
Billie is sent into the Everglades by the Seminole elders to commune with the animals and listen to the earth's message.

George, Jean Craighead. **Who Really Killed Cock Robin? An Ecological Mystery**. HarperCollins, 1991. ISBN 0-06-021890-7 Grades 3-6
Here is an ecological mystery with a message: people and nature must be kept in balance.

PICTURE BOOKS

Brown, Ruth. **The World That Jack Built**.
Dutton, 1991. ISBN 0-525-44635-4
This is a cumulative tale that presents an ecological disaster. The inevitable climax is powerful.

Christian, Mary Blount. **The Mystery of the Polluted Stream**. Illustrated by Joe Boddy. Milliken, 1991.
ISBN 0-88335-2907
The Sherlock Street kids find more than tadpoles for their class project. They find a polluted stream that calls for an investigation.

Fleming, Denise. **In the Small, Small Pond**.
Holt, 1993. ISBN 0-8050-2264-3
This book captures the activity of the inhabitants of a small pond. The birds are beautifully illustrated.

Sharpe, Susan. **Trouble at Marsh Harbor**.
Puffin, 1991. ISBN 0-14 034788-7
There is pollution in the bay. Ben works to find the source of the oil leak.

Turner, Ann. **Heron Street**.
Illustrated by Lisa Desimini. Harper, 1989.
ISBN 0-06-026185-4
Many animals live in the marsh by the sea. Little by little "civilization" takes over and only a patch of grass remains.

NONFICTION

Earth Works Group. **50 Simple Things Kids Can Do to Save the Earth**. Andrews & McNeel, 1990.
ISBN 0-8362-2301-2
This is an excellent list of hands-on activities suitable for children and adults and all "do-able."

Goldin, Augusta. **Ducks Don't Get Wet**.
Illustrated by Leonard Kessler. HarperTrophy, 1993. ISBN 0-06-445082-1
This is a great explanation about why ducks really don't get wet.

Hirschi, Ron. **Where Are My Swans, Whooping Cranes, and Singing Loons?** Bantam, 1992.
ISBN 0-553-35470-1
Readers are able to explore the wetlands of our country. Because of the frailties of the ecosystem, everyone must strive to protect all species.

Keene, Ann T. **Earthkeepers: Observers and Protectors of Nature**. Oxford University Press, 1994. ISBN 0-19-507867-5
This is a collection of portraits and contributions of environmentalists and naturalists. Also included are essays, classifications, glossary, suggested further readings, lists of conservation groups and related topics.

Taylor, Dave. **Endangered Wetland Animals**.
Crabtree, 1991. ISBN 0-86505-530-0
This is part of the Endangered Animal Series. Photographs depict the pollution that is endangering much of our wildlife.

OTHER BOOKS BY JACQUELINE B. MARTIN

Bizzy Bones and the Last Quilt. Illustrated by Stella Ormai. Lothrop, 1988. ISBN 0-688-07407-3
Bizzy lost his beloved quilt. Uncle Ezra and the orchard mice help him start a new one.

Bizzy Bones and Mooremouse. Lothrop, 1986.
ISBN 0-688-05745-4
Bizzy the mouse must stay with Mooremouse while his uncle is away. His uncle doesn't seem so bad when he rescues Bizzy.

Bizzy Bones and Uncle Ezra. Lothrop, 1984.
ISBN 0-688-03781-X
Bizzy is afraid of the wind until Uncle Ezra builds a merry-go-round turned by the wind.

Good Times on Grandfather Mountain. SRA, 1994.
ISBN 0-531-05977-4
Farmer Washburn always makes the best of everything (even when his barn blows down and all his animals run away). In the end they all return.

The Mountain That Loved a Bird

by Alice McLerran
Illustrated by Eric Carle
Simon and Schuster, 1985
ISBN 0-88708-000-6

▶ SUMMARY

A beautiful bird brings life to a lonely, barren mountain after making a pledge to the mountain to return yearly and to send generations of daughters to visit the mountain. Over the years, the barren mountain is transformed into a lush paradise that attracts wildlife, making the once-lonely mountain happy.

▶ ILLUSTRATION

Eric Carle continues to have fun with paint, paper and scissors. His creation of colorful and imaginatively textured papers forms the basis of these pictures. The rearrangement and juxtapositioning of these rich surfaces result in a type of collage that is free of ordinary imagery. For this reason the illustrations have an appeal for children and for adults. The pictures reveal a kinship with children's creative thinking.

▶ CONNECTIONS

NOVEL

In Paul Fleischman's **Seedfolks** (HarperCollins, 1997. ISBN 0-06-027471-9) a child plants a seed amongst the trash in a city lot which precipitates a whole community's involvement in a garden.

THEMES

▶ Need for love and nurturing
▶ Seeds

CURRICULUM CONNECTION

▶ SCIENCE – Ecosystems, requirements for life

LANGUAGE ARTS

COMPARING LITERATURE

▶ Read **Heron Street** by Ann Turner (see page 220). Compare and contrast the two stories. Then write a sequel to **The Mountain That Loved a Bird**. Now that the mountain is no longer barren, will it attract humans? If so, will the animals who have taken up residence there stay? How will the natural balance of the mountain be affected?

▶ Compare this story to Shel Silverstein's **The Giving Tree** (see Related Books). Who benefits in each story?

▶ Find other stories based upon promises made. Start with **Miss Rumphius** (see Related Books) by Barbara Cooney or try Dick Gackenback's **McGoogan Moves the Mighty Rock**.

▶ Compare this book to **The Gardener** by Sarah Stewart, illustrated by David Small (Farrar, 1997. ISBN 0-374-32517-0), in which a little girl transforms a rooftop into a lush garden.

▶ Transport the girl from **The Gardener** (see above) to the barren mountain. Retell the story of the **Mountain That Loved a Bird** through a series of letters, either from the mountain or the girl.

WRITING

▶ Retell this story from the perspective of the mountain or of the bird. How might the tone of the story differ if told from the mountain's point of view?

SCIENCE

▶ Investigate the migration of birds. Find out if it would be likely that a bird would stop at the same place on two consecutive migrations.

▶ Follow the migration of birds from your area. Map their routes and identify mountain ranges they may encounter. Which of them might be barren? Are there any high enough to go above the tree line?

▶ The bird says that she will not live very long. Learn about the life span of some common birds in your area.

▶ Find out what stages a barren mountain might really go through in becoming fertile. Could this really happen? What conditions would be necessary?

▶ Look at a different type of habitat, such as a field or pasture. What stages does a pasture go through in becoming a forest? Look at some fields to determine their current stage.

ART

▶ Try painting some paper with different colors and textures. Then cut and paste to create some illustrations like Eric Carle's.

▶ Find an area in your town that is relatively barren. Plan ways of beautifying it.

RELATED BOOKS

NOVEL

Fleischman, Paul. **Seedfolks**.
HarperCollins, 1997. ISBN 0-06-027471-9
Grades 3-9
A garden started when a little girl plants a seed in an empty lot brings a whole community of strangers together.

PICTURE BOOKS

Anno, Mitsumasa. **Anno's Magic Seeds**.
Philomel, 1995. ISBN 0-399-22538-2
The accent here is on math; one seed planted becomes many seeds.

Cooney, Barbara. **Miss Rumphius**.
Penguin USA, 1982. ISBN 0-670-47958-6
Young Alice promises her grandfather to do three things: She will travel to faraway places, live by the sea when she grows old and do something to make the world a more beautiful place.

Garland, Sherry. **The Lotus Seed**.
Harcourt, 1993. ISBN 0-15-249465-0
A young Vietnamese woman sees the Emperor leave the throne and decides to keep a small piece of the beauty that was there by taking a seed from the lotus pool.

Silverstein, Shel. **The Giving Tree**.
HarperCollins, 1986. ISBN 0-06-025665-6
This sentimental story centers around the love between a tree and a boy.

Turner, Ann. **Heron Street** See page 220.

Watson, Mary. **The Butterfly Seeds**.
Morrow, 1995. ISBN 0-688-14132-3
Residents of the tenement help Jake plant the seeds his grandfather gave him in the old country.

The Orphan Boy

by Tololwa M. Mollel
Illustrated by Paul Morin
Houghton Clarion, 1990
ISBN 0-899-19985-3

SUMMARY

In this Maasai (Masai) legend, an orphan boy brings luck and love to an old man shortly after a star disappears from the sky. The man's insatiable curiosity about the boy's mysterious powers causes him to violate the trust, whereupon the boy disappears, as well as the magic he brought. An afterword tells us that the boy/star is the planet Venus.

ILLUSTRATION

Each illustration, whether one or two pages in size, is a separate composition on canvas. The paint application process captures a variety of textures including the texture of the canvas. Simple sketches, principally line drawings, fill out the spaces where the text appears. In both the full- color illustrations and the black and white drawings, an outlined shape similar to a hand-made blanket hangs on the page. At the base of these blanket shapes is a border design that simulates the craft of woven beads. Native crafts are also evident in the batik-dyed hand prints, which are located inside both the front and back covers.

CONNECTIONS

NOVEL

Mary Riskind's **Apple Is My Sign** (Houghton, 1981. ISBN 0-395-65747-4) also involves trust and the betrayal of trust, although the setting is very different.

THEME

▶ Trust and the betrayal of trust

CURRICULUM CONNECTION

▶ GEOGRAPHY – Masai and nomadic cultures

LANGUAGE ARTS

WRITING

▶ Before reading the text, look carefully at one illustration such as the one where the land returned from lush to barren. List words and phrases to describe what you would see, feel, hear and smell. Use that information to write a more formal descriptive paragraph about the setting. Compare your paragraphs to the ones in the book. Do the same with a different page.

EXTENDING VOCABULARY

▶ The boy's name means Venus. Does your name have a meaning? Where does it come from?

FINDING DETAILS

▶ What clues does the author give you that tell you who the boy really is?

COMPARING LITERATURE

▶ Compare this character to the star child in **Star Mother's Youngest Child** (see Related Books).

▶ Find other stories where the point is that you don't know when you're well off, such as "The Fisherman's Wife" and "The Elephant's Child." Was there a time when you blew it because you didn't know when you were well off?

EXTENDING THE STORY

▶ The author says, "A secret known to two is no secret." Keeping a secret is never easy. Play a game where a person has a secret and the others try to uncover it through single yes or no questions.

▶ Another statement about this story might be "Curiosity killed the cat." What does that expression mean and how does it apply to this story? Find other examples in literature or life that demonstrate it.

INTERPRETING THE TEXT

▶ Look for the sections that describe the environment. Try to use the same techniques to describe an environment totally different from those in the book.

SCIENCE

▶ Locate Venus in the morning or evening sky. Could the author have used another planet or star for the character in the book? How would the story have changed if he had used Jupiter?

▶ Sketch where Venus is in the morning, using landmarks and other things in the sky to get your bearings. Sketch it again at night.

▶ Find out the origin of the planet names.

▶ Why does the planet neither flicker nor twinkle? Why do stars?

▶ Why does Venus appear in one sky at dawn and a different part at night?

▶ Compare the weather patterns in this part of Africa with the climate in your area. Are the seasons the same?

SOCIAL STUDIES

▶ Locate the scene of this story on a map of Africa.

▶ Read the book **Olbalbal** listed below to find out some of the difficulties of today's Masai life. Are these problems similar to those of any other people in the world? How can some of their problems be solved? What problems will those solutions create?

▶ We know, according to this book, that Masai raise cattle. Look for signs that show the way the Masai use the cattle. What else is essential for the way they live?

▶ Compare the clothing with the environment.

▶ Could any of these illustrations have come from where you live?

▶ In various illustrations, we get glimpses of the old man's home. Put them together to describe the house.

▶ The Masai live a nomadic life. Find out about other nomadic people in the world today. Don't forget migrant workers.

ART

▶ The texture in these illustrations is apparent. Find ways to show texture in your artwork. Try using sand, rough material, thick paint and other techniques. Try sand painting. Mix textures together for that effect.

▶ Compare these illustrations with those by the Dillons in **Ashanti to Zulu** (see Related Books).

▶ The border on each page is unique. Does it represent anything in the Masai culture? It appears to be beadwork. Try some beadwork yourself or sketch a pattern for it.

▶ Try duplicating the designs in this book with finger weaving using embroidery floss.

▶ Some of the illustrations are portraits. Look at other portraiture in books or art museums. What does a painted portrait do that a camera does not?

▶ Look at the jewelry in this book and find ways to make or design your own jewelry.

▶ RELATED BOOKS

NOVEL

Riskind, Mary. **Apple Is My Sign**.
Houghton, 1981. ISBN 0-395-65747-4 Grades 3-8
This novel also involves trust and the betrayal of trust. A boy returns to his parents' apple farm after his first term away from home at a school for the deaf.

PICTURE BOOKS

Aardema, Verna. **Bringing the Rain to Kapiti Plain**.
Puffin, 1983. ISBN 0-8037-0804-8
This rhythmic retelling of an African myth shows how another boy brought an end to a drought.

Musgrove, Margaret. **Ashanti to Zulu**.
Puffin, 1980. ISBN 0-8037-0308-2
This alphabet book reveals a great deal of information, both visually and textually, about cultures of Africa.

Moeri, Louise. **Star Mother's Youngest Child**.
Houghton, 1980. ISBN 0-395-21406-8
A lonely old woman and a star child make Christmas together.

DePaola, Tomie. **Legend of the Bluebonnet**.
Putnam, 1993. ISBN 0-399-22441-6
A Native American girl sacrifices her beloved doll to bring an end to the drought.

Grifalconi, Ann. **The Village of Round and Square Houses** See page 77.

Steptoe, John. **Mufaro's Beautiful Daughters**.
Lothrop, 1987. ISBN 0-688-04045-4
This is an African folktale in which a young king searches for a suitable wife.

NONFICTION

Margolies, Barbara. **Olbalbal: a Day in Maasailand**.
Four Winds, 1994. ISBN 0-02-762284-3
The accent here is on the dilemma of the semi-nomadic Masai, who want to cling to some of the old ways while adopting some of the new. Unfortunately, the stance is a difficult one.

Shachtman, Tom. **Growing Up Masai**.
Simon & Schuster, 1981. ISBN 0-02-782550-7
We experience the life of a Masai through the eyes of two Masai children.

Simon, Seymour. **Venus**.
Morrow, 1992. ISBN 0-688-10542-4
This is an excellent photographic and textual exploration of the planet. The information is concise and complete, and the photography is breathtaking.

Tucker Pfeffercorn

An old story retold by Barry Moser
Little, Brown, 1994
ISBN 0-316-58542-4

⚑ SUMMARY

This book is a humorous variant of the classic Rumplestiltskin tale. In a southern mining town Jefferson Tadlock spins a wild tale "to a bunch of miners," alleging that Bessie Grace Kinzalow could spin cotton into gold. The meanest and richest man in town overhears this wild story and seizes the 19-year-old widow Bessie and her baby daughter Claretta. Locked in a shed full of cotton, she knows she cannot spin it into gold. As expected, a nasty little man appears and seems to be able to help her. How Bessie outwits this nasty little man is familiar but still amusing. Southern flavor and vocabulary enhance the tone. The mystery of the disappearance of the old meany, Hezakiah Sweatt, adds a new twist.

⚑ ILLUSTRATION

These are beautifully crafted watercolors. While they are paintings, they have the nuances of graphic design.

⚑ CONNECTIONS

NOVEL

Ella Enchanted by Gail Carson Levine (HarperCollins, 1997. ISBN 0-06-027510-3) is a novel based on the fairy tale of Cinderella.

THEME

▶ Fairy tale extensions and updates

CURRICULUM CONNECTION

▶ SOCIAL STUDIES – Coal mining, organized labor issues, Appalachia

LANGUAGE ARTS

FIGURATIVE LANGUAGE

▶ Look for creative phrases, for example, "Lord o' Mercy," "my hind foot." Find other terms people use to express their feelings. Create some new expressions for surprise, sarcasm and horror.

▶ Write a paragraph in the style of the author explaining the fate of the nasty little man, Tucker Pfeffercorn. Experiment with the author's colloquial (informal) style. (Grammatical inaccuracies accepted!)

▶ Compose a letter to little Claretta to be read when she is grown. Explain the situation in which she and her mother found themselves. Speak of the courage of her mother.

EXTENDING THE BOOK

▶ Class groups of three or four students can work together to decide what happened to Hezekiah Sweatt, who "never came back," and write a news report to explain his disappearance. The report could be mystery, science fiction, romance, adventure or horror. The class chooses the best effort.

▶ Bessie Grace lived happily ever after in Cincinnati. Begin a new chapter in her life. Why was she happy? Did she miss her old home? Did she remarry? Include a section about Claretta.

VOCABULARY DEVELOPMENT

▶ The conversations here are rife with variations on words: *if'n* for *if*, *yore* for *your*, *git* for *get*, *chile* for *child*. Find other examples of this style of speaking.

▶ Speculate on why Bessie Grace is the only one who does not speak in a dialect. Are any words definitely regional?

PREDICTING

▶ There would be repercussions if Bessie had not overheard the little man's name. Could she have stopped him from taking Claretta? Did she have any support in the community? Predict some options.

▶ What would have happened if Hezakiah Sweatt had returned? How would Bessie be affected? List some possible outcomes.

COMPARING LITERATURE

▶ Begin a classroom collection of Rumplestiltskin variants.

▶ Decide how **Tucker Pfeffercorn** compares to the original as to characters, setting, refrains and chants, illustrations, exceptional vocabulary. Be sure to include similarities as well as differences.

▶ Research other tales that include verses and refrains essential to the story, such as "The Fisherman and His Wife" and "The Magic Pot."

EXAMINING ILLUSTRATIONS

▶ No one is smiling (except for some smirking by the little man). Why did the artist (author) portray all of them this way?

▶ Everyone is wearing a hat except the little man, baby and one other person. Study the hats. Do they add to the flavor of the book?

▶ Find the dark picture of Bessie Grace's house. Does it help explain her move away from the area?

▶ Except for the prices of the company store, there is not much to identify the time period. Why? Could the clothing illustrations be timeless? (The little man has a neat denim jacket.)

EXTENDING VOCABULARY

▶ Many characters have unusual names. Some are identified by roles or character, as well:

   Hashel Birdsong - hobo
   Hezekiah Sweatt - owner, richest, meanest
   Bessie Grace Kinzalow - widow woman

Decide on a title for a few people not given a specific role.

▶ Find the names that Bessie Grace tried and discarded. List the names she guessed for the nasty little man. Create some other names for him.

▶ Begin a collection of unusual names. Peruse phone books, newspapers and magazines. Do the same with nicknames.

▶ Decide if various names are affiliated with certain areas of our country, ethnic groups or physical attributes. List them.

▶ Speculate as to why the name Snow Ball was given to the 24-pound bag of self-rising flour in the company store. Find some flour names in the local market.

Social Studies

▶ Find the Appalachian Mountains on a map of the United States. Locate the west slope from southwest New York through western Pennsylvania into West Virginia, Kentucky and Tennessee. This is coal country where the majority of America's coal fields are located.

▶ Bessie Grace moved to Cincinnati. Find it on the map. Did she move very far from home? Approximate where she lived and estimate how many miles to her new home.

▶ Research life in an early mining town. Define a company town and the power of the mine owner. Have the conditions changed very much?

▶ Find out about men digging coal from deep in the earth to earn a living today. Investigate the health problems of miners.

▶ Examine facts about poverty in the area. What is the cause of most of it?

▶ Find out about church and charitable groups who work with the poor in the Appalachian areas.

RELATED BOOKS

NOVEL

Levine, Carson. **Ella Enchanted**.
HarperCollins, 1997. ISBN 0-06-027510-3
Grades 3-7
This is a full-length novel based on the fairy tale of Cinderella.

PICTURE BOOKS

Zemach, Harve & Margot. **Duffy and the Devil**.
Farrar, 1973. ISBN 0-374-318875
Duffy is the servant girl in this Cornish version of Rumplestiltskin. This Caldecott Medal winner contains bright and cheerful illustrations.

Zelinsky, Paul O. **Rumplestiltskin**.
Dial, 1986. ISBN 0-525-442650
This version is placed in a medieval setting. The illustrations resemble oil paintings.

Hendershot, Judith. **In Coal Country**.
Illustrated by Thomas B. Allen. Dragonfly-Knopf, 1987. ISBN 0-679-83479-6
Here is an authentic picture of coal country and the life of a miner and his family.

Ness, Evaline. **Tom Tit Tot**. Scribner, 1965.
In this version illustrated with woodcuts, a young girl cannot guess the name of the creature.

Dog Breath

by Dav Pilkey
Scholastic, 1994
ISBN 0-590-69818-4

▶ SUMMARY

The Tosis family love their dog, Hally. The only difficulty is the poor dog's breath. Since the family wishes to keep Hally, they attempt all sorts of ways (many involving puns and other word plays) to rid the dog of that awful breath. Hally manages to save the day, and the family finds a reasonable solution to the problem. The text is full of humor and idioms, puns and word plays, making it a silly and funny book to read.

▶ ILLUSTRATION

The cartoon format of these illustrations supports the text's wry humor. Clear and uncomplicated visual images of the Tosis family and their dog, Hally, mirror the book's message. Bright uncomplicated colors fill every page.

▶ CONNECTIONS

NOVEL

The dog in Zachary Ball's **Bristle Face** (Holiday, 1962. ISBN 0-8234-0915-5) is physically objectionable and yet becomes a hero.

THEME

▶ Eccentric and oddball characters

CURRICULUM CONNECTION

▶ LANGUAGE ARTS – Word play

LANGUAGE ARTS

VOCABULARY DEVELOPMENT

▶ Search the book for idioms. List these on chart paper along with their figurative meanings. Add to this list as other idioms appear in conversations and in other books shared in class.

▶ The name Hally, given the family's last name, certainly fits the dog in this book. What other annoying traits might dogs have and what might be appropriate names for dogs with those traits?

▶ Ask students to interview parents and older relatives to gather some expressions that they used or that they used to hear. Present them to the class to see if classmates can determine their meaning. Or consider providing students with some expressions (such as "the cat's meow") and ask them to try to determine their meanings by interviewing older family members.

▶ Generate lists of words that sound the same but are spelled differently. Think of "tricks" to help you remember the spelling and meaning of each pair.

WRITING

▶ Write advice to the Tosis family on new ways to help them deal with Hally's breath.

▶ Note the newspaper titles and headlines in the illustrations. Generate other alliterative headlines and newspaper names about the story.

▶ Use riddle books (see Related Books) to make a riddle board. Fold construction paper in half. Cut unusual and interesting shapes out of the paper, taking care not to cut the fold. Print a riddle question on the cover of the folded paper and print the answer on the inside. Try your hand at making up your own riddles. Consider hanging these in the hallway so others in your school can get a good laugh! Be sure to change your riddle board frequently. Take a close look at those riddles. What about them makes them funny? Can students identify those with puns and those with idioms?

▶ This book uses exaggeration. Try creating some exaggerations. Have students write the start of a sentence (He was so tall that...) on small slips of paper. Put these into a hat. Students draw out a slip and finish the sentence to create their mini-tall tale.

COMPARING LITERATURE

▶ Fred Gwynne's books (see Related Books) explore idiomatic, homophonic and homographic language. Share these books with the class. Ask each student to listen carefully for something someone says that could mean something totally different. Have them illustrate the phrase heard to show the way the speaker intended it and what else it could mean.

SOCIAL STUDIES

▶ Investigate real-life pets that save the day or perform heroic deeds.

SCIENCE

▶ Find out from a vet what causes bad breath in dogs and what can be done about it.

▶ Do people get bad breath? Why? Are the causes for bad breath the same for people and for dogs? Take a look at ads that sell products to improve people's breath. Do these products really work? Why or why not?

RELATED BOOKS

NOVEL

Ball, Zachary. **Bristle Face**.
Holiday, 1962. ISBN 0-8234-0915-5 Grades 4-8
The boy's dog is physically objectionable and yet becomes a hero.

PICTURE BOOKS

Gwynne, Fred. **The King Who Rained**.
Aladdin, 1988. ISBN 0-671-66744-0
A Chocolate Moose for Dinner. Aladdin, 1987.
ISBN 0-671-66741-6
A Little Pigeon Toed. Aladdin, 1990.
ISBN 0-671-69444-8
This series uses humor to look at word play in our language by illustrating homonyms literally.

Parish, Peggy. **Amelia Bedelia**.
HarperCollins, 1992. ISBN 0-06-020187-8
Amelia Bedelia's Family Album. Morrow, 1988.
ISBN 0-688-07677-7
Amelia Bedelia Goes Camping. Morrow, 1985.
ISBN 0-688-04057-8
Amelia Bedelia Helps Out. Morrow, 1979.
ISBN 0-688-80231-1
Teach Us, Amelia Bedelia. Morrow, 1987.
ISBN 0-688-80069-6
Thank You, Amelia Bedelia. HarperCollins, 1983.
ISBN 0-06-022980-2
This series concerns a woman who has an interesting interpretation of some very simple expressions and idioms. The results are always amusing.

Wood, Audrey. **Quick as a Cricket**.
Child's Play, 1989. ISBN 0-85953151
This book is a rhyming exploration of similes.

POETRY

Merriam, Eve. **Chortles: New & Selected Wordplay Poems**. Morrow, 1989. ISBN 0-688-08152-5
This book of poems about word play has alliteration, puns and a good deal more!

Aunt Chip & the Great Triple Creek Dam Affair

by Patricia Polacco
Philomel, 1996
ISBN 0-399-22943-4

SUMMARY

Everyone in Triple Creek loves television except for Eli's Aunt Chip, who doesn't even own one. Not only do all the others love television, but they love it so much that the people of the town have closed the local library and forgotten how to read. Eli's Aunt Chip has taken to bed in protest to this situation, and hasn't gotten up in the last 50 years. When she becomes aware that the folks of the town have forgotten how to read, she decides it's time she got up to do something about it!

ILLUSTRATION

Polacco manages to pack each page full of images. The compositions are of mixed media. Superimposed over various media are wonderfully drawn line details. In some cases they help complete the portraits. In other instances, they outline the many objects.

CONNECTIONS

NOVEL

Although **The Sign of the Beaver** (Houghton, 1983. ISBN 0-440-47900-2) has a different focus, the ability to read is given paramount importance by one of the characters. He knows what his grandson will need in order to survive in the new culture that is coming.

THEMES

▶ Need for reading
▶ Libraries

CURRICULUM CONNECTION

▶ SOCIAL STUDIES – Literate societies, effects of television on society

LANGUAGE ARTS

CATEGORIZING

▶ Create a chart listing all the ways the folks of Triple Creek are using books. Contrast it with another list generated by students of ways in which they use books at home and in school.

WRITING

▶ The citizens of Triple Creek have forgotten how to read. What things are they unable to do because they lack this skill? List all the places we find printed words. Write arguments to persuade the folks of this town that they should learn to read. Create posters to display around Triple Creek to persuade them.

DEBATING

▶ Stage a debate in your classroom. One team can present the argument for watching more television and the other for spending more time reading.

AUTHORS AND ILLUSTRATORS

▶ Find the authors listed in the text. What books did they write? What was the first book your students remember being able to read? What authors do they enjoy now?

▶ Read other books by Patricia Polacco. Can you find similar characters? What can you learn about the author's life from her stories?

▶ Read *The Bee Tree* (see Related Books). Have students write in their reading logs why these two books make good companions.

▶ Read the dedication on the very last page. Who is the person Polacco mentions besides her mother? Find out why she would have chosen Charlotte Huck? Write letters of gratitude to librarians in your school and community.

EXTENDING THE TEXT

▶ The author's postscript tells us that now that people in the town were now reading, Eli returned to Triple Creek to establish a newspaper that he called the *Triple Creek Herald Consequence*. Discuss why he may have chosen that title. Examine the names of your local newspapers.

▶ Look closely at the photographs in the last illustration. Compare them to characters in the book.

Read the author's dedication. What assumptions or predictions can you make? Could this story have been based on real people and events in the author's life?

SOCIAL STUDIES

▶ Investigate literacy in our country. How many adults and children are unable to read? Is this a social problem? What is being done about it? What adult literacy programs are available in your community?

▶ Research the history of television. What other "modern conveniences" were introduced at about the same time? Create a time line of the introduction of these modern conveniences.

▶ Learn about the history of your local library. Find out when it was opened, who was responsible, how it is supported.

▶ The text tells us that Aunt Chip took to her bed well over 50 years ago. Generate a list of things that could have changed in Triple Creek over those 50 years. Research your own community to determine what it was like 50 years ago and how it has changed.

▶ Interview grandparents or older friends and neighbors to find out how your neighborhood was different 50 years ago. Illustrate a "Then and Now" picture to depict what you have learned.

MATH

▶ Have each student chart time spent each week watching television and reading. Combine the data of the whole class into a graph. Graph results on a weekly basis to compare the amount of time your students spend reading to the time spent watching television. Invite students to sign contracts to increase reading time at home.

ART

▶ Examine the variety of techniques used in the illustrations. Find other illustrators who use multiple techniques. Compare. Try your hand at creating an illustration that involves several different techniques such as collage, watercolor, and pen and ink.

RELATED BOOKS

NOVELS

Speare, Elizabeth George. **Sign of the Beaver**.
Houghton, 1983. ISBN 0-440-47900-2 Grades 3-8
Matt is badly injured and stranded without food in a cabin in colonial Maine when Saknis, an Indian grandfather, rescues him. A bargain is struck; Saknis will continue to help Matt if he will teach his grandson to read.

PICTURE BOOKS

Bunting, Eve. **The Wednesday Surprise**.
Clarion, 1989. ISBN 0-395-54776-8
Grandma and Anna have a secret about books and Dad's birthday present. It isn't until the birthday that we realize that Anna has been teaching Grandma to read.

Breathed, Berkeley. **Goodnight, Opus**.
See page 34.

Heide, Florence. **Day of Ahmed's Secret**.
Mulberry, 1990. ISBN 0-688-14023-8
We watch a young boy navigate the streets of Cairo with a secret in his pocket that shows he can now write.

Thompson, Colin. **How to Live Forever**.
Knopf, 1995. ISBN 0-679-87898-X
The secret of immortality can seemingly be found on the library shelves. See page 214.

Van Allsburg, Chris. **The Wretched Stone**.
Houghton, 1995. ISBN 0-395-53307-4
The discovery of the strange, glowing stone attracts all of the ship's crew except the captain, who becomes increasingly distraught over his men's obsession. His men are no longer working and have stopped reading and story-telling in their spare time.

Williams, Suzanne. **Library Lil**.
Illustrated by Steven Kellogg. Dial, 1997.
ISBN 0-8037-1698-2
Like Aunt Chip, super tall-tale librarian Lil is exasperated when her town fails to read and chooses to watch TV instead. Unlike Chip, however, Lil takes to the streets, not her bed.

OTHER BOOKS BY PATRICIA POLACCO

The Keeping Quilt See page 163.

Thunder Cake. Putnam, 1990. ISBN 0-399-22231-6
A Russian grandmother helps her young granddaughter overcome her fear of thunder while preparing the title recipe during a storm.

The Bee Tree. Putnam, 1993. ISBN 0-399-21965-X
Grandpa has a remedy to help Mary Ellen when she tires of reading.

Pink and Say See page 167.

The Keeping Quilt

by Patricia Polacco
Simon & Schuster, 1988
ISBN 0-671-64963-9

SUMMARY

A Russian immigrant mother and family arrive in the United States. She plans to make a quilt from a basket of old clothes, telling her daughter, "It will be like having the family back home in Russia dance around us at night." The quilt is passed along from mother to daughter for four generations. It becomes a Sabbath tablecloth and a wedding canopy. When it becomes a blanket for new generations of children, it tells a family's story of love, faith and endurance. This account of the author's family could be the story of many others.

ILLUSTRATION

Sepia-colored figures are carefully drawn on textured off-white paper stock. The effect is one of recollection, or perhaps of fading diary pages. When color is used, it serves to highlight or focus on the fabric worn by the central character and, more centrally, on the quilt itself. The texture produced by conte crayon pencil on rough-surfaced paper replicates the feeling of fabrics. A variety of smooth and coarse textures as well as prints and patterned fabrics can be identified in these illustrations.

Most of the compositions are contained on single pages. The exceptions are double-page spreads that serve to highlight the story's theme. Since the shape of the book is rectangular and it is bound horizontally, the double-page illustration showing the large gathering of quilters captures the spirit of cooperation. When seen together, these caricatures, colors and quilts produce the feeling of comfort associated with folk art.

CONNECTIONS

NOVEL

In Katherine Laskey's **Night Journey** (Puffin, 1986. ISBN 0-14-32048-2), it's a samovar that is handed down through the family.

THEME

▶ Family customs and traditions

CURRICULUM CONNECTION

▶ SOCIAL STUDIES – Immigration

LANGUAGE ARTS

RECALLING DETAILS

▶ List the materials (old clothes) used to make the quilt. Match them up with the people they belonged to.

▶ Besides the obvious uses for the quilt, what unique things did it become for this family over the years?

▶ What were the traditional gifts given on special occasions and what did they signify? How do they compare to the gifts in your family?

▶ From memory, draw a small replica of the quilt. Explain the designs and their origins.

USING SEQUENCE

▶ Recall the names of the family members in generational order.

ESTABLISHING CAUSE AND EFFECT

▶ What things in the story would have changed if:
  Anna's family had not emigrated to the United States?
  The family had not stayed in New York?
  Anna had not learned to speak English?
  The family had returned to Russia?

BUILDING VOCABULARY

▶ Reread the book and find the foreign words: *babuska, challah, huppa, kulich*. Which ones are translated for us and which ones can we figure out the meaning from context?

CONTRASTING AND COMPARING

▶ Find the many traditions portrayed throughout the book. Compare the early ones with the modern ones. Which ones continued through the generations? Which ones changed? Make lists to show your findings.

WRITING

▶ Compose a letter from Anna to friends back in Russia written as she arrives in New York. Describe the scene of her arrival and her first home.

▶ Change the letter to one from Anna after the birth of her daughter Carle. Include the changes in her life.

AUTHOR STUDY

▶ Patricia Polacco often uses events in her life as inspiration for her books. Look through some of her books to see what you can tell about Ms. Polacco from her writing. What things does she think are important? Which of those do you share? You might like to write her a letter telling her about some of your family's traditions.

SOCIAL STUDIES

IMMIGRATION

▶ The Statue of Liberty is shown on the title page of the book. Find and read the sonnet "The New Colossus," some of which is inscribed on the statue. Why do you think those lines were chosen? Are immigrants still encouraged to come here?

▶ Find Ellis Island on the map and think about the 20 million or more people who came through that station. What things in America would be different today without them?

▶ Investigate your classroom's heritage. Make charts, maps and graphs to show where the different families originated. Put immigration dates into your graphics if possible.

▶ Why did they come? Various large immigrations to the United States were caused by specific factors. Find out about those and then look again at the activity above. Which of those immigrants were part of the large groups of immigrations?

HISTORY

▶ Create a family tree for Anna's family and then one for your own.

▶ Examine the clothing used throughout the book. How do the illustrations help to depict each era?

ECONOMICS

▶ Anna's family had been dirt farmers in Russia. Does that mean they raised dirt? What employment did they find in New York? Were they richer or poorer in each succeeding generation?

▶ What jobs are available for new immigrants in your area? Are they available for non-English-speaking people as well as for those who do speak that language? What help is available for new immigrants? Who provides those services?

MAPS

▶ Plot a likely route taken by Anna's ship from Russia to the United States.

MATH

GRAPHS

▶ Design a bar graph to show the number of ethnic backgrounds in the class.

ESTIMATION

▶ Estimate the time in years from the day Anna came to America up to the birth of Traci Denise.

▶ Make a time line and estimate the approximate year for each significant event in the story.

▶ Quilting is usually done using squares as the basic pattern. On paper squares, divide up the space to make interesting patterns when squares are put together.

ART

▶ A good fund-raiser for a class is the creation of a quilt to be raffled or auctioned off.

▶ You'll need to do a lot of research first about quilts. Quilt squares are the easiest to put together and will allow each person in the class to contribute.

▶ Class quilts can be simple or elaborate. It might be fun to have each person in the class design one square for a quilt. Quilting takes careful planning. Remember, the designs on it will have to be possible to recreate in cloth. Have someone who knows a lot about quilting talk to the class before, during, and after the designs are created. Children may be able to translate their own squares into cloth. If not, parents may be able or willing to help. Piecing the quilt will take some expertise, but children can do most of that stitching with guidance. Whether you tie or sew the quilt to its backing is a matter of the amount of time, skill, equipment and expertise available. Don't forget grandparents in the quest for quilt know-how. Parent groups may be available to run the actual raffle or it can become a total class activity.

▶ Arrange a quilt display in the classroom with paper designs for quilts as well as real quilts.

RELATED BOOKS

NOVEL

Lasky, Katherine. **Night Journey**. Puffin, 1986. ISBN 0-14-32048-2 Grades 3-8
A young girl learns of her family's heritage from her bedridden great grandmother.

PICTURE BOOKS

Bolton, Janet. **My Grandmother's Patchwork Quilt: A Book and Pocketful of Patchwork Pieces**. Doubleday, 1994. ISBN 0-385-3115-9
This book combines some information about quilt-making with the story of one quilt, presented to the author by her grandmother.

Coerr, Eleanor. **The Josefina Story Quilt**.
Illustrated by Bruce Degen. HarperCollins, 1986. ISBN 0-06-444129-6
A young girl traveling west with her pioneer family makes a patchwork quilt of the experiences of the trip.

Ernst, Lisa C. **Sam Johnson and the Blue Ribbon Quilt**. Lothrop, 1983. ISBN 0-688-01516-6
It isn't only women who can quilt. Sam Johnson gets the men involved in their own quilt-making activities.

Flournoy, Valerie. **The Patchwork Quilt**.
Dial, 1985. ISBN 0-8037-0098-9
Tanya learns about the quilt from her grandmother and, in so doing, learns her family history.

Harris, Deborah. **Sweet Clara and the Freedom Quilt**. Knopf, 1993. ISBN 0-679-82311-5
Clara, a slave child, is taught by Aunt Rachel to be a seamstress in the big house. She uses her time off to stitch together a map quilt with information that will help her find freedom and, maybe, her mother. See page 96.

Johnston, Tony. **The Quilt Story**.
Illustrated by Tomie DePaola. Putnam, 1985.
ISBN 0-399-21009-1
Two little girls love the same family quilt. Although generations apart, they have similar feelings for it.

Jonas, Ann. **The Quilt**.
Greenwillow, 1984. ISBN 0-14-055308-8
A little girl dreams about her quilt. Each patch comes alive as she searches for her lost dog.

Kinsey-Warnock, Natalie. **The Canada Geese Quilt**.
Dell, 1992. ISBN 0-440-40719-2
Her mother's pregnancy is a mixed delight for this 10-year-old girl whose quilt gives her a sense of belonging.

Turner, Ann. **Sewing Quilts**.
Illustrated by Thomas B. Allen. Simon & Schuster, 1995. ISBN 0-02-789285-9
Two girls and their mother work on three quilts and celebrate the moments of their lives that, like a quilt, are pieces of the whole.

Willard, Nancy. **The Mountains of Quilt**.
Illustrated by Tomie DePaola. Harcourt, 1987.
ISBN 0-15-256010-6
This is a magic quilt, created by four magicians, making it a magic carpet.

Pink & Say

by Patricia Polacco
Philomel, 1994
ISBN 0-399-22671-0

SUMMARY

Two young men meet after a Civil War battle. Pink is African American and Say is white. Pink brings the wounded Say to his home, which is not far off. There Say is nursed back to health by Pink's mother. Before they can rejoin the battle, Confederate troops arrive. Tragedy results, and the story becomes one of self-sacrifice for family and friends.

ILLUSTRATION

These are traditional illustrations that showcase colorful and well-handled mixed media techniques. Much of the detail is captured through loosely sketched lines. Among the strongest compositions are those that capture close-up views of body parts and those that employ unusual vantage points from which to observe the events. A good example of both concepts is seen in the illustration of the four clasped hands. In this composition, skillful drawings are the key to visual clarity of statement.

CONNECTIONS

NOVEL

There are many excellent Civil War novels for young people, but Patricia Beatty's **Charlie Skedaddle** (Morrow, 1987. ISBN 0-688-06687-9) might be the best follow-up to this picture book.

THEMES

▶ Friendship
▶ Sacrifice
▶ Effects of war

CURRICULUM CONNECTION

▶ HISTORY – Civil War

LANGUAGE ARTS

CAUSE AND EFFECT

▶ List the people who sacrificed something during this story. Create a cause-and-effect chain such as "Pink's mother takes in the boys and nurses Say back to health, which eventually leads to their capture."

▶ Retell the story using a "fortunately, unfortunately" pattern.

FINDING DETAILS

▶ Say's claim to fame was that he once shook the hand of Abraham Lincoln. Pink's claim to fame was that he shook the hand that shook the hand of Abraham Lincoln. What's your claim to fame?

VOCABULARY

▶ "Jumping the broom" is referred to in the text. What ceremony is that? What other customs surround a marriage?

FIGURATIVE LANGUAGE

▶ "Jumping the broom" is used to mean "wedding" in this context. Find some other expressions that stand for ceremonies and customs, such as to be "capped" (referring to a nursing ceremony), "getting hitched" and "tying the knot" (referring to wedding ceremonies).

EXTENDING THE BOOK

▶ Pink implies that he has mixed feelings about his master because his master taught him to read. Make a plus and minus list of the things the master must have done with and for Pink.

▶ Use the book **Bull Run** as reader's theater. It has many people and many voices heading into a battle of the Civil War. Make it into a full theater production.

SOCIAL STUDIES

▶ Find out the average age of soldiers during the Civil War. Contact an armed services recruiter. Find out the age requirements and qualifications needed today to join the service. Do these contrast with the requirements and age restrictions during the Civil War?

▶ The International Red Cross, Amnesty International and the rules of the Geneva Convention all strive to improve prison conditions today. Find out minimum standards for the humane treatment of prisoners today. How many of these were present at Andersonville?

▶ Pink can read, although most slaves were not allowed to learn how. What were the rights of slaves in terms of being in the army?

▶ Watch the film *Glory*, the PBS series *The Civil War*, and the movie *Gettysburg*. Find ways they relate to the action in the book.

▶ Map the North and South during the war. Trace the route of the Underground Railroad on that map. Where would slaves have been safe? What effect did the Fugitive Slave Law have on that safety?

▶ Many Civil War battle sites have been turned into memorials and tourist attractions. How does this diminish or enhance our understanding of the war?

▶ RELATED BOOKS

NOVELS

Beatty, Patricia. **Charlie Skedaddle**.
Morrow, 1987. ISBN 0-688-06687-9 Grades 5-9
Charley has longed for the glories of war, but when he finds himself part of it, he skedaddles and discovers the nature of true courage.

Lunn, Janet. **The Root Cellar**.
Puffin, 1985. ISBN 0-14-031835-6 Grades 4-9

This is a time-travel novel in which two young girls go to Washington, DC, to find a man injured during the Civil War.

PICTURE BOOKS

Lyon, George Ella. **Cecil's Story** See page 135.

See pages 98 and 137 for more books about slavery and the Civil War.

Once There Was a Tree

by Natalia Romanova
Illustrated by Gennady Spirin
Dial, 1985
ISBN 0-14-054677-4

SUMMARY

This beautifully illustrated book from the Soviet Union details the life and death of a very old tree and the animals who visit and inhabit it over the years.

ILLUSTRATION

Each page's picture or field of print is individually framed and conveys a feeling of nostalgia. Looking at these illustrations is like looking at the treasured family picture album of an earlier generation. As with photos, it is possible to look at these compositions many times and see more detail with each review. They are drawn and painted with extraordinary attention to detail. Notice the formal floral patterns that are placed at the corners of the frames of selected pages. These illustrations may remind one of the folk art of stenciling on wood to enhance the beauty of ordinary objects.

CONNECTIONS

NOVEL

Zilpha Keatley Snyder's **The Diamond War** (Dell, 1995. ISBN 0-440-40985-3) is an easily accessible novel about a group of kids who unite to save a grove of trees.

THEMES

▶ Trees
▶ Age
▶ Witnesses to history

CURRICULUM CONNECTION

▶ SCIENCE – Ecosystems
▶ HISTORY

LANGUAGE ARTS

MAKING PREDICTIONS

▶ On the first reading of the book, stop reading on page 21. Ask students to decide who owns the tree and to write a paragraph stating their case.

ORAL EXPRESSION

▶ Stage a debate with panels of students defending the animal of their choice.

EXTENDING THE STORY

▶ Have groups of students research each of the animals. Each group could generate a list of possible questions they would ask that animal. Then write a report in the form of an interview with that animal. Publish the interviews in a classroom paper, *The Forest Gazette*. Students could publish more editions of the newspaper by researching and writing interviews of other animals found in a forest. Develop another classroom publication, *Seaside Union News*, or a paper based on another habitat.

▶ Retell the story without any human influence. What other animals might have benefited from the tree if the woodcutter wasn't a part of the story? Did the woodcutter assist any animals by cutting the tree down?

▶ Near the end of the book, when a new tree has begun to grow, the chickadee, ant and bear are present. Discuss why the other animals are not included. What do they need that the young tree cannot offer?

WRITING

▶ Read **Crinkleroot's Guide to Walking in Wild Places** by Jim Arnosky. Develop a classroom big book on the "do's and don'ts" of walking in the woods. Have each student generate a rule for walking in the woods without damaging the wild plants and without affecting wildlife. Each student can contribute an illustration to the book to go with his or her rule.

MAKING COMPARISONS

▶ Have a treasure hunt. Challenge students to find picture books with bears in them. Generate ongoing charts of book titles that list books where bears are depicted realistically and where bears are depicted unrealistically.

SCIENCE

▶ If you have a wooded area near your school, divide it into an imaginary grid. Assign small groups to carefully examine a specific plot in the grid for signs of animal life. Make illustrations and notes on what is present. Examine the plot periodically and record changes. Make predictions about what may have caused the changes over time.

▶ At one point in the story, what remains of the stump glows in the dark. Try to find out why.

▶ Try to identify some of the flowers and plants in the illustrations. Do any of them grow in your area?

▶ Take a hike in the woods. Have each student choose a tree to examine closely for signs that animals have used it. Present discoveries in cause-effect statements such as "A woodpecker has been using my tree because there are holes drilled into the side of the trunk."

▶ Some of the animals in the story use the tree for a home. Find books and investigate further what some other forest creatures use for homes. Start with a book like **And So They Build** by Bert Kitchen (see Related Books).

SOCIAL STUDIES

▶ This book is from the Soviet Union. Can students find it on a map? Why or why not? Does the forest in the book look similar to forests anywhere in the United States?

▶ Find and share some Russian or Ukrainian folktales.

ART

▶ Study some Audubon prints. Do the prints remind you of the illustrations in the book?

▶ Some of the designs in the illustrations look like pressed flowers. Try pressing some flowers. Make greeting cards from the pressed flowers.

MATH

▶ Find the life span of each character in the book. Compare them on a graph. Students could make up word problems for their peers to solve, such as "What animal has a life span that is five times as long as that of the _____?"

RELATED BOOKS

NOVEL

Snyder, Zilpha Keatley. **The Diamond War**.
Dell, 1995. ISBN 0-440-40985-3 Grades 3-6
This is an easily accessible novel about a group of girls who unite to save a grove of trees. The boys want the trees cut down in order to build a baseball diamond, and the girls are equally determined to save them. The argument gets very close to violence.

PICTURE BOOKS

Edwards, Richard. **Ten Tall Oaktrees**.
Morrow, 1988. ISBN 0-688-04620-7
Over a period of time, a stand of 12 tall oak trees is cut down one by one until there are none.

Gile, John. **The First Forest**.
Worzalla, 1989. ISBN 0-910941-01-7
This book encourages us to care for each other and for the environment we share.

Hiscock, Bruce. **The Big Tree**.
Aladdin, 1994. ISBN 0-689-71803-9
This story follows the development of a large maple tree from the time of the American Revolution to the late 20th century.

NONFICTION

Arnosky, Jim. **Crinkleroot's Guide to Walking in Wild Places**. Aladdin, 1993. ISBN 0-689-71753-9
Informative, comical guide to walking in wild places safely and without causing damage.

Arnosky, Jim. **In the Forest**.
Morrow, 1989. ISBN 0-688-08162-2
This book depicts the forest at different times of the day and in different seasons. The text discusses the plants and animals that live there.

Dewey, Jennifer Owings. **Animal Architecture**.
Orchard, 1991. ISBN 0-531-08530-9
Fun and informal text explains various creatures' constructions.

Kitchen, Bert. **And So They Build**.
Candlewick, 1993. ISBN 1-56402-217-X
Here are depictions of homes of 12 different animals. Factual text explains how and why the animals build the shelters they do.

Pluckrose, Henry. **Homes, Holes, and Hives**.
Watts, 1990. ISBN 0-531-14046-6
Explore types and nature of shelters for animals through this book.

Purr: Children's Book Illustrators Brag About Their Cats

by Michael J. Rosen, Editor.
Harcourt Brace, 1996
ISBN 0-15-200837-3

SUMMARY

Forty-two well-known children's book illustrators have provided an illustration and a narrative about their felines. Some are funny, some are very sentimental, some are rather commonplace, but each one gives us some insight to the illustrator's personality. You'll recognize some of the illustrators' pets from illustrations found in their other works. Rosen's introduction offers an entertaining view of the world of cats while making the reader painfully aware of the human carelessness sometimes associated with the treatment of pets. The illustrators featured, as well as Rosen, have donated their time and effort so that proceeds from the sale of this book will provide grants to animal welfare agencies around the country.

ILLUSTRATION

This book has an inventory of illustrative styles that run the gamut from conventional to bizarre, as befits the text. They go from photo-like to cartoon in style.

CONNECTIONS

NOVEL

In Colby Rodowsky's novel, **Dog Days** (Sunburst, 1993. ISBN 0-374-41818-7), kids get excited when a famous children's author and her dog move into the neighborhood.

THEME

▶ Pets

CURRICULUM CONNECTION

▶ WRITING
▶ BIOGRAPHY

LANGUAGE ARTS

VOCABULARY DEVELOPMENT

▶ List synonyms for "brag." Review the narratives for all the cats included in the book. How many of the illustrators are truly bragging about their pets? Can you come up with a better verb to describe what each illustrator is doing in his or her narrative?

WRITING

▶ Write a classroom book on pets. Students could contribute illustrations and narratives about exceptional pets — their own or others".

▶ Write a classroom book titled *Students Brag About Their Parents* (or siblings or neighborhoods or schools).

▶ Discuss personification. Challenge learners to find examples of personification in the book. They could then try their hand at writing their own descriptions of animals and pets using personification.

▶ Discuss how the various illustrators "stretch the truth" when discussing their pets. How do these slight (and sometimes gross) exaggerations enhance the interest of the writing? Provide students with a variety of simple statements. Can these statements be rewritten using some exaggeration to make them more entertaining for the reader or listener?

▶ Make a collection of narratives titled *Cats Brag About Their Owners*.

COMPARING LITERATURE

▶ Rosen has also edited a similar book about dogs titled **Speak! Childrens' Book Illustrators Brag About Their Dogs**. Compare these two books to decide which illustrators best depict their pets and their personalities. Are any illustrators included in both books?

▶ Read **The Third Story Cat** by Leslie Baker (see Related Books) to discover more about the cat featured by Ms. Baker in this book. Then challenge students to write short stories based on other pets featured in the book.

▶ Investigate some tall tales (see Related Books) and discuss how exaggeration defines the genre by creating an outlandish tale from a mundane event. Are there examples from the book that could be considered tall tales?

▶ Challenge students to write a tall tale of their own based upon facts about their own pets.

RESEARCH

▶ Have individual students or small groups of students choose a cat from the book. Then go to the library and find as many books by that illustrator as you can. Examine the books to try to find that cat in the illustrations.

▶ Have students choose a favorite illustrator or author to research. Use the library or write to the author or illustrator's publishers to gain biographical information. Write short biographies about the subject chosen. Present first-person oral narratives to the rest of the class to share the results of the project.

SOCIAL STUDIES

▶ Investigate the Company of Animals Fund established by the editor. What organizations or agencies in your area protect the rights of animals?

▶ Try to find out where each of the illustrators featured in the book lives. Label a large wall map showing each place of residence. Allow students to add other favorite illustrators and authors to the map as they wish.

ART

▶ Gather examples of books by each illustrator featured. Try to determine methods and materials favored by the illustrators. Experiment with techniques you think would best depict your pet.

MATH

▶ Assign small groups of students to survey classrooms in your school to determine how many and what kinds of pets are owned by students and teachers. Create a graph for each classroom showing the results of the survey. Display the graphs outside each classroom. By reading the graphs, students can determine how many of each type of pet are owned and create a large wall graph showing the combined results of the surveys.

RELATED BOOKS

Kellogg, Steven. **Johnny Appleseed**.
Morrow, 1988. ISBN 0-688-06418-3
This tall tale traces John Chapman's route as he planted apple seeds across America.

Kellogg, Steven. **Paul Bunyan**.
Morrow, 1993. ISBN 0-688-12610-3
This well-illustrated book explores the tall tales of that famous logger.

Kellogg, Steven. **Pecos Bill**.
Morrow, 1986. ISBN 0-688-05871-X
This book tells the tale of a "bigger than life" cowboy with Kellogg's detailed visual additions.

Purdy, Carol. **Iva Dunnit and the Big Wind**.
Penguin USA, 1985. ISBN 0-8037-0183-7.
This comical tall tale features a pioneer woman named Iva Dunnit.

Baker, Leslie. **The Third Story Cat**.
Little, 1987. ISBN 0-316-07832-8
In this realistic story, a city cat escapes from her third-story apartment when a window is left open.

Segal, Lore. **The Story of Mrs. Lovewright and Purrless her Cat** See page 190.

Rosen, Michael J. **Speak! Children's Book Illustrators Brag About Their Favorite Dogs**.
Harcourt, 1993. ISBN 0-15-277848-9

NOVEL

Rodowsky, Colby. **Dog Days**.
Sunburst, 1993. ISBN 0-374-41818-7 Grades 3-6
Some kids get excited when a famous children's author and her dog move into the neighborhood.

Appalachia: The Voices of Sleeping Birds

by Cynthia Rylant
Illustrated by Barry Moser
Harcourt, 1991
ISBN 0-15-201605-8

SUMMARY

This is not so much a story as it is a loving portrait in words and pictures of the people and animals of Appalachia. It talks about the housing, customs and seasons of the mountain people. It may change some people's vision of life there.

ILLUSTRATION

A point-counterpoint placement of illustration and story provides the pattern for this visual and narrative accounting of Appalachia. The watercolors demonstrate the command of technical knowledge and concise detail that is the hallmark of Barry Moser's well-known print making. His use of pure white paper and watercolors testifies to a wealth of knowledge about the medium. Moser illustrates his subject matter clearly and concisely. His compositions are camera-like; however, they are the product of a very selective lens.

CONNECTIONS

NOVEL

Robert Burch's **Ida Early Comes Over the Mountain** (Puffin, 1990. ISBN 0-140-34534-5) is a delightful novel set in Appalachian Georgia.

THEMES

- Appalachia
- Mountain people

CURRICULUM CONNECTION

- SOCIAL STUDIES – Appalachia

LANGUAGE ARTS

COMPARING LITERATURE

▶ Read the story "Silver Packages" in Cynthia Rylant's book **Children of Christmas** (see Related Books). What does it tell you about life in Appalachia that confirms or negates what this book says? Go on to read **A Blue-Eyed Daisy** and **Miss Maggie** (see Related Books) and other books set in this area. Do they change your mind?

FINDING DETAILS

▶ The book talks a lot about the dogs of Appalachia. Make a list of the ways in which the people need and use their dogs.

WRITING

▶ It is obvious from this book that both the author and the illustrator love Appalachia and the people who live in it. Get a group together in your room to portray in words, pictures, or both, an area of the country with which you are familiar and which you love.

RELATING TO PERSONAL EXPERIENCE

▶ Make a list of the good and bad things about Appalachia as your home.

SCIENCE

DOGS

▶ Look carefully at the dog pictures in the book. Use a dog book to identify as many breeds as possible from the book.

GEOLOGY

▶ How did the Appalachian Mountains come to be? Were they volcanoes? Did the glaciers cause them? Find out how and why the coal became so plentiful.

SOCIAL STUDIES

▶ Locate the Appalachian Mountains on a map of the United States. They cover a lot of territory. Do you think this book is talking about all of the range or just parts of it? The bottom of the front book flap may help you.

▶ The book names a few towns in Appalachia with unusual names. Consult an atlas to find other unusual names of towns, like Sally's Backbone. Write or call the mayor's office or town hall in some of those towns to find out the source of the name. On a large map of the United States, put pins locating those towns and at the side of the map, attached to the pin by string, write the information about the town.

▶ The book talks about living in coal-mining towns. Read other books such as **Trouble at the Mines** and **In Coal Country** (see Related Books) to find out more about a coal miner's life. Is coal mining still done the way it used to be? Is it still as dangerous?

ART

▶ Most of the books by Cynthia Rylant are about Appalachia. Many different illustrators have contributed to her books. Gather as many of them as possible and notice the various illustrators' techniques. Which do you like best? Which ones best suit the text? Would more or less color have helped some of them? Why do you think the illustrator chose a particular palette of color?

MUSIC

▶ There's a rich heritage of music from Appalachia. Find and sing some of the folksongs of Appalachia.

▶ Find out about dulcimers, fiddles and banjos and the role they play in creating music from Appalachia.

▶ Find and perform some of the square and folk dances from the region.

RELATED BOOKS

NOVELS

Burch, Robert. **Ida Early Comes Over the Mountain**. Puffin, 1990. ISBN 0-140-34534-5   Grades 3-6
An eccentric housekeeper descends on this Georgian Appalachian family.

Rylant, Cynthia. **A Blue-Eyed Daisy**. Bradbury, 1985. ISBN 0-440-40927-6   Grades 4-9
These chapters actually stand individually as short stories in the life of a little girl growing up in West Virginia.

OTHER BOOKS BY CYNTHIA RYLANT

Best Wishes. Richard Owen, 1992.
ISBN 1-878450-20-4
This is a brief, excellent autobiography of Rylant with color photographs of her life and work.

Children of Christmas: Stories for the Season.
Orchard, 1987. ISBN 0-531-05706-2
These short stories all revolve around Christmas; some of them take place in Appalachia.

Miss Maggie. Dutton, 1983. ISBN 0-525-44048-8
The neighbors of Miss Maggie, especially the children, are afraid of her, but when she needs help, it's one of those mountain children who finds and helps her.

Mr. Griggs' Work. Orchard, 1992.
ISBN 0-531-07037-9
Mr. Griggs is a postmaster and he loves his work.

Night in the Country. Simon & Schuster, 1991.
ISBN 0-689-71473-4
This is almost a lullaby as the text and pictures combine to help us experience a quiet rural night.

The Relatives Came. Simon & Schuster, 1985.
ISBN 0-02-777220-9
A large family reunion results when the relatives arrive in their dilapidated car and the noise, food, chatter and love is enjoyed by all.

When I Was Young in the Mountains. Dutton, 1982.
ISBN 0-525-42525-X
The simple joys and pleasures of life in the mountains is related from the author's own childhood.

OTHER BOOKS ILLUSTRATED BY BARRY MOSER

Polly Vaughn: A Traditional British Ballad.
Little, 1992. ISBN 0-316-58541-6
A Romeo and Juliet tale set in Appalachia tells of tragic lovers one of whom kills the other.

Tucker Pfeffercorn. Little, 1994.
ISBN 0-316-58542-4
Rumplestiltskin is recast and retold in an Appalachian setting in which the villain of the piece is the coal mine owner. See page 154.

The Old Woman Who Named Things

by Cynthia Rylant
Illustrated by Kathryn Brown
Harcourt, 1996
ISBN 0-15-257809-9

SUMMARY

An old woman who has outlived all of her friends has determined that the only way to keep from being lonely is to name only those things around her that she cannot outlive. Thus, she has names for her chair, car, house and bed, but not her gate, because it has rusty hinges and won't last much longer. All is well until that stray puppy shows up at the garden gate. What if she gives it a name and becomes attached to it and then it dies before she does? The solution seems simple; feed the pup daily when it shows up and tell it to go home. One day the pup does not appear and she finds she must name it to claim it at the pound.

ILLUSTRATION

These are lighthearted, lightly colored illustrations of a whimsical nature. They exhibit mixed media ranging from watercolors to pastels and capture the feeling of sentimentality.

CONNECTIONS

NOVEL

Phyllis Naylor's Newbery Award winning novel **Shiloh** (Atheneum, 1991. ISBN 0-44-40752-4) is about a dog that won't go away.

THEMES

▶ Love
▶ Death
▶ Eccentric people
▶ Loneliness

CURRICULUM CONNECTION

▶ SOCIAL STUDIES – Problems of the elderly

LANGUAGE ARTS

COMPARING LITERATURE

▶ Investigate other books that depict lonely elders (see Related Books). Compare and contrast the characters and determine what strategies each used to curb loneliness.

FINDING DETAILS

▶ Notice the objects the old woman has named. Why were those particular objects chosen? What other objects might she have named and what would she have named them?

▶ Look closely at the illustrations of the named items. Notice their very human appearance. Now, look around your classroom and find objects to name. Illustrate those things, giving them human characteristics.

▶ Again, look at the illustrations. Focus on the old woman herself. What fashion tips and hairdressing tips could you give her? Do her clothes and hair style tell you anything about her personality?

EXTENDING THE TEXT

▶ What are the purposes of naming objects? Have you ever named an inanimate item?

▶ List 10 common everyday items. What is the origin of their names?

▶ Investigate your own name's origin.

WRITING

▶ Write arguments for and against the old woman's keeping the dog. Stage a debate in your classroom on the good and bad points of owning and caring for pets.

▶ Write a sequel to this story about another type of pet showing up at the garden gate. Would the old woman name and keep another animal?

SOCIAL STUDIES

▶ Investigate the procedures for dealing with stray animals in your community. Perhaps someone from the Humane Society can speak to your class about caring for stray animals.

▶ Find out what kinds of activities are available for the elderly in your community. Consider establishing a pen pal relationship with a group of local seniors.

▶ Plan a field trip to a home for the elderly to sing a song or to deliver handmade greeting cards before a holiday. Perhaps some of the residents of the place you visit could be invited to school to read with the children or to join them for a special luncheon.

▶ Investigate the average life span of men and women in this country. Compare this to the average life span in the last century. Contrast the life expectancy in other countries.

MATH

▶ Using warranties of common house and garden items and appliances, create a wall chart that shows the expected "life" of each. Compare these results with the stated or implied "life" in those products' advertisements.

▶ Go on a fact-finding mission in your own homes. Find and list those items you find that are (1) older than you, (2) older than your parents and (3) older than your grandparents. Be sure to include the house itself in one of the lists. What types of products seem to have the greatest longevity? Graph class results.

ART

▶ Betsy was quite a car! Design your own car and name it.

▶ Draw yourself with your own pet. Write the pet's name and the reason the pet was given that name.

RELATED BOOKS

NOVELS

Rylant, Cynthia. **Missing May**.
Orchard, 1992. ISBN 0-53-05996-0 Grades 4-9
Aunt May and Uncle Ob knew an angel when they saw one, so they brought Summer home with them after the death of her parents. This gentle novel depicts loss, love and humor.

Naylor, Phyllis. **Shiloh**.
Atheneum, 1991. ISBN 0-440-40752-4 Grades 3-9
Marty, an Appalachian boy, befriends an abused puppy in this Newbery Award winner.

PICTURE BOOKS

Kesselman, Wendy. **Emma**.
HarperCollins, 1985. ISBN 0-440-40847-4
A lonely woman discovers that if she paints pictures of the things she likes, she is not lonely any more.

Gray, Libba M. **Miss Tizzy**.
Simon and Schuster, 1993. ISBN 0-671-77590-1
The children love Miss Tizzy and visit her every day. She's different, and the adults aren't so sure that's great.

Fox, Mem. **Wilfrid Gordon McDonald Partridge**.
Kane/Miller, 1985. ISBN 0-916291-04-9
Wilfrid Gordon McDonald Partridge lived next door to an "old people's home" and was friends with all the folks who lived there. When Wilfrid heard his parents talking about one of the people losing her memory, he set out to learn what a memory is.

Stevenson, James. **Mr. Hacker**.
Greenwillow, 1990. ISBN 0-688-09217-9
Mr. Hacker thinks he doesn't have any friends, but he is a friend to many.

Cooney, Barbara. **Miss Rumphius**.
Viking 1982. ISBN 0-670-47958-6
Miss Rumphius promises her grandfather that she will live by the sea, travel to far-off places and do something to make the world a more beautiful place.

Blos, Joan W. **Old Henry**. Morrow, 1987. ISBN 0-688-06399-3
Henry's neighbors are appalled that he ignores them and allows his property to get rundown. But when they drive him away, they find themselves missing him.

Ackerman, Karen. **Song and Dance Man**
See page 1.

OTHER GOOD BOOKS BY CYNTHIA RYLANT

All I See. Orchard, 1988. ISBN 0-531-08377-2
A painter sets up his easel every day by the lake, observed by a young boy. Eventually, the boy makes his presence known to the painter.

Miss Maggie. Penguin USA, 1983.
ISBN 0-525-44048-8
The children of the mountains are afraid of Miss Maggie, but one boy becomes her friend.

Night in the Country. Simon and Schuster, 1986.
ISBN 0-02-777210-1
The sounds and sights of a country night are poetically described.

The Relatives Came. Simon and Schuster, 1985.
ISBN 0-02-777220-9
What a wonderful family reunion takes place when the relatives drive all the way from Virginia.

When I Was Young in the Mountains. Penguin USA 1982. ISBN 0-525-42525-X
In this gentle story, the author shares memories of her childhood with her grandparents in the mountains.

Tree of Cranes

by Allen Say
Houghton, 1991
ISBN 0-395-52024-X

▰ SUMMARY

Allen Say brings to life a story of two cultures coming together with respect and love. A little Japanese boy who "was not yet old enough to wear long pants" spends a gray winter day worrying about his mother's reaction to his visit to the pond. Will this rekindle her fear of his drowning? He finds her making small paper cranes—a device to make a big wish come true. Convinced she is angry at him, he is even more worried when later in the day she digs up a little pine tree and brings it to his room. As she places the cranes and candles on the tree, she tells him of the celebration of Christmas she experienced long ago when she lived in California. This Christmas memory brings gifts for both the child and the reader as two cultures blend for a moment.

▰ ILLUSTRATION

A formal balance is established through the regular placement of text on pages that are directly opposite the pages of clear and concise illustrations. The regular pattern of reading print on the left and seeing pictures on the right is visually comforting. Allen Say uses an economy of line and color to convey the sequence of events in his story.

The illustrations are crisply clean and appear to have photo images as their foundation. Images of paper-folded cranes link the Origami practice with the western counterpart of hand-crafted decorations. These illustrations are so articulate and concise that the story could be fully understood through the pictures alone.

▰ CONNECTIONS

NOVEL

Betty Bao Lord's short novel **In the Year of the Boar and Jackie Robinson** (HarperCollins, 1984. ISBN 0-0-024004-0) is about a Chinese immigrant who must combine her heritage with her new culture.

THEME

▶ Combining cultures

CURRICULUM CONNECTION

▶ SOCIAL STUDIES – Japan

LANGUAGE ARTS

MAKING COMPARISONS

▶ Contrast the gifts given by the mother and boy. Make a class list of tangible and intangible gifts and their worth.

▶ Compare the boy's punishment with that used in your household: grounded, penalties and the like.

COMPARING LITERATURE

▶ In **Where the Wild Things Are**, Max is also sent to his room. Are there any other similarities to the little boy in **Tree of Cranes**? Find books with other types of punishments.

▶ Read **Sadako** by Eleanor Coerr for another story about origami cranes. See page 59.

LEARNING OTHER LANGUAGES

▶ Find two Japanese words in the story. Define them and list Japanese words and their translations such as

Konban wa = good evening
Ohayo = good morning
Konnichi wa = hello
Sayonara = goodbye

POETRY

▶ Find and share some haiku poetry, a Japanese art form. Notice that it has lines of five syllables, seven syllables and five syllables. (Note: this will not hold true in translation.) Review the book's message and see if you can put it into haiku form. Usually haiku has an element of nature in it. Try writing other haiku verses and then printing them on paper decorated with Japanese designs.

EXTENDING THE STORY

▶ Write more details about other things the mother might have seen and done at the Christmas celebration.

▶ If the father is present in the home, what gifts might the boy give him or he give the boy?

▶ When, where and how might the boy finally use his kite?

LETTER WRITING

▶ Participate in the Peace Corps Volunteer Pen Pal Program that promotes writing between cultures. For information and addresses:
Peace Corps, Office of World Wise Schools
800/424-8580
http://www.peacecorps.gov

▶ Brainstorm for possible questions to ask your pen pal about his or her culture, town, school and home. Decide on some information your pen pal might like to have about you and the way you live.

▶ Write a short autobiography for your pen pal.

SCIENCE

▶ Are real cranes found in Japan? What kinds of cranes? Do they migrate? Where? Why are they used as a symbol of hope?

▶ What other birds and animals are indigenous to Japan?

▶ Do the surrounding waters influence the eating habits of this island nation? What type of seafood is popular there?

▶ Mother brought the pine tree into the house. Find examples of Japanese gardening and investigate the art of bonsai — the cultivation of dwarf trees.

SOCIAL STUDIES

▶ Choose a topic of traditional Japan to research: samurai, sumo wrestling, tea ceremony, calligraphy, origami or costume, for instance.

▶ Find books about World War II. How did the war cause changes in the Japanese culture?

▶ List the foods mentioned in the story: carp, tea cake, rice gruel, sour plum and yellow radishes. Compare these to a menu in an American Japanese restaurant. Compare this menu to one from an Italian restaurant.

ART

▶ Origami is the art of Japanese paper folding. Find directions or create your own for some symbols from the story: snowflake, pine tree, crane.

▶ Make a Japanese Christmas tree decorated with origami samples and samurai symbols.

▶ Reread the book and carefully examine the illustrations. Notice the simplicity and purity of each room in the house. Compare the Japanese architecture and interior decoration to that in more familiar houses.

▶ Compare Allen Say's illustrations with those of Jan Brett, Trina Hyman, and others. Can you find an illustrator whose work reminds you of Allen Say's?

▶ Make a samurai kite or some other kind of kite.

RELATED BOOKS

NOVELS

Lord, Betty Bao. **In the Year of the Boar and Jackie Robinson**. HarperCollins, 1984. ISBN 0-06-024004-0 Grades 4-8
A Chinese girl experiences culture clash when she goes with her mother to join her father in America.

Say, Allen. **The Ink-Keeper's Apprentice**.
Houghton, 1979. ISBN 0-395-70562-2 Grades 4-9
This is a fictionalized autobiography.

PICTURE BOOKS

Bang, Molly. **The Paper Crane**.
Greenwillow, 1985. ISBN 0-688-04108-6
A restaurant owner and his wife befriend a stranger who leaves them a magic origami crane.

Bierhorst, John. **Spirit Child: A Story of the Nativity**. Morrow, 1984. ISBN 0-688-09926-2
This is an Aztec version of the Christmas story, told in modern English with unique illustrations.

Coerr, Eleanor. **Sadako**.
Putnam, 1993. ISBN 0-399-21771-1
This is a picture book version of the story of the little girl dying of leukemia who tries to fold a thousand paper cranes.

Owens, Mary Beth. **Counting Cranes**.
Little, 1993. ISBN 0-316-67719-1
Although this is a counting book, it also provides an insight into the habits of the endangered whooping crane.

Sendak, Maurice. **Where the Wild Things Are**.
HarperCollins, 1963
The punishment of Max is similar to that of the child in **Tree of Cranes**.

Uchida, Yoshiko. **The Bracelet**.
Philomel, 1993. ISBN 0-399-22503-X
Here's a picture book story about the internment camps during World War II.

Wetzel, JoAnne Steward. **The Christmas Box**.
Knopf, 1992. ISBN 0-679-82789-1
In the 1950s, a father is stationed in Japan during the Christmas holidays. Back in the United States, his family misses him and enjoys the unusual presents he sends them.

Yagawa, Sumiko. **The Crane Wife**.
Morrow, 1981. ISBN 0-844-66589-4
In this Japanese folktale, a farmer marries a mysterious stranger. After many strange occurrences, it is discovered that she is really the crane he once saved.

OTHER BOOKS WRITTEN AND ILLUSTRATED BY ALLEN SAY

The Bicycle Man. Houghton, 1989.
ISBN 0-39550-652-2
A group of Japanese children is first frightened and then entertained by their first visit from American soldiers.

Grandfather's Journey. Houghton, 1993.
ISBN 0-395-57035-2
American and Japanese heritages are brought together. The story traces two quests: the narrator's and that of his grandfather, each torn between two cultures. See page 184.

Lost Lake. Houghton, 1992. ISBN 0-395-63036-3
Luke and his father are disgusted by the tourists who spoil the secluded lake near their home.

Grandfather's Journey

by Allen Say
Houghton, 1993
ISBN 0-395-57035-2

SUMMARY

The lifetime of a Japanese man is recounted by his grandson. The grandfather travels to America and falls in love with his new home, but his longing for Japan eventually takes him back there. Wherever he is, he tends to be homesick for the other place. The grandson also grows up to love two different countries.

ILLUSTRATION

Viewing these illustrations is like perusing a painter's portfolio of works. All of these illustrations are carefully crafted compositions of landscapes and figures with emphasis on a variety of portraits. Allen Say handles both watercolor and tempera paint in the classical manner, creating a calm and quiet mood with his painting style. In each separate page and composition, the lettering is clearly distinct from the pictures.

CONNECTIONS

NOVEL

Many novels revolve around a person caught between cultures. Gloria Whelan's **Goodbye, Vietnam** (Knopf, 1992. ISBN 0-679-82263-1) is a short, accessible novel that is a logical step from this picture book.

THEME

▶ Caught between cultures

CURRICULUM CONNECTION

▶ HISTORY – Immigrants

LANGUAGE ARTS

WRITING

▶ Interview a grandparent or elderly friend. Write and illustrate a biography of events in that person's life or illustrate it with photographs if possible.

▶ Create autobiographies titled "_____'s Journey." After writing a sequence of important events in your life, try creating "photo-like" pictures to go with each event.

▶ Look at the symbol on the sleeve of the grandfather's kimono. It is shown both on his kimono when he is a young boy and again when he is an old man. Do some research to try to find its meaning. Look at some other Japanese symbols and writing. Try making name tags for desks using Japanese symbols.

EXTENDING THE STORY

▶ The grandfather and later the grandson seem to be homesick regardless of what country they are in. Write stories about a time when you were homesick. What were the things you missed about home when you weren't there?

MAKING COMPARISONS

▶ Create timelines of the grandfather's life and of the grandson's life. Examine both to find the parallels between the two men's lives.

▶ Find as many books as you can that depict stories of families immigrating to the United States. How are the experiences of the different families similar?

SCIENCE

▶ The grandfather in the story raises songbirds. Find out what kinds of songbirds are native to Japan. Compare these to the kinds that can be found in your community. Are there any similarities? Why did the grandfather stopped raising songbirds?

▶ Learn about the weather and climate in Japan. How do they compare to the weather where you live? What types of major storms occur in Japan? How are they different from storms in your area?

▶ The Japanese have a reputation for having very healthful diets. Look into Japanese cuisine. Try some traditional Japanese foods. What makes their diet more healthful than that of other cultures? What can we learn from the Japanese about eating foods that are more nutritious for us?

SOCIAL STUDIES

▶ Locate Japan on a world map to discover that it is composed of many small islands. Map two very different routes from Japan to the United States by boat — one traveling east and one traveling west. Use the map key to determine the distance of each route. Which is shorter?

▶ Do the same by next measuring the shortest route by air in each direction.

▶ Learn about Ellis Island. Do you have relatives who came through Ellis Island? Find where your ancestors came from. Mount small pictures of class members around a world map, and stretch yarn from each photo to the country of origin.

▶ Invite someone to talk to your class about immigrating to this country and about the differences between the two countries.

▶ In Japan, families of boys hang carp-shaped kites outside their homes on Children's Day. Learn about other Children's Day customs. Discuss why only families of boys did this. Why is the grandmother not mentioned in the story, even though she does appear in some of the illustrations?

▶ Use the war, articles of clothing worn and the generations of the family to estimate the approximate time period from the beginning to the end of the story. Retell the story with illustrations and captions on a time line.

▶ Study the illustrations of the grandfather's travels and use travel guides, textbooks and encyclopedias to guess the state that is the location for each illustration.

▶ Find items in your homes that were made in Japan.

▶ Many modes of transportation are depicted in the story — steamship, train and riverboat. On a blank map of the United States, plan an itinerary that would allow visitors to see as much of the country as possible. Develop symbols to use on your maps to show different modes of transportation.

▶ Look at travel brochures and photos of California. Also look at California's location on the map in relation to Japan. Why did the grandfather chose to settle in California after traveling around our country? What about California may have reminded him of home?

▶ On page 10 of the book, the grandfather is "bewildered and yet excited" by huge cities of factories and tall buildings. Why were there none of these in Japan at that time? Are there now?

▶ Take a look at traditional Japanese clothing. Find out if people of modern Japan still wear the same types of clothing.

MATH

▶ The grandfather didn't see land for three weeks when he came to our country. Find out how many miles the grandfather traveled each day. Then create math word problems for others to solve. For example, if it took the grandfather three weeks to travel from Japan to California, how long would it have taken him to travel from California to Hawaii?

ART

▶ Look at the origami boat shown on the inside cover page of the book. Try your hand at the Japanese art of paper-folding as well as other Japanese art forms such as calligraphy and kite-making.

▶ RELATED BOOKS

NOVELS

Say, Allen. **The Ink-Keeper's Apprentice**.
Houghton, 1979. ISBN 0-395-70562-2 Grades 4-9
This is a fictionalized autobiography.

Whelan, Gloria. **Goodbye, Vietnam**.
Knopf, 1992. ISBN 0-679-82263-1 Grades 4-9
Mai's family escapes from war-torn Vietnam and we are witness to the journey of these boat people.

PICTURE BOOKS

Ackerman, Karen. **Song and Dance Man**
See page 1.

Castle, Caroline. **Grandpa Baxter and the Photographs**. Orchard Books, 1993.
ISBN 0-531-05487-X
Grandpa Baxter and his grandson find Great Grandpa Doodle's famous photo album and cancel their plans for the day to learn about their family history.

Coerr, Eleanor. **Sadako**.
Illustrated by Ed Young. Putnam, 1993.
ISBN 0-399-21771-1
Hospitalized with leukemia, a child in Hiroshima races against time to fold 1,000 paper cranes to verify the legend that doing so will make a sick person become healthy. See page 59.

Hamanaka, Sheila. **Peace Crane**.
Morrow, 1995. ISBN 0-688-13815-2
A young African-American girl learns about the story of Sadako and the Peace Crane, and she wishes it could carry her away from the violence of her own world.

Say, Allen. **Tree of Cranes**.
Houghton, 1991. ISBN 0-395-52024-X
This picture book by the same author also revolves around cultural conflict. See page 181.

Uchida, Yoshiko. **The Bracelet**.
Philomel, 1993. ISBN 0-399-22503-X
A Japanese-American second grader is sent to an internment camp with her family during World War II. When she loses a bracelet that a friend has given her, she learns that she doesn't need the physical reminder of that friendship.

Watson, Mary. **The Butterfly Seeds** See page 235.

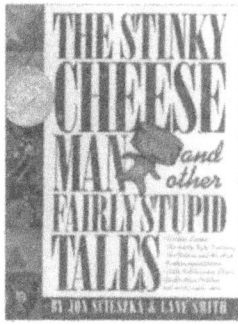

The Stinky Cheese Man and Other Fairly Stupid Tales

by Jon Scieszka
Illustrated by Lane Smith
Viking, 1992
ISBN 0-670-84487-X

SUMMARY

This humorous book of revisionist fairy tales is perfect for a diverse group of elementary school boys and girls. The 10 complete stories are clever, amusing, and true to the title: "fairly stupid." These zany stories give children the opportunity to enjoy some modern tales taken from the traditional. These 10 unique versions feature modern "hip" changes, combinations of more than one tale, new and different endings, and truly unusual twists.

ILLUSTRATION

The visual impact of this book is akin to some advertising. It contains a calculated mish-mash of lettering sizes and colors giving the impression of a catalog packed with stories in various type faces. The equally inventive illustrations substitute surreal representations for the known and predictable images usually associated with these tales. Lane Smith uses mixed media with airbrush and paint spatter techniques.

CONNECTIONS

NOVEL

For **Stinky Cheese Man** the most logical longer book to go to is not a novel but any good collection of fairy and folktales.

THEME

► Fairy tale extensions

CURRICULUM CONNECTION

► LANGUAGE ARTS – Writing

LANGUAGE ARTS

COMPARING LITERATURE

▶ Reread and examine the various characters in this book. Brainstorm for words to describe each character.

▶ Find the original stories that served as take-off points for this book. Brainstorm for words describing each of the original characters. Compare the two lists.

▶ Read other humorous versions of various fairy tales (see Related Books.) Decide what techniques the author used to make them funny: updates, reversals, surprise endings.

ANALYZING A STORY

▶ Design a story map and choose a character. Decide on a structure that shows character, goal, problem, solution. Compare maps and discuss likenesses and differences.

▶ Illustrate each segment of your story map. Invite others to put pictures in your map.

▶ Develop a story map for a current TV show. Sitcoms work very well.

▶ If you think this book was funny, note the points in the story where you smiled or laughed. Compare your list with those of other readers. Analyze those points in the story. How did the author and illustrator create the effect you laughed at?

LANGUAGE DEVELOPMENT

▶ Develop a semantic map. Choose a focus word from the story and add the necessary boxes. For example:

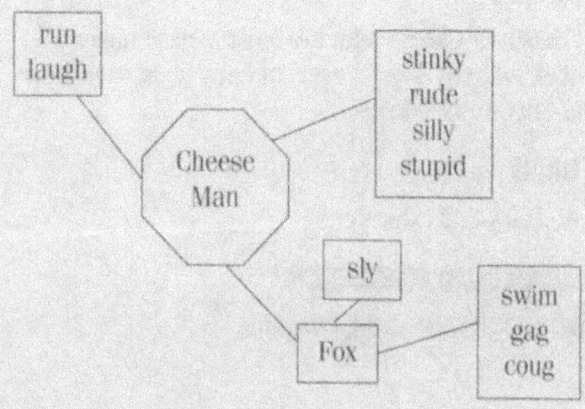

▶ Reverse the rules. After the boxes are filled, decide on the character that the words portray.

CLASSIFICATION

▶ Compile an ongoing class collection of books. Classify them in groups: folktales, fairy tales, fables, traditional stories sequels, transformations. These books could also be classified by countries.

WRITING

▶ Choose a favorite book or story from the class collection. Working together, compose a story modeled on **The Stinky Cheese Man**. Change the characters, gender, setting, goal or moral. After the final edit, print the stories as a class book.

▶ In **The Stinky Cheese Man**, various sizes and kinds of print help to tell the story. Would changing the print in such a way help your story? Try it.

▶ Use print to show meaning of individual words. Can you print the word "stinky" in such a way to make it look smelly? Try it with other words from the text.

▶ Use print to show meaning of various book or story titles.

▶ Can you print your own name in such a way as to show what you are like?

▶ Many folktales lend themselves to sequels (see Related Books). Choose a favorite and write a part two for it. Talk about movie and television sequels.

SOCIAL STUDIES

▶ Research to find out the country of origin for each of the tales in the book. Classify each country according to continent and locate it on the world map. Find out about conditions in that country at the time when the tale is believed to have originated.

RELATED BOOKS

Cole, Babette. **Prince Cinders**.
Putnam, 1989. ISBN 0-399-21882-3
Prince Cinders does all the housework and is always being teased by his brothers. In this spoof he even goes to the ball.

Galdone, Paul. **Jack and the Beanstalk**.
Houghton, 1982. ISBN 0-89919-085-5
This is the conventional folktale version of the story.

Kellogg, Steven. **Chicken Little**.
Morrow, 1987. ISBN 0-688-07045-0
Kellogg uses the illustrations to construct a subplot to his version of the tale.

Ross, Tony. **The Boy Who Cried Wolf**.
Dial, 1985. ISBN 0-8037-0193-4
This is a humorous version of the old fable. Willy cries "Wolf!" all right(every time he's asked to do something he doesn't want to do. When the hungry wolf, in dinner jacket, arrives, he eats everybody.

Ross, Tony. **Stone Soup**.
Dial, 1990. ISBN 0-8037-0890-4
This is a tongue-in-cheek version of the story in which a hen and a wolf are the protagonists.

Zemach, Harve & Margot. **Duffy and the Devil**.
Farrar, 1973. ISBN 0-374-31887-5
This Caldecott medal winner is a Cornish version of Rumplestiltskin.

OTHER BOOKS BY JON SCIESZKA

The Book That Jack Wrote. Illustrated by Daniel Adel. Viking, 1994. ISBN 0-670-84330-X
This "update" tells of a blind rat that falls into Jack's book, setting off a chain of events in which each character is killed until nothing is left but the book. Characters from other children's books are in the story.

The Frog Prince Continued. Illustrated by Steve Johnson. Puffin, 1994. ISBN 0-14-054285-X
This is a humorous sequel to the familiar folktale.

The Good, the Bad, and the Goofy. Illustrated by Lane Smith. Viking, 1992. ISBN 0-670-84380-6
Joe, Fred and Sam are transported back to the Chisholm Trail of 1869.

Knights of the Kitchen Table. Illustrated by Lane Smith. Viking, 1991. ISBN 0-670-83622-2
This is the first of the Time Trio books in which Joe, Fred and Sam travel through time. In this case it's to the court of King Arthur.

The Not-So-Jolly-Roger. Illustrated by Lane Smith. Viking, 1991. ISBN 0-670-83754-7
The third Time Warp Trio book brings them to the Spanish Main.

The True Story of the Three Little Pig.
Viking, 1989. ISBN 0-670-82759-2
This is the wolf's version of the story. It was all a misunderstanding.

The Story of Mrs. Lovewright and Purrless

by Lore Segal
Illustrated by Paul O. Zelinsky
Knopf, 1985
ISBN 0-394-86817-X

◢ SUMMARY

Mrs. Lovewright is convinced that a cat is just what she needs, and she knows exactly what she wants in a cat. However, when she acquires a cat via Dylan from the grocery store, she discovers that her new pet has a mind of its own. She wanted a cat that would sit on her lap and purr, but her new cat seems to be without a purr and more aggressive.

◢ ILLUSTRATION

These are period drawings that follow the action of the story from calm to chaos. The transition takes place in about the center of the book, where the cat is springing from Mrs. Lovewright's lap. The endpapers give a nice sense of the story, and even the cover captures the time with its use of a sort of woodcut frame of lettering.

◢ CONNECTIONS

NOVEL

Lois Lowry's **Stay: Keeper's Story** (see Related Books) is about a dog who is often a misfit in his home.

THEMES

▶ Reality vs. dreams
▶ Unloveable pets
▶ Loneliness

CURRICULUM CONNECTION

▶ SOCIAL STUDIES – Problems of the elderly

LANGUAGE ARTS

WRITING

▶ Write advertisements for the perfect pet. Be specific about exactly what you want in your new pet. Describe appearance, likes, dislikes, size and personality of the pet you want.

▶ Write advertisements for the perfect pet owner. Again, be very specific. Choose the kind of pet you want to be when you write your advertisements.

▶ Create two bulletin boards. Title one "Pets Wanted" and the other "Pet Owners Wanted." Match want ads to connect pets with appropriate owners.

▶ Write detailed descriptions of your own pet. Include specific details of your pet's attributes and habits, omitting the pet's name. Display the descriptions along with a photo if possible. Invite classmates to nominate a possible name for the pet based on its personality. Vote to choose favorite names for everyone's pets.

▶ Rewrite the story from the perspective of Purrless. Now, rewrite the story from Dylan's perspective. Compare the three stories, focusing on the emotions and feelings of the character whose perspective the story is told from.

▶ Write quotes showing what Purrless would say to Dylan each time Mrs. Lovewright complains about him.

CLASSIFYING

▶ Generate a wall chart showing what Mrs. Lovewright wanted in a cat and what she got. Discuss what attributes we may choose in a pet and what attributes we have to accept.

EXTENDING THE STORY

▶ Do you think Mrs. Lovewright has had previous experience being a pet owner? Why or why not? What advice would you give to people who are about to acquire their first pet?

▶ Notice that Mrs. Lovewright's wardrobe is limited at best, and Dylan delivers her groceries. Why? What does Mrs. Lovewright do all day? Are we seeing her only at night and thus seeing only the robe and nightgown?

▶ How is the passage of time depicted in this book?

▶ Examine the conversations that take place throughout the story between Dylan and Mrs. Lovewright. List these quotes. Can the story be understood simply through these conversations?

VOCABULARY DEVELOPMENT

▶ Create a wall-sized semantic map based on cats. While with a group choose a category such as attributes, breeds, cat roles, wild felines, famous cats or cats in literature.

SCIENCE

▶ Investigate wild members of the cat family. Do any live in your area? Do wild cats demonstrate any of the same behaviors as domestic cats?

▶ Consider watching the EyeWitness video about cats.

SOCIAL STUDIES

▶ Discuss the roles that cats have in homes and in businesses. What are some of the reasons people own cats?

▶ Find out what rules govern owning and caring for cats in your community. Discuss whether you think the rules are fair or unfair.

▶ Are there rules in your home about taking in pets? Why do most families set a limit on the number and type of animals they allow? Write a letter of argument persuading your family to allow a pet into your home.

▶ RELATED BOOKS

NOVEL

Lowry, Lois. **Stay: Keeper's Story**.
Houghton, 1997. ISBN 0-395-87048-8 Grades 3-6
This is a dog's story, told in first person, by a very talented mutt.

PICTURE BOOKS

Rosen, Michael J. **Purr: Children's Book Illustrators Brag about their Cats**. Harcourt, 1996.
ISBN 0-15-200837-3
The title says it all! See page 172.

Hall, Donald. **I Am the Dog; I Am the Cat**
See page 87.

Anello, Christine. **The Farmyard Cat**.
Heinemann, 1990. ISBN 0-86896-392-5
This is a humorous story about a hungry cat whose misadventures lead to a chain reaction involving a series of farm animals.

Baker, Leslie. **The Third Story Cat**.
Little, 1990. ISBN 0-316-07836-0
This is a realistic story about a city cat who lives in an apartment.

Gruber, Terry. **Working Cats**.
Lippincott, 1979. ISBN 0-397-01376-0
This book is simply a series of black and white photographs of various cats that "work" at places like libraries, pet stores and flower shops.

Pilgrims of Plimoth

by Marcia Sewall
Atheneum, 1986
ISBN 0-689-31250-4

SUMMARY

Sewall tells the story of the Pilgrims and their first settlement at Plimoth (Plymouth today) through the eyes of one of the settlers. The text has the formality echoing the word use of the time. Her beautiful watercolors extend the text and give it solidity. Although not done in journal or diary format or in the present tense, the book has a personal tone as the narrator tells us of the births and deaths and major events on the voyage and during that first year. Later, we shift narrators as we learn first of the responsibilities and deeds of the menfolk and then of the women. Children, too, get their voice in a following chapter of this picture book.

ILLUSTRATION

The imagery and color in these illustrations reflect Sewall's careful research about the Pilgrims. Illustrations in many picture books have a sameness to them that is not present here. Some illustrations are attractive because of their color schemes; others, because of the costume information they contain; and still others, because of technical information. An example of the innovation can be seen in the two-page spread depicting the snowstorm.

CONNECTIONS

NOVEL

Patricia Clapp's **Constance: A Story of Early Plymouth** (Peter Smith, 1993. ISBN 0-8446-6647-5) is a good novel set in Plymouth Colony.

THEMES
- ▶ Community
- ▶ Survival
- ▶ Immigration
- ▶ Early settlers

CURRICULUM CONNECTION
- ▶ HISTORY – Pilgrims, early settlers

LANGUAGE ARTS

COMPARING LITERATURE

▶ Read **People of the Breaking Day** (see Related Books) for a point of view from the Native Americans living in the Plymouth area before the arrival of the Pilgrims.

▶ Read Kathryn Lasky's novel **A Journey to the New World: The Diary of Remembrance Patience Whipple** (see Related Books).

▶ Compare the events in **Pilgrims of Plimoth** with those in the picture book **Stranded at Plimoth Plantation** by Bowen (see Related Books).

▶ Make a time line using information in these and other books about the people and the time.

SPELLING

▶ Why is "Plimoth" spelled differently in the title of this book than it is on maps of today?

▶ Find some of the original writings of the Pilgrims and see how many variant spellings you can find. When did spelling become standardized?

VOCABULARY DEVELOPMENT

▶ Some of the words used in the book are not the same as you would use. Decide what each of them means and find a modern or more common synonym for those words.

SOCIAL STUDIES

▶ Make a list of important people of the time, starting with the ones in the book. You might want to add such names as Thomas Hooker, Ann Hutchinson, Massasoit, Miles Standish, John Winthrop and Squanto. Beside each name list what the person is famous for.

▶ Read the Mayflower Compact to find out the concerns of the Pilgrims before the settlement began. The Pilgrims built their first dwellings of wattle and daub plastered on wood frames. Read about their first homes and then construct small wooden house frames. Use clay, sand and straw to replicate wattle and daub houses. What will you use for a roof?

▶ Make a scale model of the first settlement at Plymouth.

▶ Pilgrims used several means to preserve food. Core and dry some apples, or dry some herbs such as thyme or rosemary from the supermarket.

▶ The living history museum at Plimoth Plantation is a wonderful place to visit. If that is not possible, write to the museum for further information about the way the Pilgrims lived. Find out what current research is being done.

▶ The settlement at Plymouth was the result of a business agreement between the settlers and their sponsors in England. Find out what they agreed to do and decide whether or not the settlement was successful according to those terms.

▶ Take one of the passengers on the Mayflower and follow his or her life as far as possible. How long did the person live? Did he or she stay at Plymouth for his or her entire life? Did he or she have children? Are there living descendants of this person?

▶ Make one of the dishes cooked by the early settlers such as succotash, red flannel hash, johnnycake or Indian pudding.

▶ Make a relief map of the area south of Boston. Locate major and minor rivers and lakes. Did the Pilgrims choose the best spot for their village?

▶ The Pilgrims formed a community in which there were strict rules. What different communities do you belong to? What are the rules?

SCIENCE

▶ List the crops and foods that were available to the Pilgrims that first year in Plymouth. What nutritional needs did they fill? Which ones went unfilled? What effect would that have had on their health?

MATH

▶ On a map of Massachusetts, find the Pilgrims' first landing spot on Cape Cod. Then locate the present city of Plymouth. Measure the distance between the two. Calculate how long it would take to cover that distance by land and by sea, then and now.

MUSIC

▶ Find out what musical instruments were available to the Pilgrims. Find out what songs they might have sung and what dances they knew how to do. The museum at Plimoth Plantation can help you find this information.

RELATED BOOKS

NOVELS

Bowen, Gary. **Stranded at Plimoth Plantation 1626**. HarperCollins, 1994. ISBN 0-06-022541-6
Grades 3-9
Christopher Sears is on his way to Jamestown when he is stranded at Plimoth Plantation six years after the arrival of the Mayflower. There he is taken to the Brewster house and we get his observations of life there in the form of a journal

Clapp, Patricia. **Constance: A Story of Early Plymouth**. Peter Smith, 1993. ISBN 0-8446-6647-5
Grades 5-9
We read an imaginary journal kept by a young girl in one of the Pilgrim families of Plymouth.

Lasky, Kathryn. **A Journey to the New World: The Diary of Remembrance Patience Whipple**. Scholastic, 1996. ISBN 0-590-50214-X Grades 3-6
This is one of a series of books by Kathryn Lasky that personalize historic events.

Wisler, G. Clifton. **This New Land**. Walker, 1987. ISBN 0-8027-6727-3 Grades 5-9
This novel centers around the experiences of Richard, a 12-year-old boy, who sails with his family on the Mayflower.

NONFICTION

San Souci, Robert. **N. C. Wyeth's Pilgrims**. Chronicle Books, 1991. ISBN 0-87701-806-5
Wyeth's murals are used as the illustrations for this succinct text, which uses the writings of William Bradford as a source for information.

Roop, Connie & Peter. **Pilgrim Voices: Our First Year in the New World**. Walker, 1995. ISBN 0-8027-8314-7
Bradford's **Of Plymouth Plantation** and **Mourt's Relation** are made accessible to young readers through this adaptation of their text.

Sewall, Marcia. **People of the Breaking Day**. Atheneum, 1990. ISBN 0-689-31407-8
The Wampanoag people were living in southeastern Massachusetts when the Pilgrims arrived. This volume reveals their lives, beliefs and customs before the arrival of the Europeans.

Waters, Kate. **Samuel Eaton's Day: A Day in the Life of a Pilgrim Boy**. Scholastic, 1993. ISBN 0-590-46311-X and **Sarah Morton's Day: A Day in the Life of a Pilgrim Girl**. Scholastic, 1991. ISBN 0-590-42634-6
Using photographs taken at the Plimoth Plantation Living History Museum, these books relate the different existences of two young members of the colony.

Homeplace

by Anne Shelby
Illustrated by Wendy Anderson Halperin
Orchard, 1995
ISBN 0-531-06882-X

SUMMARY

A grandmother tells a story almost 200 years long about how her great-great-great-great-grandpa built her family home and farm. The reader perceives the growth and change over the years and feels the love expressed in the history of this family. Every double-page spread tells the story of another generation. A wonderful sense of place and time is portrayed in the text and illustrations together. There is enough here to interest both younger and older readers.

ILLUSTRATION

There are so many images packed into these pages that they serve as a scrapbook or sketch pad collection. Where images are superimposed on other images, a patchwork quilt of visual data is created. Rooms, attic, barn, loft, fields and farm: name it and it's the storage space for a great assortment of characters and objects. The compositions are colorful drawings packed with detailed information that requires visiting them again and again in order to see all that they contain. On selected pages composite drawings reveal both inside and outside views. This is similar to how a child's X-ray drawings mingle time and space in composition. Look again. There's even more to see.

CONNECTIONS

NOVEL

Paul Fleischman's **The Borning Room** (HarperCollins, 1991. ISBN 0-06-023762-7) is a novel in which a room sees the births and deaths of many generations.

THEME

▶ Home

CURRICULUM CONNECTION

▶ HISTORY & SCIENCE – Discoveries and inventions

LANGUAGE ARTS

WRITING

▶ If you were selling this house, what would you use as a sales pitch? Write a newspaper ad describing the best features.

▶ Choose a room in the house and a generation on which to concentrate. Write a description for that time period. Stress furniture, cooking styles or recreational activities. When finished, compare your descriptions with those of others in the class.

▶ Write a diary or journal entry that might have been written by a young person living in the house during a given time period. Date it and include appropriate clues to the picture or page from which you are working.

▶ Skip ahead a few generations from the end of this book and imagine any modernization that would have been made by new occupants.

EXTENDING THE BOOK

▶ Which period was the happiest for the family? Were they happier when they had more conveniences?

▶ Suppose that a group of later ancestors had moved away or that the next generation had had no children. What might happen to the house?

DEVELOPING VOCABULARY

▶ Collect as many proverbs as possible that refer to home: "Home is where the heart is," for instance. Do the same with the word *house*.

▶ With a group, prepare a semantic map. Choose your own main word, for example, *homeplace*, or *1910* or *ancestors*. Decide on categories and classifications. Share and compare your maps with those of other groups.

▶ Locate the similes in the book. Is there a pattern here?

RECALLING DETAILS

▶ Find clues that show change and modernization both inside and outside the house. Find out what year each innovation occurred.

▶ Watch the two quilts throughout the book.

▶ Locate objects related to time throughout the book.

▶ On the last double page, match the objects in the illustrations to those pictured and dated at the bottom. Locate others and place them in the time line.

▶ Create a treasure hunt quiz based on the illustrations of the book

DRAMA

▶ Decide on a generation. Make props and clothing to identify the time period. Choose names for the family members. Create appropriate dialogue for a day in the life of the ancestors of that period.

SOCIAL STUDIES

USING MAPS

▶ On a map of the United States, choose an area that seems to have the same climate as the place in the book. Explain your choice of locations for the book. Cite your research to defend your choice, such as weather, crops, time of settlements.

HISTORY

▶ List every invention pictured. Date each one and explain its importance. Identify the inventor, if possible.

GEOGRAPHY

▶ List other types of home places around the world. How are they suited to their environments?

ART

▶ Create a quilt using flowers and plants of a given area or one depicting toys or inventions over the years.

▶ Invent a character from a particular generation. Research and design appropriate clothing for all occasions for that character.

➤ RELATED BOOKS

NOVELS

Field, Rachel. **Hitty, Her First Hundred Years**.
Dell, 1990. ISBN 0-440-40337-5 Grades 4-9
This Newbery Award winner tells the story of the life of a wooden doll.

Fleischman, Paul. **Borning Room**.
HarperCollins, 1991. ISBN 0-06-023762-7
Grades 4–9
We view several generations of a family through the events in one room in an Ohio farmhouse.

PICTURE BOOKS

Bunting, Eve. **Fly Away Home**.
Houghton, 1993. ISBN 0-395-66415-2
A homeless man and his young son find a temporary home in an airport.

Desimini, Lisa. **My House**.
Holt, 1994. ISBN 0-8050-3144-8
A house is shown variously draped in snow, leaves, clouds and shadows. It seems alive and real in all seasons of the year.

Dragonwagon, Crescent. **Home Place**.
Simon & Schuster, 1990. ISBN 0-02-733190-3
The life of a long-ago family is drawn into the present when a modern family finds remnants of an old homestead deep in the woods.

Polacco, Patricia **The Keeping Quilt** See page 163.

NONFICTION

Rounds, Glen. **Sod Houses on the Great Plains**.
Holiday, 1995. ISBN 0-8234-1162-1
Rounds' lighthearted illustrations accompany a factual text about how the houses were built and what it was like living in them.

Sierra

by Diane Siebert
Illustrated by Wendell Minor
HarperCollins, 1991
ISBN 0-06-021639-5

SUMMARY

Here we have a poetic look at a mountain range from the mountain's point of view. The unique perspective of the prose is continued in the unusual perspectives of the illustrations. This book combines geography geology, ecology and poetry.

ILLUSTRATION

Each desert animal is visually captured in full detail and situated in landscape compositions that are cleanly spacious. The close-up images of hawk and bear are Wyeth-like in drawing skill and Audubon-like in attention to detail. Notice how the repeated use of extended horizontal compositions link a full page with a half page of illustration and offer a distinctive format or layout. The text is consistently reserved for the remaining half page of space. On some pages the composition may appear interrupted, while in most, the expanded illustration adds to the sense of spaciousness.

CONNECTIONS

NOVEL

Carolyn Reeder's **Grandpa's Mountain** (Simon & Schuster, 1991. ISBN 0-02-775811-7) is about a range far from the Sierras, but the love for that area is just as strong.

THEMES

▶ Unusual perspectives
▶ Mountains

CURRICULUM CONNECTION

▶ GEOGRAPHY
▶ SCIENCE – Geology and ecology

LANGUAGE ARTS

USING FIGURATIVE LANGUAGE

▶ Find the parts in the book where the mountain compares itself to other things such as a guard and a human body.

READER'S THEATER

▶ Use the book for reader's theater, giving a page to each person for reading and interpreting aloud. Find slides or other pictures to illustrate your page and let the audience view your choices while they listen to the poem.

COMPARING LITERATURE

▶ Siebert and Minor have done two other books similar to this one. Find and read them and decide which one interests you the most.

▶ Both Siebert and Minor offer different perspectives of the desert, mountains and plains. Decide how Minor does in pictures what Siebert does in words. Which part of the book is done first, do you think?

WRITING

▶ In this book we see things from the point of view of the mountain. Try your hand at viewing something else in nature, such as a river, from a nonhuman point of view. You could make a list of other things that come in contact with the river, words that describe a river in various moods or in different seasons and places the river travels. Then write a poem or story using your list.

▶ Take one of the animals or plants that the mountain refers to and do another book from its perspective.

SCIENCE

▶ The mountain lists both predators and prey that exist on the mountain. Make an interesting chart using pictures or graphics to show these animals and their relationships to each other.

▶ Was your area ever affected by glacier activity? What ponds, lakes, rocks and other geologic effects are still visible?

▶ Make a web such as the one started showing how all the things mentioned in the book relate to one another. Take one section of the chart and enlarge it and then add greater detail to it showing even more relationships.

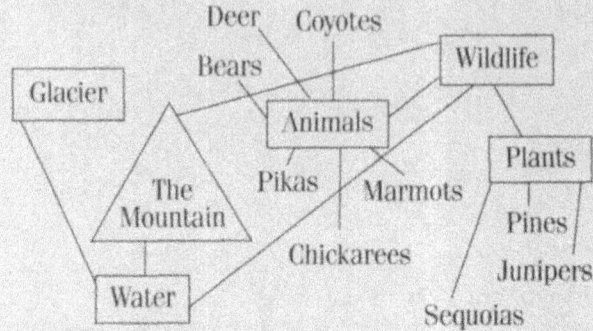

▶ If one or more of the elements on your chart should cease to exist, what would be the effect on the other items of your chart?

▶ Look carefully at a small area that is relatively wild. Find something alive in that area and write a series of backward cause-and-effect statements such as "There is an ant. The ant is here because the soil is sandy. The soil is sandy because a river once flowed through here. A river once flowed through here because the ground is low. The ground is low because a glacier dug it out." See how far back you can go.

▶ Find one aspect of the mountain as described in the book that interests you. Read other books about it, watch videos on the subject, and find a way to present what you have found to the others in the class.

▶ The mountain says that it will die. Do mountains die? Are they born? How can scientists tell how old a mountain is? How old are the nearest mountains?

▶ List the sports associated with mountains such as skiing, snow-boarding, hiking.

▶ What are the features of the mountains in various national parks?

SOCIAL STUDIES

▶ Find the place on a map where this mountain might be. Find rivers and glaciers that might be the ones referred to in the book.

▶ The book ends with the thought that humans can change the fate of the mountain. How can this be?

▶ John Muir's life had an effect on wilderness areas. Can you find out what it was and then find others whose lives had similar beneficial effects on our wilderness?

RELATED BOOKS

NOVEL

Reeder, Carolyn. **Grandpa's Mountain**.
Simon & Schuster, 1991. ISBN 0-02-775811-7
Grades 4-9
When Carrie's grandfather's property in the Blue Ridge Mountains is confiscated by the government for the creation of Shenandoah National Park, he vows never to give up his land.

PICTURE BOOKS

Baylor, Byrd. **A God on Every Mountain Top: Stories of Southwest Indian Sacred Mountains**.
Scribner, 1981.
These traditional stories are presented in poetic form and describe the relationship of the various Indian nations to the mountains.

McLerran, Alice. **The Mountain That Loved a Bird**.
Picture Book Studio, 1991. ISBN 0-88708-000-6
A bird lights on a barren mountain and the mountain loves it. However, since there is no food available there, the bird must leave. On a later visit the bird drops a seed and the mountain becomes a life-sustaining place. See page 148.

NONFICTION

Simon, Seymour. **Icebergs and Glaciers**. Morrow, 1987. ISBN 0-688-06186-9
Simon's usual clear and interesting text combines with magnificent color photographs to explain the nature of these phenomena, making this an excellent resource.

Talmadge, Katherine. **John Muir: At Home in the Wild**. 21st Century Books, 1993.
ISBN 0-8050-2123-X
Muir's life story includes his crossing of Muir Glacier, as well as the events that led him to found the Sierra Club and crusade to preserve the Yosemite Valley.

OTHER BOOKS BY DIANE SIEBERT AND WENDELL MINOR

Heartland. HarperCollins, 1989.
ISBN 0-690-04730-4
Here it's the land of the great plains that speaks to us through poetry and illustrations, giving us a look at the farms and cities of America's Midwest.

Mojave. HarperCollins, 1992. ISBN 0-06-443283-1
The perspective of the desert itself is the focus of this book of striking prose and artwork.

Mufaro's Beautiful Daughters

by John Steptoe
Lothrop, 1987
ISBN 0-688-04045-4

▶ SUMMARY

The king in a West African country has decided to take a wife. In this tale "the most worthy and beautiful daughters in the land are invited to appear before him." Mufaro, one of the villagers, has two beautiful but very different daughters: Manyara, who is always in a bad temper, is ambitious and mean; Nyasha is not only beautiful but kind and helpful. Mufaro declares that only the king should choose between them. Manyara's trickery does not help as she goes about ignoring various magical happenings. The reader realizes from the outset who will be the queen, but it is great fun to read about a certain servant in the new queen's household.

▶ ILLUSTRATION

These illustrations are almost inventories of the land and culture of Africa. The most interesting treatments are in the costumes, particularly the white robes on many of the characters, where the use of hatching and cross-hatching is extensive and effective.

▶ CONNECTIONS

NOVEL

Ella Enchanted (HarperCollins, 1997. ISBN 0-06-027519-1) is a novel based on Cinderella.

THEMES

▶ Beauty

▶ Trickery

▶ Contests

CURRICULUM CONNECTION

▶ SOCIAL STUDIES – Folk literature around the world

LANGUAGE ARTS

COMPARING AND CONTRASTING

▶ Compare the reaction of each sister to Nydha the snake, the hungry little boy, the old woman and each other.

▶ Make a chart contrasting the character and personality traits of the two sisters.

COMPARING LITERATURE

▶ This story is a Cinderella variant. Find and read other versions of the tale (see Related Books). What makes them Cinderella tales? Do they all have poor and abused girls? Is there always a fairy godmother? Do they all end with a wedding? What things are valued?

VOCABULARY DEVELOPMENT

▶ In the story, we learn that Mufaro means "happy man," Nyasha means "mercy," Manyara means "ashamed," and Nyasha is "snake." Each name seems fitting for each character. Research other names; for example, Native American names are almost always descriptive (Running Bear), as are the names in fairy tales (Cinderella, Snow White). Find others.

▶ Investigate the names of family members and classmates. What do they mean? Why were they given? Are they appropriate?

DRAMA

▶ This story is ideal for dramatizing. The two main characters are strong, and the supporting characters are interesting. There is some dialogue and plenty of opportunity to add more. The set, costumes and props can be simply made. Perform it as reader's theater or as a play.

RELATING TO PERSONAL EXPERIENCE

▶ One sister cannot seem to relate to anyone. She seems to be selfish and overbearing. The other seems almost perfect. Is there sibling rivalry here? Is the father oblivious?

EXTENDING THE STORY

▶ Relate what happens to the newlyweds. Do you think they really love each other?

▶ What kind of work did "Manyara the servant" have to do after the story? Did the father return to his village? Do the king and queen ever return for a visit? Is Nyasha happy without her animal friends and her little garden? Did Nyasha's life change forever?

COMPARING LITERATURE

▶ These themes or motifs occur in the story. Add other related books to these examples:

sibling rivalry (one-sided) – "Cinderella"
young girl taming animals – "Snow White"
choosing a queen – "Princess and the Pea"; "Cinderella"
animal becoming royalty – "Frog Prince"

FINDING DEEPER MEANINGS OR THEMES

▶ Choose a moral to the story for *both* Nyasha and Manyara. Should Manyara have been warned beforehand? Would she have heeded the warning? Finally, choose or create one moral for the entire story.

SOCIAL STUDIES

▶ The illustrations were inspired by the ruins of an ancient city in Zimbabwe.

▶ Locate Zimbabwe on a map of Africa:

List neighboring countries.

Identify the zone in which it lies and investigate the climate and temperature.

Examine the illustrations and identify and list the wildlife and plants shown.

Research the present-day vegetation and animal life and compare to the ones in the book.

▶ Research the modern history of Zimbabwe:

What is the background of April 17, 1980, as Independence Day for Zimbabwe?

What was Rhodesia?

Find out about the government of Zimbabwe. Is there still a king?

▶ If the small village lay across a river and half a day's journey from a city, what is it called today? Decide the location on a present-day map.

SCIENCE

FLORA AND FAUNA

▶ Using guidebooks, identify some of the brightly plumed birds, the towering trees, and the flowers you see in Steptoe's illustrations.

▶ Recall what crops Nyasha grew in her garden. Decide what type of climate and soil were needed for them to flourish.

RELATED BOOKS

NOVEL

Levine, Gail. **Ella Enchanted**.
HarperCollins, 1997. ISBN 0-06-027519-1
Grades 3-7
This is a novel made from the Cinderella story that works.

PICTURE BOOKS

Aardema, Verna. **Misoso: Once Upon a Time Tales from Africa**. Illustrated by Reynold Puffins. Hamish Hamilton, 1994. ISBN 0-67983430-3
This collection of African tales is entertaining as well as eloquent. There is a glossary as well as an explanation of the origin of each.

Lewin, Hugh. **Jafta and the Wedding**.
Illustrated by Lisa Kopper, Carolrhoda.
ISBN 0-87614-210-2
A young South African boy describes all the events of his sister's wedding. The stress is on home and family.

Musgrove, Margaret. **Ashanti to Zulu: African Traditions**. Illustrated by Leo and Diane Dillon. Dial 1976. ISBN 0-803-70308-2
This stunning book is a Caldecott Medal winner. The captions are outstanding, as are the illustrations, in explaining many facets of African life.

CINDERELLA VARIANTS

(These are just a few of the many variants available.)
Climo, Shirley. **The Egyptian Cinderella**.
HarperCollins, 1992. ISBN 0-06-443279-3
Climo, Shirley. **The Korean Cinderella**.
HarperCollins, 1993. ISBN 0 06-020432-X
Greaves, Margaret. **Tattercoats**. Crown, 1990.
ISBN 0-517-58026-8

Oram, Hiawyn. **The Second Princess**.
Illustrated by Tony Ross. Western Publishing Co, 1994. ISBN 0-307-17513-8

This is a humorous look at two sisters, one of whom is very tired of being the second best princess. After many adventures and mishaps, the parents proclaim a solution amenable to both.

Perrault, Charles. **Cinderella or the Little Glass Slipper**. Illustrated by Marcia Brown. Simon and Schuster, 1954. ISBN 0-689-70484-4
This version of the classic story is a Caldecott Medal winner. The illustrations enhance this wonderful rendition of the tale.

OTHER BOOKS BY JOHN STEPTOE

Daddy is a Monster ... Sometimes.
Lippincott, 1980. ISBN 0-064-43042-1
The children's father finds a way to turn into a scary monster. But it occurs only when someone in the family is noisy or messy.

Stevie. Harper, 1969. ISBN 0-874-99050-5
A little boy explains the many problems that his younger foster brother causes. Ultimately he admits that he misses him very much.

The Story of Jumping Mouse. Lothrop, 1984.
ISBN 0-688-01902-1
This is a Plains Indian legend. A mouse is transformed and finds a new land. There are mysterious black and white illustrations. See page 205.

BOOKS ILLUSTRATED BY JOHN STEPTOE

Adoff, Arnold. **All the Colors of Race**.
Lothrop, 1982. ISBN 0-688-11496-2
The poems here are strong. A young girl born of a mixed marriage expresses her feelings and thoughts.

Greenfield, Eloise. **She Come Bringing Me That Little Baby Girl**. Lippincott, 1974.
ISBN 0-064-43296-3
Kevin is not happy about his new baby sister. His uncle's stories gives him insights to help him overcome his resentment.

The Story of Jumping Mouse

by John Steptoe
Mulberry, 1983
ISBN 0-688-08740-X

SUMMARY

This Native American folktale tells of the quest of a little mouse who dreams of finding the far-off land. On his way he is often tempted to give up the dream. He gives away his sight and his smell to other noble beasts, but his dream is strong and he achieves his quest, thanks to the help of a frog. The story can be taken as an allegory of age and death or as the simpler story it seems to be at first glance.

ILLUSTRATION

Drawing skill and mastery of the elements of line and value result in spectacular illustrations. Steptoe is a master of composition, filling the pages as though the images were of cropped photographs.

CONNECTIONS

NOVEL

Lynd Ward's wordless novel **The Silver Pony** (Houghton, 1992. ISBN 0-395-64377-5) is a quest story that can also be considered allegorical.

THEME

▶ Quests

CURRICULUM CONNECTION

▶ SOCIAL STUDIES – Native American folklore

LANGUAGE ARTS

ANALYZING THE STORY

▶ This is a quest story: a character has a goal and sets out to achieve it. While on the quest, the character is both helped and hindered. Make a chart similar to the one below about **The Story of Jumping Mouse**.

The Title	The Quest	Helpers	Hindrances
The Story of Jumping Mouse	the far-off land	the frog the fat mouse the bison the wolf	his lack of sight & smell

▶ When you think about it, many stories are quests. Look at **Amelia's Road** (page 10), **Dandelions** (page 44), **Way Home**, and other titles as quests. Look at novels such as **The Lion, the Witch and the Wardrobe** and **The Search for Delicious** (see Related Books) as quests. Many of the King Arthur stories are quest stories as well. Put the information about some of those books into the chart above.

COMPARING LITERATURE

▶ This folktale is similar to many in which a character helps others and is rewarded. Read **Rainbow Crow** (see Related Books) and compare it to **The Story of Jumping Mouse** and then find others which follow that pattern.

▶ If you think about it, this story could be talking growing old and dying. Some older people lose some of their senses, as does Jumping Mouse. The far-off land could be heaven. Read Paul Goble's **Beyond the Ridge** (see Related Books), a different Native American look at death and dying. Find other stories that deal with the same subject. Write a poem or story or create a painting that shows your thoughts on the subject.

▶ This is one of many folktales from the Native American cultures. Find and tell others. Compare them as to plot, theme and characters.

DEVELOPING VOCABULARY

▶ The bison talks about "the shadows of the sky" as dangers for the mouse. What might he be referring to?

SCIENCE

▶ The bison's sense of sight and the wolf's sense of smell are, of course, important to their existence. What are the enemies of both of these animals and what, in turn, do those animals prey upon? Find a way to show the food chains of which either or both of these animals are a part.

▶ Is there a jumping mouse in real life? If so, what are its habitat and food chain?

▶ The mouse becomes an eagle, which certainly has a keen sense of sight and great flying power. Does it have a sense of smell? Do any birds have the ability to smell?

▶ There are animals and plants in the illustrations of **The Story of Jumping Mouse** that are not mentioned in the text. Identify as many of them as you can and put them on a list. Looking at that list, can you figure out the scene of the story? How far would Jumping Mouse have had to travel to reach those different areas?

SOCIAL STUDIES

▶ The bison was an animal of extreme importance to the Native Americans. What happened to the huge herds of bison that once were found in North America? What's being done to preserve the species? Are bison an endangered species?

ART

▶ John Steptoe chose to illustrate this book in black and white instead of color. For **Mufaro's Beautiful Daughters** (see page 202), he chose to use color. What would the addition of color have done to Jumping Mouse? If you did it in color, what tints and shades of color would you have used? Look at **The Silver Pony** (see Related Books), a wordless novel also done in black and white. Do you think Lynd Ward had the same reasons as Steptoe did for choosing to illustrate his book that way?

▶ Look at some black and white photographs such as those by Ansel Adams. Try some black and white drawings and paintings yourself. Is it more or less challenging to create effects without the use of color in your work?

RELATED BOOKS

NOVELS

Adams, Richard. **Watership Down**.
Simon & Schuster, 1994. ISBN 0-02-700030-3
Grades 4-9
This fantasy about rabbits can also be considered an allegory.

Babbitt, Natalie. **Search for Delicious**.
Farrar, 1985. ISBN 0-374-46536-3 Grades 4-9
Galen's quest is at the behest of the king. He is to poll the kingdom for the definition of "delicious." This is a funny, satirical novel.

Lewis, C. S. **The Lion, the Witch and the Wardrobe**.
Simon & Schuster, 1988. ISBN 0-02-758120-9
Grades 4-9
This is the first in a series of books about the conflict between good and evil, with many quests embedded in the plot.

Ward, Lynd. **The Silver Pony**.
Houghton, 1992. ISBN 0-395-64377-5 Grades 3-9
This wordless novel is the story of a quest and is done completely in black and white.

PICTURE BOOKS

Altman, Linda. **Amelia's Road**
Lee & Low, 1993. ISBN 1-88000-04-0
See page 10.

Goble, Paul. **Beyond the Ridge**.
Simon & Schuster, 1989. ISBN 0-02-736581-6
We follow the spirit of a Plains Indian woman as she begins the journey to the next life.

Hodges, Margaret. **Saint George and the Dragon**.
Illustrated by Trina Schart Hyman, Little, 1984.
ISBN 0-316-36789-3
Trina Hyman received the Caldecott Award for this quest story.

Van Laan, Nancy. **Rainbow Crow**.
Knopf, 1989. ISBN 0-394-89577-0
This folktale is also a quest. The beautiful crow sacrifices her beauty and voice in order to bring fire to the animals.

OTHER BOOKS BY JOHN STEPTOE

Mufaro's Beautiful Daughters See page 202.

I Had a Lot of Wishes

by James Stevenson
Greenwillow 1995
ISBN 0-688-13705-9

SUMMARY

An old man declares, "When I was young I had a lot of wishes." Even though some wishes were impossible, he wished them anyway. Many of his wishes were to make things happen (to be a G-man and capture gangsters). Some were to make things stop, like hoping his parents would stop arguing about nothing. He explains at least four "possible" ways to make wishes come true, familiar to most people. After a summer at camp he wishes he could stop wishing. There is a happy conclusion when this "grown-up boy" decides that probably most of the truly significant wishes he made long ago really did come true.

ILLUSTRATION

This book is done along the lines of an illustrated diary. The format is that of a personal sketchbook. There's an economy of medium use somewhat similar to the work of Jules Feiffer.

CONNECTIONS

NOVEL

Jane Langton's **The Fledgling** (HarperCollins, 1980. ISBN 0-06-440121-9) portrays a girl with one wish — to fly.

THEMES

▶ Memoirs

Growing up

CURRICULUM CONNECTION

▶ HISTORY – 1930s and 1940s

LANGUAGE ARTS

EXTENDING THE STORY

▶ The boy used four possible ways to make wishes: cake candles, tooth fairy, evening star and wishbone. Canvas friends, family and classmates and add to the list.

▶ Many people use magic objects as charms to make wishes, e.g., stones, jewelry, rabbit's foot. Research other magic "touchstones."

▶ Decide if the Disney songs "make sense": "Wishing Will Make It So" or "When You Wish Upon a Star" (your dreams come true). Add to these titles with proverbs, quotations, poems, other songs about wishes.

USING FIGURATIVE LANGUAGE

▶ At summer camp, they told ghost stories. Create "spooky" stories. Take turns telling or reading them to the class.

▶ When the boy said goodbye to all his friends, their pictures are shown with their names. Choose four or five of them to describe in detail.

USING CATEGORIZING AND CLASSIFICATION

▶ Assemble a collection of various fables and fairy tales and other books in which wishes are featured. Add those wishes that are mentioned in threes.

▶ Read and then index the "wishing" section. Classify the various types. Include wishes that come true, wishes that don't come true, childhood wishes, adult wishes, serious wishes, frivolous wishes and lifesaving wishes.

▶ Share the results: If granted, were they used wisely? Foolishly? In anger? Greed? If not, were the consequences serious?

▶ In the book, the boy classifies his wishes. Find his five kinds of wishes. Classify these as do-able or impossible, or name the ones that were given a 50:50 chance.

EXPANDING THE STORY

▶ This boy grows to be an old man. Write about his present life. Does he spend time wishing? Where does he live? With whom? Does he have grandchildren? Is he happy?

▶ His childhood friends were David, Dorothy and Bill. Does he still have contact with them? What happened to them?

EXAMINING THE ILLUSTRATIONS

▶ What technique did the artist use? Find out and make some watercolor sketches of people in your life.

▶ Sometimes it's a little difficult to find details. Were his camp friends all boys? What about the counselors? On the last page, decide if there are grandchildren. Are they girls or boys? Speculate what kind of dog Jocko was.

SOCIAL STUDIES

▶ Camp Wampasohee was an overnight boat trip from New York City to Cape Cod in Massachusetts. Using a road map, decide how long the trip was. Is it shorter by boat or car?

▶ Choose various areas in New York State and map out a trip to Cape Cod.

▶ Decide on an area in the United States and again trace the route to Cape Cod.

▶ Study the location of the camp (Cape Cod). List the advantages of a camp in this area. What activities would be possible? Speculate on the advantages and disadvantages, if any.

▶ Describe various summer camps you've attended. Where were they? How far away? Did the location have any bearing on the activities, i.e., swimming, climbing, horseback riding?

▶ Why did the trip home take two days? Estimate the year in which this trip took place. Are there any other hints to help place the time period? What about the Roosevelt button and the plastic pickle pin?

▶ At summer camp "they made you make things you don't want to make." Compose a set of directions for someone who would be forced to make something.

▶ Choose any school projects that require directions and write clear and concise instructions for completing them.

▶ The boy said goodbye to his camp friends. There were 13 children illustrated with their names. Most are boy's names. Are there any "unisex" names? What about Sam?

▶ This could have been a boys' camp. Brainstorm the advantages and disadvantages of girls only, boys only, or mixed.

▶ This camp had some negatives, including "bossy counselors." Find other negatives. List all the positives (include setting). Which negatives turned to positives?

▶ Name the "good stuff" his father had on his desk. Which objects were hints about his profession as an architect?

▶ List desk items for various professions, such as librarian, secretary, artist, doctor.

▶ Have computers changed desk uses? How?

SCIENCE

▶ What foods were shown that the boy in the story didn't like? Are any of these served today? Do they fit into the major food groups in the food pyramid?

▶ Plan a menu that would please the whole class and would contain the five food groups.

▶ Interview the cooks. What are the favorite and least favorite foods in your school?

MATH

What percentage of the class eats school lunch? What percentage of the whole school?

▶ RELATED BOOKS

NOVELS

Langton, Jane. **The Fledgling**. HarperCollins, 1980. ISBN 0-06-440121-9 Grades 3-6
A little girl named Georgie wishes to fly. After meeting a mysterious Canada goose, she gets her wish.

Maclachlan, Patricia. **Sarah Plain and Tall**. HarperCollins 1985. ISBN 0-06-024102-0
Grades 3-6
Everyone in the family has a wish, even Sarah, the mail-order bride. This Newbery Award winner is wonderful to read aloud.

Maclachlan, Patricia. **Arthur, for the Very First Time**. HarperCollins, 1980. ISBN 0-06-024047-4
Grades 3-6
Arthur spends the summer with his aunt and uncle and learns as much about himself as he does about the farm.

Paulsen, Gary. **Winter Room**.
Orchard, 1989. ISBN 0-531-08439-6 Grades 5-9
A young boy's extended visit on a farm in northern Minnesota teaches him a lot about wars fought miles away.

Paulsen, Gary. **Popcorn Days and Buttermilk Nights**.
Lodestar, 1983. ISBN 0-525-66770-9 Grades 4-9

A boy works with his uncle at the blacksmith's forge to create magic for the kids in town after a hard harvest season.

PICTURE BOOKS

Cooney, Barbara. **Miss Rumphius**.
Puffin, 1985. ISBN 0-14-050539-3
Miss Rumphius lived to carry out all her dreams, including making the world more beautiful.

Houston, Gloria. **My Great Aunt Arizona**
See page 99.

Rylant, Cynthia. **When I Was Young in the Mountains**. Dutton, 1982. ISBN 0-525-44198-0
The author remembers what it was like growing up in the mountains in a coal-mining family.

Say, Allen. **Grandfather's Journey** See page 184.

OTHER BOOKS BY JAMES STEVENSON

Don't You Know There's a War On.
Greenwillow, 1992. ISBN 0-688-11394-2
Fun No Fun. Greenwillow, 1994. ISBN 0-688-11674-4
Higher on the Door. Greenwillow, 1987.
ISBN 0-688-06637-2
These picture books all relate the author's memories of growing up in the 1930s and 1940s.

The Araboolies of Liberty Street

by Sam Swope
Illustrated by Barry Root
Crown, 1995. ISBN 0-517-56960-4

SUMMARY

In this town, the houses are all neat, the people are well behaved, and there is safety. There is also fear, however, because of General Pinch and his wife, who are ever watchful for any deviation from the norm. Bellowing "I'll call in the army!" at any misbehavior, no matter how slight, the general and his wife are able to keep everything under control and everyone under their thumbs. Then the Araboolies move in next door to the Pinches. They don't understand the language and, what's more, they don't care! Their carefree existence, which violates all that the Pinches hold dear, is bound to bring about a confrontation. And so it does. There's a didactic message here, but it's so exuberantly and humorously presented that we absorb it and, as a result, we laugh at the "Pinches" we encounter.

ILLUSTRATION

Barry Root's illustrations reveal a skilled painter and colorist who has great experience with color mixing. For example, surfaces that read as an off-green color are really the result of mixing of pigment on paper using two primaries(yellow and blue. The fun is to figure out how other colors are achieved.

CONNECTIONS

NOVEL

Kendall's **The Gammage Cup** (Harcourt, 1990. ISBN 0-15-230575-0) involves a need for conformity and the rebellious group that refuses to comply.

THEMES

▶ Conformists and nonconformists

CURRICULUM CONNECTION

▶ HISTORY – McCarthy Era

LANGUAGE ARTS

EXTENDING THE TEXT

▶ In this book even the title is ironic: There is no liberty on Liberty Street. Look in your town for other inadvertently ironic names. Are there elm trees on Elm Street? Is the town square square?

▶ One child in the story persuades the others to rally. How did this happen? What are some ways to persuade others to follow you? Have you ever done things as part of a group that you would not have done alone?

▶ Find some mottoes or lines from speeches that persuaded others to react or act in some way: "Give me liberty or give me death," "I have a dream," "Win one for the gipper."

▶ Think about the things in your own basement, garage or attic that you have been able to use in the plot of the book. Which could you muster within 10 minutes?

COMPARING LITERATURE

▶ Find and read other books about conformity such as **Sneetches**, **Rebel** (see page 16) and the chapter in **Wrinkle in Time** (see Related Books) about the planet where everybody does the same thing at the same time.

▶ Find and read such books as **Old Henry**, **The Big Orange Splot**, **Shaker Lane** and **Miss Tizzy**, which are all about non-conformists. See related books.

OTHER LANGUAGES

▶ The Araboolies are not worried about the army, because they don't understand the language spoken there. Ask people who speak different languages to direct you blindfolded through a maze of crackers on the floor using a language you do not understand. By the end of the maze, which words or phrases do you now understand?

SOCIAL STUDIES

This neighborhood has strict rules of behavior and appearance, thanks to the domination of one family. What rules exist in your neighborhood? Who makes them? Are there zoning laws? Noise pollution controls?

▶ Investigate planned communities such as Levittown and Celebration City. What are the advantages and disadvantages of living in such regulated communities?

▶ What's the difference between a neighborhood watch program and vigilante groups?

▶ The army in this book follows orders without question. Is that a good thing? Should all armies follow orders at all times? After World War II, many war criminals claimed that they were merely soldiers following orders. Did they have a choice?

▶ In the story, the parents were held back by the army and the threat of the army even if the children were not. They locked and barred their doors. Is this what they did in China, Hungary or Bosnia during recent uprisings? What choice did these real people have?

▶ During the 1950s there was much fear that Communism was a destructive force in American society. Find out about the McCarthy era and its effect on society.

▶ During the uprising in Tienamin Square in China, one person stopped a tank. How?

ART

▶ Make a classroom mural of a street with real individuality. Let individuals design and cut out a building for the mural.

MUSIC

▶ Find and sing the song "Little Boxes" by Malvina Reynolds, recorded in the 1970s by several artists. It's about people who are complete conformists living in houses that are just alike.

RELATED BOOKS

NOVELS

Kendall, Carol. **The Gammage Cup**.
Harcourt, 1990. ISBN 0-15-230575-0 Grades 4-8
A society of tiny people demands conformity in the color of the clothing and houses and one group rebels and is banished. This exiled group eventually uncovers a dastardly plot against the minipins and rescues them.

L'Engle, Madeline. **A Wrinkle in Time**.
Dell, 1976. ISBN 0-440-99805-0 Grades 4-9
This is a novel about many things including the strength within the individual. When Meg and Charles are looking for their parents, they view many different ways of life including complete conformity.

Lowry, Lois. **The Giver**.
Houghton, 1993. ISBN 0-395-64566-2 Grades 5-9
A futuristic society appears to be perfect, but the price these people have paid for it is too great.

Robinson, Barbara. **Best Christmas Pageant Ever**.
HarperCollins, 1988. ISBN 0-06-440275-4
Grades 3-6
The pageant was going well until the Herdmans took over and taught everyone a lesson.

PICTURE BOOKS

Baillie, Alan. **Rebel** See page 16.

Blos, Joan. **Old Henry**.
Morrow, 1987. ISBN 0-688-06399-3
At first, the neighbors are delighted when Henry moves into the derelict house, convinced that he will fix it up to look like the rest of the houses; however, Henry likes it just the way it is.

Dr. Seuss. **Sneetches**.
Random, 1961. ISBN 0-394-80089-3
The need to be just like everybody else is ridiculed deliciously in this book; the only one to profit by this mania is Sylvester McMonkey McBean.

Gray, Libba. **Miss Tizzy**.
Simon & Schuster, 1993. ISBN 0-671-77590-1
The adults in the neighborhood are upset by Miss Tizzy's nonconformist ways, but the children adore her.

Pinkwater, Daniel. **The Big Orange Splot**.
Hastings, 1992. ISBN 0-8038-9346-9
One man's individuality spreads out from his most unusual house until the whole neighborhood becomes involved.

Provensen, Alice and Martin. **Shaker Lane**.
Puffin, 1990. ISBN 0-14-050713-2
One area of town is inhabited by people who are not as anxious to be conventional and neat as the rest of the town is. So, when one area of town needs to be flooded out, guess which area goes?

How to Live Forever

by Colin Thompson
Knopf, 1995
ISBN 0-679-87898-X

➤ SUMMARY

Here is fantasy about a huge library with one lost book. Acting out the title, **How to Live Forever**, a boy named Peter and his cat Brian spend two years in search of that lost book. Peter and his family actually reside within one of the books in the library. As this fantasy unfolds, we travel through many of the come-to-life books and meet their inhabitants, who also come to life as the library closes each night. When Peter and Brian finally discover the fate of the lost book, he is faced with the most important decision of his young life: Should he read the book or not?

➤ ILLUSTRATION

Details, details details. Peter begins his journey at what appear to be the gates of the British Museum. There's a wonderful playfulness of scale contrasting predictable size relationships with imaginative ones in juxtaposition. At one point, Peter may think he's going into a Chinese garden, but it's really the Willow Tree Plate. One monotone figure has Peter sitting on a chair with the rest of the bizarre illustration in full color. There are no major art movements that are not represented somewhere here. The spatial games of Escher are evident, as are various Japanese portrayers of Mt. Fuji.

➤ CONNECTIONS

NOVEL

Tuck Everlasting by Natalie Babbitt (Farrar, 1979. ISBN 0-374-37848-7) is a novel that also involves characters destined to live forever.

THEMES

▶ Time
▶ Living forever

CURRICULUM CONNECTION

▶ LITERATURE – Many references to various well-known books and their characters

LANGUAGE ARTS

WRITING

▶ After reading the story, study the illustrations. Choose a favorite book that you would like to visit in that library after closing time. Write a short narrative explaining why you chose that book and which characters you wish to spend time with and why.

EXTENDING THE BOOK

▶ Notice the titles of the books on the cover. Hunt for more book titles related to the concept of time. Who can come up with the longest list of time titles? You might wish to do the same with song titles or clichés related to time.

VOCABULARY DEVELOPMENT

▶ Take time to read some of the titles the author has included in his illustrations. Most of them are puns based on titles of real books. Take a book title list and rewrite the titles making your own puns.

▶ Peter winds up speaking to the Ancient Child. His "title" in itself is an oxymoron. Discuss what an oxymoron is. Think of other oxymorons such as jumbo shrimp, army intelligence.

FINDING DETAILS

▶ By examining the illustrations, find where the author has included his initials and the year he drew the illustration? Study each page carefully and you might be able to find it every time!

DEBATING

▶ "Should Peter read the book or not?" Use a graphic organizer titled "Persuasion" with a space for you to write your response to the question whether Peter should or should not read the book. The remainder of the organizer should be divided into four sections, each titled "Reason." Come up with four legitimate reasons to defend your argument. Now divide your class into two groups, those in favor and those opposed to Peter reading the book. Each group will critique the written responses to choose the four most convincing arguments. Have a spokesperson from each group present their argument to the rest of the class. After hearing both sides, vote to determine what more people want. Have any opinions changed as a result of this mini-debate?

COMPARING LITERATURE

▶ Can you find other books related to or taking place in libraries? Start with **Aunt Chip and the Triple Creek Dam Affair** by Patricia Polacco (page 160) and **Library Lil** (page 162).

MATH

▶ Peter and Brian spent two years looking for the lost book. How many nights did they spend doing this? Assuming that they spent four hours each night in the library, how many hours, minutes and seconds were they involved in the search?

▶ The record card disappeared 200 years ago. How many decades is that? Years? Days? Hours? Minutes? Seconds?

SOCIAL STUDIES

▶ How are books organized in your library? Is it possible to remove a single card from your filing system and erase all permanent record of that book?

▶ What are the possible ways to locate a particular book or a book on a specific topic in the library?

▶ Compare the old card catalogues to the new computer databases. Now you can locate books not only in your own library, but all over the country.

▶ Peter was finally assisted in finding the lost book by four old men in front of a row of ancient Chinese books. Examine the illustrations for other indications of Chinese culture.

RELATED BOOKS

NOVELS

Avi. **Who Stole the Wizard of Oz?**
Knopf, 1981. ISBN 0-394-84992-2 Grades 3-6
A book is missing from the library, and two children follow the clues to the culprit.

Babbitt, Natalie. **Tuck Everlasting**.
Farrar, 1979. ISBN 0-374-37848-7 Grades 4-8
This novel tells the tale of a family destined to live forever after drinking water from a spring.

Miles, Betty. **Maude and Me and the Dirty Book**.
Avon, 1991. ISBN 0-380-55541-7 Grades 3-6
An innocent book becomes a controversial one in this novel about censorship.

PICTURE BOOKS

Polacco, Patricia. **Aunt Chip and the Triple Creek Dam Affair** See page 160.

Polacco, Patricia. **The Bee Tree**.
Putnam, 1993. ISBN 0-399-21965-X
This tale teaches a young girl that sweetness can be found between the pages of a book.

Rahaman, Vashanti. **Read for Me, Mama**.
Boyds' Mill, 1997. ISBN 1-56397-313-8
A little boy loves the stories his mama reads(but she cannot read.

Williams, Suzanne. **Library Lil**.
Dial, 1997. ISBN 0-8037-1698-2
When a storm knocks out the television in town, Library Lil takes over.

Dakota Dugout

By Ann Turner
Illustrated by Ronald Himler
Simon & Schuster, 1985
ISBN 0-02-789700-1

SUMMARY

The book begins with these two sentences: "Tell you about the prairie years? I'll tell you, child, how it was." A well-dressed Victorian lady tells about life on the Dakota prairie. She traveled, first alone by train, and then with her husband Matt by wagon, to the sod house which was their first home. When she saw it, she cried at the sight of the gloomy dwelling of earth strips. She talks about the way it was made and the paper window that gave so little light. She tells of their joy when, after a year of backbreaking work tilling the soil, prosperity enabled them to build a clapboard house "with windows like suns." The memory of the beauty and hardship of the prairie life never leaves the woman.

ILLUSTRATION

Solid drawing is the basis for these illustrations. The compositions are straightforward representations of the text, organized and arranged as though they are part of a portfolio, each composed in an orderly fashion, centered on a single page, and contained within the line of a simple frame. By building his forms with line density, Ronald Himler creates a full-value scale of dark to light.

CONNECTIONS

NOVEL

The same author's **Grasshopper Summer** (Simon, 1989. ISBN 0-02-789511-4) gives more details about life in a sod house.

THEME

▶ Homes and shelters

CURRICULUM CONNECTION

▶ HISTORY – Westward movement, prairie settlements

LANGUAGE ARTS
DESCRIPTIVE WRITING

▶ Characterize Matt and his wife during their first year on the prairie. What do you know about each of them?

▶ List the good and bad qualities of the sod house.

▶ Describe the occasions when the weather was observed in the text.

▶ List some words that might describe the feelings of Matt and his wife when the corn finally grew.

BUILDING VOCABULARY

▶ When the corn grew, the couple saw "dresses, buggies, and gold." Did they really? What happened when their dreams disappeared? Can you write or find some morals about that experience?

▶ Matt and his wife never gave up in spite of the many hardships. Can you find a proverb that might describe their experience?

▶ The woman says, "Sometimes the things we start with are best." How does that compare with your family's experiences? What would you say about that expression? Have you ever known that to be true for you?

▶ Reread the text and find and explain these expressions:

"windows like the sun"
"tocked like a busy heart"
"green spreading faster than fire"

▶ Find other phrases you like in the story and read them aloud.

USING CAUSE AND EFFECT

▶ This story lends itself to speculation. What if:

The woman had not even tried to live in the sod house?

The setbacks they endured convinced them to return to the city?

The corn never grew?

The cattle died?

Matt gave up and never built the clapboard house?

No one successfully lived in a sod house?

SOCIAL STUDIES

▶ Decide on the time period that Matt and his wife lived in the sod house. Use hints in the story for verification. Use other books to compare clothing styles of the women in the city street. Find out when the peak time was for sod houses on the prairie.

▶ Draw a time line of the important events in the history of the United States. Mark the Westward Movement and the time of this book especially.

▶ Research the effort made by the pioneers to clear the land and settle it. Who was there before them? What happened to those people? Would their view of the sod houses be the same as this woman's?

▶ Research the Homestead laws. Speculate on the reasons why this couple might have chosen the Dakota Territory for their home.

SCIENCE
ANIMALS

▶ A number of animals are mentioned or pictured in the story. Find and list them and decide what effect, if any, the westward movement had on their lives.

▶ What animals were used by settlers for food? Show the food cycle as affected by these animals. Could the settlers have survived without them?

CLIMATE

▶ Locate the Dakota Territory on a map from 1776-1867. Find out about the weather in that area. Check recent papers and TV weather reports for further information. Decide on the effect of current weather on sod houses, if they still existed.

▶ Investigate the type of food, clothing and shelter appropriate for the pioneers in this territory. Why didn't they build log cabins as eastern settlers frequently did?

▶ Investigate the various "grasshopper plagues" that descended on the settlers. What effect did they have? Why don't they occur these days? What "plagues" do occur? Find out about the Mediterranean fruit fly in the California area, mad cow disease and bird flu.

ART

▶ Using real sod, replicate a sod house in miniature. Try to use the materials described in the book for windows, floors, roof and walls.

▶ Do the same for a clapboard house of the era.

RELATED BOOKS

See **Dandelions** on page 44 for more books on this subject.

NOVEL

Turner, Ann. **Grasshopper Summer**.
Simon, 1989. ISBN 0-02-789511-4 Grades 3-6
This novel gives more details about life in a sod house.

NONFICTION

Conrad, Pam. **Prairie Visions: The Life and Times of Solomon Butcher**. HarperCollins, 1994.
ISBN 0-06-446135-1
This nonfictional pictorial biography of a photographer on the prairie shows many settlers outside their sod and clapboard houses and gives much information about the many people who came to the prairie to make their homes and livings there.

Rounds, Glen. **Sod Houses on the Great Plains**
This is an excellent, accesssible book on the subject.

OTHER BOOKS BY ANN TURNER AND RONALD HIMLER

Nettie's Trip South. Simon & Schuster, 1987.
ISBN 0-02-789240-9
Taken from a diary of the author's great-grandmother, this book describes a trip she took to Virginia, where she saw the effects of slavery for the first time. See page 223.

Katie's Trunk. Simon & Schuster, 1992.
ISBN 0-02-789512-2
This picture book, set in the time of the Revolutionary War, tells a simple story with a big message: Humanity can transcend the effects of war.

OTHER BOOKS WRITTEN BY ANN TURNER

Apple Valley Year. Simon & Schuster, 1993.
ISBN 0-02-789281-6
Hard-working apple farmers show us one year of their lives in this quiet picture book.

Christmas House. HarperCollins, 1994.
ISBN 0-06-023429-6
Each part of the old house tells us of a Christmas memory.

Grass Songs. Harcourt, 1993. ISBN 0-15-136788-4
In free verse, with beautiful illustrations by Barry Moser, the author gives a poetic look at the prairie as seen through the eyes of pioneer women.

Grasshopper Summer. Simon & Schuster, 1989.
ISBN 0-02-789511-4
This short novel describes more fully the same time and area as **Dakota Dugout** does, but through the lives of one family coping with disaster and some success on the prairie.

Heron Street. HarperCollins, 1989.
ISBN 0-06-026184-6
The author traces the changes in an eastern swamp from the Revolution to the present. See page 220.

Heron Street

by Ann Turner
Illustrated by Lisa Desimini
HarperCollins, 1989
ISBN 0-06-026184-6

SUMMARY

A marsh by a sea is home to many animals and birds until progress turns it into a noisy city. As the city encroaches, the animals are forced to move. The process takes place over the course of many generations.

ILLUSTRATION

The drawings of the objects and figures capture the subject matter in a static fashion, while the color is used in a powerfully imaginative way. In certain illustrations that use of color is reminiscent of Marc Chagall. The illustrations themselves, when seen from page to page, establish a predictable pattern.

CONNECTIONS

NOVEL

Jean George's **Talking Earth** (HarperCollins, 1983. ISBN 0-06-440212-6) involves the changes in the Everglades due to human encroachment.

THEME

▶ Effects of progress

CURRICULUM CONNECTION

▶ SCIENCE – Effects of civilization on ecology

LANGUAGE ARTS

USING FIGURATIVE LANGUAGE

▶ Find out what "onomatopoeia" is. Generate examples from the story and allow students to add more. Why is the use of onomatopoeia an effective writing technique?

▶ List street names from your own community. Do the names seem to fit the streets? For example does your Elm Street have elm trees along it? Why might your streets have been originally named as they were? Can you come up with more appropriate names?

COMPARING LITERATURE

▶ Read **Letting Swift River Go** by Jane Yolen (see page 245). How is this book different from **Heron Street**? List some of the reasons why communities were eliminated to create the Quabbin Reservoir. Are the reasons valid? What effect might the creation of Quabbin have on wildlife? Hold a mock town meeting to discuss the pros and cons of the idea.

SCIENCE

▶ What other animals might have been found in this marshy area? Make a chart listing the possible inhabitants. What would attract them to the area, and what food they would find there?

▶ The folks in this story built a town on a marsh. Investigate your local laws and regulations regarding building on wetlands. What are the restrictions? Are they fair?

▶ Make a chart showing animals that used to be in your locale and are no longer present. Why? Look at the wildlife that remains. What keeps them there?

▶ Find out if there are wetlands in your area. What defines a wetland? What rules govern its use?

SOCIAL STUDIES

▶ Look at your own neighborhood. How has it changed within your own memory? Interview an older member of the community to find out how things have changed. Then write "Before and After" stories or charts and illustrate them.

▶ Find the illustration in the book where the men are beginning to build. What other buildings would be needed to create a complete community? List them and then prioritize the list in order of importance. Would you build a hospital before building a library? Present an argument to defend your choices.

▶ Study the illustrations to determine the approximate years in which the changes took place.

▶ What might the settlers have done to protect the wildlife in the area? Make a list of regulations for developing a new community that might allow progress and at the same time protect the wildlife

ART

▶ Use watercolors to sketch and paint a variety of water fowl.

▶ Design a model of the ideal community. How does the model work with nature?

▶ Draw before-and-after illustrations of your neighborhood or of an imaginary setting.

▶ Look at examples of architecture. Look at pictures of buildings and determine what weather conditions prompted their design.

RELATED BOOKS

NOVEL

George, Jean. **Talking Earth**.
HarperCollins, 1983. ISBN 0-06-440212-6
Grades 4-8
A Seminole girl is sent into the Everglades to learn to embrace her heritage.

PICTURE BOOKS

Cherry, Lynne. A **River Ran Wild**.
Harcourt, 1992. ISBN 0-15-200542-0
The story of the Nashua River in New England and its pollution and clean-up.

Yolen Jane. **Letting Swift River Go** See page 245.

Martin, Jacqueline Briggs. **Washing the Willow Tree Loon** See page 145.

NONFICTION

Isaacson, Philip. **Round Buildings, Square Buildings, Buildings that Wiggle Like a Fish**.
Knopf, 1990 ISBN 0-394-89382-4
This book explores various architectural styles around the world.

OTHER BOOKS BY ANN TURNER

Dakota Dugout See page 217.

Nettie's Trip South

by Ann Turner
Simon & Schuster, 1987
ISBN 0-02-789240-9

▷ SUMMARY

This book is based on the diary of the author's great-grandmother, Nettie, and is presented as a letter to her friend Addie. When she was 10 years old, Nettie took a trip from Albany, New York, to Richmond, Virginia, where she experienced the sights and sounds of the South in pre-Civil War days. Slaves with no last names lived in crowded slave quarters and did back-breaking work in the cotton fields. The most sickening event was the slave auction. Nettie writes, "If we slipped into a black skin like a tight coat, everything would change." Nettie's trip ends with her realization that the images she has seen will haunt her forever.

▷ ILLUSTRATION

These traditional illustrations are strong examples of drawings in graphite. The illustrations are photograph-like compositions that extend the text.

▷ CONNECTIONS

NOVEL

There are at least two connections between this book and Joan Blos's **A Gathering of Days: A New England Girl's Journal, 1830 - 1832** (Simon & Schuster, 1990. ISBN 0-689-71419-X): Both are stories told as journals and one of the characters in each is a slave.

THEMES

▶ Slavery
▶ Letters

CURRICULUM CONNECTION

▶ HISTORY – Slavery

Language Arts

RECALLING DETAILS

▶ Write a short biography of each of the travelers – Nettie, Julia and Lockwood. Include descriptions, age, personality traits and any other pertinent information.

▶ If you were Lockwood, what would you write in a newspaper article about this trip? What do you think he meant when he said, "I've seen all I need to see"?

▶ What do you think were Tabitha's feelings when she met Nettie in the hotel and when she waved goodbye?

▶ Make a list of the ways in which slaves were meant to think of themselves as less than human.

VOCABULARY DEVELOPMENT

▶ Brainstorm the sights, sounds and smells of the South in this story. List them in chart form. Add those that are implied as well as those stated in the text.

▶ Find the figurative phrases in the book and explain what they mean: "sharp tongue," " slipped into a black skin," "face like the oak."

MAKING COMPARISONS

▶ Compare the attitude of Nettie toward slavery with one that a Virginia white girl of the time might have.

WRITING

▶ If you haven't already done so, start a journal. React to this book and other reading in your journal. Will you share it with others or keep it private?

Social Studies

▶ Was there slavery in the North? Why did it last longer in the South?

▶ John Adams used the Declaration of Independence to defend Cinque after he led a slave rebellion. Watch clips from *Amistad*. What about Morgan Freeman's character? He's supposed to be a composite of many abolitionists. What beliefs did abolitionists share?

▶ Research the role of the North in slavery. For instance, the cotton mills of the North needed the cotton produced by the slaves in the South. Compare that to current American use of goods made in other countries by cheaper labor.

▶ Make a map showing the states and territories of the United States in 1861, coloring the slave states and free states differently.

▶ Research as many different kinds and conditions of slavery as you can find: house slaves, field slaves, living conditions, abuse, paternalistic treatment, humane treatment, opportunities for freedom: purchase, deed and escape.

▶ Find the names of as many well-known historic figures as possible, especially U. S. presidents, who were slave owners. Find portraits of them and make a bulletin board display. Under each portrait, list the person's accomplishments as well as his role in slavery.

▶ Read the Preamble to the Declaration of Independence. How do you think slave owners would handle that part about "life, liberty, and the pursuit of happiness"?

MAP READING

▶ Nettie traveled by train from Albany, New York, to Richmond, Virginia. Could she do it today? Trace the possible route on a map. What cities might she have seen on her way there?

HISTORY

▶ Design a time line of key dates in U. S. civil rights history. Illustrate it appropriately. Add flags, photographs and biographies.

RELATED BOOKS

PICTURE BOOKS

Boulton, Jane. **Only Opal: The Diary of a Young Girl**. Putnam, 1994. ISBN 0-399-21990-0
These are excerpts from a five-year-old girl's diary from the lumber camps of Oregon (see Related Books).

Lawrence, Jacob. **Harriet and the Promised Land**. Simon & Schuster, 1993. ISBN 0-671-86673-7
With dramatic poster-like illustrations and narrative poetry, Lawrence brings the life of Harriet Tubman closer.

Winter, Jeannette. **Follow the Drinking Gourd**. Knopf, 1988. ISBN 0-394-99694-1
This is a book about slaves using the Underground Railroad, but the leader is a white man.

NOVELS

Blos, Joan. **A Gathering of Days: A New England Girl's Journal, 1830 - 1832**. Simon & Schuster, 1990. ISBN 0-689-71419-X Grades 3-6
This book is referenced for two reasons: It's a journal, as is **Nettie's Trip South**, and it deals with a runaway slave.

Collier, James. **Jump Ship to Freedom**. Delacorte, 1981. ISBN 0-440-44323-7 Grades 5-9
This novel tells of the buying and selling of slaves around the time of the Revolution.

Fritz, Jean. **Brady**.
Puffin, 1987. ISBN 0-14-032258-2 Grades 4-8
Brady has trouble keeping secrets, but when he finds out that his father is a conductor on the Underground Railroad, the keeping of secrets is vital.

NONFICTION

McMullan, Kate. **The Story of Harriet Tubman, Conductor on the Underground Railroad**. Illustrated by Steven James Petruccio. Dell, 1991. ISBN 0-440-40400-2
This moving, well-written biography begins with her owner's hiring Harriet out to another white family in Maryland and ends with her death. It's a memorable account of a fascinating and heroic woman.

McKissack, Patricia & Fredrick. **Christmas in the Big House, Christmas in the Quarters**. Scholastic, 1992. ISBN 0-590-43027-0
The actual living conditions of slaves on a Virginia plantation in 1859 are the focus of this picture book.

Whiteley, Opal. **Opal: The Journal of an Understanding Heart**. Tioga, 1984. ISBN 0-935382-52-6
This is the full journal that was excerpted for **Only Opal** (see Boulton above).

Other Books by Ann Turner and Ron Himler
Dakota Dugout See page 217.

Katie's Trunk. Simon & Schuster, 1992. ISBN 0-02-789512-2
This picture book, set in the time of the Revolutionary War, tells a simple story with a big message: Humanity can transcend the effects of war.

Bad Day at Riverbend

by Chris Van Allsburg
Houghton, 1995
ISBN 0-395-67347-X

SUMMARY

This deceptively simple picture book is a puzzle or maybe even a joke, but it leaves the reader smiling and maybe thinking about what's real and what is illusion (a typical reaction to many of Van Allsburg's books.) This one, however, is a visual departure for him. Something awful is happening at Riverbend. Horses, cattle and people are being covered with a mysterious, greasy substance. It's up to the sheriff to find out just what it is. There are clues for both reader and sheriff, but the ending for many will be a surprise.

ILLUSTRATION

Van Allsburg (and youngsters) understand that the purpose of having a coloring book is to have fun with color. The most relevant images are the childlike drawings of the cowboys and horses superimposed on the staid coloring book images.

CONNECTIONS

NOVEL

Sid Fleischman's **Jim Ugly** (Greenwillow, 1984. ISBN 0-688-10886-5) also involves a puzzle in the old West.

THEME

▶ Puzzles and riddles

CURRICULUM CONNECTION

▶ HISTORY – Old West

LANGUAGE ARTS
FINDING DETAILS
▶ After you've read the book and solved the puzzle, go back to look for clues that could have helped you solve it earlier.

▶ Who's doing the coloring? The answer is in the book but not on the pages.

▶ Look carefully at the pictures on each page. If the text were not there, as it probably would not be in a real coloring book, what might each picture have for a caption?

COMPARING LITERATURE
▶ In this book, the point at which reality and fantasy meet is the spot where the crayon touches the paper. Look for other books where there is such a transition point. Make a bulletin board that shows these points such as the wardrobe in **The Lion, the Witch and the Wardrobe**, the keyhole in the medicine chest in **The Indian in the Cupboard** and the mirror in **Through the Magic Mirror**. Sometimes these transition points are more obvious in time fantasies. Add some examples to your bulletin board and indicate the sources.

▶ This book is a puzzle involving perspective. Look at **Zoom** and **Black and White** (see page 138) for more perspective play, and then find other books where the reader is fooled in that way.

▶ In some books, the reader is not fooled, but a character in the book is. Look at the story in **Owl at Home** where Owl can't figure out those bumps at the foot of his bed. Find others where the reader is in on the joke, but the character is not.

▶ Although this book looks very different from anything else Chris Van Allsburg has done, there is a similarity in plot to some of his books. Read **Jumanji**, for instance, and think about the way you feel at the end of the book. Is it in any way similar to the way you feel at the end of this one? (See Related Books.)

SCIENCE
▶ When the crayon is used on the coloring book, the coloring book changes, but so does the crayon, which is now slightly worn down because of that action. Make a list of other actions that result in change that is less immediately obvious. For instance, when a car is driven over a paved road, what changes? The road? The tire? The car? The atmosphere? Take one of the actions on your list and illustrate the changes, going as far as you can to identify the reactions.

SOCIAL STUDIES
▶ The name of this community, Riverbend, is probably descriptive. There is, no doubt, a river that bends in that area. Look through an atlas and list other towns having similarly descriptive names. Write to the Chamber of Commerce in one or more of those towns or cities to find out if the description is still accurate. What is the origin of the name of your city, county and state?

▶ This book is set in the Old West. Find other picture books with the same setting.

ART
▶ Although not many picture books are quite as similar to coloring books as this one, there are many in which, if you look closely, you can see that the pictures were probably first outlined and then colored in by the artist. Check **In the Night Kitchen** and the work of Kevin Henkes, for instance. Then look at James Stevenson's **Don't You Know There's a War On**, which is done very differently. Look closely at several picture books to see if you can tell which came first, the line or the color.

▶ Chris Van Allsburg's style of illustration varies considerably in his work. Assemble as many of his books as possible. Put books with similar styles in separate piles. How many piles do you get? Which style do you like best? If **Polar Express** had been illustrated in the same style and media as **Bad Day at Riverbend**, what effect would it have had on the mood of the book? (See Related Books.)

▶ Look for fine art that uses the same medium, style or technique that appears in one of Van Allsburg's books.

▶ Lots of people discourage coloring in coloring books. They feel that, while fun for some kids, it really isn't a good thing to do very often because it makes some of us dissatisfied with our own art and less willing to experiment with art. What do you think? Can you defend your answer?

RELATED BOOKS

NOVELS

Banks, Lynne R. **The Indian in the Cupboard**.
Avon, 1982. ISBN 0-380-60012-9 Grades 3-5
This first in a series of books about a boy and his toy Indian uses an antique key and lock as the entry point to fantasy.

Fleischman, Sid. **Jim Ugly**.
Greenwillow, 1984. ISBN 0-688-10886-5 Grades 3-6
A puzzle is the focus in this novel about the old West.

Lewis, C. S. **The Lion, the Witch and the Wardrobe**.
HarperCollins, 1994. ISBN 0-06-440499-4
Grades 3-6
This first in a series of books about Narnia uses the wardrobe as the point of entry to Narnia.

PICTURE BOOKS

Browne, Anthony. **Through the Magic Mirror**.
Greenwillow, 1992. ISBN 0-688-10725-7
Strange things are seen when you walk through a mirror.

Henkes, Kevin. **Chester's Way**.
Puffin, 1989. ISBN 0-14-054053-9
This is just one of many books by Kevin Henkes, who often uses pen outlines with filled-in color.

Lobel, Arnold. **Owl at Home**.
HarperCollins, 1975. ISBN 0-06-023948-4
In this easy-to-read book of short chapters, the reader is often in on the joke but Owl is not.

Sendak, Maurice. **In the Night Kitchen**.
HarperCollins, 1985. ISBN 0-06-443086-3
Although this book is done in full color, it has a coloring-book appearance.

Stevenson, James. **Don't You Know There's a War On**. Greenwillow, 1992. ISBN 0-688-11383-4
This is a good book about civilian behavior during World War II, but it's included here because the art is watercolor with no outlines.

Van Allsburg, Chris. **Jumanji**.
Houghton, 1981. ISBN 0-395-30448-2
This book, like many by Chris Van Allsburg, has a turnabout ending that may leave the reader grinning.

OTHER BOOKS BY CHRIS VAN ALLSBURG

See page 138.

The Stranger

by Chris Van Allsburg
Houghton Mifflin, 1986
ISBN 0-395-42331-7

SUMMARY

It is late summer when Farmer Bailey accidentally hits a man while driving his truck down a country road. The man is quite clearly shaken, so Farmer Bailey brings him home to care for him. According to the doctor, the accident victim has lost his memory but should be all right in a few days. The Baileys care for the man, who doesn't seem to be able to speak and who apparently is beginning to enjoy life with the Baileys. Although he seems nice enough, some strange things occur. He doesn't seem to sweat or tire, regardless of the heat or the amount of work he does. Wild rabbits hop right to him rather than running away from him. A draft is felt in the room when the man blows on his soup to cool it. Signs of fall, apparent in the distance, can't be seen or felt around the Baileys' farm. When the stranger abruptly leaves the Baileys' farm, fall comes instantly.

ILLUSTRATION

Van Allsburg uses a format for this picture book in which the illustrations face the text. Both text and illustration appear matted or framed by clean double lines or clean white paper borders. The illustrations are meticulously crafted renderings of visual images that mirror the text. Each picture captures the story's essence in a frozen time frame.

CONNECTIONS

NOVEL

In Mollie Hunter's brief novel **A Stranger Came Ashore** (HarperCollins, 1977. ISBN 0-06-022652 8), another family takes in a stranger, but they live to rue the day.

THEMES

- Puzzles
- Seasons
- Kindness to strangers

CURRICULUM CONNECTION

- HISTORY – Treatment of strangers in history

Language Arts

INTERPRETING THE TEXT

▶ Who or what is the stranger?

COMPARING LITERATURE

▶ Go on a treasure hunt for stories with strangers in them. Create a list of clues to start the searchers off. For example, "This story includes a stranger who appears in a yellow suit and attempts to extort the woods from Winnie's family." (**Tuck Everlasting** by Natalie Babbitt. Farrar,1975. ISBN 0-374-37848-7)

VOCABULARY DEVELOPMENT

▶ Create a semantic map around the word *autumn*. Include categories that involve the senses, such as "looks like, sounds like, feels like, tastes like, and smells like." Use this poetry frame for a "Senses Poem":

Autumn feels like_____
It smells like_____
It tastes like_____
It looks like_____
It sounds like_____

WRITING

▶ Write imaginative poems rich in language. For example, "Autumn smells like a piping hot sweet potato pie fresh from the oven on a cold, crisp October afternoon."

▶ Retell the story from the stranger's point of view.

▶ Discuss the concept of personification. Is the stranger a strong example? Write a story about another stranger who perhaps represents another season. What if summer were delayed due to an accident on the Bailey's farm?

▶ Write "Personification Poems." Become a symbol of autumn such as leaves, scarecrows or pumpkins and write poems in the first person. For example, "I am the wind. I race through the dry cornfields, wrestling with the stalks."

▶ Divide your class into three groups. Have one group generate a list of pros and cons to living in a place that experiences four distinct seasons. Have another group do the same for a place where it's always winter and the third group do the same for a place where it's always summer. Then create a book by writing "Fortunately" and "Unfortunately" statements. For example, the summer group might include a page in their book that says, "Fortunately, we can go swimming in the lake on any day of the year. Unfortunately, we can never go ice skating on that lake."

Science

▶ Investigate causes of memory loss. Was the doctor in this book accurate when he seemed to attribute the Stranger's memory loss to a bump to the head?

▶ What are some signs of fall in your area? If the story's location had been changed to a desert, would the impact of the Stranger's presence have been the same?

▶ What does the term "Indian Summer" mean? Does it relate to this story?

▶ List the indicators of fall in this story. Brainstorm to generate others not mentioned. Look into folklore as it applies to predicting the weather. Is there any truth to things such as judging the severity of the coming winter by the thickness of animals' fur?

▶ Find out what causes leaves to change color. Do certain types of trees change to particular colors in autumn? Are there trees that do not turn to typical fall colors in the Fall?

Social Studies

▶ As the stranger was unable to speak, how could he have communicated with the Baileys? Investigate various ways of nonvocal communication including American sign language, Morse code, body language, the printed word and international symbols. Is there a communication system that seems more efficient?

▶ Given characteristics of the Bailey farm, the landscape, and the visual indications of the weather changes, is it possible to make an educated guess about where this story could have been set? Find those locations on a map.

▶ What types of climate and weather create the changing of seasons? Look on a map of the United States to determine what states in our country experience four distinct seasons. Look at a world map. What other countries of the world might experience season changes similar to the location in this story?

ART

▶ Create autumn shadow boxes. Collect dried weeds, seed pods, colored leaves, abandoned bird's nests, beehives (with the help and advice of parents!) to display creatively in a shoe box that has been lined with yellow, orange or brown paper. Boxes could be displayed in your school library or cafeteria for everyone's pleasure.

▶ Create a wall-size mural depicting an autumn landscape. Use brushes and paint and lots of sponges and paints in seasonal colors and see what happens!

▶ RELATED BOOKS

NOVELS

Hunter, Mollie. **A Stranger Came Ashore**.
HarperCollins, 1977. ISBN 0-06-022652-8
Grades 4-9
This stranger brought real danger to the chieftain's daughter.

Spinelli, Jerry. **Maniac Magee**. Little, 1990.
ISBN 0-316-80722-2 Grades 3-9
Maniac Magee is the stranger who ran into town and changed it forever in this Newbery Award winner.

Paterson, Katherine. **Jip: His Story**.
Dutton, 1996. ISBN 0-525-67543-4 Grades 4-8
Jip has longed forever to know his father, who may be the mysterious but somehow threatening stranger in town.

PICTURE BOOKS

Arnosky, Jim. **Every Autumn Comes the Bear**.
Putnam, 1993. ISBN 0-0399-22508-0
Here is a realistic depiction of a bear in its woodland environment as it searches for a place to sleep during the cold months ahead.

Blos, Joan. **Old Henry**.
Morrow, 1987. ISBN 0-688-09935-1
This stranger who moves into the neighborhood refuses to adapt to his neighbors' standards.

Browning, Robert. **Pied Piper**
There are many editions of this old tale about a stranger who came to the village to rid it of rats.

Bunting, Eve. **Man Who Could Call Down Owls**.
Simon & Schuster, 1984. ISBN 0-02-715380-0
A stranger with the mysterious power to communicate with birds meets with tragedy.

Swope, Sam. **The Araboolies of Liberty Street**
See page 211.
This picture book relates what happened when a strange family incited a neighborhood confrontation.

Wreck of the Zephyr

by Chris Van Allsburg
Houghton, 1983
ISBN 0-395-33075-0

▶ SUMMARY

This story, told by an old man to a younger one, explains why the ruins of a sailboat are found high above the sea on a cliff. He tells of a boy in the village, years ago, who was an excellent sailor. One day, in a storm, the boy saw boats being sailed above the waves. He demanded to know how it was done, and an islander taught him how. When the boy did it himself, he sailed too high and the boat crashed against the cliff, breaking the boy's leg. After that, the boy tried in vain to sail above the waves. The old man telling the story may be that very boy.

▶ ILLUSTRATION

The illustrations are classic Van Allsburg. His mastery of composition, especially the elements of texture, value and color, are where his skills are best demonstrated. His traditional choice of rectangular and horizontal compositions is reflected in the shape of the book itself.

▶ CONNECTIONS

NOVEL

The story told by Moss's father within the short novel **Guests** (Hyperion, 1994. ISBN 0-7868-0047-X) by Michael Dorris is a pourquoi tale that explains why people no longer live together

THEMES

▶ Human reach exceeding its grasp
▶ Ambition
▶ Vanity

CURRICULUM CONNECTION

▶ LITERATURE – Mythology

LANGUAGE ARTS
WRITING
▶ The story leaves many questions unanswered. Write a sequel that answers some of those questions and poses new ones.

▶ What does the person listening to this story do with that information? Is it a reporter? Will he or she now join the quest?

DRAWING CONCLUSIONS
▶ What do you know about the boy as a result of reading this book? Would you like him for a friend? Do you know anyone, including yourself, who would have done the same thing? Do you know anyone who would have stopped sooner?

EXTENDING VOCABULARY
▶ Investigate the name *Zephyr* and determine why it might be chosen as the name of a sailboat.

▶ Make a glossary of sailing terms.

▶ Draw a diagram of a sailboat, labeling the parts.

FINDING AND READING POETRY
▶ There are thousands of poems about the sea and the feeling it gives humans. Read enough of those poems to find a favorite and share it with the class either orally or visually.

COMPARING LITERATURE
▶ In this story, as in many others by Chris Van Allsburg, there is visible proof that the events might have been real. What evidence is here? Find the evidence in other books by Van Allsburg listed below. Find other books where the author uses a similar technique.

▶ This is a story about a person who went one step too far. Compare it to the story of Icarus in Greek mythology.

▶ Read the wordless novel **The Silver Pony** (see Related Books). Are the boys in both stories similar?

▶ Find other stories where the person didn't know that enough was enough. Try **The Fisherman and His Wife**.

▶ This is a quest story. Someone decides what he or she wants and sets out to do it. Usually, in the quest story format, a character is not immediately successful in achieving the quest. It is difficult and takes practice, or things intervene to prevent its being easily achieved. Find similar quest stories and fill in the chart as you do further reading.

The Questor	The Quest	Interveners	Result
a boy	to sail above the waves	getting the skill	he sails too high
Icarus	to fly	getting wax wings	he sails too high

SCIENCE
▶ One type of boat can sail above the waves. Find out about hovercraft. How do they work? Where are they being used successfully?

▶ There was a storm at sea in the story. Find out about the various storms that are threats to sailing. Are there some seasons where they are more frequent? Make a list of the different kinds of sea storms. Do they have different names on land?

SOCIAL STUDIES
HISTORY
▶ Research some famous voyages that interest you. Try the *Kontiki* raft trip or the *Hesperus* wreck about which Longfellow wrote a poem. Many of the early European explorers' trips are well documented and make good research topics.

▶ Investigate famous ship disasters such as the *Titanic* and the *Maine*.

GEOGRAPHY
▶ Look at charts of the ocean near Cape Hatteras to see some of the wrecks there. Are any of those wrecks recent? Why is that such a dangerous area?

▶ Where might the village in this story be? Are there any clues in the story?

MUSIC
▶ The musical *The Man of La Mancha* is about a quest, and the song "Impossible Dream" may apply to this story. Listen to it and decide if it changes your feeling about the boy in this story.

RELATED BOOKS

NOVELS

Dorris, Michael. **Guests**.
Hyperion, 1994. ISBN 0-7868-0047-X Grades 4-9
This novel about a Native American boy contains a pourquoi folktale.

Ward, Lynd. **The Silver Pony**.
Houghton, 1973. ISBN 0-395-14753-0 Grades 3-6
In this wordless novel, a boy and his winged horse fly too high and meet with disaster.

PICTURE BOOKS

Van Allsburg, Chris. **Ben's Dream**.
Houghton, 1982. ISBN 0-395-32084-4
In a dream Ben sees many of the wonders of the world as well as his friend Margaret. When he wakens, he learns that she has had the same dream.

Van Allsburg, Chris. **The Garden of Abdul Gasazi**.
Houghton, 1979. ISBN 0-395-27804-X
Alan is minding the dog for the day, and when the dog enters the house of a mysterious magician, Alan follows. Does Abdul Gasazi change Fritz into a duck? There may be proof.

Van Allsburg, Chris. **Polar Express**.
Houghton, 1985. ISBN 0-395-38949-6
After an adventure at the North Pole that might have been a dream, the boy finds a bell under the tree as evidence that it was real.

Van Allsburg, Chris. **The Wretched Stone**.
Houghton, 1991. ISBN 0-395-53307-4
Captain Hope has recorded the events of a mysterious voyage on which a mysterious glowing stone transfixed his sailors. The analogy to a television set is obvious.

OTHER BOOKS BY CHRIS VAN ALLSBURG

Jumanji. Houghton, 1981. ISBN 0-395-30448-2
A board game gets the children in terrible trouble. Fortunately, they follow directions.

Just a Dream. Houghton, 1990. ISBN 0-395-53308-2
A boy dreams that many of the great landmarks of the United States are being destroyed because of the lack of concern about the environment.

The Mysteries of Harris Burdick. Houghton, 1984.
ISBN 0-395-35393-9
Mr. Burdick apparently had some great stories in mind when he left these pictures and their accompanying captions with the publisher. Unfortunately, he then disappeared leaving us to imagine the content of the stories.

The Stranger. Houghton, 1986. ISBN 0-395-42331-7
A mysterious mute stranger stays with the family for a while and, while he is there, the seasons do not change.

The Sweetest Fig. Houghton, 1993.
ISBN 0-395-67346-1
Be careful what you wish for is the point of this book, in which a cruel dentist is given magic figs that will make his dreams come true. Before he can eat the second one, his dog eats it and becomes his master.

Two Bad Ants. Houghton, 1988.
ISBN 0-395-48668-8
This is an ant's-eye view of a human's kitchen.

The Widow's Broom. Houghton, 1992.
ISBN 0-395-64051-2
A widow uses trickery to retain her magic broom.

The Butterfly Seeds

by Mary Watson
Morrow, 1995
ISBN 0-688-14132-3

SUMMARY

Jake's family immigrates to the United States, leaving his grandfather behind. Jake's greatest treasure is a box of "butterfly seeds" his grandfather gives him to plant in America. He needs to be resourceful in order to plant and grow the seeds, but eventually his seeds provide a magical reminder of his grandfather back home.

ILLUSTRATION

A series of well-composed paintings of easily recognizable places and things, these illustrations complement and reflect accurately the content of the text. The story and the pictures cultivate a nostalgic view of a particular time as well as the immigrant experience.

CONNECTIONS

NOVEL

Seedfolks (HarperCollins, 1997. ISBN 0-06-027471-9) is a novel about how a few seeds made a neighborhood a community.

THEME

▶ Heritage

CURRICULUM CONNECTION

▶ HISTORY – Immigrants

LANGUAGE ARTS

COMPARING LITERATURE

▶ Find other stories about relationships with grandparents. Have students write about personal experiences with a grandparent.

WRITING

▶ Write "Grandparent Wanted" ads. Display with illustrations of the ideal grandparent.

▶ Write couplets about butterflies. Mount couplets on large butterfly cutouts and hang from the ceiling.

▶ Read **The Very Hungry Caterpillar** by Eric Carle (see Related Books). Write a more realistic and sophisticated picture book on the life cycle of the butterfly.

▶ Jake treasures his butterfly seeds because they remind him of his grandfather. Bring something into school that you treasure because it reminds you of someone special in your life. Write short narratives telling why the object is important. Make a display of the objects with the students' writing.

▶ Study the illustrations. Develop a chart to compare and contrast Jake's home in New York City with the home he left.

ORAL EXPRESSION

▶ Ask students to pretend that they are leaving their home to move to another country and that they will be allowed to bring only three small personal things with them. Let them take turns telling the rest of the class what they would bring and why.

▶ Play the "I packed my bag to go to _____" game. Other students in turn add to the list something they would bring and state why they would bring it.

SCIENCE

▶ Study the life cycles of butterflies. Create flip-books showing the stages in the life of a butterfly.

▶ Contact a science supply company and purchase the necessary things to hatch butterflies in your classroom. Make a celebration of setting them free when they are ready.

▶ Study the anatomy of flowers. Construct diagrams of flowers with all the parts labeled. Dissect real flowers to find and identify the parts.

▶ Look through seed and flower catalogs and flower identification books. Find out what flowers are more attractive to butterflies and why. Look for flowers that have butterfly-like names. Are they named that because they attract butterflies or because of their appearance?

▶ Plant window boxes at school and try to attract butterflies.

▶ Take a field trip to a local park or public garden. Look for butterflies. Try to identify the butterflies you see and the plants or flowers they are on or near.

SOCIAL STUDIES

▶ Look at the illustrations for clues about where Jake's family came from. Make educated guesses about the family's original home and tell why you've made that guess. Is the name of the ship they came on a clue?

▶ Cite other immigrant groups and the reasons they came at various points in history.

▶ Discuss Jake's experience at Ellis Island. Why were the children examined? What might have happened if the children were found to be unhealthy?

▶ Discuss the sense of community in Jake's new home. What contributions did other members of the community make to help Jake succeed in growing his butterfly seeds.

ART

▶ Use colored tissue paper and black construction paper to create "stained glass" butterflies to decorate your classroom windows.

▶ Invent and illustrate flowers named after insects or animals. For instance, what might a "bumblebee daisy" look like?

RELATED BOOKS

NOVELS

Fleischman. **Seedfolks**.
HarperCollins, 1997. ISBN 0-06-027471-9
Grades 4-8
This is a brief novel that tells how one seed got a neighborhood to act as a community.

Lasky, Kathryn. **The Night Journey**.
Puffin, 1986. ISBN 0-14-032048-2 Grades 3-9
This short novel spans three generations and tells of a family's escape from a pogrom carrying a precious samovar that becomes a symbol of their past.

PICTURE BOOKS

Anno, Mitsumasa. **Anno's Magic Seed**.
Putnam, 1994. ISBN 0-399-22538-2
In this mathematical story, two seeds produce enough food to feed a family.

Carle, Eric. **The Very Hungry Caterpillar**.
Putnam, 1981. ISBN 0-399-20853-4
A very hungry caterpillar becomes a butterfly.

Garland, Sherry. **The Lotus Seed**.
Harcourt, 1993 ISBN 0-15-249465-0
Her grandmother saw the Vietnamese emperor on the day he lost the throne and took a seed from the imperial garden to remember the occasion. That seed becomes a symbol of hope for the entire family as they make a new life in America.

George, Jean Craighead. **The Moon of the Monarch Butterflies**. HarperCollins, 1993 ISBN 0-06-020817-1
In this 48-page book, the emphasis is as much on the environment as it is on the monarch butterfly it follows.

Sandved, Kjell. **The Butterfly Alphabet**.
Scholastic, 1996. ISBN 0-590-48003-0
In this photographic alphabet, the letters are found in close-ups of butterfly wings.

Say, Allen **Grandfather's Journey**
See page 184.

Waiting for the Evening Star

by Rosemary Wells
Illustrated by Susan Jeffers
Dial, 1993. ISBN 0-8037-1398-3

▶ SUMMARY

Rosemary Wells states on the book jacket that she and Susan Jeffers have gone to rural Vermont to search for a past where "innocence lived in the hearts of our children." She found it there and has written a touching depiction of the life of a family in a remote Vermont village during the early 1900s, as seen through the eyes of the younger brother of the family. While younger brother Berty is content with Vermont farm life and feels that they have everything they could possibly want or need, his older brother Luke yearns to see the world that he knows lies on the other side of the mountains. Wells gives us a close look at life on the farm throughout all the seasons of the year and depicts the strong sense of community that existed in rural New England.

▶ ILLUSTRATION

There is a classical approach to these illustrations. The foundation for each picture is superb drawing abilities. The meticulous pen lines are used to sculpt forms of figures and landscapes. These tones are built on background of subtle color washes. The book's actual dimensions make it inviting to handle.

▶ CONNECTIONS

NOVEL

Wells makes numerous references to life on the farm being cyclical, stating that time turned like a wheel. This concept is strongly presented in **Tuck Everlasting** by Natalie Babbitt (Farrar, 1975 ISBN 0-374-37848-7).

THEMES

▶ Circles and cycles

CURRICULUM CONNECTION:

▶ SCIENCE – Life cycles

LANGUAGE ARTS
WRITING

▶ Read the poem "Under the Elms" that appears on the first page of the book. Write a short statement telling what the poet's message is for you. Why might she have chosen that title?

▶ The phrase "The year turned like a wheel" appears on the first page of the text. Discuss similes. Find other examples of similes related to time throughout the book. Choose one of them for a topic sentence for a short paragraph. Display the writing on a bulletin board titled "The Times of our Lives."

▶ Find other similes in the story not associated with the passing of time, such as "carrots as fat as thumbs." Write your own similes and illustrate them to include in a class book of similes. You might want to take a look at Wood's **Quick as a Cricket** for a possible format (see Related Books).

▶ Try your hand at writing a short poem that uses similes and metaphors to describe your own neighborhood or community or to describe a specific event in their lives.

▶ Retell the story on a bulletin board by creating a time line of Berty's childhood. Each student could retell and illustrate an important event in his or her life.

▶ Make a list of unfamiliar vocabulary from the story that you think may be unique to that time period such as *milch, ice house, buttery* and *paraffin*. Interview parents, grandparents and friends to try to find meanings and or descriptions of the terms. Then decide as a group which terms truly are unique to the time period, which are unique to rural New England life and that are simply unfamiliar words or terms.

COMPARING LITERATURE

▶ Read **Lucy's Summer** by Donald Hall (see Related Books), which is about a young girl living at the same time as Berty in a town in rural New Hampshire. Compare and contrast Lucy's and Berty's lives. Write a short realistic story based on the format of The City Mouse and the Country Mouse.

▶ Examine the text for all the techniques that the author employs to indicate the passing of time. Also look for the same indications in the illustrations. Hunt for other books that show the passage of time over an extended period of a character's life. Can they find other techniques that authors use to show passing time. For example, Chris Van Allsburg depicts the passing of time through dates on a daptain's log in **The Wretched Stone**.

SOCIAL STUDIES

▶ Create a "Then and Now" wall chart. Under the "Then" side list the activities that the family and community are involved in such as cutting blocks of ice from the pond, gathering maple sap and making butter. Complete the "Now" side of the chart as you discuss how we access those same products and services today.

▶ Given the time frame of the story, determine in what war Luke intended to fight when he left Vermont. Find out when that war actually ended. Do you think Luke actually got to France before the war ended?

▶ Find other books that depict American life in the period following the war. Predict how the family's life may have changed in the following years.

▶ Revisit the text for the purpose of more closely examining this community's economic system. List examples of how the families there obtained goods and services. Organize the information you find under categories that include growing, harvesting, raising, bartering, buying, selling, making. Compare this chart with our lives today. Are there similarities as well as differences? Which of these practices may still be found today? Come up with examples of bartering that take place today. Find out which families in your class are involved in occupations that provide services or create products.

▶ Berty's family cuts blocks of pond ice to keep their own food cool during the warm months and to ship to faraway places. Discuss the methods used for gathering and saving ice for future use. Investigate the history of refrigeration. Do any families still own old-fashioned iceboxes? Do any families still refer to their refrigerators as "iceboxes"?

▶ Berty's family obviously lived without a refrigerator. Generate a list of as many other modern conveniences as you can think of that were not available at that time. Find out when each was invented. Decide which of them may have been available to Berty in his lifetime.

SCIENCE

▶ Berty's family collected "fiddleheads" and other greens from the wild. Find out what fiddleheads really are. Do they grow in your area? What natural foods may be found in your community? Try to find out, collect them and sample some.

▶ Study the process of gathering maple sap and creating maple syrup. How does the process used today differ from the technique used in Berty's community? Is maple syrup produced near where you live? If so, visit a maple sugar farm for a first-hand look at this interesting activity. What parts of our country are commonly known for maple sugar production?

MATH

▶ Make a list of imaginary events that may have taken place in Berty's life after the story ends. Begin each event with the words, "When Berty was ___ years old" and determine what year each event took place. Also write a list of events that begin with the words, "In the year _____," and determine how old Berty was when the event took place.

▶ RELATED BOOKS

NOVEL

Babbitt, Natalie. **Tuck Everlasting**.
Farrar, 1975. ISBN 0-374-37848-7 Grades 3-9
This story about the tragedy of not following nature's cycles is a classic.

PICTURE BOOKS

Hall, Donald. **Lucy's Summer**.
Browndeer Press, 1995. ISBN 0-15-276873-4.
This is a realistic story based on the life a young girl growing up in rural New Hampshire in the early 1900s.

Hall, Donald. **Old Home Day** See Page 90.

Schertle, Alice. **Maisie**. Lothrop, 1995.
ISBN 0-688-09310-8.
This is another story that shows the life of a girl from her birth though her 90th birthday.

Shelby, Anne. **Homeplace** See Page 196.

Van Allsburg, Chris. **The Wretched Stone**. Houghton, 1991. ISBN 0-395-55307-4
The passage of time is depicted in this book through the entries in a ship captain's log.

Wolff, Ferida. **Seven Loaves of Bread**.
Morrow, 1993. ISBN 0-688-11112-2.
This book comically illustrates what can happen when the bartering system goes awry.

Wood, Audrey. **As Quick as a Cricket**.
Childs Play, 1990. ISBN 0-85953-306-9
This is a rhyming exploration of common similes.

Encounter

by Jane Yolen
Illustrated by David Shannon
Harcourt, 1992
ISBN 0-15-225962-7

▶ SUMMARY

In this book, Jane Yolen recreates the discovery of America from the point of view of a Taino Indian boy. It is believed that this Taino culture was established and a civilization existed long before Christopher Columbus landed on San Salvador. It is an innocent world where the natives welcome the strangers with gifts, only to be rewarded with "a serpent's smile." The young boy understands more than the tribal adults. He grows old telling his story and trying to warn other native groups about the duplicity of the strangers. This is the story of a gentle people who lose their land to invaders.

▶ ILLUSTRATION

These are traditional images and colors used in a photo album format. They complement the story successfully. A particularly powerful illustration is the one in which the skin of the native child is starkly contrasted with that of the Caucasian hand of the explorer.

▶ CONNECTIONS

NOVEL

Michael Dorris' **Morning Girl** (Hyperion, 1992 ISBN 1-56282-284-5) is set in the same culture before the arrival of Columbus.

THEMES

- ▶ Culture clash
- ▶ Columbus
- ▶ Change

CURRICULUM CONNECTION:

- ▶ HISTORY – Explorers, Columbus

LANGUAGE ARTS

FINDING DETAILS
▶ Decide exactly when the little boy became convinced of the evil of the soldiers.

▶ Review the thoughts of the young Taino boy. Explain how he seemed to know what was in the heart of the strangers.

WRITING
▶ Take any other event in history and write about it from a different point of view.

▶ Describe the Zemis and its importance in the life of the little boy.

USING CAUSE AND EFFECT
▶ How might history have been changed if:

Columbus had reached India?

There were no other explorers to the new world?

The natives had expelled the strangers from their land?

The strangers did not leave and were assimilated into the native culture?

Columbus and his men were killed soon after they landed?

USING COMPARISON AND CONTRAST
▶ Decide which traits were most influential in creating the type of world in which we now live.

▶ Create a list of attributes that would exemplify the best leader for the island.

RECALLING DETAILS
▶ Identify these objects described by the little Taino boy:

spit sticks into the sand (flags)

shells with tongues (bells)

round pools that gave a man back his face (mirror)

woven things that fit upon a man's head (hat)

▶ Reread and find the other objects so described.

▶ Find other objects and use the boy's description to create a riddle.

USING DESCRIPTIONS
▶ Find the ways the Taino boy described the ships, for example, "The great winged birds with voices like thunder."

▶ Reread and retell the various descriptions of the strangers by the boy.

INTERPRETING THE TEXT
▶ What gifts did the chief give to the strangers and why? (For example, balls of cotton thread to bind them to friendship.)

▶ Explain why the natives thought that "the strangers were not quite human beings."

USING SIMILES AND METAPHORS
▶ There are several similes and metaphors in this book, for example, "hair growing like bushes" (simile), "the skin was moon to my sun" (metaphor). Find examples of similes and metaphors and substitute your own ideas, such as "hair like *silk*."

COMPARING LITERATURE
▶ Collect some of the books relating to the discovery of America. Class members can search for those that are "politically correct" (blaming Columbus and the white man for the sad plight of the natives in the New World). Others can report on the books that stress the legacy as well as the superiority of the Europeans.

SOCIAL STUDIES

▶ Research the four voyages of Columbus. Briefly describe and date each one.

▶ Find out about:

foods native to the Americas that became staples around the world

animals not familiar to the strangers

plants of the New World, including the drugs derived from them

▶ The Europeans were more advanced technologically, yet the natives were accustomed to various ferocious battles. Try to explain how a handful of newcomers managed to conquer millions of people with ease.

▶ Design a time line of explorers after Columbus. Include Magellan, Balboa, Vespucci, Cabot and others. Identify the country of origin of each one and the area of exploration.

▶ On a map of the world:

Trace and mark the route of each explorer and his destination.

Compare Columbus' route to the Americas and his intended voyage to the Indies.

▶ Research the Spaniards who followed Columbus to the Americas, namely Pizarro and Cortez.

▶ Compare the fate of the Aztecs and Incas to the destiny and fortunes of the Native Americans.

▶ Investigate the importance of gold in the journeys of each explorer.

▶ Make copies of a relief map of the world. Mark the identifiable areas of the known world in the time of Columbus. Include countries, oceans, mountains, rivers and seas. Speculate and then trace various routes Columbus would have taken.

▶ Challenge Columbus's discovery of the New World. Research some of the various claimants: Brendan the Bold, an Irish priest; Leif Ericsson, a Viking explorer, among others. Plan a debate and argue the various sides.

RELATED BOOKS

NOVELS

Conrad, Pam. **Pedro's Journal**.
Scholastic, 1992. ISBN 0-590-46206-7 Grades 3-6
This fictional journal sticks closely to the facts of Columbus's first voyage but retains the perspective of a cabin boy.

Dorris, Michael. **Morning Girl**.
Hyperion, 1992. ISBN 1-56282 284-5 Grades 4-8
This novel is narrated by two Taino children. When a journal entry is revealed, attributed to Christopher Columbus, the story takes a dramatic turn.

Dorris, Michael. **Guests**.
Hyperion, 1994. ISBN 0-7868-0047-X Grades 4-8
This brief coming-of-age story includes the protagonist's fury at the presence of Colonial guests at a festival.

NONFICTION

Brenner, Barbara. **If You Were There in 1492**.
Bradbury, 1991 ISBN 0-02-712321-9
This book offers much detailed information about life in Spain prior to the voyage of Columbus and about the voyage itself.

Fritz, Jean. **Where Do You Think You're Going, Christopher Columbus?** Putnam, 1980.
ISBN 0-399-20723-6
As in all her brief biographies, Fritz uses humor and conscientious research to give us a picture of the man and his dream.

Fritz, Jean, et al. **The World in 1492**.
Holt, 1992 ISBN 0-8050-1674-0
This version of Columbus's discovery transports the reader to certain cultures that might have been forgotten. The many authors show that the European-centered view might be too narrow.

Sis, Peter. **Follow the Dream: The Story of Christopher Columbus**. Knopf, 1991
ISBN 0-679-806288
The stunning illustrations in this picture book biography dominate the book.

OTHER BOOKS BY JANE YOLEN

The Ballad of the Pirate Queen. Illustrated by David Shannon. Harcourt, 1995.
ISBN 0-15-200710-5
This is a dramatic seafaring poem. Anne Bonney and Mary Reade were real pirates. They sailed on the *Vanity* and were captured and tried in Jamaica. It all takes place in 1720.

Bird Watch. Illustrated by Ted Lewin. Philomel, 1990. ISBN 0-399-21612-X
This is a wonderful collection of poetry celebrating birds with beautiful illustrations and poems.

Owl Moon. Illustrated by John Schoenherr. Philomel 1987. ISBN 0-399-21457-7
In this Caldecott Award-winning book, a father and son share the adventure of owling. The poetic language and illustrations are outstanding.

Piggins. Illustrated by Jane Dyer. Harcourt, 1987.
ISBN 0-315-261685-3
Piggins, a proper English (pig) butler, solves a mystery in an English home.

Sleeping Ugly. Illustrated by Diane Stanley. Philomel, 1981. ISBN 0-698-20617-7
Plain Jane becomes the favored princess. Miserella the beautiful but hateful one is taught a lesson.

Letting Swift River Go

by Jane Yolen
Illustrated by Barbara Cooney
Little Brown, 1992
ISBN 0-316-96899-4

SUMMARY

In order to build Quabbin Reservoir, which was to serve as the water supply for Boston, four small New England towns had to be completely destroyed. This is the story of how it was done, seen through the eyes of Sally Jane, a young girl living in one of those towns in the early 1930s. The steps are painful, but no blame is assigned here. The city was not wrong for needing water and the townspeople were not wrong for giving up their lands; it was done to make things better. The reader is left to decide whether or not progress was made.

ILLUSTRATION

Watercolor washes are the basis for these illustrations. The details and textures are achieved by using a variety of illustrative techniques. Barbara Cooney uses mixed media and a variety of application methods to achieve unique textures and critical details. The element of color is used to designate seasons as well as the time of day. It is also employed to establish the mood for the events shown in the illustrations.

CONNECTIONS

NOVEL

Mollie Hunter's novel, **The Walking Stones** (Harcourt, 1996 ISBN 0-15-200995-7), involves the proposed flooding of a valley and the actions of a mysterious creature of the past to save it.

THEME

► Price of progress

CURRICULUM CONNECTION:

► HISTORY – Local history
► SCIENCE – Water

LANGUAGE ARTS

FINDING DETAILS

▶ Find the words in the first part of the book that tell you why Sally Jane lets the water run out of her cupped hands. Do the words mean the same thing both times?

USING FIGURATIVE LANGUAGE

▶ There's an old saying that goes, "When progress is made, a price has been paid." Who paid the price here? Was it worth it?

VOCABULARY DEVELOPMENT

▶ Where does the word *reservoir* come from? What does it mean?

SCIENCE

WATER

▶ Where does your water come from? What's done to the water before you get it? What's being done to keep the water cleaner before processing? What can you do?

▶ This project was done to create a water supply for Boston. Could they have used it for waterpower as well? How?

SOCIAL STUDIES

PROGRESS

▶ Think about a reservoir, shopping area or housing development in your area. What used to be there? Who owned it? What happened on that land before its current development? Who changed it? Was the change necessary? For whom? Who benefited? Who lost? Were there other alternatives with more benefits and fewer losses?

▶ Seldom does anyone say, "I'm going to tear down that shopping center and put in a farm." Could that happen? Could towns such as the ones in this book be recreated? Why or why not?

MAPS

▶ Find Quabbin Reservoir on a topographical map. It's the largest human-made body of water in New England. Find the city of Boston on the same map and figure out how the water gets from Quabbin to the city. Which routes would you use for the pipes and why? Remember that water flows downhill.

▶ Examine a topographical map of your area. Which river could be dammed that is not currently being used that way? What areas would then probably be flooded? In what order would they flood? What other effects would your creation of a new body of water have? Are there more pluses or minuses? In your opinion, should the dam be built?

▶ Build a model of clay or plaster of Paris of your area as accurately as possible using the topographical map. When it has hardened, flood it and see if your predictions were accurate.

ORAL HISTORY

▶ Talk to someone from your grandparents' generation. Ask the person to walk or ride with you around your area and tell you about the way things used to be: the people, buildings, farms, woods and rivers. How does this person feel about the changes? Take notes or use a tape recorder to help you remember what he or she has told you.

▶ Do the same with someone from your parents' generation. Are their feelings the same?

▶ Quabbin Reservoir project was part of the WPA, an organization which provided employment during the Great Depression. Research the organization. What projects, if any, were completed in your area through the WPA? Are there similar organizations today?

MATH

▶ Follow the money in this book. Who had it? Where did it come from? What were the major expenses? Who profited? Who lost? Who's making money from it today? Make a chart to show the flow of money as a result of the building of Quabbin Reservoir.

RELATED BOOKS

NOVEL

Hunter, Mollie. **The Walking Stones**.
Harcourt, 1996. ISBN 0-15-200995-7 Grades 4-8
The Bodach is said to have special powers but tells Donald that "Magic is something that happens when everything is right to happen." Surely it should happen now with the peaceful valley about to be flooded by the engineers. This fantasy mixes ecology and magic with great mystery.

PICTURE BOOKS

Cherry, Lynne. **A River Ran Wild**.
Harcourt, 1992. ISBN 0-15-200542-0
We follow the Nashua River, which is not far from Swift River, from the first viewers and settlers through the changes civilization brought to it until it is a polluted mess. A campaign to clean up the Nashua succeeds in bringing it back to a cleaner condition.

Cole, Joanna. **The Magic School Bus at the Waterworks**. Scholastic, 1986. ISBN 0-590-40361-3
As in the other Magic School Bus Books, Cole and Degan give a fictional context for a great deal of factual information, in this case, the way water is made ready for human use.

Dragonwagon, Crescent. **Home Place**.
Simon & Schuster, 1990. ISBN 0-02-733190-3
A family, walking in the woods, finds a group of daffodils and realizes that a home must once have stood there. They imagine the family and how they lived.

Provensen, Alice. **Shaker Lane**.
Puffin, 1990. ISBN 0-14-050713-2
Shaker Lane may not be the prettiest area of town, but it's home to a lot of people and they pay the price when a reservoir is needed for their town.

Pryor, Bonnie. **The House on Maple Street**.
Morrow, 1987. ISBN 0-688-06380-2
Children find an arrowhead near their house and imagine the same scene 300 years ago when it would have been relatively untouched wilderness. Page by page we follow the area through history until we are back in the present.

NONFICTION

Ardley, Ned. **Dams**.
Garrett, 1990. ISBN 0-944483-75-5
This historical and technological examination of dams features clear text, photographs and diagrams.

Dorros, Arthur. **Follow the Water from Brook to Ocean**. HarperCollins, 1991. ISBN 0-06-021598-4
This picture book follows the earthbound part of the water cycle from melting snow on a mountaintop to the ocean and, along the way, we get information about water supply and pollution.

Honkers

by Jane Yolen
Illustrated by Leslie Baker
Little, Brown, 1993
ISBN 0-316-96893-5

▶ SUMMARY

In this picture book set at the turn of the century, a timid and frightened Betsy is sent to her grandparents' farm to await the birth of a sibling after her mother's difficult pregnancy. At the farm young Betsy witnesses the birth and eventual departure of three goslings. The parallel between the growth and independence of the geese and that of Betsy is clear.

▶ ILLUSTRATION

These illustrations are the picture-image counterpart to the literal text and are juxtaposed facing the text on opposite pages. They are composed of soft watercolor washes and are limited to muted color tones. The medium and color contribute to a serenity of the story's portraits and landscapes. The backgrounds in these compositions employ misty washes, while the foreground figures are given greater detail by means of fine-pointed watercolor brushes. Notice that the printed pages are balanced by the illustrated pages, with one exception. As the story begins, the geese are shown on the same page flying above the introductory text.

▶ CONNECTIONS

NOVEL

There are many coming-of-age or self-realization books, and this picture book could lead to any of them. There's a fairly strong parallel between this story and the novel **House of Wings** by Betsy Byars (Viking, 1972. ISBN 0-14-031523-3).

THEMES

▶ Birth
▶ Pets
▶ Farm

CURRICULUM CONNECTION

▶ SOCIAL STUDIES – Farm life, economics

LANGUAGE ARTS

EXTENDING VOCABULARY

▶ Betsy is nicknamed Little Bit. Discuss the nicknames of people in your class. Find out why they are called those nicknames. Who named them? Categorize the nicknames according to their origins: something they did, a variation of their first name, a variation of their last name, a physical feature. Also chart people's like or dislike of their names and nicknames.

▶ Betsy calls her grandparents Nana and Grandy. Chart a list of names students in your class call their grandparents. Find out what names on the list represent other languages.

COMPARING LITERATURE

▶ Read **Owen** by Kevin Henkes. How are the two stories similar? Would either book have been better if illustrated by the other artist? Why or why not?

▶ Tell a five-minute story of something you have done with a grandparent. Do it in a circle and have the "teller" call on another person to retell the tale. Then open it up to the whole group to ask questions. Perhaps the "teller" will discover he or she has a story worth writing down.

▶ Betsy plays checkers and Spit in the Ocean with her grandfather. What games or activities can adults and children enjoy together?

▶ Betsy was packed off for the summer with a trunk of clothes, three reading books and her silky blanket. Make a list of things you would want to take if you were going away for the summer. Break your list into two categories of "Things Needed" and "Things Wanted." Compare lists.

▶ Play a game of "I packed my bag to go to Nana and Grandy's and in it I put an (apple)." Each person repeats the previous items and adds something to the bag that begins with the next letter of the alphabet.

SCIENCE

▶ Investigate Canada geese and their migration patterns. Learn about domestic geese. How are they similar and different?

▶ Hatch some eggs in your classroom. Your local 4-H Club may be able to help you obtain the necessary equipment. Study the incubation cycle in the process. Keep a journal of your observations.

▶ Grandpa smells the change coming from summer to fall. List clues your senses tell you about a change in season. For example, what are the smells of spring, summer, fall, winter? What are the sounds associated with each season?

▶ Discuss why Betsy does not keep her gosling as a pet. What makes a good pet and what does not? Why are wild animals such as geese not the best pets?

SOCIAL STUDIES

▶ Study the illustrations carefully. Can you date the story based on clothing and mode of transportation? Look at a variety of other books that obviously take place in past time periods. Can you create a time line depicting the titles? Provide books (see Related Books) such as **When I Was Young in the Mountains** by Cynthia Rylant, **Oxcart Man** by Donald Hall and **Island Boy** by Barbara Cooney.

MATH

▶ Grandpa tells Betsy that a goose egg takes 25 days to hatch. Read **Chickens Aren't the Only Ones** by Ruth Heller. Find out and chart the incubation period for a variety of different animals. Sequence the list from shortest to longest amounts of time. Create word problems for each other to solve. For example, How many more days does it take for a _____ to hatch than for a _____?

RELATED BOOKS

NOVELS

Byars, Betsy C. **The House of Wings**.
Viking, 1972. ISBN 0-14-031523-3
Left with an uncommunicative grandfather while his parents settle their new home, Sammy finds himself engrossed in the battle to save the life of a blind crane and finds himself and his grandfather in the process.

MacLachlan, Patricia. **Arthur for the Very First Time**. HarperCollins, 1980. ISBN
Ten-year-old Arthur is sent to stay with his eccentric aunt and uncle and changes from the timid boy nicknamed "Mouse" to Arthur, for the very first time.

PICTURE BOOKS

Hall, Donald. **Oxcart Man**.
Live Oak Media, 1984. ISBN 0-941078-41-8
A farmer loads up his family's produce onto an oxcart and journeys to Portsmouth, where he sells and barters everything including the ox.

Heller, Ruth. **Chickens Aren't the Only Ones**.
Putnam, 1993. ISBN 0-448-40454-0
This is a graphically beautiful book that explores eggs and egg-layers of all sorts.

Henkes, Kevin. **Owen**.
Greenwillow, 1993. ISBN 0-688-11449-0
Owen's parents make numerous attempts to separate Owen from his security blanket before he goes off to school.

Hughes, Shirley. **Dogger**.
Lothrop, 1988. ISBN 0-688-07980-6
A little boy loses his stuffed animal and is inconsolable.

Lyon, George Ella. **Cecil's Story**.
Orchard, 1991. ISBN 0-531-05912-X
A boy waits at the neighbors' for his father, a wounded soldier in the Civil War, to come home. In this book a lapse of time is shown through the development of a chicken egg. See page 135.

Rylant, Cynthia. **When I Was Young in the Mountains**. Dutton, 1982. ISBN 0-525-42525-X
The author relates childhood memories of growing up in the mountains.

OTHER BOOKS BY JANE YOLEN

Owl Moon. Philomel, 1987. ISBN 0-399-214577
As a rite of passage, a child goes with his father owling at night.

Letting Swift River Go See page 245.

The Seeing Stick See page 251.

The Seeing Stick

by Jane Yolen
Illustrated by Remy Charlip and Demetra Maraslis
HarperCollins, 1975
ISBN 0-690-00596-2

▶ SUMMARY

The Emperor offers a fortune in jewels to any person who can help his blind daughter see. Many people attempt to help her, but it is an old man with his "seeing stick" who finally provides a means for the young girl to understand and appreciate the world around her. The fortune is given away, but the old man stays.

▶ ILLUSTRATION

These beautiful, rich drawings are sensitive value studies reflecting the subtle drawing techniques of the Eastern culture.

▶ CONNECTIONS

NOVEL

Theodore Taylor's **The Cay** (Doubleday, 1987. ISBN 0-385-07906-0) also has a wise blind man.

THEME

▶ Coping with disabilities

CURRICULUM CONNECTION

▶ SOCIAL STUDIES – Physically challenged individuals

Language Arts

EXTENDING THE LITERATURE

▶ Show the cover of the book. Make predictions about the story based upon the title and the jacket illustration. Can the setting and characters be determined?

▶ Present the story without showing the illustrations. See how many realized that the old man was blind himself. What words or descriptions hinted at his blindness? Would the story have had a different impact if the old man could see?

▶ Show the illustrations (without rereading the text) that start as black and white, then are in color, and that finally become black and white again. Can students determine when in the story and why the illustrations change?

▶ Again review the illustrations. Note that the seeing stick itself serves as the illustration for a major portion of the story. Construct a travel journal for the old man based upon the images carved in the stick.

BUILDING VOCABULARY

▶ Brainstorm attributes that would be important to use when describing objects for someone who is unable to see them. Practice using these attributes by playing a guessing game. Write the names of common objects on small scraps of paper and put these into a basket. Each student will draw one of the pieces of paper and describe what the object looks like so that the others in the class can guess.

▶ The text contains some vocabulary that might be unfamiliar such as *citadel, ascended, incantations* and *stropped*. Can the meaning of these words be determined from their context? Find a synonym for each of these words. Plug the new words into the text. Do they make sense? Use a dictionary to determine the accuracy of the synonyms. Providing that they are accurate, decide whether the original words or the synonyms sound best.

Social Studies

▶ Locate China on a world map. The text refers to the walled city of Peking. Is it on the map? Did the author invent a fictional location for the story? Why would any city be walled?

▶ Investigate the Great Wall of China. Where is it, who built it, and why?

▶ Using the objects shown in the illustrations of the seeing stick itself and the directions in the text, can you determine a possible route for the old man's journey?

▶ What is an emperor? How is China ruled today?

▶ Use a wok to cook Chinese vegetables and sample them using chopsticks.

▶ How did physically challenged people get around on their own before the Americans with Disability Act? What changes occurred in your school? In your city?

Art

▶ Try carving images into bars of soap or other soft material. Can others identify the carved objects by their feel?

▶ Make paper kites in the shapes of dragons or birds and fly them on Children's Day, June 1.

▶ Try the "three perfections" — calligraphy, poetry and painting. Perhaps a simple poem could be illustrated in watercolors and highlighted with Chinese symbols.

Science

▶ Perhaps a local ophthalmologist or optometrist could speak to the class about how our eyes work.

▶ The old man used the sense of touch to bring the princess happiness and an appreciation of the world around her. In what ways could her other senses have brought her an awareness of her surroundings?

▶ Why might a blind person call a cane a "seeing stick"? Why are canes carried by the blind usually white? Try using one to navigate the classroom and school hallways.

RELATED BOOKS

NOVELS

Taylor, Theodore. **The Cay**.
Doubleday, 1987. ISBN 0-385-079060
An old African-American man, Timothy, teaches an arrogant rich boy, Philip, to survive after a shipwreck, although he is blind.

PICTURE BOOKS

Louie, Al-Ling. **Yeh Shen: A Cinderella Story from China**. Philomel, 1982. ISBN 0-399-20900 X
In this version of the well-known story, Yeh Shen escapes through the use of magic fish bones.

Wolff, Ferida. **The Emperor's Garden**.
Tambourine,1994. ISBN 0-688-11651-5
When the villagers build a garden to honor the Emperor, they argue over who has made the most important contribution to this tribute.

Young, Ed. **Lon Po Po** See page 257.

Yolen, Jane. **The Emperor and the Kite**.
Putnam, 1988. ISBN 0-399-21499-2
The smallest daughter of the Emperor helps her imprisoned father.

NONFICTION

Cotterell, Arthur. Eyewitness Books: **Ancient China**.
Knopf, 1994. ISBN 0-679-86167-X
Chapters in this book include topics such as clothing, food and drink, the Silk Road. and festivals and games. As is true of all the books in this series, there are hundreds of color photographs that will allow even poor readers to gain information.

Ganeri, Anita. **Body Science**.
Dillon, 1992. ISBN 0-87518-576-2
This well illustrated book uses a question-and-answer format to explain the workings of the human body including the eye.

Savage, Stephen. **Adaptation for Survival—Eyes**.
Thomson Learning, 1995. ISBN 1-56847-349-4
Simple text and wonderful color photographs inform readers how human and animal eyes function.

Steele, Philip. **Journey through China**.
Troll, 1991. ISBN 0-8167-2113-0
Color photographs enhance the text, which informs the reader about life in modern-day China.

Ward, Brian R. **The Eye and Seeing**.
Watts, 1981. ISBN 0-531-04290-1
Color illustrations and a glossary combine with readable text to provide information about the human eye.

Waterlow, Julia. **China-A Study of an Economically Developing Country**. Thomson Learning, 1995.
ISBN 1-56847-340-0
Color photographs, maps, sidebars and informative text give facts about China.

OTHER BOOKS BY JANE YOLEN

See page 250.

Wings

by Jane Yolen
Illustrated by Dennis Nolan
Harcourt, 1997
ISBN 0-15-201567-1

▶ SUMMARY

This is the story of Daedalus and Icarus, beautifully told. There's a rhythm in the narrative punctuated on each page by a sentence about the gods who watch it all. More background information is included than usual in this myth's retelling, and it can serve as an introduction to a study of many myths

▶ ILLUSTRATION

These illustrations appear as traditional renderings with a sense of nostalgia—visual themes with roots in illustration about mythology, theology and nature. Of particular note is the use of dual images with the subtle background images in contrast to the stronger figures in the foreground. The pattern of the print page facing the illustration page is a traditional one.

▶ CONNECTIONS

NOVEL

Paul Fleischman's **Dateline: Troy** (Candlewick, 1996. ISBN 1-56402-469-5) makes an excellent connection to **Wings**. It tells the story of the Iliad and makes a modern connection to the mythology.

THEME

▶ Greek and Roman mythology

CURRICULUM CONNECTION

▶ HISTORY – Ancient Greece
▶ SCIENCE – Flight

LANGUAGE ARTS

MAIN IDEA

▶ Is there a moral to this story? Compose some.

FINDING DETAILS

▶ Can the characters of the myth see the gods we see? What makes you think so?

▶ The story says that Daedalus had many occupations: sculptor, inventor and architect, for instance. Find examples of his skill in the illustrations of **Wings**.

▶ There may be a mistake in this story. Read the part about the ant and the shell and see if you think there's a mistake.

WRITING

▶ Read some newspaper obituaries. Then write obituaries for Daedalus and Icarus.

▶ Using a computer, make a class database of the gods and goddesses of Greek and Roman mythology.

POETRY

▶ Find and read W. H. Auden's poem "Musee des Beaux Arts," which refers to the painting by Bruegel referred to below. Does the poem make the painting easier to understand?

VOCABULARY

▶ Yolen refers to "hubris" as being present in all versions of this myth. Find out what it is and then find examples of hubris in other myths.

▶ The minotaur is only one of mythology's many monsters. Find others and make a bulletin board display of as many types as possible. Along the edges of the bulletin board, place information about the gods and heroes who interacted or fought with each of them.

▶ Find traces of mythology in our common words — cereal, atlases, gases.

COMPARING LITERATURE

▶ The idea of aiming too high or flying too high is present in many pieces of literature. Read **Rainbow Crow**, **The Silver Pony** and **The Wreck of the Zephyr** (see Related Books). Find the parallels in those books and then look for others in literature.

▶ Threading the shell is almost impossible. Find other difficult tasks in literature.

SCIENCE

▶ The maze in this book is referred to as a "labyrinth." Find examples of that term in games and other books. One part of the human ear is called a labyrinth. Can you see why?

▶ B. F. Skinner was just one of many psychologists who have used mazes. How did he use them? What information did he gain from his experiments? Do scientists still use them? Find out about the maze in an IQ test called the WISC 3.

▶ Icarus flew so high that the wax in his wings melted. How hot does wax have to get in order to melt? How soft would it have to get in order to release the feathers? Design experiments to check your estimates.

▶ Find feathers of both songbirds and birds of prey. Swinging a single songbird feather through the air usually produces a sound. Owl feathers make no sound. Why would this be an advantage for an owl? Why not the soundless quality for other birds?

▶ Compare the shape of various bird wings with airplane wings. What principles of physics are they using?

▶ Look at daVinci's illustration of a man with bird wings. Would his design for flight have worked? Why or why not?

SOCIAL STUDIES

▶ There's a line in the book that states, "Not even a prince can kill a prince." Is that true? Find examples of murder by kings and princes.

▶ The tower that imprisoned Daedalus and Icarus is just one of many towers in literature and in the real world. Find as many as possible and make a display showing what you have learned.

ART

▶ Locate Bruegel's painting "Landscape with the Fall of Icarus" at **http://sunsite.unc.edu/wm/paint/auth/bruegel/** on the Web. In it we see only the feet of Icarus as he falls into the sea. What do you think Bruegel is trying to show here?

▶ Research mazes and then design some of your own.

RELATED BOOKS

NOVELS

Fleischman, Paul. **Dateline: Troy**.
Candlewick, 1996. ISBN 1-56402-469-5 Grades 4-9
Fleischman tells the story of the Iliad in a straightforward manner and then makes visual parallels to the action through newspaper articles of recent history.

Ward, Lynd. **The Silver Pony**.
Houghton, 1973. ISBN 0-395-14753-0 Grades 3-9
This is a wordless novel in which a winged horse is urged to fly too high.

PICTURE BOOKS

Van Allsburg, Chris. **The Wreck of the Zephyr**
See page 232.
A boy learns to sail above the waves and goes too high.

Van Laan, Nancy. **Rainbow Crow**.
Knopf, 1989. ISBN 0-394-89577-0
A crow loses its beautiful feathers by bringing fire back to the earth.

OTHER GOOD MYTHOLOGY BOOKS

Climo, Shirley. **Atalanta's Race**.
Clarion, 1995. ISBN 0-395-67322-4
The tale of the race for the hand of Atalanta is beautifully illustrated and told.

D'Aulaire, Ingri and Edgar. **Book of Greek Myths**.
Doubleday, 1962. ISBN 0-385-01583-6
Nobody's done a better compilation of these classic myths for young readers.

Fisher, Leonard Everett. **Theseus and the Minotaur**. Holiday, 1988. ISBN 0-8234-0703-9
Here's an extension of the focus book that pays more attention to Theseus.

Orgel, Doris. **Ariadne, Awake!**
Viking, 1994. ISBN 0-670-85158-2
Another closely related tale, this one focusing on Ariadne.

Lon Po Po: A Red-Riding Hood Story from China

by Ed Young
Putnam, 1989
ISBN 0-399-21619-7

SUMMARY

This Caldecott Award-winning book is a wonderful retelling of an ancient Chinese tale. The comparisons to the traditional European "Red Riding Hood" as well as other folktales involving wolves and innocents are obvious. In this version, a mother leaves her three daughters to visit their granny after instructing her children to close the door and latch it. A wolf disguised as their Po Po (grandmother) tricks them and enters the house. The eldest and most clever daughter soon sees through the disguise and plots the wolf's destruction. With the help of her sisters she succeeds and the wolf meets his well-deserved fate.

ILLUSTRATION

Watercolors and pastels are the principal media in these soft and subtle illustrations. Superimposed on the book's vertical pages are subdivided sections or multiple panels that create horizontally connected sequences. Double-page spreads are divided variously into two-, three- and four-paneled arrangements. In all multi-sectioned compositions, the wolf's image can be found. In some of the illustrations the wolf is easy to see, while in others a bit more searching is necessary. The book's jacket is also two-paneled and shows the wolf coming around the jacket from back to front. To fully appreciate these illustrations, a second or third scanning is necessary.

CONNECTIONS

NOVEL

Wolf by Gillian Cross (Holiday, 1991. ISBN 0-8234-0870-1) explores many of our concepts about wolves in the context of a good story.

THEME

▶ Variants of familiar tales

CURRICULUM CONNECTION

▶ SOCIAL STUDIES – World cultures and folktales

LANGUAGE ARTS

INTERPRETING THE BOOK

▶ Reread the dedication of the book and decide what the author means by it. Find other tales where the wolf has the same role.

▶ Locate as many stories as possible involving wolves (see Related Books). Chart the roles as to "wicked" and "sympathetic."

▶ After reading the text and examining each illustration, divide the story into sections.

▶ With the help of the panels, list the important events in each section.

EXTENDING VOCABULARY

▶ List as many wolf expressions as possible. Don't forget "wolf at the door," "crying wolf," and "wolf in sheep's clothing." Explain the meaning and origin of as many as possible.

COMPARING LITERATURE

▶ The wolf disguises himself as an old woman. Find other books in which wolves don disguises and describe them. See Related Books.

▶ Read other versions of Red Riding Hood. Chart their similarities and differences.

▶ Find and read "The Wolf and the Seven Kids." Compare the settings, families and disguises with this story.

▶ What about this story makes it a Red Riding Hood tale?

FINDING THE MAIN IDEA

▶ List morals that might be taken from this tale for the wolf, the children and the mother. For instance:
   Mother: Put everything in writing.
   Children: Listen to your mother.
   Wolf: Don't underestimate your victims.

RELATING TO PERSONAL EXPERIENCES

▶ Would you have let the wolf enter the house? What would have prevented you from doing so?

FINDING CAUSE AND EFFECT

▶ Tao and Paotze unlatched the door. What if:
   They had listened to their mother?
   Shang had not relit the candle?
   Chang had not coughed? (Was the cough a pre arranged signal?)
   The wolf was not hungry for gingko seeds?

SCIENCE

TREES

▶ Investigate gingko trees and prepare a display. Describe and show the shape of the leaf. Where are these trees found? How is the gingko tree used in China? How are they used here? What is the seed called? How do people use it for food?

▶ If the story had been set in your part of the world, what seeds should have been used?

WOLVES

▶ What is there about a wolf that causes it to be used so often in tales as a villain? Are the characteristics of wolves in the wild consistent with their characterization as villains?

▶ On a map of the world, show areas where wolves can still be found. What is their natural habitat? How do you feel about the reintroduction of wolves to Yellowstone National Park? Would you feel the same way if you lived near it?

▶ What's happened to the wolf's natural environment in America?

ART

▶ Look at the image of the wolf on the dedication page. Why do you think Ed Young created that particular illustration?

▶ Find and list all the images of the wolf in the book. Compare your list with the others in the class. Which ones did you miss?

▶ What effect do the paneled pages create? Examine panels by other artists in books and museums. Look at triptychs and oriental screens.

▶ Divide a piece of your own artwork into panels. Divide any artwork that way. Do you like the differences it makes? Does it matter whether you created it to be divided or did it as an afterthought?

▶ Compare Ed Young's artwork in this book with the work he did in **Seven Blind Mice** and **Sadako** (see Related Books). Which is more similar?

RELATED BOOKS

NOVELS

Burgess, Melvin. **Cry of the Wolf**. Morrow, 1990. ISBN 0-688-11744-9 Grades 5-9
What if there were only one wild wolf left in England and one man whose compulsion it was to kill it?

Cross, Gillian. **Wolf**.
Holiday House, 1991. ISBN 0-8234-0870-1
Grades 5-9
Casey's mother and her new family are engaged in educating the public about wolves. We explore fairy tale wolves as well as real ones.

PICTURE BOOKS

Goodall, John S. **Little Red Riding Hood**.
Simon & Schuster, 1988. ISBN 0-689-50457-8
Half and full pages alternate to tell this wordless version of Red Riding Hood.

Hyman, Trina Schart. **Little Red Riding Hood**.
Holiday, 1983. ISBN 0-8234-0470-6
This is the traditional version of the tale with Hyman's exquisitely detailed illustrations.

Marshall, James. **Red Riding Hood**.
Puffin, 1993. ISBN 0-14-054976-5
In Marshall's funny version, Grandma has an expanded role and she's a real reader.

Mosel, Arlene. **The Funny Little Woman**.
Dutton, 1972. ISBN 0-525-30265-4
In this folktale from China, a little woman intent on her household tasks is disturbed by supernatural creatures.

OTHER BOOKS ILLUSTRATED BY ED YOUNG

Coerr, Eleanor. **Sadako**.
Putnam, 1993. ISBN 0-399-21771-1
Young's illustrations add poignancy to this true story of a victim of the bombing of Hiroshima.

Frost, Robert. **Birches**.
Holt, 1988. ISBN 0-8050-0570-6
Young's illustrations for this classic poem are misty and beautiful.

Leaf, Margaret. **Eyes of the Dragon**.
Lothrop, 1987. ISBN 0-688-06155-9
A great artist paints a dragon on the village wall. A little boy's grandfather wants him to put in the dragon's eyes, but that's taboo.

Louie, Al-Ling. **Yeh Shen: A Cinderella Story from China**. Philomel, 1982. ISBN 0-399-20900-X
This version of the folktale has Yeh Shen escaping from her misery through the use of magic fish bones.

Yolen, Jane. **The Emperor and the Kite**.
Putnam, 1988. ISBN 0-399-21499-2
The youngest and smallest daughter of the Emperor helps her imprisoned father.

Yolen, Jane. **The Girl Who Loved the Wind**.
Harper, 1987. ISBN 0-06-443088-X
A merchant's efforts to keep his beautiful daughter in prison are foiled by the wind.

Young, Ed. **Seven Blind Mice**.
Putnam, 1992. ISBN 0-399-22261-8
Young's own version of "The Blind Men and the Elephant" utilizes totally different techniques from those he uses in his other books.

Title, Author & Illustrator Index

Aardema, Verna 153, 204
Ackerman, Karen **1**, 3, 46, 83, 137, 180, 186
Across America on an Emigrant Train 33
Adams, Richard 207
Adaptation for Survival – Eyes 253
Adler, David 64
Adoff, Arnold 204
Adrift 18
Adventures of High John 98
Aesop 131
Aesop's Fables 128
After Columbus 76
Against the Storm 122
Agee, Jon **4**
Ahlberg, Allan 33, 34, 36
Ahlstrom, Mark E. 49
Alex & the Cat 83, 89
Alexander & the Wind-Up Mouse 125
Alexander, Lloyd 7, 131
Aliki 116
All I See 6, 119, 180
All the Colors of Race 204
Allen, Thomas B. 3
Almost Famous Daisy **117**
Altman, Linda Jacobs **10**, 12, 207
Amazing Armored Animals 40
Amelia Bedelia 6, 159
Amelia's Road **10**, 207
Among the Dolls 125
Ancient China 253
Ancient Egypt 68
Ancient Rome 143
And So They Build 171
Anello, Christine 192
Annie & the Wild Animals 40
Anno, Mitsumasa 92, 125, 128, 150, 237
Anno's Aesop 128
Anno's Magic Seeds 150, 237
Anno's Mysterious Multiplying Jar 125
Anno's USA 92

Antle, Nancy 46
Appalachia: The Voices of Sleeping Birds **175**
Apple Is My Sign **151**
Apple Picking Time 12
Apple Valley Year 219
Araboolies of Liberty Street **211**, 231
Araminta's Paint Box 3, 46
Ardley, Ned 247
Are We Almost There 27
Ariadne, Awake 256
Arly 12
Arly's Run 12
Armadillo from Amarillo 40
Armadillo Rodeo 37
Armadillos & Other Unusual Animals 40
Armstrong, Jennifer 96
Arnold, Caroline 21, 55
Arnold, Tim 70
Arnosky, Jim 134, 171, 231
Arthur for the Very First Time 210, 250
Ashabranner, Brent 12
Ashanti to Zulu 153, 204
Atalanta's Race 256
Atkin, S. Beth 12
**Aunt Chip & the Great Triple Creek
  Dam Affair** **160**, 216
Autumn Street 24, 64, 86
Avi **13**, 15, 55, 216

Baa 140
Babbitt, Natalie .. 36, 110, 129, 207, 214, 238, 240
Bad Day at Riverbend 140, **226**
Baillie, Allan **16**, 213
Baker, Leslie 174, 192
Baker, Olaf 76
Ball, Zachary 157
Ballad of the Pirate Queen 244
Bang, Molly 183
Banks, Lynne Reid 18, 228
Banshee Train 31

Banyai, Istvan	140
Baron, Kathy	67
Barron, T. A.	83
Bash, Barbara	55
Bat	55
Bat in the Dining Room	55
Bat-Poet	53
Bats, Creatures of the Night	55
Bawshou Rescues the Sun	18
Baylor, Byrd	**19**, 21, **22**, 24, 27, 40, 110, 125, 201
Bear Called Paddington	125
Beats Me, Claude	43
Beatty, Patricia	168
Beautiful Land	46
Bee Tree	162, 216
Ben's Dream	234
Benjamin's Barn	36
Berlioz the Bear	40
Berson, Harold	9
Bess's Log Cabin Quilt	104
Best Christmas Pageant Ever	213
Best Town in the World	40
Best Wishes	177
Beyond the Cellar Door	3
Beyond the Chocolate War	16, 18
Beyond the Ridge	73, 207
Beyond the Western Sea	55
Bicycle Man	183
Bierhorst, John	183
Big Orange Splot	213
Big Tree	171
Billiland, Judith Heide	**93**
Bjork, Christina	119
Birches	259
Birchman, David F	**25**
Bird, the Frog & the Light	**13**
Birdseye, Tom	**28**
Birdwatch	95, 244
Bizzy Bones & Mooremouse	147
Bizzy Bones & the Last Quilt	147
Bizzy Bones & Uncle Ezra	147
Black & White	**138**
Black Hawk, Sac Rebel	18
Black Stallion	76
Blackberries in the Dark	1, 3, 83
Blos, Joan	3, 180, 213, 223, 225, 231
Blossom Culp & the Sleep of Death	9
Blow Away Soon	**108**
Blue Willow	10, 12
Blue-Eyed Daisy	177
Bodkin, Odds	31
Body Science	253
Bolton, Janet	166
Bond, Michael	125
Bone Wars	21, 71
Bonjour, Mr. Satie	6
Bonvillain, Nancy	18
Boodil My Dog	89
Book of Pigericks	128
Book That Jack Built	189
Borning Room	67, 90, 196
Boston, Lucy	21
Boulton, Jane	52
Bowen, Gary	195
Boy Who Cried Wolf	189
Boys' War	137
Bracelet	61, 183, 186
Brady	225
Breakout	143
Breathed, Berkeley	**34**, 162
Brenner, Barbara	244
Brett, Jan	**37**, 88
Brian's Winter	134
Briggs, Raymond	18
Brimmer, Larry D.	12
Bringing the Rain to Kapiti Plain	153
Bristle Face	157
Brooke, William	128
Brooke, William J.	6
Brooks, Bruce	83
Brown, Brian	143
Brown, Kathryn	**178**
Brown, Marcia	9
Brown, Margaret Wise	36
Brown, Ruth	147
Browne, Anthony	225
Browning, Robert	231
Bruchac, Joseph	49
Brush with Magic	4
Bryan, Ashley	98
Buck, Pearl	131
Buehner, Caralyn	**41**
Buehner, Mark	**41**
Buffalo Woman	73
Build Your Own Toys	125
Bull Run	138
Bunting, Eve	3, 15, **44**, **47**, **50**, 67, 104, 162, 198, 231
Burch, Robert	175
Burgess, Melvin	259
Burma	18

Burnford, Sheila 89
Butterfly Alphabet 237
Butterfly Seeds 116, 150, 235
Butterworth, Oliver 21
By the Dawn's Early Light 3
Byars, Betsy 7, 47, 116, 248

Caleb and Kate 43
Call Me Francis Tucket 113
Campbell, Joanna 76
Canada Goose Quilt 104, 166
Cannon, Janell **53**
Carle, Eric **148**, 237
Carpenter, Nancy **145**
Carter, Dorothy 58
Carter, Jimmy 95
Castle 140
Castle, Caroline 186
Cat That Walks by Itself 89
Catalanotto, Peter **135**
Catching the Wind 110
Cathedral 140
Catrow, David **123**
Caught in the Crossfire 95
Cay 86, 251
Cazet, Denys 6
Cecil's Story 95, **135**, 168, 250
Celia's Island Journal 67
Cesar Chavez 12
Chalk Doll 122
Charlie Drives the Stage 113
Charlie Skedaddle 168
Chen, Ju-Hong **28**
Cherry, Lynn 40, 92, 222, 247
Chester's Way 228
Cheyenne 73
Chicken Little 189
Chickens Aren't the Only Ones 250
Children Just Like Me 61, **120**
Children of Christmas 177
China 253
China Year 122
Chinese Mirror 30
Chocolate Moose for Dinner 6, 159
Chocolate War 16, 18
Chortles 159
Christian, Mary Blount 147
Christiansen, C. B. 80
Christmas Box 183
Christmas House 219

Christmas in the Big House 98, 225
Cinderella 204
Circle of Love 73
City 140, 143
Clapp, Patricia 193
Clare, John D. 143
Classical Rome 143
Clements, Andrew 58
Cleopatra 58
Clever Kate 9
Climo, Shirley 56, 204, 256
Cobblestone Magazine 137
Cochran, Oren 134
Coerr, Eleanor 59, 86, 166, 183, 186, 259
Cohen, Caron 76
Cole, Babette 189
Cole, Joanna 247
Collier, James 225
Colman, Penny 64
Conrad, Pam 19, 21, 46, 244
Constance: A Story of Early Plymouth 193
Cookcamp 107
Cooney, Barbara 52, 62, 65, 101, 150, 180,
   210, 225, **245**
Corduroy 125
Cormier, Robert 16, 18
Cotterell, Arthur 253
Counting Cranes 183
Cowboy & the Black-Eyed Pea **111**
Cowboys 113
Coyote Dreams 43
Crane Wife 183
Crews, Donald 33
**Crinkleroot's Guide to Walking
   in Wild Places** 134, 171
Cross, Gillian 257
Cry of the Wolf 259

d"Aulaire, Ingri & Edgar 256
Da Vinci 119
Daddy Is a Monster Sometimes 204
Dakota Dugout 45, 80, 104, **217**
Dams 247
Dancing on the Table 3
Dandelions **44**, 52, 67, 104
Dangerous Promise 52, 73
Danziger, Paula 55
Dark Harvest 12
Darkness & the Butterfly 80
Dateline: Troy 254

Day of Ahmed's Secret 95, 162
Dean, Julia 67
Dear Hildegarde 119
Dear Mr. Blueberry 119
Death of the Iron Horse 46, **71**
DeFelice, Cynthia 83
DePaola, Tomie 6, 76, 83, 116, 153
Desert Is Theirs 24, 40
Desert Voices 24
Desimini, Lisa 198
Di Wu **16**
Diamond War 169
Did You Hear the Wind Sing Your Name 110
Digging Up Tyrannosaurus Rex 21
Dodd, Anne 110
Doesn't Fall Off His Horse 3
Dog Breath **157**
Dog Days 172
Dogger 250
Don't You Know There's a War On 210, 228
Don't You Turn Back 80
Dorris, Michael 232, 241, 244
Dorros, Arthur 110, 247
Doyle, Peter 143
Dr. Seuss 213
Drac and the Gremlin 18
Dragonwagon, Crescent 55, 67, 80, 198, 247
Dreadful Future of Blossom Culp 9
Dream Wolf 73
Dreams 43
Ducks Don't Get Wet 147
Duffy & the Devil . . . .?????????????
Dunlop, Eileen 67

Earle, Ann 55
Earthkeepers 147
Edwards, Richard 171
Egyptian Cinderella 56, 204
Eight Hands Round 104
Eleanor 62
Eleanor Roosevelt 64
Ella Enchanted 154, **202**, 204
Emberley, Rebecca **68**
Emily & the Enchanted Frog 83
Emma 3, 6, 101, 119, 180
Emperor & the Kite 259
Emperor's Garden 253
Encounter **241**
Endangered Wetland Animals 147
Enormous Egg 21

Erickson, John 37, 113
Ernst, Lisa Campbell 83, 166
Escape from Slavery 98
Estes, Eleanor 24
Everett Anderson's Goodbye 80
Every Autumn Comes the Bear 134, 231
Everybody Needs a Rock 21, 24
Exploding Frog 15
Eye & Seeing 253
Eyes of the Dragon 259

Fables **126**, 131
Fairy Rebel 18
Family Apart 52, 73
Fanny's Dream **41**
Farber, Norma 83
Farley, Walter 76
Farm Summer 1942 . . . . 62, **84**
Farmyard Cat 192
Father Water, Mother Woods 134
Feel the Wind 110
Fenner, Carol 6
Field, Rachel 198
Fifty Simple Things Kids Can Do
 to Save the Earth 147
Finn's Island 67
First Dog 40, 88
First Forest 171
First Look at Bats 55
Fisher, Leonard Everett 73, 256
Fledging 208
Fleischman, Paul . . . 33, 67, 90, 138, 148, 196, 254
Fleischman, Sid 25, 27, 107, 226
Fleming, Denise 147
Fletcher, Jane Cowen 9
Flossie & the Fox 131
Flourney, Valerie 166
Fly Away Girl 80
Fly Away Home 52, 198
Follow the Dream 244
Follow the Drinking Gourd 225
Follow the Water from Brook to Ocean 247
Footprints & Shadows 110
Fortune-Tellers 7, 131
Fossil 21
Fossil Snake 21
Fossils 21
Four Dollars & Fifty Cents 113
Fox & the Crow 131
Fox 49

Fox Song	49
Fox Went Out on a Chilly Night	49
Fox, Mem	83, 180
Fox, Paula	98
Foxes	49
Fradin, Dennis	73
Franklin Delano Roosevelt	64
Fraser, Mary	73
Freedman, Russell	46, 64
Freeman, Don	55, 125
Freight Train	33
Fritz, Jean	137, 225, 244
Frog Prince	15
Frog Prince Continued	189
Frost, Robert	259
Frosted Glass	6
Fun No Fun	210
Funny Little Woman	259
Galdone, Paul	189
Games They Played	27
Gammage Cup	211
Gammell, Stephen	**1**, 3
Ganeri, Anita	253
Garden of Abdul Gasazi	234
Garland, Sherry	150, 237
Gates of the Wind	110
Gates, Doris	10, 12
Gathering of Days	223, 225
Gauch, Patricia Lee	95, 137
George, Jean Craighead	147, 220, 237
Georgia Music	**81**
Get Rich Mitch	125
Ghost Belonged to Me	9, 31, 33
Ghost Train	33
Ghosts I Have Been	9
Gila Monsters Meet you at the Airport	113
Gile, John	171
Gilson, Jamie	122
Ginsburg, Mirra	30
Girl Who Loved the Wind	110, 259
Girl Who Loved Wild Horses	73, **74**
Giver	13, 15, 213
Giving Tree	150
Gladiator	143
Goble, Paul	46, **71**, 73, **74**, 207
God on Every Mountain Top	201
Goldilocks & the Three Bears	40
Goldin, Augusta	147
Good Times on Grandfather Mountain	147

Good, The Bad & the Goofy	189
Goodall, John S.	259
Goodbye Vietnam	184
Goodbye, My Island	67
Goodman, Joan	141
Goodnight Moon	34
Goodnight Mr. Beetle	36
Goodnight Opus	**34**, 162
Gordon, Sheila	77
Grandaddy & Janetta	83
Grandaddy's Place	3, 83
Grandfather's Dream	83
Grandfather's Journey	61, 116, 183, **184**, 210, 237
Grandfather's Rock	83
Grandpa Baxtere & the Photographs	186
Grandpa's Mountain	101, 201
Grandpa's Song	83
Grass Songs	219
Grasshopper on the Road	128
Grasshopper Summer	44, 217
Gray, Libba Moore	101, 180, 213
Great Carnival Caper	27
Great Grey Owl	134
Great Pumpkin Snatch	95
Greaves, Margaret	204
Green Magician Puzzle	27
Greenfield, Eloise	204
Greenfield, Eloise	3
Grifalconi, Ann	77, 153
Griffith, Helen	3, 81
Grimm Brothers	15
Growing Up Masai	153
Gruber, Terry	192
Gryski, Camilla	27
Guess Who My Favorite Person Is	24, 27
Guests	232, 244
Gwynne, Fred	6, 15, 159
Hahn, Mary Downing	64, 86
Hall, Donald	61, **84**, **87**, **90**, 101, 134, 192, 240, 250
Halperin, Wendy Anderson	**196**
Hamanaka, Sheila	61, 186
Hank the Cowdog	37, 113
Hankin, Rosie	27
Harriet & the Promised Land	98, 225
Harris & Me	86
Harris, Geraldine	**58**, 166
Harvey, Brett	46
Haseley, Dennis	3
Hatchet	134

Hattie the Backstage Bat 55	Huynh Quang Nhuong 122
Have You Seen My Duckling 40	Hyman, Trina Schart 3, 7, 259
Heartland 201	
Heartlight 83	**I Am the Dog; I Am the Cat** 87, 92, 134, 192
Heide, Florence Parry **93**, 134, 162	**I Dream of Peace** 95
Heller, Ruth 56, 250	**I Had a Lot of Wishes** **208**
Hello, My Name Is Scrambled Eggs 122	**I Sing for the Animals** 73
Hendershot, Judith 156	**I Was Born About 10,000 Years Ago** 107
Henkes, Kevin 15, 228, 250	**I'm in Charge of Celebrations** 24, 40
Henry David Thoreau 18	**Icebergs & Glaciers** 201
Henry, Marguerite 74	**Ida Early Comes Over the Mountain** 175
Henry, Matthew **13**	**If You Are a Hunter of Fossils** **19**, 24, 110
Her Seven Brothers 73	**If You Made a Million** 125
Here Comes McBroom 107	**If You Traveled on the Underground Railroad** .. 98
Heron Street 92, 147, 150, 219, **220**	**If You Were There in 1492** 244
Heyer, Marilee 30	**In Coal Country** 156
Hicyilmaz, Gaye 122	**In Summer Light** 117
Hidden House 125	**In the Face of Danger** 52
Higher on the Door 210	**In the Forest** 171
Himler, Ron **50, 102, 217**	**In the Night Kitchen** 228
Hiroshima No Pika 61	**In the Small, Small Pond** 147
Hirschi, Ron 147	**In the Year of the Boar & Jackie Robinson** 181
His Majesty, Queen Hatshepsut 58	**Incredible Journey** 89
Hiscock, Bruce 171	**Incredible Painting of Felix Clousseau** 4
Hitty, Her First Hundred Years 198	**Indian Winter** 46
Hodges, Margaret 207	**Ink-Keeper's Apprentice** 6, 183, 186
Hodgman, Ann 55	**Iron Horse** 73
Holg, Stan 73	**Iroquois** 122
Holmes, Burnham 12	Isaacs, Anne 105
Home Place 67, 80, 198, 247	Isaacson, Philip 80
Homeplace **196**, 240	**Island Boy** **65**, 101
Homes, Holes & Hives 171	**Island of the Blue Dolphins** 67
Honkers 86, **248**	**It Could Always Be Worse** 9
Hopkinson, Deborah **96**, 104	**It's Hard to Read a Map** 89
Hopscotch Around the World 27	**Iva Dunnit & the Big Wind** 174
Horner, Jack 21	
House of Wings 248	**Jack & the Beanstalk** 189
House on Maple Street 247	Jacobs, Leland 36
Houston, Gloria **99**, 210	**Jafta and the Wedding** 204
How Does It Feel to Be Old 83	James, Betsy **108**
How Many Days to America 52	James, Simon 119
How Many Miles To Jacksonville 33	James, Simon 143
How Much Is a Million 125	Jarrell, Randall 53
How Pizza Came to Queens 114	Jeffers, Susan **238**
How to Live Forever 162, **214**	**Jigsaw Jackson** **25**
Howard, Ellen **102**	**Jim Ugly** 226
Hughes, Shirley 250	**Jip: His Story** 231
Humphrey, Paul 27	**John Brown, Rose & the Midnight Cat** 89
Hundred Dresses 24	**John Henry** 107
Hunter, Mollie 229, 245	**John Muir** 201

Johnny Appleseed 174	Langton, Jane 208
Johnston, Tony 6, 33, 67, 83, **111**, 166	Lankford, Mary D. 27
Jonas, Ann 166	LaPlaca, Annette 27
Josefina Story Quilt 166	Lasky, Kathryn . . 3, 21, 71, 110, 114, 163, 195, 237
Journey through China 253	**Last Snow of Winter** 6
Journey to the New World 195	**Last Train** 33
Jukes, Mavis 3	Laundrie, Amy 76
Jukes, Mavis 83	Lawrence, Jacob 98, 225
Jumanji 6, 228, 234	Leaf, Margaret 259
Jump Ship to Freedom 225	Lee, Jeanne M. 30
Just a Dream 234	**Legend of Scarface** 76
	Legend of the Bluebonnet 76, 153
Katie's Trunk 219, 225	**Legend of the Milky Way** 30
Keats, Ezra Jack 43	Lester, Julius 98, 107
Keene, Ann 147	**Letting Swift River Go** 222, **245**, 250
Keeping Quilt 104, **163**	Levine, Carson 156
Keeping Secrets 52	Levine, Ellen 98
Keller, Holly 83	Levine, Gail 204
Kellogg, Steven 107, 113, 174, 189	Lewin, Hugh 204
Kendall, Carol 213	Lewin, Ted **93**, 95
Kent, Zachary 137	Lewis, C. S. 207, 228
Kesselman, Wendy 3, 6, 101, 119, 180	Lewis, Kim 33
Khalsa, Dayal Kaur **114**	**Library Lil** 162, 216
Kidd, Richard **117**	**Lights on the River** 12
Kidnapped in Rome 143	Lindbergh, Reeve 37
Kids Games 27	Lindenbaum, Pija 89
Kimmel, Eric 113	Lindsay, William 21
Kinda Blue 80	**Linnea in Monet's Garden** 119
Kindersley, Anabel & Barnabas 61, **120**	**Lion, the Witch & the Wardrobe** 207, 228
King Who Rained 6, 159	Lionni, Leo 125
Kinsey-Warnock, Natalie 76, 104, 166	**Little Red Riding Hood** 259
Kipling, Rudyard 89	Littlechild, George 76
Kiss the Dust 95	Lobel, Anita 9
Kitchen, Bert 171	Lobel, Arnold **126, 129**, 228
Klaveness, Jan 3	**Log Cabin Quilt** **102**
Kneeknock Rise 129	Lohf, Sabine 125
Knights of the Kitchen Table 189	**Lon Po Po** **257**
Kodama, Tatsuharu 61	London, Jonathan **132**
Korean Cinderella 204	Lord, Betty 181
Kotzwinkle, William **123**	**Lost Lake** 183
	Lotus Seeds 150, 237
L'Engle, Madeleine 28, 30, 213	Louie, Ai-Ling 259
Laird, Elizabeth 95	Louie, Ai-Ling 30
Lamb, Susan Condie **99**	Love, Anne 46, 104
Land I Lost 120	Lowell, Susan 70
Land of Dreams 43	Lowry, Lois 15, 24, 64, 86, 89, 192, 213
Land of Hope 43	**Luckiest Kid on the Planet** 83
Land of Promise 43	**Lucy's Summer** 92, 240
Lane, Margaret 49	Ludwig, Warren 111
Langley, Andrew 143	Lunn, Janet 137, 168

Lyon, George Ella 95, **135**, 250	**Mitten** 40
Lyttle, Richard B. 27	Moeri, Louise 153
	Mojave 201
Macaulay, David 58, **138, 141,** 143	Mollel, Tololwa M. **151**
MacDonald, Fiona 73	**Moon of the Monarch Butterflies** 237
MacLachlan, Patricia 101, 210, 250	**More Alex & the Cat** 89
Magic School Bus at the Waterworks 247	Morin, Paul **151**
Maisie 240	**Morning Girl** 241, 244
Man Who Could Call Down Owls 52, 231	Mosel, Arlene 259
Maniac Magee 30, 231	Moser, Barry **87, 90, 154,** 175
Many Stars 27	**Motel of the Mysteries** 143
Mara Daughter of the Nile 56, 58	**Mother Jones** 64
Margaret Mead 64	**Mountain That Loved a Bird** **148,** 201
Margolies, Barbara 153	**Mountains of Quilt** 166
Marie, D. 98	**Mouse Views** 134
Markle, Sandra 55	**Mr. Griggs' Work** 177
Martin, Jacqueline Briggs **145,** 222	**Mr. Hacker** 180
Maruki, Toshi 61	**Mud Pony** 76
Mason, Cherie 49	**Mufaro's Beautiful Daughters** 153, **202**
Maude & Me & the Dirty Book 216	Muhlberger, Richard 119
Mayo, Edith 64	Munsch, Robert 43
McBroom Tells the Truth 25, 27	Murphy, Jim 33, 137
McDonald, Megan 95, 101, 122	**Murphy's Island** 67
McFarland, John 15	Murrow, Liza Ketchum 3
McGraw, Eloise 58	Musgrove, Margaret 153, 204
McKenna, Colleen 67	**My Daniel** 19, 21
McKissack, Patricia 98, 131, 225	**My Grandmother's Patchwork Quilt** 166
McLerran, Alice 70, **148,** 201	**My Great-Aunt Arizona** **99,** 210
McLoughlin, Wayne **132**	**My House** 198
McMillan, Bruce 134,	**My House Has Many Stars** 122
McMillan, Kate 225	**My Mother's House** 80
McNeese, Tim 46	**My Prairie Christmas** 46
Medieval Feast 116	**Mysteries of Harris Burdick** 234
Merriam Eve 159	**Mystery of the Polluted Stream** 147
Midnight Fox 47	
Migrant Family 12	**N. C. Wyeth's Pilgrims** 195
Migrant Farm Workers 12	Naylor, Phyllis Reynolds 178
Mike Fink 107	Ness, Evaline 156
Miles, Betty 216	**Nettie's Trip South** 98, 219, **223**
Mill 140	Neville, Emily 122
Million-Dollar Bear **123**	**Night in the Country** 177, 180
Milton, Joyce 55	**Night Journey** 3, 114, 163, 237
Ming Lo Moves the Mountain 129	**Night of the Gargoyles** 52
Minor, Wendell 47	**Night Thunder & the Queen of the Wild Horses** 76
Misoso 204	**Nightjohn** 98
Miss Maggie 177, 180	**Nineteenth Century Railway Station** 73
Miss Rumphius 101, 150, 180, 210	Nixon, Joan Lowry 41, 43, 50, 52, 73
Miss Tizzy 101, 180, 213	**No Turning Back** 55
Missing May 180	Nolan, Dennis **254**
Misty of Chincoteague 74	**Nothing But the Truth** 15

Nothing Grows Here	68
Not-So-Jolly Roger	189
Nunes, Susan	43
O'Dell, Scott	67
Oibalbal	153
Old Banjo	3
Old Henry	3, 180, 213, 231
Old Home Day	**90**, 240
Old Woman Who Named Things	**178**
On the Wings of Peace	61
Once in a Wood	128
Once on This Island	67
Once There Was a Tree	**169**
Oneal, Zibby	117
Only Opal	52, 101, 225
Oram, Hiawyn	204
Orgel, Doris	256
Orle, Sandra	110
Orphan Boy	151
Osceola	18
Our Golda	64
Ousseimi, Marta	95
Owen	250
Owens, Mary Beth	183
Owl Moon	244, 250
Ox-Cart Man	89, 92, 101, 250
Paper Crane	183
Paper John	6
Parish, Peggy	6, 159
Parnall, Peter	**19, 22**, 24
Patchwork Quilt	166
Paterson, Katherine	231
Paul Bunyan	113, 174
Paul, Ann	104
Paulsen, Gary	86, 98, 107, 113, 132, 134, 210
Peace Begins with You	95
Peace Crane	61, 186
Pearce, O. L.	40
Pearson, Susan	27
Peck, Richard	9, 33
Peck, Robert Newton	12
Pecos Bill	113, 174
Pedro's Journal	244
People of the Breaking Day	195
People of the Sacred Arrow	73
Perrault, Charles	204
Peterson, Beth	55
Pied Piper of Hamlin	231
Piggins	244
Pilgrim Voices	195
Pilgrims of Plimoth	**193**
Pink & Say	95, 137, 162, **167**
Pinkwater, Daniel	213
Pinocchio's Sister	3
Pluckrose, Henry	171
Polacco, Patricia	95, 104, 110, **160, 163, 167**, 216
Polar Express	234
Polly Vaughn	177
Pomerantz, Charlotte	122
Pondlarker	15
Popcorn Days & Buttermilk Nights	210
Potato Man	95, 101
Prairie Visions	46, 219
Prehistoric Life	21
Prince Cinders	189
Princess & the Frog	15
Princess & the Pea	113
Provensen, Alice & Martin	213, 247
Pryor, Bonnie	247
Purdy, Carol	174
Purr: Children's Book Illustrators Brag About Their Cats	**172**, 192
Pyramid	58, 140
Quick As a Cricket	159, 240
Quilt	166
Quilt Story	166
Rahaman, Vashanti	216
Rainbow Crow	207, 256
Randall's Wall	6
Ransome, James	**96**
Rappaport, Doreen	98
Ray, Deborah K.	12
Read for Me, Mama	216
Rebel	**16**, 213
Red Fox Running	**47**
Red Hawk's Account of Custer's Last Stand	73
Reeder, Carolyn	101, 137, 199
Reiser, Lynn	76
Relatives Came	3, 177, 180
Rhodes, Frank	21
Rice, Eve	128
Rise & Fall of Adolf Hitler	18
Riskind, Mary	151
River	134
River Ran Wild	92, 222, 247
Roberts, Allan	21

Robinson, Barbara	213
Rodowsky, Colby	172
Rogers, Jean	67
Roman News	143
Rome Antics	141
Roop, Connie & Peter	195
Root Cellar	137, 168
Root, Barry	**211**
Rose in My Garden	131
Rose, Ted	**31**
Rosen, Michael J.	**172**, 174, 192
Rosie the Riveter	86
Ross, Tony	131, 189
Round Buildings, Square Buildings	80, 222
Rounds, Glen	46, 70, 113, 198, 219
Ryder, Joanne	76, 110
Rylant, Cynthia	3, 6, 101, 119, **175**, 177, 180, 210, 250
Sadako & the Thousand Paper Cranes	59, 86
Sadako	59, 183, 186, 259
Saint George & the Dragon	207
Sam Johnson & the Blue Ribbon Quilt	166
Sami & the Time of Troubles	**93**
Samuel Eaton's Day	195
San Souci, Daniel	**25**
San Souci, Robert	58, 76, 195
Sanchez, Enrique O.	**10**
Sanders, Eve	122
Sandved, Kjeli	237
Sanfield, Steve	98
Sarah Morton's Day	195
Sarah Plain & Tall	99, 210
Savage, Stephen	253
Say, Allen	6, 61, 116, 122, **181**, 183, **184**, 210, 237
Schertle, Alice	240
Scholes, Katherine	95
Schwartz, Alvin	27
Schwartz, David	125
Scieszka, Jon	15, 70, **187**
Search for Delicious	207
Second Princess	204
Secret Garden	52
Seedfolks	148, 235
Seeing Stick	250, **251**
Segal, Lore	174, 190
Selsam, Millicent	55
Sendak, Maurice	36, 183, 228
Seven Blind Mice	128, 259
Seven Loaves of Bread	240
Sewall, Marcia	193
Sewing Quilts	166
Shachtman, Tom	153
Shades of Grey	135
Shadows of Night	55
Shaker Lane	213, 247
Sharmat, Marjorie	113, 125
Sharpe, Susan	147
She Come Bringing Me That Baby Girl	204
Shed, Greg	**44**
Shelby, Anne	**196**, 240
Shiloh	178
Shin's Tricycle	61
Ship	140
Shirer, William	18
Shrinking of Treehorn	134
Shub, Elizabeth	9
Siebert, Diane	33, **199**
Sierra	**199**
Sign of the Beaver	160
Silver Pony	205, 234, 256
Silverstein, Shel	150
Simon, Seymour	153
Simon, Seymour	30, 110, 201
Singer, Marilyn	89
Sioux	46
Sis, Peter	244
Slave Dancer	98
Slawson, Michele	12
Sleator, William	125
Sleeping Ugly	43, 244
Small Pig	131
Small, David	6
Smith, Lane	**187**
Smithsonian Book of the First Ladies	64
Sneetches	213
Sneve, Virginia Driving Hawk	46, 122
Snyder, Zilpha Keatley	169
Sod Houses on the Great Plains	46, 198, 219
Something	36
Song and Dance Man	**1**, 83, 180, 186
Song of Stars	**28**
Songs from Home	141
Sootface	58
Sowler, Sandie	40
Speak: Children's Book Illustrators Brag About Their Dogs	174
Speare, Elizabeth	160
Speirs, John	27
Spier, Peter	43, 49
Spinelli, Jerry	30, 143, 231

Spirit Child	183
Stanley, Diane	58
Star Mother's Youngest Child	153
Stars	30
Stay: Keeper's Story	88, 192
Steal Away	96
Steele, Philip	253
Steig, William	43
Stellaluna	**53**
Stepping on the Cracks	64, 86
Steptoe, John	153, 204, **205**
Stern, Philip Van Doren	18
Stevenson, James	81, 180, **208**, 228
Stevenson, Janet	113
Stevie	204
Stinky Cheese Man	**187**
Stolz, Mary	58
Stone Soup	9, 131, 189
Stonewall	137
Story of Harriet Tubman	225
Story of Jumping Mouse	204, **205**
Story of Mrs. Lovewright & Purrless Her Cat	174, 190
Story of the Battle of Shiloh	137
Stranded at Plimoth Plantation	195
Stranger	**229**, 234
Stranger Came Ashore	229
Strangis, Joel	83
Stringbean's Trip to the Shining Sea	119
Stroud, Virginia	3
Swamp Angel	**105**
Sweet Clara & the Freedom Quilt	96, 104, 166
Sweetest Fig	234
Swope, Sam	**211**, 231
Table Where Rich People Sit	22, **125**
Tafuri, Nancy	40
Talbot, Charlene	52
Talking Earth	147, 220
Talking Peace	95
Talmadge, Katherine	201
Tarot Says Beware	7
Tattercoats	204
Taylor, Dave	147
Taylor, Paul	21
Taylor, Theodore	86, 251
Tears for Ashan	98
Teller of Tales	128
Temple Cat	58
Ten in a Bed	34, 36
Ten Mile Day	73
Ten Tall Oaktrees	171
Terrible Things	15
Thaxter, Celia	67
There's a Bat in Bunk Five	55
There's a Batwing in My Lunchbox	55
Theseus & the Minotaur	256
Thesman, Jean	68
Thief Who Hugged a Moonbeam	9
Third Story Cat	174, 192
This Land Is My Land	76
Thomas, Jane Resh	12
Thompson, Colin	162, **214**
Three Billy Goats Gruff	70
Three Cool Kids	**68**
Three Little Javelinas	70
Three Little Wolves & the Big Bad Pig	70
Through the Magic Mirror	228
Thunder at Gettysburg	95, 137
Thunder Cake	110, 162
Time Train	33
Tin Heart	137
Tin-Pot General	18
To Be a Slave	98
Toad Is the Uncle of Heaven	30
Tom	83
Tom Tit Tot	156
Tony's Bread	116
Toor, Rachel	64
Tracks Across America	73
Train Song	33
Train to Somewhere	**50**
Trapped in Tar	21
Tree of Cranes	122, **181**, 186
Tree of Time	67
Treeful of Pigs	131
Trivizas, Eugene	70
Trouble at Marsh Harbor	147
Trouble River	116
Trouble with Trolls	40
True Story of the Three Little Pigs	70, 189
Tuck Everlasting	110, 214, 240
Tucker Pfeffercorn	154, 177
Turner, Ann	44, 80, 92, 98, 104, 147, 150, 166, **217, 220, 223**
Twelve Days of Christmas	40
Two Bad Ants	134, 234
Uchida, Yoshiko	61, 183, 186
Unbuilding	140

Underground 140	When the Rivers Go Home 95
Unriddling 27	When the Wind Stops 110
Untold Tales 126	Where Are My Swans 147
Untold Tales 128	Where Do You Think You're Going Christopher Columbus 244
Van Allsburg, Chris 6 134, 140, 162, **226, 229,** **232**, 234, 256	Where the Buffaloes Begin 76
Van Laan, Nancy 207, 256	Where the Wild Things Are 36, 183
Velveteen Rabbit 125	Whinny of the Wild Horses 76
Venezia, Mike 119	Whiteley, Opal 225
Venus 153	Who Really Killed Cock Robin 147
Very Hungry Caterpillar 237	Who Stole the Wizard of Oz 216
Vesey, A. 15	Why the Chicken Crossed the Road .. 140
Village of Round & Square Houses **77**, 153	Widow's Broom 234
Viola, Herman 76	**Wild Fox** 49
Voices from the Fields 12	**Wild Mustang** 76
Voices of the Wild 132	**Wildfires** 110
Vojtech, Anna **108**	**Wilfrid Gordon MacDonald Partridge** 83, 180
	Willard, Nancy 166
Waber, Bernard 119	**William & the Good Old Days** 3
Waddell, Martin 125	Williams, Margery 125
Wagner, Jenny 89	Williams, Sherley 12
Waiting for Rain 77	Williams, Suzanne 162, 216
Waiting for the Evening Star 238	Williams, Vera 119
Walk Together Children 98	**Wings** **254**
Walking Stones 245	**Winter Room** 210
Ward, Brian 253	**Winter Whale** 76
Ward, Lynd 205, 234, 256	Winter, Jeanette 225
Washing the Willow Tree Loon **145**, 222	Wisler, G. Clifton **This New Land** 195
Waterlow, Julia 253	Wiswell, Phil 27
Waters, Kate 195	**Wolf** 257
Watership Down 207	Wolff, Ferida 240, 253
Watkin, Richard 143	Wood, Audrey 159, 240
Watson, Mary 116, 150, 235	**Woodsong** 132
Wave 131	**Words of Stone** 15
Way Things Work 140	**Working Cats** 192
Weaving of a Dream 30	**Working Cotton** 12
Wednesday Surprise 3, 162	**World in 1492** 244
Wells, Rosemary **238**	**World That Jack Built** 147
Western Wagon Train 46	Wormser, Richard 73
Wetzel, JoAnne 183	**Wreck of the Zephyr** **232**, 256
What Makes a Monet a Monet 119	**Wretched Stone** 162, 234, 240
What Was It Like Before Television .. 27	Wright, David K. 18
What Was It Like Before The Telephone 27	**Wringer** 143
What's Your Name 122	**Wrinkle in Time** 28, 30, 213
Whelan, Gloria 184	Wyllie, Stephen 33
Whelan, Gloria 67	
When Grandpa Kissed His Elbow 83	Yagawa, Sumiko 183
When I Was Young in the Mountains 101, 177, 180, 210, 250	**Year of the Ranch** 70
	Year on Monhegan Island 67
	Yeh-Shen 30, 253, 259

Yolen, Jane ... 43, 86, 95, 110, 222, **241, 245, 248, 251, 254,** 259
Yonder 67
Young, Ed **59,** 128, 253, **257**

Zane, Alex 18
Zekmet the Stone Carver 58
Zelinsky, Paul **105,** 156, **190**

Zemach, Harve 156, 189
Zemach, Margot 9, 189
Ziesk, Edra 64
Zipping, Zapping, Zooming Bats 55
Zolotow, Charlotte 110
Zoom 140
Zoom Upstream 58
Zwerger, Lisbeth 128

Subject & Skills Index

Adaptation 53
Advertising 26, 82
Africa 152
Agriculture 11, 84, 136
Allegory 15
Ambition 232
Analyzing 188, 206
Ancient Greece 254
Ancient Rome 142
Animals 133, 179, 218
Appalachia 99, 154, 175
Architecture 141
Armadillos 37
Art 5, 8, 20, 66, 72, 75, 97, 117, 118, 139, 153, 165, 206, 227, 252, 255, 258
Artists 4, 117
Astronomy 28, 152
Atom Bomb 60
Attributes 39, 78, 87, 146
Author Study 51, 139, 161, 165, 173

Baltimore, MD 81
Bats 53, 54
Beauty 23, 202
Betrayal 151
Biography 63, 172
Birds 14, 66, 149, 185, 249, 255
Blindness 251
Bullies 16, 211
Burma 16, 17
Butterflies 236

California 186
Cameroon 7
Camouflage 39
Categorizing 8, 88, 161, 209
Cats 87, 172, 190
Cause & Effect 8, 60, 91, 103, 139, 164, 168, 218, 242, 258
Cemeteries 91
Changes 90, 108, 129, 220, 227, 241
Characterization 29, 70
China 252

Cinderella Variants 56
Civil War 135, 167
Classifying 29, 54, 188, 191
Clothing 8, 17, 64, 121, 185, 194
Coal Mining 154, 176
Columbus, Christopher 241
Communication 26, 94, 114, 115, 230
Community 16, 65, 90, 91, 145, 160, 193, 212, 221, 245
Comparing Literature 5, 11, 14, 26, 32, 35, 38, 42, 45, 51, 54, 57, 63, 75, 83, 85, 91, 100, 103, 109, 112, 124, 136, 139, 142, 149, 152, 155, 158, 173, 176, 179, 182, 188, 194, 200, 203, 206, 212, 215, 221, 227, 230, 233, 236, 239, 242, 249, 255, 258
Comparisons 29, 32, 69, 78, 94, 106, 115, 121, 133, 164, 170, 182, 185, 203, 224, 242
Conflicting Cultures 71
Constellations 30
Copyrights 35
Cotton 97
Courage 16, 59
Cowboys 39, 112
Cranes 60, 182
Cultures 30, 71, 77, 120, 181, 184, 241, 257

Dance 2
Death 60, 108, 178
Debate 215
Descriptions 69, 242
Desert 19, 23
Details 8, 26, 42, 51, 78, 82, 94, 97, 124, 139, 164, 168, 176, 179, 197, 215, 224, 227, 242, 246, 255
Dictators 16
Dogs 87, 158
Dreams 35, 41, 72, 190

Eccentrics 157, 178, 211
Ecology 133, 199, 220,
Economics 11, 164, 248
Ecosystem 138, 146, 148, 169, 200, 221
Egypt, Ancient 56

Elderly People 2, 81, 82, 178, 190
Elections 17
Ellis Island 185
Emotions 29, 45, 103
Environment 132, 218
Estimating 45, 165
Evaluating Literature 2
Experiments 112
Extending Literature 11, 14, 17, 23, 26, 29, 38,
    42, 45, 54, 66, 69, 72, 91, 94, 103, 106, 112,
    124, 139, 146, 152, 155, 161, 168, 170, 179,
    182, 185, 191, 197

Fables 13, 126, 203, 209, 212, 215, 252
Fact & Fiction 48, 127
Fairy Tale Extensions 34, 68, 111, 154, 257
Falcons 57
False Identity 53
Family . . . 22, 42, 50, 65, 82, 85, 91, 121, 163, 229
Fantasy vs. Realism 26, 127
Farms 84, 240, 248
Figurative Language 29, 72, 75, 106, 109, 155,
    168, 200, 209, 221, 246
Flight 254
Flowers 100
Folk Tales 202, 205
Food 114, 194, 210
Food Chains 47, 48, 54, 133
Fossils 19, 109
Foxes 47
Friendship 167
Frogs 14

Gardening 148
Genre 14, 106, 127
Geography 105, 151, 175, 199, 227, 233
Geology 90, 176, 199
Georgia 81
Getting Meaning from Illustration 2, 5, 35, 48,
    115, 130, 142, 155, 209
Ghost Stories 31
Glaciers 91
Government 17
Grammar 2, 29, 136
Grandparents 1
Graphs 165

Haiku 60, 182
Health 11
Hiroshima 60

Hobbies 26, 123
Holocaust 17
Home 10, 44, 50, 78, 120, 130, 196, 217
Homesteading 41, 44, 45
Horses 74

Icarus 254
Idioms 5
Illustrator Study 51, 112, 136, 161, 173, 206
Immigrants 114, 163, 184, 193, 235
Impossible Tasks 111, 129
Inanimate Objects 4
Inferences 82, 97, 103, 130
Interpreting the text 17, 57, 109, 127, 152,
    230, 242, 258
Interviews 2, 26, 85, 121, 161
Invention & Discovery 65, 196

Japan 59, 181, 185

Labor Unions 154
Leaders 64, 142
Lebanon 93
Legends 28, 31
Leisure 26, 85, 161
Letters 69, 118, 182, 223
Libraries 160, 215
Life Cycles 108, 238
Lists 23
Literacy 161, 168
Literary Devices 124
Loneliness 44, 178
Love 42, 148, 178

Maps 10, 35, 51, 54, 57, 60, 66, 78, 85, 100,
    103, 106, 116, 118, 121, 136, 165, 176, 197, 209,
    224, 243, 246, 252
Markets 142
Masai 151
Math 2, 11, 20, 22, 32, 35, 45, 54, 82, 85, 124,
    136, 170, 179, 249
Maze 255
Memories 84, 208, 230
Migrant Workers 10
Migration 149, 249
Milky Way 28, 30, 35
Mistaken Identity 37
Moh's Hardness Scale 20
Money 22, 23, 121, 124
Morals 29

Music	2, 39, 45, 81, 82, 85, 176
Myths	13, 28, 232, 254
Native Americans	45, 71, 74, 75, 133, 205
Needs	22
New York City	63, 116
Nomads	151
Numbers	23
Occupations	1, 8, 20, 23, 32, 42, 105, 121, 133
Oil Spills	146
Omens	60
Oral Expression	88, 170, 236
Origami	60, 182
Orphans	50
Paleontology	20
Parodies	34, 35, 126
Parts of Speech	29
Peace	94
Perspective	87, 132, 138, 141, 199
Pesticides	11
Pets	172, 176, 190, 248
Pilgrims	193
Plains	44
Poetry	233, 255
Point of View	48, 138
Pollution	145
Pourquoi Tales	77
Prairie	44, 45
Predator/Prey	133, 200
Predicting	88, 118, 155, 170
Problem Solving	130
Progress	245
Proverbs	68, 69
Puns	142
Puzzles	26, 226, 229, 255
Quests	205
Quilts	96, 102, 163
Railroad	32, 72
Readers' Theater	200
Reading, Importance of	14, 160
Recycling	68, 70
Research	173
Resistance	16
Rocks	19
Rome	141
Roosevelt, Eleanor	62
Rules & Laws	17, 212
Russia	170
Safety	32
School	99, 121
Seasons	48, 229, 249
Seeds	149
Senses	206, 249, 251
Sequence	8, 146, 164
Shelter	78, 109, 130, 217
Similes	2, 60, 242
Size	54, 106
Slavery	96, 223, 224
Spelling	194
Statistics	51, 136
Storytelling	31
Surveys	35, 116, 173
Survival	193
Symbolism	51
Talent	25
Tall Tales	25, 105
Teaching	99
Television	160
Texas	37, 39
Time	135, 169, 214
Toys	124
Tracks	48
Trains	32
Transformation	4, 74, 206
Transportation	133, 185
Travel	99, 117
Trees	169, 258
Tricksters	129, 202
Truth	13
U. S. History	2, 44, 50, 62, 71, 84, 100, 102, 193, 196, 208, 211, 217, 223, 224, 246
Ugly Ducklings	62
Underground Railroad	96
Values	22, 72, 123
Vaudeville	2
Vocabulary	5, 8, 14, 17, 20, 26, 29, 35, 38, 42, 48, 54, 57, 63, 66, 69, 82, 88, 100, 103, 112, 121, 124, 127, 133, 139, 146, 152, 155, 158, 164, 168. 173, 188, 191, 197, 203, 206, 215, 218, 224, 230, 233, 246, 249, 252, 255, 258
Volcanoes	79

War 93, 94, 135, 167
Washington, D. C. 35
Waste Disposal 70
Water 91, 245
Wealth 123
Weather 8, 79, 109, 130, 185, 218, 231, 233
West Africa 7
Westward Movement 46, 102, 217
Wild Flowers 45
Wild West 26, 226
Wind 109
Wisdom 129
Wolves 258

Women's Roles 41, 105, 130
Woods 170
Word Play 157
World War II 59, 63, 85, 182, 239
Writing 2, 5, 8, 11, 14, 20, 23, 32, 35, 51, 54,
   63, 69, 75, 78, 85, 88, 100, 103, 109, 115, 118,
   121, 127, 133, 136, 142, 146, 149, 152, 158,
   161, 164, 170, 173, 176, 179, 185, 188, 191, 197,
   200, 215, 218, 224, 230, 233, 236, 239, 242,
   255

Zimbabwe 203